RICKEY

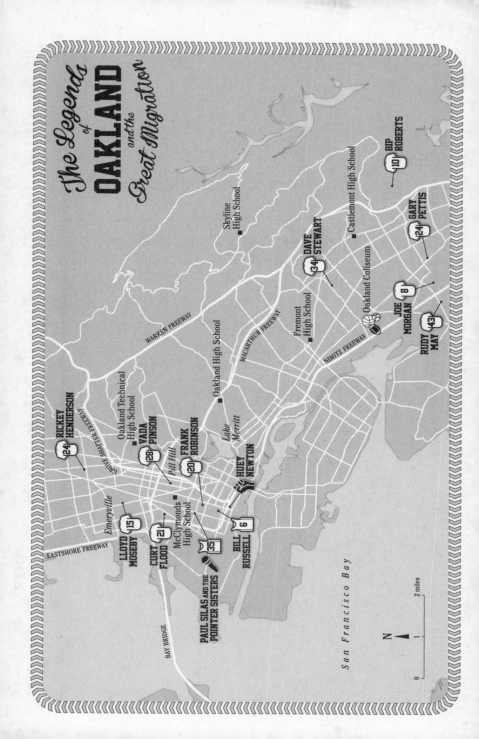

Also by Howard Bryant

Full Dissidence: Notes from an Uneven Playing Field

The Heritage: Black Athletes, a Divided America, and the Politics of Patriotism

The Last Hero: A Life of Henry Aaron

RICKEY

The Life and Legend of an
American Original

◆

Howard Bryant

MARINER BOOKS
New York Boston

The Henderson family Christmas card appears courtesy
of Pamela Henderson. Rickey Henderson's induction speech into
the Baseball Hall of Fame appears courtesy of Rickey Henderson.

HarperCollins books may be purchased for educational, business, or
sales promotional use. For information, please email the Special Markets
Department at SPsales@harpercollins.com.

A hardcover edition of this book was published in 2022 by Mariner Books.

FIRST MARINER BOOKS PAPERBACK EDITION PUBLISHED 2023.

Designed by Chloe Foster
Image of Rickey Henderson on page viii © Brad Mangin
Map by Mapping Specialists, Ltd.

Library of Congress Cataloging-in-Publication Data has been applied for.

ISBN 978-0-06-326866-1

23 24 25 26 27 LBC 5 4 3 2 1

For Pedro Gomez

"You see how an airplane lands? That's me. I'm like an airplane."
— Rickey Henderson

Contents

Prologue

YOU COULD SAY that Rickey Henderson was destined to be a gift. The surviving details of Christmas 1958, all tangled and swirled in legend, conspired to make the simple fact that Rickey, of all people, being born on Christmas Day felt preordained. One story said it snowed so hard on the South Side that Thursday night in Chicago that just reaching the hospital was an ordeal. Another said Rickey was so unexpected, so calm and quiet in Bobbie Earl's belly and not yet ready to join the world, that neither she nor his father, John Henley, had any reason to expect a Christmas birth. Even if the details were not exactly fact, the stories were true in their own way; Rickey *was* on his own schedule, and, as would be a defining characteristic of over a quarter-century of professional baseball, he was born with the element of surprise, capable of transforming the calm into the chaotic, always a step ahead of an unsuspecting world.

It was true that Bobbie never made it to a hospital bed in time to deliver Rickey, and it was true that it was Christmas—but there was no blizzard. It didn't snow at all that week—by the weekend the papers reported temperatures in the 50s. Bobbie wasn't taken by surprise by Rickey either. She knew her boy was coming. From the very start she knew Rickey better than Rickey knew himself; this was true even before she ever gave him a name. The most important detail was, of course, indisputably true: on Christmas night 1958, in an Oldsmobile on the way to the hospital, Bobbie Earl, just 19, gave birth to her fourth child, Rickey Nelson Henley, who introduced himself on cue, with an irresistible flair.

The chaos myth surrounding Rickey's birth served everybody—*what a debut!* It was a good, clean story, a dramatic opening act fitting for the man

destined to be the greatest opening act in baseball history. In subsequent retellings, that night resembled a wacky sitcom, all the characters scrambling
before everything works out harmlessly in the end. Even his birth certificate
carried intrigue—a friend recalled it stating his name as "Boy Henley," a
routine placeholder that virtually never finds its way into the official paperwork. Maybe that was fitting too, because Bobbie eventually gave Rickey, the
Christmas baby born in a car, an additional sprinkle of Hollywood magic,
naming him after that clean-cut white kid with the guitar who made all the
girls melt, 1950s teen heartthrob Ricky Nelson.

Thus it was that Rickey had a specialness and a story a little more fan-
tastic, a little grander—and he knew it. In later years he would remind everybody that he was set apart. Who else could brag about the day they were
born? "You know Rickey was born on Christmas Day!" he would sometimes
say when making a grand entrance into the clubhouse—but in the quiet moments, in the right light, he could tell his origin story at ground level, without the gritless predestiny, with a sobriety that suggested the tale wasn't so
cute, not quite so family-friendly. "Yes, I was born in a car, but I was born in
a car because my father was out gambling instead of getting us to the hospital. When he got to the hospital, he came in fussing to see my mother, acting
all crazy. 'Where my wife? She's having a baby!' The nurse said, 'You better
calm yourself down. The boy's already in the backseat.'"

John Henley would be out of the family picture before Rickey was three.
Bobbie had gone back home to Pine Bluff, Arkansas, to live on her mother's
farm. Rickey recalled John Henley with a bittersweet resignation as "a man
who liked the streets," and his allegiance to the street life was greater than his
fidelity to his growing family.

While Bobbie charted a new course to get out of Arkansas, Rickey's ear-
liest memories were of being raised by his grandmother on the farm, surrounded by livestock, riding hogs and chasing chickens, high times for a
little kid, but Pine Bluff was a nowhere town for Black people. There were no
jobs, and segregationists were waging a violent last stand against integration.
Rickey was born a year after the governor, Orval Faubus, blocked the doors
of Little Rock's Central High School, refusing to comply with the federal
mandate to integrate public schools and forcing President Dwight Eisenhower to deploy federal troops to escort Black students to class. Pine Bluff
was just 45 minutes south of Little Rock, and there the white leadership confronted the landmark 1954 *Brown v. Board of Education* decision with hostile

obfuscation, employing a series of stalling tactics to delay school integration for nearly five years, reinforcing its filibusters with extralegal muscle—White Citizens' Councils, Ku Klux Klan chapters, and unaffiliated vigilantes who knew they could menace Black neighborhoods without consequences from the law.

"I don't know how they did it," Rickey recalled of the women raising him. "With all that stuff going on down there," he said, his mother "had to get away." While Rickey was in elementary school, Bobbie began crafting her second act—heading 2,000 miles west, to Oakland, California.

For Black people the exodus from the South was as defining and American a journey as arriving at Ellis Island was for the Europeans, the Italians, the Poles, and the Irish who flooded the Eastern Seaboard in the 19th century, then became white and proudly American. Ellis Island was the first chapter of their American story, the place where hope and America became synonymous. The arrival of millions of Black people in far-flung cities across the country represented a similar journey with similar possibilities, yet those who joined the Great Migration had always been treated as unwelcome intruders, their presence linked to the various collapses of socioeconomic policies in cities across America, which had got along just fine before the Black people showed up. That was a slice of history being told by the whites for the whites. For the descendants of slavery (and in many cases, ex-enslaved), leaving the South for Chicago or Philadelphia, or New York, Los Angeles, or Oakland, and stepping off that train was *their* Ellis Island.

In 1900, 90 percent of Black people in America lived in the Deep South. Within a decade, they would begin remaking America with one of the greatest mass movements in recorded human history. The Great Migration was a hope, but it was also a revolution for Black people in search of an America yet undiscovered, the one promised in the textbooks and the fancy speeches, the America where hard work and industry would translate into opportunity no matter who you were—without being in danger of getting shot for trying to vote.

It wasn't until the early 1940s, with the world engulfed by war, that the San Francisco Bay Area became a destination for Black folks, but when it happened, the transformation was staggering. According to the 1940 census, Oakland was 2.8 percent Black and 95.3 percent white. The allure of jobs in the war economy made Oakland attractive, however, to Black migrants. Historians would later call it "chain migration": one family member would settle in a place, create an anchor, and several relatives would follow. Word was out that there was work in Oakland—on the docks and shipyards in Oakland, Alameda, and the port of Richmond as well as in the canneries and later, as the government began to expand in the postwar boom, the post office. By 1950, 81 percent of Black people living in the Bay Area had been born in the southern states.

Their exodus made a political statement. Black people weren't just looking for good jobs but leaving something very specific and unique to them: violence at the hands of white southerners—the corrupt lawmakers, the extralegal mobs who ignored the law with the encouragement of the police and the courts, and the political and social systems that disenfranchised them. Their movement away from all that rejected the assumption that their origins as an owned and permanent underclass meant they should be comfortable staying that way. They were leaving behind the notion that they were unentitled to be American.

No group of Black people came to Oakland at a higher percentage than the Louisianans, and with good reason. In the early part of the 20th century, the violence against Black people in the late 1800s was still fresh in the institutional memory of Black communities. The violence occurred so frequently that, into the 1950s, southern newspapers often ran a blotter of Black people killed while attempting to vote or register other Blacks to vote. The blotter served the dual purpose of recording the killings and warning any ambitious Black people to reconsider getting involved in voting rights. Black Louisianans still remembered firsthand the Colfax Massacre of 1873, when white militias killed more than 150 Black people while overthrowing Republican governments following the Civil War. The next year, in Red River Parish, another white mob, the White League, killed 10 people in the Coushatta Massacre of 1874 for the same reason—to return Black people to the subjugated class. In Coushatta, the mob accepted the resignation of six white Republican officeholders, made a deal with them to leave town, and then killed them as they fled the city limits. Monte Poole, the Oakland native who would grow up to be a prominent sports columnist with the *Oakland Tribune*, recalled the family stories his mother would tell of her grandfather surviving Natchitoches, a small city a few miles over from Coushatta, and 30 minutes south of Shreveport. "I used to hear it at barbecues all the time. My great-grandfather, well, he was a motherfucker. And I mean that. White folks knew the name. Bob Dixon. You didn't mess with Bob Dixon. The implication was that he dusted a couple of guys too." The Poole family left Louisiana and settled in Oakland in 1952.

Just two and a half hours from Pine Bluff, Monroe, Louisiana, into the 1900s was notorious for its lynching of Black residents, its poll taxes, and its insistence on violence to keep Black people in place. In the post-Reconstruction years, only four counties in the entire country unleashed more violence against Black people than Ouachita Parish, and the white residents of the county seemed determined to become number one. That distinction of being first in the terrorizing of Black people also went to Louisiana—to Caddo and Bossier Parishes, where Shreveport was located. Joe Dumars, born in Shreveport in 1963, who went on to become an NBA champion and Hall of Famer with the Detroit Pistons, remembered hearing about the lynchings in Caddo and Bossier from family members as a kid. For decades, generations of Black people from the parishes heard the stories from the elders.

One Ouachita resident, Charles Russell of Monroe, arrived home to hear his wife tell him that she had been accosted by a policeman in broad daylight for "dressing too fancy." "Who do you think you are, nigger? Dressing like a white woman," the cop told Katie Russell. "Get out of town before sundown or I'll throw you in jail." Charles Russell decided to leave Monroe. He chose Oakland, and when he saved enough money, Russell sent for his wife and children. In retelling this story, Charlie Russell's eldest son, the future 11-time NBA champion Bill Russell, wrote, "The memory lingers on of the five-year-old boy who watched that woman sitting in the kitchen of her home, trying to understand, trying to comprehend this unwarranted viciousness. Faced with this, and being a man and the head of the house, my father struck out for freedom. He went to Oakland, California."

Tired of the humiliations, another resident, Rev. Walter Newton, left Monroe for Oakland in 1945. Of his father, Walter's son, the future Black Panther Party cofounder Huey Pierce Newton, wrote, "My father was called crazy for his refusal to let a white man call him 'nigger' or to play the Uncle Tom or to allow whites to bother his family. 'Crazy' to them, he was a hero to us."

Black Texans left for Oakland at a nearly similar rate to Black Louisianans, and for similar reasons. Curt Flood came from Houston, and Joe Morgan from the little Texas town of Bonham, population 6,349. In 1939,

Lula Mae Shaw left Silsbee, a little Texas town right outside of Beaumont, as racial tensions over jobs simmered, highlighted by the Beaumont Race Riot of 1943. White employees at the Pennsylvania Shipyard, already upset about having to compete with Black workers for jobs, attacked Black employees and Black neighborhoods after a specious rumor circulated that a Black man had raped a white woman. At the end of two days of unrest, three people lay dead and more than 50 people were injured. By then, Shaw had settled in West Oakland with her 10 children, including her youngest child, future baseball legend Frank Robinson. The same year as the Beaumont attack, George and Thelma Seale, living 19 miles to the south in Port Arthur, relocated to Oakland with their eight-year-old son Bobby, who, with Huey Newton, would be the future Black Panther Party's other cofounder.

When Bobbie Earl returned to Pine Bluff to move the entire family to Oakland, the state of Arkansas was already infamous as a national symbol of white resistance to integration, but the attitudes underlying white violence—by police, the Ku Klux Klan and its splinter factions, and a hostile white public—had existed in that part of the South for centuries. The 1921 attack on Tulsa's Greenwood District would be the most remembered—because it had the unforgettable nickname "Black Wall Street," which stood as a symbol of white rage toward Black aspiration—but Tulsa was no outlier. Black Oklahomans remembered Tulsa, but Black Arkansas remembered Elaine, the 1919 massacre of nearly 200 Black men, women, and children by white vigilantes and soldiers dispatched to the town of Elaine, on the Missouri border, by Arkansas governor Charles Brough after Black sharecroppers formed a union to protest unfair wages and predatory work practices.

"Listen, you never forget," recalled former baseball All-Star Lloyd Moseby. The Mosebys headed for Oakland for the same reasons as the Newtons, the Russells, and the Robinsons. "We're a little different. I got a lot of Indian in me, so we were some of the few people who owned land in Arkansas because it was Indian land—but we still got treated the same. We were from Portland, Arkansas—little place. You'd never, ever find it. We were between Monroe, Louisiana, and Greenville Mississippi, each within 40 minutes. Think about what I just said: Louisiana, Mississippi, Arkansas. So, my dad pretty much worked for nothing.

"The way I got to California was my sister had had enough. She no longer wanted to say 'Yes, ma'am' and 'No, sir' and all this crap, and it got to the point where my mother felt my sister was going to get hurt, maimed, or killed. So she sent her off to my [other] sisters, who lived in Oakland, and then we followed."

Bobbie Earl had the same idea, leaving Pine Bluff for Oakland and following the quarter-century-long path of Black people who traveled west to realize their chance at something better. It was a path that remade Oakland, as well as her family. "Going to California," Rickey recalled, "was a one-way trip."

Book One

_____

"YOU MUST NOT KNOW
WHO I AM."

ONE OF RICKEY'S first recollections of Oakland was of being teased. Being laughed at was nothing uncommon because kids were always the cruelest, especially to newcomers, but it wasn't the teasing he remembered most about those days. It was *why* he had been singled out: it was the Arkansas in him. He arrived as a 10-year-old, in 1969, and even though so many of the Black families had also come from the South, a good number of the children had been in Oakland so long that it was the only home they knew, and an increasing number of their younger brothers and sisters had been born in Oakland. So when Rickey arrived at Washington Elementary School in North Oakland, the initial reaction to him was almost universal: damn, was this new kid *country.*

"They all spoke so *proper,*" Rickey recalled. "And I got self-conscious because everybody acted so different from where I came from. Here I am, talking the way I talked, and in California they were all so *refined.*"

Bobbie Earl settled in North Oakland, at 742 Alcatraz Avenue, near the corner of Alcatraz and Shattuck Avenue on the Berkeley border, and soon her mother moved from Pine Bluff to Oakland too. There were five boys—Tyrone, Alton, John, Rickey, and Douglas. Bobbie had also met a man, Paul Henderson, a truck driver for General Motors, with whom she had two more children, the girls Glynnes and Paula. Bobbie found work at Peralta Hospital up on Pill Hill in North Oakland. (The close proximity there of the Providence, Peralta, and Merritt Hospitals had given Pill Hill its name.) To the Black people settled in Oakland, North Oakland was an upgrade from West Oakland, which was often considered the roughest part of town. West Oakland was certainly the most congested part of the city, and the original epicenter of Black Oakland. North Oakland, on the Berkeley border, was nicer and had an added bonus: there was a playground, Bushrod Field, right down the street.

Rickey initially felt out of place in Oakland—it was too fast, too sophisticated—and when he spoke and let the Arkansas out, well, that sealed it. With anybody new, however, especially with boys, sports were the equalizer. That was where the nobodies became somebodies, where the teasing stopped once you got on the field and served up some business, and now the teasers wanted you on their team. One day when the kids met up at Bushrod and started picking sides—for football, touch or tackle, and baseball, with a hardball, tennis ball, or basketball—Rickey was there. So who was gonna take the new kid? Could he even play?

The first day Rickey showed up to Bushrod, the star wasn't even there. That title belonged to Fred Atkins, the best player in the neighborhood, but he was busy that day. Fred wore the crown—he was the reigning Washington Elementary Athlete of the Year, sixth grade—but he had a doctor's appointment or some such engagement that kept him from showing up at the field, as they all usually did right after school. When Fred got to school the next day, nobody was talking about him anymore—they weren't even sure he was still the man. Everyone was talking about the new kid who just moved in, Rickey Henley.

The new kid was *good*, they said, and the way they put that extra emphasis on *good*, that meant Rickey wasn't just good. That meant Rickey was *special*. They told Fred this kid Rickey was so good that it had already been decided without him: he and Rickey could never be on the same team—it was the only way the teams could be fair. It also meant, indirectly, that with Rickey on the other team, Fred's team had a chance to lose. Rickey had already moved in on Fred's territory and Fred hadn't even seen him play.

"You have to remember," Fred Atkins recalled, "I used to play with the older kids, so I was primed. They were all talking about this new dude, Rickey Henley. I figured, 'Lemme test this guy out. Let me see if this guy is the real deal.' We were playing football. He hit me so hard he knocked me into a tree. So, first of all, I found out he was strong. He was a real athlete. And then *he* realized he had to watch *me*—because most guys getting knocked into a tree wouldn't show up for more. You knock somebody into a tree and they quit. He needed me. I needed him, and from then on, we were inseparable."

During Washington Elementary flag football games, Rickey would get five or six touchdowns. By halftime. "He used to just run," recalled Mike Hammock, who ran the community center at Bushrod for 15 years. "Rickey was so good, they just couldn't keep playing him. They had to sit him down." In a very short time everybody knew Rickey could play, but what did that really mean in a place like Oakland, where one guy getting a sniff of top-level competition was hardly news?

Rickey may have been the new kid, but Fred Atkins had arrived in town only a couple of years earlier. After stops in Virginia and New York back east, his father Orlando was stationed in West Oakland at the Oakland Army Base. The Atkins family first lived on 16th and Chestnut, and Fred wanted to follow his brother to McClymonds High School and be part of the legend.

Over at McClymonds High School, originally on 14th and Adeline in the heart of West Oakland, they had an outfield of Frank Robinson, Vada Pinson, and Curt Flood. All of them would play in the major leagues. And all of them would make the All-Star team and reach the World Series. Robinson and Bill Russell were teammates on the McClymonds basketball team. Lee Lacy played in four World Series over 16 years in the big leagues and won one with Willie Stargell on the 1979 Pirates, and another Mack kid, Willie Tasby, bounced around the big leagues for six years—even hit 17 bombs one year for the '61 Senators. Mack would forever be known as "the School of Champions"—a dynasty the local kids wanted to join.

The reasons why one school produced that much top-shelf, All-Star, Hall of Fame talent—or more specifically, the implausibility of it—fed the legend. Fans and future scholars of the great game of sports concluded that it was inexplicable that so many world-class players could hail from such a small footprint, and they decided that Oakland was just one of those random outliers where the universe conspired to create wonder. This, of course, was not true. West Oakland's dominance in sports was not the least bit implausible nor fantastical. The reason was not coincidence. The reason was segregation.

For nearly the entire first half of the 20th century, Oakland was an overwhelmingly white port town run by a conservative business and political class—as exemplified by the city's largest newspaper, the *Oakland Tribune,* whose building, the Tribune Tower, could be seen from every angle of the city as it rose up from 12th and Franklin Streets. The *Tribune*'s publisher, Joe Knowland, was a powerhouse figure in Oakland and California Republican

politics, and his paper supported the city's business class. As Oakland became a major shipping center it also became a formidable union town, and
the *Tribune* would undermine the unions with generally hostile coverage.
Whenever the unions pressed for improved working conditions, the *Tribune*
would accuse them of being Communists.

Two of the city's great cultural exports were writers. One was Gertrude
Stein, credited with famously saying of Oakland, "There's no there there"
(even though she was talking about the remnants of her own past, not cri-
tiquing the city). Stein was a major voice of her time who called the great
Paul Robeson a friend even while referring to Black people as "niggers" in
correspondence with mutual friends. Stein nevertheless insisted in these letters that the two got on fabulously.

The other was Jack London. The city's most famous literary son, London
sat ringside at Rushcutters Bay on December 26, 1908, in Australia when
Jack Johnson destroyed the Canadian Tommy Burns in the 14th round of
their heavyweight fight. Johnson became the first Black heavyweight champion of the world. "Personally, I was with Burns all the way. He is a white
man, and so am I. Naturally I wanted to see the white man win," London
wrote in the *Australian Star* two days after the fight under the subhead, "The
Negro's Smile." London urged the retired champ Jim Jeffries to un-retire and
beat Johnson so as to "remove that golden smile from Johnson's face" and
restore the purity and dominance of the white race. "Jeff, it's up to you," London wrote in the same article. In framing the necessity to defeat Johnson as
a matter of preserving white superiority, Oakland's own Jack London coined
the term "the Great White Hope." London's urgings didn't do much good,
though. Jeffries did indeed come out of retirement, and when they fought in
1910, Johnson knocked Jeffries right back into it.

In reaction to the onrush of Black migration from the South, Oakland's
housing agencies and banks erected strict racial covenants, both by code
and custom, to funnel the city's booming new population of working-class
Black arrivals overwhelmingly into West Oakland, which quickly became
the heartbeat of Black Oakland. The porters and redcaps working the trains
for the Union Pacific and Southern Pacific Railroads lived there, as did the
Black women working as domestics in the big, stately homes on the Clare-
mont and Piedmont sides of town. The final Bay Area stop on the Union
Pacific, West Oakland literally provided the first glimpse of Oakland for the
Black people who had made the 2,000-mile trek west in search of work on

the docks as longshoremen or at the Oakland Army Base, which sat at the Port of Oakland, jutting into the San Francisco Bay.

Black folks had been invited to come to Oakland. Many of the shipyards recruited Black southerners, enticing them to relocate by offering, though never guaranteeing, two essential benefits: a wage and a roof. Oakland offered possibility—and even, it seemed, a voice. In solidarity with union workers, and in the hope that his dream of an interracial American labor force that rejected both racial and class divisions could be realized, Paul Robeson in 1942 sang "The Star-Spangled Banner" at the Moore Dry Dock Company in West Oakland—one of the shipyards that recruited and hired thousands of Black workers to offset labor shortages during the war years.

Seventh Street was West Oakland's commercial epicenter, from Eula's Powder Puff Beauty Salon at 1727 Seventh Street to the Square Deal Furniture Company ("What's in a Name?") at 924 Seventh Street. As the Black population increased, West Oakland took on the nickname "the Harlem of the West." Of course, in the 1940s any town with a growing Black population and a couple of jazz clubs referred to itself as the Harlem of the West. Just across the Bay Bridge, San Francisco's Fillmore District called itself the same thing. So did Five Points, Denver's Black nightclub district, and of course so did the legendary stretch of nightclubs that ran along Central Avenue in Los Angeles.

Seventh Street had its dry cleaners, shoe stores, and beauty shops, as well as its restaurants and nightclubs, speakeasies, and smoke shops. That many of the businesses were Black-owned confirmed for some the decision to move west. Fresh off a cross-country run, the porters would show up on Seventh Street with some money in their pockets to spend and exciting stories to tell about traveling the United States. Being a Pullman porter was a prestigious gig for Black men, for not very many people could say that they had seen the country. Being part of the famed Brotherhood of Sleeping Car Porters was also a chance to make history. Few Black people had ever collectively bargained over job conditions and salaries.

Seventh Street was the invaluable social hub of a new immigrant community for those who had recently moved there. On Seventh Street, a chance conversation might connect them to someone from back home. The man they called the "Mayor of West Oakland" was Harold "Slim" Jenkins, who had left Monroe, Louisiana, and arrived in Oakland during World War I. He ran Jenkins' Corner (which was also known as Jenkins' Supper Club) at 1748

Seventh Street, at the corner of Wood Street, and also managed the Wolf Smoke Shop down the street at 1714 Seventh, which by nightfall turned into the Wolf Club. In 1950, a waitress at Jenkins' Supper Club, Esther Brown, who had arrived in Oakland from Texas as a 22-year-old, opened up her own place, Esther's Breakfast Room, which would later become another well-known Oakland jazz hotspot, Esther's Orbit Room.

For first-run movies, you had to go to 1620 Seventh Street, on the corner of Seventh and Peralta, to the Lincoln Theatre, but when the big acts came through Oakland, like Dinah Washington or Louis Jordan, they played at one of Slim's joints. Jenkins was a gambler and an operator, a man who had his hand in everything and knew everyone. Lest anyone think Jenkins wasn't aspirational, he was also part of the Oakland business class and a member of the NAACP. William Knowland, who succeeded his father Joseph as publisher of the *Tribune,* came to Jenkins' Supper Club, as did, at least once (went the word), the president himself, Franklin Delano Roosevelt.

For a time, West Oakland was seen as an improvement for Black newcomers—but only in comparison to the conditions they had fled. The speed of the Great Migration coupled with city resistance to building more housing stock led almost immediately to overcrowding, however, and Black people arriving in Oakland soon encountered structural barriers similar to what caused them to leave the South in the first place. In his book *American Babylon: Race and the Struggle for Postwar Oakland,* the author Robert Self details Oakland's descent into nearly complete segregation. "In 1950, 90 percent of Oakland's Black residents lived in 22 percent of its census tracts in West and North Oakland." In the early 1940s and 1950s, even the vast tract of East Oakland was largely unavailable to Black citizens, and Oakland's segregation was virtually complete.

The biggest beneficiary of that heavy segregation of Black people into West Oakland was McClymonds High. The great McClymonds coach George Powles was undoubtedly an influential figure, and indeed the Mack Warriors were the School of Champions, but Frank Robinson, Vada Pinson, Curt Flood, and Bill Russell all ended up at McClymonds for one reason: it was the only public high school in the neighborhood, and Black people were discouraged or outright prevented from living anywhere else in Oakland.

Frank Robinson lived at 1515 Myrtle, almost across the street from Mc-Clymonds. "It was a regular house with a regular garage, except that eight families were living in the eight rooms and one family was living in the garage," Bill Russell wrote of his living conditions in the Acorn projects of West Oakland, upon arriving in Oakland. "Pigs and sheep and chickens were raised in the backyard. A rotten, filthy hole. A firetrap with lights hanging off uncoated wires. It was the only place we could find." Huey Newton, another recent transplant from Monroe, wrote similarly of his first two houses in West Oakland. "The first house I remember was on the corner of fifth and Brush streets in a rundown section of Oakland . . . The floor was either dirt or cement. I cannot remember, but it did not seem to be the kind of floor 'regular' people had in their homes . . . Later, when we moved into a two-room apartment on Castro and Eighteenth streets . . . I slept in the kitchen. Whenever I think of people crowded into a small living space, I always see a child sleeping in the kitchen and feeling upset about it; everybody knows that the kitchen is not supposed to be a bedroom. That is all we had, however. I still burn with the sense of unfairness I felt every night as I crawled into the cot near the icebox."

Having left Hope, Arkansas, the Silas-Pointer family lived six blocks away from the Newtons on two floors of a duplex at 18th and Adeline—home to 15 people in all. The girls—Bonnie, June, Anita, and Ruth—were such standout singers at the West Oakland Church of God at the corner of 10th and Myrtle Streets that even early on the Pointer Sisters had their eye on being professional singers. Their first cousin, Paul Silas, who lived downstairs, was a standout power forward at McClymonds, and before he became an NBA champion with the Boston Celtics, Silas was playing by 1965 in the National Basketball Association for the St. Louis Hawks—against Bill Russell.

Meanwhile, white West Oaklanders had fled. In 1938, 648 white students were enrolled at McClymonds. By 1948, the number was down to 50, a 92.2 percent decrease. During that same period, Black enrollment at McClymonds increased 593 percent, from 115 students to 797. Making West Oakland into a ghetto was a staggeringly deliberate process.

There were a few pockets of Black transplants who had found a way to avoid West Oakland, North Oakland, and South Berkeley—where virtually all of the Black people in Oakland lived before 1960—but their move into a community almost ensured that white families would move out. "We were one of the first Black families to move into our new neighborhood," Joe Morgan recalled about moving to East Oakland in 1948 as a five-year-old. "Soon after our move, the neighborhood, sure enough, became all Black. They didn't call it 'redlining' then, and no organizations protested, but this

was the all-too-common pattern that developed in northern cities." Monte
Poole, whose father landed a job at the Oakland Army Base in the early
1950s, also found housing in Brookfield Village in East Oakland.

The Black community that took shape in Oakland confronted hostility
with action—within the job market as Black employees attempted to join
and influence the labor movement, and with political action by fighting dis-
criminatory practices in housing and employment. One of the leaders was
C. L. Dellums, who left Corsicana, Texas, in the 1920s and came to the Bay
Area, first to San Francisco before settling in Oakland. Dellums had a high-
class job for Black people at the time: he worked as a porter for the Southern
Pacific Railroad. As a member of the Brotherhood of Sleeping Car Porters,
Dellums was second in command in the national leadership to the famed
A. Philip Randolph and was chair of the local NAACP. Another legendary
figure and rights advocate in Oakland was the attorney and later Alameda
County judge Clinton White—who would one day bankroll one of Rickey's
youth baseball teams. Protest and community very quickly developed in the
DNA of an emerging Black Oakland transitioning from its southern roots to
something uniquely Californian.

The city's reaction to the waves of African American arrivals was to re-
trench through housing. Oakland's white homeowners feared that mixed-
race neighborhoods would affect property values—or more accurately, the
city's banks and real estate brokers and the *Tribune*'s editorial page stoked
such fears. White homeowners sold and fled to the racial safe havens of
Albany, El Cerrito, and San Leandro, bordering cities whose real estate industry would not sell to Black buyers in numbers that might threaten the
white majority. The best-known white enclave was Piedmont, a city within
the city of Oakland that did not welcome Black residents.

The whites who did not flee the city sought additional protection from
the onrush of Blacks—which in the early 1960s, according to the census,
was 22 percent of the population—by redrawing the city's enrollment map
so that students attending Skyline, the new high school, would be drawn
almost exclusively from the Oakland Hills. By not enrolling students from
the valley below the hills, the new high school was virtually guaranteed to be
overwhelmingly white when it opened in 1961.

As West Oakland sagged, the city did not support its Black residents
but instead allowed the bulldozers of its friends in private development to
raze huge swaths of land. The death knell for West Oakland as a thriving

Black community came with the construction of the Bay Area Rapid Transit (BART) elevated line, which was placed right down Seventh Street, destroying the heart of West Oakland's busiest Black thoroughfare. The shiny new transportation system also bypassed Black neighborhoods on its way through the East Bay to San Francisco. That was yet another blow for the city, which had already built the Cypress Structure (aka the Cypress Freeway) and bulldozed the Acorn District of West Oakland, wiping out thousands of housing units.

The number of Black people moving west from the South had tapered off by 1970, the year Rickey turned 12. That year would be considered by historians the official end of the Great Migration, which had transformed the style, flavor, and identity of Oakland and made the city an epicenter of Black political, creative, and artistic thought. The novelist and poet Ishmael Reed moved to Oakland in 1970. Richard Pryor resurrected his comedy career in Oakland. The boxer George Foreman trained in Oakland. And there were so many Black Texans and Louisianans in Oakland that Black people called Oakland "New Orleans West."

Bushrod was where all the kids played, and sports (at least for a time) protected them from the streets. "When Freddy and Rickey were coming up, it was the biggest field. It was like a stadium," Mike Hammock recalled. "It was the only place that had an indoor gym, and we had two 90-foot baseball diamonds. The Oakland Raiders used to practice there. It was their facility in 1961. Locker rooms, equipment, everything. All at Bushrod." Rickey and Fred would play one-on-one hoops until it got dark. When the sun went down, they'd play indoors—at least until the grown-ups came in and shut the lights out. Things could get a little edgy at Bushrod, where the street life crept inexorably closer to the kids, turning the boys too quickly into men. There was baseball, but there were also roughnecks, dice games, and some throwdowns when tempers flared—fist to knife to gun. Rickey loved the dice. When Bobbie saw Rickey gambling, she would invoke John Henley and tell her son that it was the one characteristic he inherited from his father.

The fear of the streets devouring the boys (and even more perilously—because there were fewer encouraged and accessible diversions—the girls) was omnipresent, and everyone knew a cautionary tale firsthand. Those Oakland playground legends—like West Oakland's famous Demetrius "Hook" Mitchell, who had so much hang time he used to hold exhibitions where he'd jump over cars and dunk—would always be better ballplayers than the guys on TV, with their bubble-gum cards and big contracts, because the life caught them. The margins were so thin, with everything decided by a hair. "The temptation was everywhere," Fred Atkins recalled. "Rickey and I kept each other grounded. Either he wanted to go and I didn't, so we didn't, or I wanted to get into something and he didn't, so we didn't. And almost every time one of us kept the other from hitting the streets we'd hear a story a few days later about how something happened that we might have been right in the middle of."

There was a rumor that as the Black population increased, the Oakland Police Department intentionally hired white southerners, men who were raised to be enthusiastic and unconflicted about handling a Black populace through intimidation. Soon it became an open secret that the OPD was stoking preexisting hostilities by harassing the Black community with impunity. "Generally, Negroes regard the police as their natural enemies," Oakland's NAACP chair C. L. Dellums told a committee investigating the police shooting of an unarmed Black man in 1949.

Huey Newton, 22 years old in 1964, had an idea: the city wouldn't monitor the police, so Black people needed an organization that would do it. If the city was going to deprive Black residents of necessary services, Black residents needed an organization that would provide them. If the business leaders of America were going to suffocate poor communities with capitalism, Black communities needed an organization that would take a communal approach to community building. Newton met David Hilliard in 1964 and Berkeley High's Bobby Seale two years later. In light of the city government's redevelopment initiatives and unresponsive approach to police violence against Black and brown citizens—concerns Dellums had voiced nearly 20 years earlier—Newton, Hilliard, and Seale formed the Black Panther Party for Self-Defense. If police were going to position themselves in the Black community as an occupying force, the Black Panther Party would pledge to protect it from the occupiers. "You'd see them walking up and down the street," Fred Atkins recalled. "They were a part of the community, like a club. Some of our friends we went to school with, they were part of it. It was a strong presence."

Within this environment the second wave of Oakland's athletic dynasty came of age. The players weren't the only people who became legends.

George Powles, who coached both the basketball and baseball teams, became a household name as not only the beneficiary of insanely talented kids but as a white man who actually cared about them as people.

It helped that the enormous shadow cast by the first wave of Oakland's athletic dynasty allowed local kids to see that the big leagues weren't some faraway daydream. One of George Powles's American Legion teams (for 16- to 18-year-olds) had Robinson, Pinson, and Flood in the same outfield, and they came home with the championship trophy (obviously!). Joe Morgan graduated from Castlemont in 1961 and within 18 months was playing in the big leagues as a 19-year-old against Hank Aaron, Willie Mays, Roberto Clemente, and Sandy Koufax for the Houston Colt .45s (who soon came to their senses and renamed the team the Astros). By 1965, Willie Mays's last sensational season, another Castlemont kid, 20-year-old lefty pitcher Rudy May, reached the big leagues and would stay there for 18 years.

The kids played all the major American sports, but the center of their world was baseball. For Oakland boys, baseball was in their bloodstream long before they hit high school. There were two main baseball leagues—Babe Ruth (for 13- to 15-year-olds) and Connie Mack (for the high school juniors and seniors, the 16- to 18-year-olds)—and a local company, Bercovich Furniture, sponsored many good teams in those leagues. Owner Sam Bercovich was perhaps the biggest name in Oakland youth sports. He had taken over the family business from his father, Edward Bercovich, who founded the store in 1906. For virtually the entire 20th century, there wasn't a kid who stepped onto a ball field in Oakland who wasn't touched either directly or tangentially by Bercovich Furniture. Legend had it that Sam Bercovich bought Curt Flood an $8 bike so he could get to Oakland Tech every day after transferring there from McClymonds. It was Bercovich who paid for uniforms year after year, and for the equipment, bats, balls, and gloves. It was Bercovich who brought so many of the kids together—and it was Bercovich Furniture that supported so many good teams that everyone wanted to play for them. Morgan and Robinson played for Bercovich Furniture. Even as a teenager Frank was ornery, but everybody wanted him on their team—because Frank could hit. Bercovich got him.

Rickey and Fred never played for Bercovich. They played in the Babe Ruth League, for the Bercovich team's rival, Porta House. When Rickey played in the Connie Mack League, Judge Clinton White sponsored the team. "He bought all the uniforms. He was like a real owner," Fred Atkins recalled. "He went on trips. Paid for everything. Wore a three-piece suit on the field. The judge." Rickey's uniform read "NAACP" across the front.

With whites fleeing to the suburbs, the children of the Migration now lived all over the city, and Black people could aspire to leave West Oakland on better financial terms. Oakland was growing up as the kids did. After 13 years in Kansas City, and 11 years after the Giants moved from New York to San Francisco, Oakland got its own major league team when Charlie Finley moved his ball club, the Athletics, to the city. There he ditched the gray, blue, and red uniforms in favor of green and gold unis, with white shoes. The baseball establishment would laugh at those white shoes—until Oakland became a powerhouse.

Two years before the Athletics came to Oakland, in 1966, the city built a stadium, the Oakland–Alameda County Coliseum, to be the new home for the A's and the American Football League Raiders. (Sam Bercovich could be seen on the sidelines before Raiders games hanging out with his pals Al LoCasale and *el jefe*, Al Davis.) In 1971 the NBA San Francisco Warriors also moved to Oakland—though, fearful of the negative connotations of the name Oakland, the team opted to rename themselves the Golden State Warriors.

The city was full of ballplayers. The North Oakland kids commiserated on the Bushrod field at 59th Street and Racine, between Telegraph and Shattuck, right next to Rickey's house. When Lloyd Moseby's family left Arkansas, they wound up living close to Rickey's family, up on 53rd at the corner of San Pablo. Moseby came from a little town named Portland (population 662) about two hours south of Pine Bluff. Moseby arrived in Oakland in 1969 as a 10-year-old around the same time as Rickey, and when his country drawl slipped out, as Rickey's did, the teasing started. That sometimes meant throwing hands. "They used different words than we used, so you had to fight," Moseby recalled. "They used slang we never heard of. So you had to fight. I had a stutter, so now you had to fight about that too."

Lanky and strong, Moseby was called "Shaker," but the nickname had nothing to do with baseball. The Shaker got his name because, on the basketball court, he could shake anyone off the dribble and be gone, straight to the hoop.

At 58th and Grove Streets (renamed MLK Boulevard in 1984), just three blocks west from Bushrod, lived "the Quiet One," Gary Pettis, another silky-smooth player on both the basketball court and the baseball diamond. On the fast break, Pettis would just look at the ball-handler and point to the sky. Wherever the pass arrived—too high, too low, or just right—Gary Pettis would catch the ball in stride and find a way in midair to make any shot, no matter how awkward, look natural, like it was always part of the plan.

The Pettis family was part of the Great Migration too. Like Huey Newton and Bill Russell, Gary Pettis's mother was from Monroe, Louisiana; his father was from Little Rock, Arkansas. Fred Atkins's family would move from West Oakland to 58th and Dover, a block and a half away from Gary Pettis. A few blocks from them, at 55th and Market, was one of the Oakland offices of the Black Panther Party. "It was a very political time revolving around racism and equal rights. It was everywhere, so quite naturally seeing the Panthers on TV we had to go see if we could get a look at them in person," Pettis recalled. "It just so happened we didn't have to look very far."

Closer to Bushrod but past the city limits to the north and into Berkeley was another group of players. The Berkeley boys, who used to play at San Pablo Park, didn't take a backseat to anyone. Like McClymonds back in the day, all you had to say was "Berkeley High" and people acted like the Yankees were in town. Everyone was talking about one of the Berkeley boys, this kid Glenn Burke, who could do it all. Everything he did out there was easy—at least he made it look easy. They all looked up to Burke, who was six years older than Rickey, as another example of the pathway. Everybody said Burke was going to the majors.

There were two more kids crushing the Berkeley leagues: Claudell Washington and the little infielder Mack Neal Babitt II. Everybody called Babitt "Shooty," and the baseball people figured the nickname came from being a good batsman who could take the outside pitch and "shoot" it into the gap. An educated guess, but in fact the nickname came from the Berkeley High and former Boston Celtics forward Don Barksdale, who was also a DJ. Barksdale would open his shows by exclaiming, "Shooty-Rooty-Booty!" When his father Mack repeated Barksdale's opening to his infant son, the little boy would just laugh. Every time he heard the word "shooty," out came the laughter—and the nickname stuck.

The Berkeley boys could play, and they had their own first wave dynasty: Chuck Cooper, Earl Lloyd, and Sweetwater Clifton, one of the first five Black players in the NBA, and Barksdale (whose father was a Pullman porter in West Oakland), the first Black NBA All-Star. In the legendary 1967 NFL ti-

tle game between Dallas and Green Bay, with Tom Landry on one sideline,
Vince Lombardi on the other, and Bart Starr in the middle of the famous
Ice Bowl, it was Cornell Green from Berkeley High who was playing for
the Cowboys. His older brother Elijah played in the big leagues and was the
first Black player to play for the Boston Red Sox. (Everyone called Elijah
"Pumpsie" and nobody knew why—not even him.) And there was the pug-
nacious Billy Martin, the Italian kid who everyone knew played with Mantle
and Yogi and won all those World Series titles. Before the migration of Black
people into Oakland, it was at Bushrod where Billy Martin learned to play
baseball.

Oakland was a haven for baseball players during Rickey's time. Down
near the Coliseum site, at 2512 Havenscourt Boulevard in East Oakland,
lived a catcher, Davey Stewart. The word was, when he was 12, his throws
from behind the plate were so strong they called him "Smoke." Dave Stewart
was part of the sports mix in Oakland, but he didn't play in the Oakland
Athletic League. His mother didn't trust the Oakland schools to educate her
boy—and also didn't trust that the odds of losing him to the streets were
in her favor. So Davey ended up at St. Elizabeth's, the Catholic school on
35th Avenue, over in the Fruitvale District.

There was the younger kid Leon Roberts—his father Leon II was also
a Panther. Leon hung out with Gary Pettis's little brother Stacy. He lived
over by the Oakland Zoo and the new MacArthur Freeway, also known
as Interstate 580 of the Eisenhower Interstate Highway System, which was
completed in 1963, the year Leon was born. Everybody called Leon "Bip"—
because of his diminutive stature, word had it. (In fact, he got his nickname
from his mother, Wilma Jean, who came to Oakland from Natchez, Louisiana. She called him "Bip," not because he was peanut-sized, but because as
a toddler he used to say "a little bip" instead of "a little bit.") Bip was a little
thing of a hitter who would grow to be just five-foot-seven—Joe Morgan's
size, but small for a big leaguer—yet somehow he could lash line drives, and
he might even surprise you and clear the fence.

If you lived in North Oakland, you played at Bushrod. In East Oakland,
McConnell was the place. Greenman Field, over by the newly constructed
Coliseum, had some action—but the best comp was at Bushrod. When Gary
Pettis was in the seventh grade, the Pettis family moved from North Oak-
land south to East Oakland, but instead of settling in at Greenman, he still
took the AC Transit bus all the way back up to North Oakland to keep play-

ing at Bushrod. Sometimes he'd fall asleep on the long ride home, miss his stop, and wind up in San Leandro. It got to be that his mother would give him an emergency dime so he could call home.

Everybody respected Rickey as a baseball player, but he would say he didn't even really like baseball. There were times, in fact, when he said he hated it. When the A's won the World Series in 1972, in only their fifth year in Oakland, and won it again in 1973 and then again in 1974, Rickey was all about football. His team was the Raiders, who were always playing for championships. No team reflected Oakland toughness like the Raiders. Around town, baseball was king, but Rickey was known as "the Football Kid."

Rickey would play baseball, but only if somebody asked. In his 1992 autobiography *Off Base: Confessions of a Thief,* written with the veteran Bay Area baseball writer John Shea, Rickey said that, before even arriving in Oakland, he played baseball as an obligation to his older brother Tyrone. "I first played baseball only because I was forced to by Tyrone. It was back in Arkansas. He was the only other athlete in the family, and sometimes he'd have nobody else to play catch with. So, he'd throw a glove on me and drag me along. I didn't want to play, but he made me. And then he fired the ball at me. I'd get mad and fire it back. He'd throw it harder at me, and I'd throw it harder back at him. That's how I started playing baseball."

In later years, he would tell a different story, but with the same theme. "I played in Little League and all that. I was a good baseball player. It was Fred Atkins who said, 'You play baseball, and I'll come and play football with you.' I said, 'Deal.' He came to play football, and he was getting killed! Every time he tried to play quarterback, throwing bad balls, I mean getting *killed*—bad deal for him. He said, 'I ain't doing that no more.' So I came and played baseball."

It was also true that Fred played football so he and Rickey could hang out more, and it was no exaggeration to say that he was indeed getting demolished on the football field. "There's no doubt in my mind Rickey could have been one of the greatest football players ever," Fred Atkins recalled. "The football coach at Tech, Wayne Brooks, looked at me and put me on the line because he said I had 'lineman's hands.' Here I am weighing 155 pounds, and they've got me blocking for Rickey. Rickey could pick me up with one hand. Rickey ran for a thousand yards one year and we put *nothing* in front of him. That's how good he was. He got all those yards by himself."

The Football Kid got his name not just for loving the game, but for loving one player above all others: one Mister Orenthal James Simpson, aka the Juice, aka O.J. There weren't many places you could go in America and *not* see O.J. He was the most electrifying player in college at the University of Southern California. In 1973, when Rickey was 14, O.J. was the first player to rush for 2,000 yards in a season (in a 14-game season, it should be noted). He was the pitchman for cars on TV, for orange juice in magazines, for cowboy boots and cleats on the back page of comic books. He was everywhere.

O.J. and Rickey played the same position, even though O.J. made you miss him and Rickey would never pass up a chance to flatten you. Rickey played for contact, like the time in the seventh or eighth grade when all the kids were playing in the driveway and Rickey went out to catch a pass, stretching out to the end of the driveway, stretching . . . stretching . . . and— *bam!*—ran headfirst into a car. "Rickey ran directly into a parked car," Fred Atkins recalled. "We were all standing over him, looking at him, and we're like, 'Damn, you're not knocked out?' He got up and kept on playing. Rickey was like Jack Tatum or Ronnie Lott or something."

There was something else about O.J. that drew Rickey in—he was local. O.J. grew up in public housing right across the Bay Bridge in the Potrero Hill projects, on the western slope of the Hill. If a San Francisco kid could be the most famous football player in the world, why couldn't a kid from Oakland?

People knew it was possible. When Rickey attended Oakland Technical High School, they came to see him in action. Everybody had a Rickey story. Kids who wouldn't be caught dead in North Oakland were attending Tech games, just to get a glimpse of him. "Rickey was all-world, and people will laugh, but he was more dangerous on the football field than baseball," recalled Dennis Dixon Sr., who attended Fremont High and played against Rickey in baseball and basketball. "What kind of runner was Rickey? He had all the skills, but he used to run over you. Run right through you—then took off. He had them big old thighs—ran the ball like Earl Campbell." Mike Hammock, who was a couple of years older than Rickey, just remembered him as a little adolescent tank. "Rickey was the same size as a big leaguer as he was in elementary school. Big kid."

Even as a teenager, when everyone else looked all gangly, a painful lost collection of elbows and knees, Rickey as a teenager had a body from the heavens—five-foot-ten, 175 pounds—a gift that would make people feel even worse about themselves when he said he didn't even lift weights or work out much to make it that way.

In later years, people who weren't there would say they were, just to get in on the ground floor of the phenomenon. Rickey would tear up the Oakland Athletic League. A punt return and a touchdown against Oakland High. A blast off-tackle to destroy Castlemont. The scholarship letters piled up. Rickey said he had over 100 scholarship letters to play football, a number he would later amend upwards to 125. (Maybe even 150!) The Raiders were his team, O.J. was his guy, and football was his life.

Rickey played basketball too, but only to stay in shape, he would say. He'd call it a win-win: he could look at the girls—and have the girls get a good look at him in a tight pair of shorts.

Even though Rickey favored football, the baseball coaches knew how valuable Rickey was to their teams. Hank Thomasson, Rickey's Connie Mack coach, would literally provide door service for his players. He'd come to Rickey's house to drag him out of bed for big games—and bring breakfast. Fred would talk up baseball to Rickey, who would just reply, "Gotta concentrate on football." One piece of the Rickey legend would need correcting: it was true football was his favorite sport, but whatever sport he was playing at the moment was the sport that came first—and once the game started, Rickey was all business.

"Now, Rickey will tell you he didn't care about baseball, basketball, but he was tremendous," Lloyd Moseby recalled. "But no matter what, he had to win. Ping-pong? He had to win. We play dominoes, he has to win. No matter what it was—jacks—he had to win. Talk to anyone, and those stories will be consistent. Rickey always had to win."

For a time, baseball seemed destined to hold the same place in his life as basketball—just something to do when he wasn't playing football, another way to give the girls a chance to wink at him. But it was clear that baseball meant something more to him. When Bobbie caught him not doing his chores, she would spank him, and Rickey would recall wiping the tears from his face, then heading right back to the baseball field. Then came the day at Tech, when the pot got sweetened.

"There was this counselor, Mrs. Wilkerson. I was just playing, just sitting around not doing nothing, looking at basketball, and they had an Easter tournament," he recalled. "She brought me in the office and told me, 'We're a little short on players. Can you come out and play baseball?'

"I said, 'I don't want to play baseball.'

"Back in them days, you better get a job. She offered me a quarter. Hits, runs, stolen bases—a quarter each. I said, 'I'm about to make me some money. I'mma bout to make some money *and* don't have to work.' And I ain't lying. I had two hits, three, four stolen bases. Two, three runs every time I came out. Now I had lunch money to go get me something to eat!"

Tommie Wilkerson was one of those community angels who the world forgets but the kids never did. She knew Rickey from when he first arrived at Washington Elementary, and by the time Rickey arrived at Tech, she was there too. She even had a son named Rickey. He played baseball too, on the East Oakland fields at Fruitvale with Dave Stewart. Tommie Wilkerson used to attend the Oakland Tech games with a pocketful of quarters. Her deal with Rickey wasn't special—it was heartbreaking that so many kids didn't have walking-around money, so she gave a little something to all the kids who stole bases or the pitchers who did a good job—but it was Rickey who cleaned her out. Usually she would owe him around three bucks, but there was that day Rickey ran wild and she owed him $5.25. "I just wanted him to grow up a clean young man. I wanted him to have spending money so he could have things that a youngster needed—lunch money, a jacket, a gown at graduation time. I didn't want a lack of money to stand in his way."

With something to play for now, Rickey was all in on baseball—and that was when things got weird. When he and Fred first began playing Babe Ruth, Rickey was playing a year behind his friend. The same was true when they ventured north and played in the Berkeley leagues. Then the year Fred was promoted from ninth grade to the tenth, Rickey the eighth-grader was suddenly in the tenth grade too. "One year he was behind me," Atkins said. "The next year we were side by side." One plausible explanation was that his grade was adjusted because his birthday fell so late in the year. Another was that it was possible his birthday may have changed. As was once customary, children born at home often had two birth dates—the actual date of birth and the day the birth was recorded. Rickey was born in a car, and thus his birthday and his official birth date may have been different. The hint of mystery added to the legend of Rickey. Fred Atkins would give it the side-eye and laugh. *How old was Rickey, really?*

That was also the same year a story became legend that didn't quite seem true: Rickey Henderson, newly minted sophomore and local legend, was cut from the Oakland Tech baseball team.

The new baseball coach, Bob Cryer, was Tech's driving and training instructor. The word was that Cryer knew nothing about baseball and probably wasn't the school's first choice to coach the team, but he was the only one
who said yes. Before anyone stretched, caught, or hit a ball, Cryer literally
chose his varsity team by lottery, pointing out kids at random ("You, and
you, and *you* to the JV"). One of the kids banished to the JV field was Rickey.

"Rickey was a Babe Ruth legend," Fred Atkins recalled. "We all told him
he was making a mistake, that Rickey belonged on the varsity." While the
players pleaded with Cryer that there was no way Rickey belonged at the
kids' table, 15-year-old Rickey interrupted his new coach, a grown man, in
midsentence and said to him, "You must not know who I am."

Then Rickey showed him who he was.

"The varsity and JV fields went back to back," Atkins remembered. "There
was no fence separating the two fields. The JV and varsity center fielders
stood back to back. So you know what Rickey did? Whenever there was a fly
ball to center from the varsity field, Rickey would spin around from the JV
field and catch it.

"When we were wrapping up, the coach said, 'Did everybody hit? Is there
anybody that didn't hit?' Rickey raised his hand, even though he was supposed to be on the JV. He ran in and grabbed a bat—and all you could hear
off the bat was *Ping! Ping! Ping! Ping!* He was hitting *rockets.* When he was
finished, Coach looked at Rickey and said, '*You!* You come with us.'"

2

WHILE RICKEY SIFTED through the volume of college offers, thinking about the Pac-8, the Big 10, and, of course, the NFL, his buzz as a football player expanded beyond the tight borders of the Oakland Athletic League. Along all three sides of the Bay—in San Francisco, down the Peninsula, and in the East Bay—people knew Rickey's name. Even some of the older heads had been hearing about this kid from Oakland Tech who bruised defenders and left onlookers with memories. Mike Norris, the star pitcher from Balboa High in San Francisco whom the A's drafted in the first round, was one of them.

Norris was now in the big leagues as a 20-year-old, but even the big leaguer came up to North Oakland to check Rickey out. That was the way with the special ones. The virtuoso trumpeter Miles Davis referred to it in music as "that thing." There was just something different about the way Rickey moved—through the crowd, through a defensive line, from first to third. He made people pay attention. Even as a teenager, Rickey had "that thing."

Another San Franciscan besides Mike Norris was taking notice of Rickey during his senior year of 1975, when he was a running back on offense, a kick returner on special teams, and a linebacker on defense. Freshman Pamela Palmer and a girlfriend loved football so much that they reached out to Wayne Brooks, the Oakland Tech football coach, and he gave them both jobs as statisticians. Pamela's job was to record the Bulldogs' defensive stats.

Pamela lived on Pill Hill at 31st and Telegraph in North Oakland. The Palmers had followed the same pattern as Rickey's family. Her great-aunt owned a Victorian at Sacramento and Lyon Streets in the Pacific Heights

District, back when many Black families owned property in that part of town. The word was that only light-skinned Blacks could live in Pacific Heights. As Mike Norris recalled, the saying back in the day was that to live in Pacific Heights you had to be "light, bright, and almost white," but to Pamela that was just talk. "My aunt was brown-skinned, and most of the neighbors were brown, not light," Pamela recalled. "You know how Black folks come out as one solid color or a rainbow of brown shades? That was my family. All shades."

Pamela had moved to North Oakland when she was in middle school. She didn't much like baseball but understood at once its importance in Oakland. She first starting hanging around Bushrod during the Easter tournament—the same annual event where Tommie Wilkerson bribed Rickey to participate for the shorthanded Oakland Tech squad—and eventually Pamela got a summer job at the Oakland Parks and Recreation Department.

Baseball was too slow for Pamela. Too slow and too boring. "I'd watch the games and then just ask myself, 'Am I watching this wrong? When is *something* going to *happen?*'" Football was more accessible, with its athleticism, its speed, its contact—and contact was Rickey's game. Rickey didn't evade the defense and step out of bounds. He wasn't one of those backs who were too pretty, too soft. Rickey bulldozed his way through opponents. And on defense? He wanted to lay people out.

Pamela's job was to keep the statistics of the game, run the stat sheets upstairs to the broadcast booth, and occasionally call the scores in to the *Tribune* so Tech's games could appear on the agate page. (Who didn't want to see their name in the paper?) The first time she took notice of Rickey Henderson, star running back of the Oakland Technical High School Bulldogs, he wasn't running through tacklers but rolling the bones. In the middle of a dice game (at school!), Pamela, the freshman, introduced herself to the Biggest Man on Campus, even though he was three grades above her.

"They used to call me 'Squeaky' because of my voice. It had that high pitch to it," she recalled. "I saw Rickey. I walked him all the way to class that day, and I told him, 'You're not supposed be out here.' It's true, I was just a freshman, but I had a little spark to me. I think that's why his mother liked me. She figured I could keep up."

It was one thing to be a local sensation. The schools were full of kids who peaked in high school. (And when those local heroes aged and their glorious pasts became their mundane presents, all the bars across America were filled with them too.) In other places, for the best players in town, that last senior-year touchdown was as good as it was going to get for the rest of their lives. In Oakland, especially Black Oakland, where it felt like everybody was a three-star athlete, careers weren't expected to end after high school for the best players. High school was just the beginning.

Rickey first believed he had pro-level talent around the eighth grade, when he was 13 or so, and it was then that he began thinking about his future in those terms. Meanwhile, school was something of an annoyance. The classroom was the only place in his life where he couldn't win all the time, couldn't just channel that hypercompetitiveness and will himself to success. He always felt sure in math, but when he was reading, the words sometimes looked like a jigsaw puzzle. On the field, his confidence sustained him, but in the classroom Rickey spent more time hiding what he didn't know. Sometimes concealing his subpar academic output did not require much effort. With the school, the teachers, everybody, getting caught up in what their touchdown maker could do on the field, no one was going to interfere too much. "They pushed me through," Rickey has admitted, "especially if we had a game that week."

Viewing himself as a future pro instead of an eager fan might explain why Rickey always remembered that time when the great Reggie Jackson stiffed him for an autograph. Rickey and Fred were spending more time around the A's because a new friend, Lewis Burrell, had gotten them tickets to the Coliseum a couple of times. Lewis was from East Oakland, got bounced from Fremont High, and wound up at Oakland Tech. Once he was at Tech, Fred said, he told them, "'You guys are supposed to be the athletes. If you need anything let me know.' He was low-key about it, and we said, 'Yeah, right.'"

What Lewis didn't advertise was that he was the A's batboy and his little brother Stanley was Charlie Finley's eyes and ears. The players had a nickname for Stanley—they called him "Hammer" because they thought the kid looked like "Hammerin' Hank" Aaron. They also had another nickname for him: "Pipeline," as in the pipeline to Charlie Finley. That was better than calling him a "snitch." When Lewis kept telling Rickey and Fred to let him know if they needed anything—hats, balls, bats, all the swag—they grew intrigued. "He said, 'Y'all need some batting gloves? The ballplayers give it to me,'" Fred Atkins said. "'At the end of the season, they just give us free stuff. And now we were listening because we had some raggedy stuff. And

Lewis came by with a duffel bag full of stuff. We started going over to his house, and we got free tickets to A's games, and from that point on we were all close."

Being around the ballpark was cool, and the swag was even better, but Rickey didn't see himself as some neighborhood shrimp begging for Reggie's time. Even if he admired what other players were doing, he wasn't a spectator. He saw himself as a future peer, destined to be a one-name guy just like him. *Reggie. Mickey. Willie . . . RICKEY.* The great ones, they didn't *need* last names. *Rickey.* That sounded good. It sounded so good he started calling himself just Rickey. Plus, he wasn't really being cocky. It was true that Rickey wasn't a sports fan in the classic sense. Rickey saw the sports field as a place where *he* was the one who should be doing the dominating, where the watchers came to watch *him.*

In addition to her football duties, Pamela used to keep time for the Tech track team with the stopwatch around her neck. She remembered the time Rickey came out to the track on a whim and Coach Brooks, who doubled as Tech's track coach, called out his best runner to face Rickey. Rickey *dusted* the school champ in the 100-yard dash—just made him look like he was standing still. Turned him into a totem pole. That fed into another Rickey story: after school, Rickey would practice his speed by racing the school bus home. "He could just do things that no other player could do. The sport didn't matter," Pamela remembered. "Any sport he played, he just played exceptionally well. Any time there was competition, he just couldn't lose. He had to win. It was always about being better."

The scouts camped out in Oakland. There were the full-time scouts who knew to make the special trip to the East Bay to see a kid firsthand. They were the grizzled old baseball men who drove the hard miles across America to find talent and were not easily impressed, for they had seen different variations of the same kid—big fish in his own pond, but unable to swim once the water got deep. Having them show up wasn't exactly a compliment because they were so impatient (and was it really possible to project a kid's future in nine innings?) that they probably missed on more ballplayers than they hit. Those scouts were called "performance scouts"—if a kid didn't perform the day they happened to be in the stands, well, they weren't coming back for a second look. The bird-dog scouts were the real eyes and ears of a town for a pro ball club. They were the ones who stuck around, took the time to get to know a player, to know his family—and they often got a bonus if a kid they recommended made the grade.

If in the old days it seemed as if Cincinnati owned exclusive rights to Oakland, it was because they did. On their side the Reds had George Powles, the best, most respected pair of eyes in town, and as a result Frank Robinson, Curt Flood, Vada Pinson, and Joe Gaines, as well as Tommy Harper, who was across the estuary over in Alameda crushing balls at Encinal High, all ended up in Cincinnati. Bobby Mattick would go down in baseball history as the Reds' super-scout who signed them, but that happened because the kids trusted his local man Powles—and more importantly, their parents trusted him—and because George Powles steered the best athletes to Bobby Mattick.

By the time scouts had come around to look at Rickey, McClymonds no longer had exclusive run of the place. Segregation had no longer packed the city's Black talent exclusively into West Oakland, and in the second wave the talent was more widely dispersed throughout the city. Furthermore, unlike in Powles's heyday, when the advantage of ground-level information was key to beating the competition and a phone call and a handshake could lead to a contract, the rest of the big leagues now had their eye on Oakland. Also indirectly limiting the influence of local legends like George Powles was the amateur draft instituted in 1965 to keep the Yankees and Cardinals from hoarding all the talent with their vast reach and resources. Knowing about a kid first no longer conferred an exclusive advantage because he might be gone before a team's slot came up in the order. In the United States, teams that wanted to control scores of kids without having to compete with or pay very much to other teams for their services could no longer easily do so. Baseball would go to Latin America for that.

In later years, it wouldn't seem possible, but there was one team everyone would look back on in wonder. It was Hank Thomasson's Connie Mack team. People said it was the best-ever collection of talent, a superlative that didn't get thrown around easily in Oakland. The team was dynamite. Dave Stewart was on it. So was Gary Pettis. Fred Atkins was quickly shedding the nickname "Shorty" with a mighty growth spurt and becoming, at over six feet tall, a fearsome pitcher for the team. A speedster named Danny Liggins was the center fielder. Another kid, Cliff Wherry from Oakland High, was the shortstop. The team also included Steve Moore from Fremont High and Rickey Henderson, the Football Kid. And Rickey didn't always start. Another Oakland High kid, Lloyd Moseby, aka the Shaker, was on the team too—as the batboy.

"I got cut when I was 10, and I got cut when I was 11. And I saw Rickey and Fred—that was Rickey's guy. And Fred, Fred Atkins was a hell of a pitcher," Moseby recalled. "So, I saw these guys play. I wasn't playing yet. I kept getting cut. So I asked, 'Can I batboy for you?' He said 'Sure,' and I got cut. And got cut again, and when I kept coming back, he said, 'How can a kid be that motivated?' I wanted to play."

Like Rickey and the rest of them, Dennis Dixon had lived the Black Oakland migration story. His mother was from Little Rock, his father from Houston. The family arrived in Oakland in the late 1950s "to find a better life," Dennis would say. They settled in West Oakland, at 25th and Grove (a few blocks away from members of the funk band Sly and the Family Stone), before moving to East Oakland in 1968. Dixon went head-to-head with Lloyd Moseby on the basketball court; with Gary Pettis in Babe Ruth (Dixon recalled that he played for the Phillies and Pettis for a team sponsored by Granny Goose, the potato chip company, but Pettis actually played for the Braves, sponsored by the television station KTVU); with Dave Stewart on the mound when, he swears, he drove a line drive back up the box in a game against St. Elizabeth's (by that time they called Stewart "the King of St. Elizabeth's"); and with Rickey, on the basketball court and the baseball diamond. Dixon also believed he had plus-talent and, in his eyes, big league ability (his son Dennis Dixon Jr. would one day win Super Bowls as a member of the Pittsburgh Steelers and Baltimore Ravens), but at the time he didn't want to leave home. Dixon would live in the Bay his entire life.

In a serious Oakland-level understatement, Dixon was never short of confidence. "In all the years I played baseball, from Little League through high school, I never struck out," Dixon recalled. "Never. Seriously. Not once. And I batted leadoff. Even when I pitched, I hit leadoff. And I had a serious glove—and speed. I played against Rickey for the first time in an all-star game together as a 15-year-old. He was a nightmare. You couldn't get Rickey out. Speed, a quick bat. He was just awesome."

There was always something different about these Oakland kids—and about Oakland in general. They never backed down, not in the street and not on the field (*"You must not know who I am"*). Having played against each other since elementary school and seen so many in the group gain the opportunity to play Division I or professional ball, they knew their training ground was no small pond for big fish; aware that they were playing against potential professionals in middle school, they knew they had to bring it—or get embarrassed. They knew if they could bring it against these players in their neighborhoods who were being signed by major league teams, they could compete against anyone in the country. Oakland kids had a reputation for knowing how to shine when the lights came on (*Ping! Ping! Ping! Ping! "You! You come with us!"*), and that was a quality the scouts were looking for. All the Oakland kids—those like Rickey and Moseby, who had come to Oakland when they were old enough to remember the journey from the South, and those like Gary Pettis and Dave Stewart, who were born in Oakland but whose families were from the South—had absorbed the rhythms and cadences of the city and shared a distinctive Oakland personality.

In 1940, Oakland counted 8,462 Black people as residents. By 1970, Rickey's first year in middle school, the number had swelled to 124,710. By the time Rickey was old enough to drink, Oakland's Black population was 159,351, or 47 percent of the city—a 1,783 percent increase in 40 years. Much of the blood in Black Oakland was originally southern, but the kids also possessed that California expectation of being free, unrestricted by the caste systems of the South and the North; they were seduced by the newness and possibilities of California, just like the prospectors before them.

Black migration to California wasn't the same as the pre- and postwar exoduses from the South to the East Coast or to Chicago and Detroit; those places were already established. California after the war represented an exciting new frontier in the American story. Blacks who migrated there, however, would be reminded that, regardless of time zone, there was no promised land for Black people within America's borders. Black people changed the city of Oakland, and in turn the city, and its often hostile reaction to the Blacks moving in, shaped them, hardening them and giving them another layer of toughness. Oakland embodied a certain national schizophrenia: the aspirations of California combined with the crushing segregation of the North and, particularly in the case of law enforcement, the southern tendency to use violence to intimidate Black people.

Besides the appeal of its good weather, California was also attractive because of the zero-sum nature of its geography: if California didn't work out, there was literally nowhere else to go. That was why reinvention was such a big part of the California mythology: the state represented the *tabula rasa*, the fresh start. For the Black people picking up stakes in Texas, Louisiana, and Arkansas, the move 1,500 miles to the West Coast was supposed to bring a permanent improvement. Any other move was going backward, not only physically if they moved back east but also psychologically, returning to a place meant to be left behind. For Black people in particular in the postwar years, Oakland presented a strange blend of expression, possibilities, and freedom as well as restrictions and tensions that created a unique type of Black American. California had to work. They were home now.

Rickey's generation was young, and they were imbued with the spirit of Oakland. Gary Pettis, who was only eight months older than Rickey, knew they had all dodged a bullet, literally, by being too young to serve in Vietnam. By the time the scouts began projecting a potential future for them in baseball, America had already done away with the draft, in 1973. Still, the kids remembered a ferocious time in America, and the volatility on their own streets, such as when police savagely beat antiwar protesters who shut down the Oakland Induction Center on October 17, 1967.

Oakland kids were defiant, wholly independent, creative outsiders with an irreverent style. It made sense to Lloyd Moseby that the Black Panther Party—a direct challenge to a fearsome institution—was formed in Oakland by Bobby Seale and Huey Newton, two southerners whose families came west for better, only to be faced with humiliation and subpar living conditions similar to what they had left in the South. The Oakland kids especially remembered the look and aura and presence of the Black Panther Party. "They were our heroes because they represented change," Moseby said. "We wore the naturals, with the picks, and we saw how much [the authorities] made sure they got rid of them. Look at how many of them they put in jail, for a long time, for nothing. Angela Davis, Huey Newton. Bobby. They showed us the way."

The kids saw the Panthers, armed to protect them. They saw what the police and the FBI did to them—Bobby Seale, Eldridge Cleaver, and the rest—and they saw it up close. "I lived a block or two away from one of their headquarters," Pettis said. "We used to walk by there, and you might see Angela Davis or Huey Newton on a given day. Even though we were young, politics seemed to be ingrained into our systems because of the color of our skin." Pamela recalled the influence of the Panthers on the community as well. Her mother used to pack the breakfasts and lunches for school lunch programs that the Panthers pioneered. When Oakland Police infamously killed 17-year-old Panther Bobby Hutton in a shootout two days after the assassination of Martin Luther King, Jr., the confrontation occurred at 1218 28th Street in West Oakland, the home of Nelly Pierre—11-year-old Dave Stewart's great-grandmother. For more than a half-century, the family would keep the bullet-filled couch where police opened fire upon entering the house.

Nor was it a coincidence to Pettis that it was Curt Flood who challenged baseball's reserve clause, the 100-year-old claim of baseball's owners to a right to control players in perpetuity. Taking on this fight came, at least in part, from the Oakland in him. Flood refused to report to the Phillies, sued baseball, and took his case to the Supreme Court, where he lost by a 5–4 decision. But he had shown the players who did not believe that they could have a say in their careers, that a different reality was possible. (Boston's Carl Yastrzemski famously called Flood selfish; Willie Mays was making $180,000 a year and didn't want to get involved.)

The boldness of the Panthers and Flood's lawsuit against baseball represented to Pettis the spirit of the Black migration from the South to Oakland. A challenge to an entire industry and its economic system could only have come from a person who had traveled as Flood had—fleeing the hostility and indignities of Texas for West Oakland, only to discover that the place of promise for Black people was full of the same barriers, limitations, and violence through other means. Not everyone had it in them. Frank Robinson was no revolutionary and didn't want the real world to enter the game. "A lot of Negro groups have criticized me for it," Frank Robinson wrote in his 1968 autobiography *My Life Is Baseball*. "But I don't think baseball should be a fight for anything but baseball." Flood, on the other hand, was an inspiration: if Curt Flood could not move to freedom, he would will it to existence.

Now professional baseball wanted Oakland's ballplayers. Word had gotten around about Fred Atkins, who remembered feeling like a rock star when he stepped onto the baseball diamond. "You'd look into the stands, and your paths crossed with the scouts so much you'd say, 'Hey, there's the scout from the Tigers,' Or, 'Hey, there's the scout from the Angels.' They were just camped out." People said Atkins threw as hard as Dave Stewart, maybe even harder. Stewart, as competitive as anyone, didn't argue. Word had also gotten around that the Yankees—the lordly Yankees—were looking at Fred. Their scout was Wayne Morgan, who lived down past San Jose, in Morgan Hill, just an hour south.

A Berkeley High kid, Ruppert Jones, went in the third round to the Royals in the 1973 draft. Then the Dodgers, who had already drafted Glenn Burke, took the catcher Davey Stewart in the 16th round of the 1975 draft. By this point, he was called Dave, but his friend Rickey still called him Davey (and for the next half-century would be the only one allowed to do so). At the suggestion of the great Sandy Koufax, the Dodgers took away Stewart's catcher's mitt, sent him to the Bellingham Dodgers of the Northwest League, and converted him into a pitcher.

Claudell Washington was the true natural. He didn't even play on the Berkeley High team, and everybody knew why: Claudell never went to class. Unlike Rickey, he wasn't fueled by the game, the pure competition of it. He just happened to be so ridiculously good at it (the die-hard who busted his ass and couldn't produce one swing like Claudell's might have said *unfairly* good at it) that he was major league material without even always going 100 percent. Washington was working as a janitor when James "J.J." Guinn, a Berkeley policeman and part-time scout for the A's, signed him as a 17-year-old free agent. When Washington got the call to the big leagues from Double-A Birmingham, he told his roommate Mike Norris, "Send me my records because I ain't coming back." By the time he was 19, Washington was in the major leagues hitting .300 and winning the 1974 World Series, the last of the A's three straight titles.

Everybody assumed that Rickey's path was to the NFL, but Jim Guinn wasn't exactly convinced. Charlie Finley's area bird dog had already struck gold signing Claudell Washington, and now he had been hanging out at Bushrod, watching Rickey, almost certain he was seeing something of value that no one else did.

In his own way, Guinn identified Rickey because he was one of them—a product of the Migration who had world-class athletic talent. Jim Guinn was born in Jefferson, Texas, in Marion County, a small East Texas town in the middle of nowhere, between Tyler and Shreveport. Growing up there, he saw firsthand how the Jim Crow South destroyed the aspirations of Black people, economically and psychologically. His father saw Black residents who had owned land for decades after emancipation losing their property to whites, through shady bookkeeping, force, or both. He told his son that losing your property was the first sign of losing everything, of being part of a permanent underclass with no self-determination, no future.

Young Jim was taught early that whites expected subjugation to be an understood condition of the Black man. He remembered as a boy watching his father having to stop and face the street if a white woman happened to be approaching in his direction. When Jim asked his father one Saturday morning why he was subjected to this humiliating local custom, the older man explained that if he didn't go along with it, if he made eye contact with a white woman, he'd be thrown in jail—at best. At school the following Monday, 11-year-old Jim Guinn refused to recite the Pledge of Allegiance—especially that hogwash about "with liberty and justice for all." His father was called to the school, where he admonished his son and forced him to recite the pledge, though Jim pleaded with his father not to force him to swear allegiance to a lie. J. J. Guinn never forgot his father's response. "My daddy used to tell me, 'If I don't raise you, the white man will. I owe you this.'"

Young Jim obeyed his father, but he recited the final line, "*With liberty and justice for all*," with such sarcasm that the teacher and the class were even further offended by his defiance. That same year, 1948, seven years before the infamous murder of Emmett Till in Mississippi, the elder Guinn sent his son to California to live with his sister in West Oakland at 32nd and Hannah Streets—and quite possibly saved the boy's life in doing so.

Jim Guinn played locally in the Oakland Police Department league, and after the family moved out of West Oakland, he was a standout at Berkeley High. In high school he made an important contact that would be beneficial years later—he was classmates with Bobby Seale, and his sister was best friends with Bobby's sister Betty. After attending Santa Rosa Junior College, he was signed by Philadelphia in 1957, the same year the Phillies became the last team in the National League to integrate. Guinn was assigned to Salt Lake City, of the Class C Pioneer League.

"I was the only Black player on the team, and there was one hotel I was allowed to stay. The manager was a guy named Cliff Dapper—he wound up raising avocados in California with Duke Snider," Guinn recalled. "I was all of 19 years old. He briefed us on the game, looked at me, and said, 'When you get to first, take your lead, but don't get nigger rich.' That meant don't stray too far from your place and get picked off. He walked me back to the hotel and apologized for what he said, but being from the South, I was insulated, because I'd already seen the worst of it."

Jim Guinn batted .287 in 451 minor league games. He played in Salt Lake City, Olean, and Elmira in the New York Penn League, in Asheville in the Sally League, and in Williamsport of the Eastern League, but he never got the call to the big leagues. Unless you were a superstar like Richie Allen, the

Phillies did not promote Black players through the ranks. "They would sign them and just leave them there and release them. When I got signed, they signed like 30 Blacks and immediately released 16 of them . . . In Asheville down in the Sally League, one of my teammates said to me, 'Hey, Jimmy, we're playing these niggers from Charleston, South Carolina. All them niggers can run, and you can't see them at night.' It was just part of the conversation. And the guy who said it, he liked me. He was just being open with it. Being 20, 21 years old, I took offense, but I never expressed it."

After seven years in the minors, Jim Guinn returned to California, but he stayed on in baseball as a part-time scout for the Phillies. Then Charlie Finley offered him the same job with the A's in 1969. By then, he had joined the Berkeley Police Department, where he soon discovered that the humiliations were not confined to an occupation, area code, or zip code. As enlightened as California (and Berkeley in particular) liked to consider itself, Black people in Berkeley knew the racial hierarchy in the city.

Once, when Guinn was in the patrol car with a white cadet, a call came across the dispatch with the code "TNA." Guinn knew his radio codes, like 10-17 (request for gasoline) and 10-71 (shooting), but TNA was unfamiliar to him. Over time the code had been used more frequently, as in "TNA in progress." When his young partner asked him if the term bothered him, Guinn was forced to admit he didn't know what TNA meant. Sheepish at first, the young trainee finally told Guinn that the abbreviation stood for "Typical Nigger Activity." "I almost left the department because I'd heard it so many times. I was shocked because we had the greatest admiration for the Berkeley Police Department because their standards were high. You had to have a BA to be on the force, and we had college men from Cal and Stanford, and still this."

Despite the volatility of those years and the distrust between the Black community and police, Jim Guinn developed an understanding with Black residents. He refused to replicate the common behavior of the earlier generation of Black policemen, who believed that an unspoken prerequisite of their job was to be even more aggressive with Black citizens than the white policemen were. Guinn wasn't going to be that Black cop beating on Black kids. He would look for talent and use his connections with the game to give players the chances he might have had in better times. He also benefited from his sister's friendship with Betty Seale, Bobby's sister. "That was a big advantage," he recalled. "No trouble with the Panthers."

• • •

The scouts who watched Rickey had no doubt they were watching a gifted athlete, but they were unconvinced about him as a baseball player. Doubt was baked into their DNA—scouts never missed a chance to emphasize what a player *couldn't* do. Rarely did they see what a player *was,* or what he *could* be. Once they saw a deficiency in a player, they always seemed absolutely certain it could never be overcome ("He'll never hit for power"). So they were doubtful that 17-year-old Rickey would ever make the big leagues. Too many problems, they said. He had that weird batting right–throwing left combination that virtually no successful position players had. (Cleon Jones of the Mets was a notable exception, as was that game-throwing cheater of the early 1900s, the Yankees' Hal Chase.) Throwing left-handed, he couldn't play an infield position, except for first base, but at his height (Rickey was already at his full height, five-foot-ten, as a high school senior) and with his superior athletic skills, who was going to waste Rickey at first base, home of the clods? They were also convinced that, by batting right and throwing left, Rickey wouldn't generate sufficient bat power, because his dominant hand, his left, was on the bottom of the bat, not the top, where it needed to be. Of course, Rickey could have batted left-handed as a kid, but he hit right-handed for two reasons: to be like Willie Mays, and because everyone else did.

Then came the day the Dodgers came to see Rickey during an Oakland Tech game against Skyline. As Jim Guinn recalled, it wasn't Dick Hager or Dick Hanlan, the two full-time Dodger scouts who lived in the area and had scouted Dave Stewart, who came but most likely the scouting director, Bill Brenzel, himself from old Oakland, before the Migration. Brenzel attended Fremont High in the 1920s, when Black residents were virtually nonexistent in the city—and those who did live there certainly did not live in East Oakland—and he even played in the big leagues for a minute. Brenzel was a performance scout. He showed up, sat right down, and waited for Rickey to show him what he had. Brenzel introduced himself to J. J. Guinn, who was seated next to him. Guinn would recall that Brenzel's countenance said it all: *Important Guy. With the Dodgers.* The Dodgers always created a buzz.

Andrew Robinson was the Skyline pitcher that day. He was also the Titans' starting quarterback and knew Rickey well from football, having played against him in Babe Ruth—Rickey for Porta House, Robinson for

Bercovich. Robinson, no slouch athlete himself, was heading to Washington State on a football scholarship. He could attest to Rickey's electricity and recalled a game in which Rickey ran back the opening kickoff against Skyline. He and his team had the last laugh, though, rolling to a blowout, "something like 45 to 7."

Robinson got Rickey in his first at-bat, striking him out on a curveball. Rickey looked even worse his second time up, striking out again. As Rickey walked back to the dugout, Brenzel was done. He was a performance scout, and Rickey hadn't performed. Guinn would remember that, as Brenzel stood up, he heard the scout mutter something to the effect of "I've seen enough" and "got a plane to catch." Then he left.

And that was how J. J. Guinn and the Oakland A's got the inside track on signing Rickey Henderson. In his third at-bat Rickey crushed a long home run. In his fourth, Rickey hit another one, this one rocketing even farther. By the time it landed, Bill Brenzel was probably settling into his plane seat, enjoying the pre-takeoff beverage service. "If he'd have stayed," Jim Guinn recalled, "Rickey would have been a Dodger."

"I got him the first two times, and then he put it out, like way out there," Robinson recalled. "Those balls ended up in the middle of the football field. Rickey was always a great player. Never did anyone think he'd be the greatest leadoff hitter of all time, but there were so many great athletes then. It was a great time growing up."

Another time Jim Guinn showed up to take a look at Rickey, and Hank Thomasson, who was then coaching Rickey in American Legion ball, told Guinn he must have made a mistake.

"He said, 'Rickey? You're looking at the wrong guy. The best player here is the center fielder.' That kid's name was Danny Liggins. I think the Cardinals drafted him. I said, 'Maybe I have to look at other guys, but I'm not looking at the *wrong* guy.'"

J. J. Guinn watched Rickey for 20 games, 140 innings in all, and maintained a good line of communication with the family. He had to go through his mother Bobbie because Rickey was still a minor—nothing could be done without Bobbie's consent. On April 19, 1976, two months before the 1976 draft, Guinn submitted his scouting report to the A's. The Oakland A's scouting card consisted of 10 categories for evaluating position players presented in two columns: present level and future projection. The report was based on a scale of 2 to 8, with 8 being "outstanding" and 2 being "poor."

Guinn gave Rickey's running speed his highest rating of 7 (Very Good), both in the present and projected for the future, and gave him a 5 (Average) for his baseball instinct and aggressiveness. He reported both Rickey's fielding ability and hitting ability as a 3 (Well Below Average) at present, and his present power, baserunning, arm strength, arm accuracy, and range all as 4 (Below Average). In no area of the game, however, did Guinn project Rickey to be below average in the future, and he projected Rickey's range and baserunning to increase to a 7 (Very Good). In other words, Guinn felt that Rickey had room to grow. His assessment contained the following summary:

STRENGTHS:
Henderson has a lot of athletic ability. He is an outstanding athlete in three sports, baseball, basketball, and football. He has very good speed and an average throwing arm. I feel that his throwing arm will improve when he learns to extend it. He also has some power at the plate, but cannot be considered a power hitter at the present time although he has the basic physical qualities to become one. Henderson has very good lateral range in the outfield, which is mainly due to his speed. He also has very good baseball instinct, which is evident in his baserunning. Acceleration and speed are the main qualities that are needed to become an outstanding baserunner. Henderson possesses both of these qualities. I would like to project a good future in baseball for this youngster.

WEAKNESSES:
Henderson needs a lot of work on his hitting techniques. He crouches too low and tilts his bat too far behind his head. He has a fairly good swing, but it is often not quick enough due to the position of his bat; he over strides a lot, especially on breaking pitches and off-speed pitches. These problems, I feel, can be corrected with some sound hitting instructions. In the outfield, he has problems on balls that are hit directly over his head. Again, with the good speed that he possesses he will probably overcome these problems.

He has an unusual combination that is seldom seen in the major leagues. That is, he throws left-handed and bats right-

322222

handed. The only active player that stands out in my mind with that combination is Cleon Jones. This does not concern me because he demonstrates potential from the right side.

"You're not watching a kid to see if they can hit. You're watching him to see if he *will* have the ability to hit," Guinn recalled. "And once you determine they have that ability, then it's about making adjustments as the competition increases and the pitchers get better. You cannot scout what's inside someone. If you don't have the guts to hit, you can have the great swing [but] you're not gonna hit anything. Rickey had all that. Curt Flood was an excellent hitter at 12, 13 years old, but very few guys are. Willie Stargell was nearly sent down permanently because he didn't hit."

In his report, Guinn concluded:

> In my opinion, Henderson is the best looking prospect in the Alameda County Athletic League and the Oakland Athletic League. I am impressed with this youngster mainly because of his all-round athletic ability. He is an athlete. I am not aware of the availability of other top prospects throughout the country, nevertheless, I recommend the Oakland Athletics draft this youngster no lower than "AA."

Whatever enthusiasm Jim Guinn had for Rickey was not exactly shared by the A's, at least not in the tangible way that enthusiasm is shown in all things sports and business—an urgency to keep Rickey from other teams by aggressively drafting him and making sure he'd sign by offering a generous signing bonus. Rickey hadn't even yet graduated from high school, but he was about to engage in a battle he'd be in for the rest of his professional life: defining his worth.

Just before graduation, Bobbie had a family friend who was in the finance business take a look at the offers coming in. Rickey knew he was going to be drafted and knew what he could do on the football field, so he wasn't concerned about his future. After making his calculations, the financial planner and Bobbie decided that it would take $100,000 for a baseball team to sign Rickey.

• • •

The A's of 1976 were a dynasty in name only. They had won their division again the year before, but when a younger, surprising Boston caught them in the playoffs and knocked them out in a sweep, everybody knew it was only a matter of time before the Swingin' A's were a wrap. (After the Red Sox sweep, rumor had it that Reggie Jackson and several other teammates congratulated Tom Yawkey—and begged him to take them away from Oakland, and owner Charlie Finley.)

The end felt especially inevitable that December, when arbiter Peter Seitz ruled in favor of players Andy Messersmith and Dave McNally in a case brought on their behalf by the Major League Baseball Players Association: at long last players had won their right to change teams once their contracts expired. The glory days of three straight championships in Oakland were the first casualty, dusted away by Curt Flood's revenge—the howl and lightning of free agency. Catfish Hunter was already gone to the Yankees for big money. Reggie had departed as well, also to the Yankees for big money, but only after Finley first traded him and Ken Holtzman to Baltimore for Don Baylor. Those in what was left of the great core—Vida Blue and Rollie Fingers, Joe Rudi and Bert Campaneris—were still hanging on, but Finley knew free agency meant he now had to pay them the old-fashioned American way. If he didn't pay them what the market said they were worth, he'd lose them for nothing, so he was trying to get rid of them too.

When Guinn made his presentation about Rickey to Syd Thrift, the A's farm director, Thrift was unimpressed. When Guinn was done talking about how much he liked the kid and detailing all of his accompanying upsides, Thrift told Guinn he'd take Rickey if he was available—in the fourth round. There were three other guys he *really* had his eye on. Thrift's urgency about Rickey sounded about as pressing as raking the leaves on a Sunday with a full slate of football on TV—he'd do it *if* he got around to it. Just in case there was any ambiguity about how the A's felt about Rickey, Thrift (you couldn't invent a better last name for someone working for the parsimonious Charlie Finley) ended the mystery by telling Guinn he had $10,000 to sign Rickey. That was fourth-round money.

Ten grand sounded like a lot, especially to a high school senior who four years earlier played baseball for a quarter per stolen base. Ten Gs was also what the great Hank Aaron signed for, and being in the same company as the Hammer also sounded special—except that it was 1952 when Henry signed with the Boston Braves for his $10,000.

Jim Guinn knew Rickey was worth more than what Finley was offering, and he knew teams often tried to sign players for less than their worth. After all, baseball had made an industry off of the practice for a century. What was appalling to Guinn was the racial and class-based exploitation of this practice, which he felt was at work during the process with Rickey but couldn't quite articulate. The true reason for this practice finally became clear for Guinn years later during an A's organizational meeting. "We were looking at potential prospects, and with each name that came up, one of the guys in the meeting would ask if the player came from a single-parent home," Guinn recalled. "He said, 'Get the single mothers . . . Look for the single moms . . . Always good to get a single mom because they're going to jump at the first amount—and then we can lowball them.' I almost quit on the spot. I don't usually speak up in a group like that because I prefer to talk to people in private, but I said right there, 'I thought we were offering contracts based on the merit and level of their ability? Isn't that what we're supposed to be doing?'"

The Rickey baseball story, passed down over the years like a family heirloom, went like this: He chose baseball over football because Bobbie feared he would get hurt playing football. Rickey, the Good Son, said he abided by Bobbie's choice because "she never makes a bad decision." All of this was generally true, but there was another component of the decision to sign with the A's: the classroom. Rickey didn't have the grades to go directly from Oakland Tech to Division I football. With his less than stellar academic performance, his road to the pros was now convoluted and much riskier— through the junior college circuit to the big-time college game and then, more distantly, the NFL. But adding another step to the journey raised the risk of injury: Rickey could shatter his knee at some Podunk junior college and blow the whole thing. Baseball was the surer, safer bet. What Finley offered wasn't a lot, but in baseball Rickey was going to get paid immediately. Guinn's advice to Bobbie would have been for Rickey to not sign and to play baseball at junior college before going back into the draft. But Rickey took the bird in hand: accepting $10,000 from the A's, he was now a professional athlete—but he would never forget he was worth significantly more than the money he'd accepted.

On draft day in 1976, somebody *did* get their 100-large—but it wasn't Rickey. The Astros selected Floyd Bannister first overall, signing him for $100,000. Back then, only first-overall picks got the hundred grand Rickey

wanted. The Angels drafted Ken Landreaux sixth overall and signed him
for $82,500. The Cardinals took a burly kid named Leon Durham and gave
him $37,500, and the Dodgers—whose scout had only had time enough for
Rickey to watch two at-bats—took a catcher, Mike Scioscia, with their first-
round pick. Scioscia signed for $44,500.

As the rounds passed, Rickey remained on the board. The Tigers took
a shortstop, Alan Trammell, with their first pick of the second round. The
Mets took a pitcher, Mike Scott. Of the 24 picks of the third round, only
eight would ever play in the majors, and only two—Max Venable, picked
67th overall by the Dodgers, and the Twins' John Castino (58th)—would
appear in at least 500 big league games.

Rickey was the final pick of the fourth round, 96th overall. History
would show only six other players selected ahead of him in that round—
Jim Pankovits, Dan Petry, Keith Drumright, Bob Pate, Brian Allard, and
Ted Wilborn—reaching the majors, and only the ornery right-hander Petry
made a real career out of it. None of Syd Thrift's first three picks ahead of
Rickey, the ones he *really* had his eye on—Thomas Sullivan, Brian Duffy,
and Al Minker—ever reached the major leagues, and Sullivan and Duffy
never even *signed* with the A's.

The A's were going after the big bodies: Duffy and Minker were six-five
and six-six, respectively. Picking them was consistent with the old baseball
adage: "Little guys have to prove they can play; big guys have to prove they
can't." Of course, there were stories like that throughout sports, and they
didn't end with Rickey in his own draft. Two other players, fifth-rounder
Jack Morris, and seventh-rounder Ozzie Smith, were selected after Rickey,
and a third, Wade Boggs, went not only after Rickey but also after Rickey's
best friend, Fred Atkins—who was drafted by the Yankees with the 160th
pick, six slots before Boggs. Calling drafting an imprecise science was being
extremely kind to the baseball talent evaluators—and insulting to the word
"science."

Nevertheless, Rickey and Fred had now graduated from Oakland Tech
and signed contracts to play professional baseball, Rickey with the hometown A's, Fred with the legendary Yankees.

For signing Rickey and Claudell Washington, Jim Guinn received neither
a raise nor a bonus (nor a gold-wrapped piece of candy) from the A's. He
remembered Charlie Finley's rationale for not rewarding him in five words.
"He said, 'You'll never do that again.'" Still, signing Rickey vindicated J. J.

Guinn. Having been in baseball in some capacity his whole life, he believed it was the unique road he had taken in the game and his experience as a former player that enabled him to see something in Rickey that not only did his own organization fail to see, but so did the rest of baseball. The full-time professionals believed that 95 other players had a better chance of making an impact on the game than Rickey.

"The biggest difference between Rickey and everybody else was his attitude," he recalled. "Rickey had something I could identify with. Rickey had that will to win. He didn't back down from anybody. When I asked Claudell what he wanted to accomplish in the game, he said he wanted to hit .300 in the big leagues once. He didn't say 'every year.' He said 'once.' Well, he did it in his first year. Mission accomplished. He could have set his sights so much higher. Now, Rickey? When I asked Rickey the same question, as a 17-year-old, he said to me point-blank—again, as a 17-year-old, mind you—he said, 'I want to be the greatest base stealer of all time.'"

3

IN ANY LEGENDARY life, there is a flashpoint moment when the star becomes separated from the mortal rest, the heads turn, and the people who weren't really paying attention get the heads-up, a special stock-tip whisper in the ear: *Get in on this early.* Those who listen can always say they were there on the ground floor before the rest of the legend fell deliciously into place.

For Rickey, that moment occurred on May 26, 1977, when the Modesto A's were up against the Fresno Giants. It was just A ball, the California League. Rickey was 18. That was the night when all of the signature Rickey touches coalesced into one spectacular package they'd be talking about for years. For anyone who watched or played against Rickey, the traits had already been there, of course, but as big as Rickey was in Oakland, he was still area-code big, local hero big. From this night forward, a roadside sign was metaphorically parked over his head. He was serving notice.

The score didn't matter—A's 13, Giants 12—but it was a football score for the Football Kid. Rickey ran: he stole seven bases that night. Swiped seven bags—never got caught. A gleaming seven-for-seven. There was the trash talk—a harbinger that Rickey was not just going to be good, but was going to let you know it too—directed specifically at Fresno catcher Wayne Cato, the man he had tortured all night. Cato was griping at the A's bench, especially the Modesto manager, Tom Treblehorn, so Rickey figured Cato had it coming. "We figured he needed to be taught a lesson, that's all," Rickey said afterward.

But Cato had the red ass for a particular reason. A couple nights earlier, the A's were getting killed by another football score, 22–7, but kept on stealing bases in a blowout. That violated the unwritten baseball etiquette: you don't show guys up, and you don't pad stats in meaningless situations.

Moreover, it was the way Rickey stole bases—all balls and impunity and total disregard for the physics of it all that said a ball travels faster through the air than a man can run on foot. Offending physicists around the globe, Treblehorn would say Rickey simply *outran* the ball. He'd only been in the minors for a half-hour, but there was immediately something about Rickey's style that embarrassed even professional players. Rickey reminded everyone that he had shown the Giants mercy that night: he would always recall that night by saying he *could* have stolen an *eighth* base, but when he broke for second the hitter executed a perfect hit-and-run and lined a single. In his telling, there was the flash of the stolen bases and the substance of the production—Rickey had three hits and scored four runs that night.

Everybody was talking about seven steals, but Rickey's night was just more of what he had been doing all season writ large. When he told J. J. Guinn he wanted to be the best base stealer of all time, he wasn't just dreaming. Rickey entered professional baseball in the record-breaking business. He had stolen so many bases the first two months of the season that he was already being projected to break the California League single-season stolen-base record, set by California Angels prospect Thad Bosley, who had stolen 90 bags a year earlier for Salinas. On his stolen-base frenzy, Rickey had tied what was believed to be the single-game stolen-base record in all of American recorded professional baseball—minors, majors, independent leagues (but not Negro League, whose stats were not considered to count, not because the players weren't professionals but because they were Black). That record had been set a couple of years earlier, in 1975, by New York Mets rookie Lee Mazzilli with Visalia.

The A's couldn't pitch (they would give up more than 1,000 runs that year in 140 games), but they could run. For the entirety of the 1977 season, the A's were challenging the team all-time single-season stolen-base record of 372. On top of that, Rickey was hitting .391 for a while during one stretch.

Now, instead of just showing up in game stories and agate type, Rickey was a player the local feature writers showed up for, and their stories began showing up in bigger places. He was an exciting player, to be certain, but it was still A ball, and the California League at that (the ball flew out of the yard, especially in high-altitude Reno), but Rickey was rolling and people were starting to watch—and project.

A'S HAVE FARMHAND WHO'S QUITE A STEAL

MODESTO, Calif. (AP)—When Charlie Finley heard what Rickey Henderson, an Oakland farmhand, was doing to the California League, the A's owner said, "Maybe we should bring him up right now."

But Finley, who is busy enough changing managers and playing personnel at the major league level added, "I don't make those decisions."

The good news for Modesto fans and bad news for pitchers is that Henderson will stay a while. There's high-level optimism but also caution in the case of the outfielder who was batting .370 and had 47 stolen bases, including seven in one game, in 50 games this season through last weekend.

"We definitely feel he'll make the big leagues, but he's just 18. We can't rush him," says Norm Koselke, Finley's farm director.

A year earlier, the A's had sent 17-year-old Rickey to Boise in the Northwest League for short-season A ball. Rookie ball, they called it. He had never been away from home, and there were few if any places in the country more foreign to Oakland than Boise, a desolate outpost in the baseball landscape that was barely surviving as a minor league city. Boise was in its second year as an A's affiliate, and some nights there'd be more people at the post office than in the stands at the ballpark.

Before Rickey left for Boise, Tommie Wilkerson stopped by the house on Alcatraz to bring him a care package—socks, supplies, and things—and Bobbie would from then on refer to Tommie as a "godmother" to Rickey. Bobbie would visit periodically. Pamela was still in high school, so Rickey would be going to Idaho solo.

Fred Atkins was all the way across the country, playing for Oneonta, the Yankees' short-season A-ball affiliate in the New York–Penn League. Fred was on his own journey to the big leagues. "I was ready to take off," he said. "Just like Rickey."

Two best friends who were both climbing their way to the top made for another improbable story and added to the legend of Oakland, but Fred was carrying a big secret: his right shoulder was killing him, and the current pain was only the half of it. His shoulder had been killing him for years, really since middle school. That meant he was already hurt when the Yankees drafted him. At Tech, Rickey served as Fred's personal physician, trying to get his arm loose before games. Gary Pettis would thank Bob Cryer, the Oakland Tech coach, for ruining Atkins. "He ran Fred out there every day. *Every. Single. Day,*" Pettis recalled.

Fred concealed his injury from virtually everybody, but finally, during spring training, the Yankees sent him up to New York for an MRI of his right shoulder. He went to the famed Yankee Stadium while he was there. The Yankee doctors found nothing wrong with the shoulder. Maybe it was this, perhaps it was that, but it was nothing serious. Maybe he had a tired arm. Or maybe he was one of those kids who deep down wasn't sure he *really* wanted to pitch. Maybe he didn't want it bad enough. With Rickey in Boise, Fred pitched two games for Oneonta, starting one, 3.60 ERA. His shoulder was in agony, though, and the Yankees, unable to pinpoint the issue, sent him back to California.

In Oakland, Fred went to an A's game, and the connected Burrell boys, Lewis and Stanley, brought him into the Coliseum clubhouse, where Fred met Mike Norris. A's team trainer Joe Romo gave Fred a quick once-over and suggested that he go to Los Angeles to see Dr. Frank Jobe, *the* Frank Jobe, who two years earlier had famously and successfully performed elbow ligament replacement surgery on Dodgers pitcher Tommy John. Jobe was also a pioneer in the field of reconstructive shoulder surgery.

"When I got to LA, Dusty Baker's in the weight room. Him and I get to talking. They shoot the X-rays. They put the X-ray up, and they showed me it right there, just like I thought: calcium deposit in my shoulder," Atkins recalled. Eventually, he underwent shoulder surgery, which ended his baseball career.

"The Yankees told me I didn't want to pitch. They gave me a cortisone shot, which I never would have taken had I known what that stuff does to you. Two days later, they release me, and Rickey says to me, 'Man, if you can't come back, I'll play for both of us.' That's the kind of friend he was."

Jim Guinn was uncertain how the A's would handle Rickey, considering that few people in the organization thought he could hit professional pitching well enough to be considered a serious immediate prospect. Everybody knew Rickey was a mama's boy, but they also believed that even if he got homesick and missed Bobbie, his competitiveness would sustain him. Rickey wasn't going 600 miles to get embarrassed.

The Boise manager was 27-year-old Tom Treblehorn, himself just two years removed from playing and only two years older than Lee Sigman, the oldest player on the team. Treblehorn was so young that two years earlier, in Lewiston, Idaho (where the A's affiliate played before moving to Boise), he'd been teammates with one of his Boise players, the second baseman Darrell Woodard. Boise was a bunch of kids, with Rickey being the youngest player on the team. Another kid, the first baseman Eric Attaway, was also from Oakland, from Fremont High, and had also been signed by J. J. Guinn. Attaway played just 11 games.

In the beginning, Rickey did not know whether Treblehorn was an ally. Jim Guinn was convinced he was not. During an organizational meeting, Guinn recalled, an early memo from Treblehorn was shared in which he expressed his doubt that Rickey would have the offensive capabilities to play above Double-A. But Treblehorn, a former catcher who came up in the Angels' system, watched Rickey closely for the 46 games he played in Boise. Rickey led the team in stolen bases with 29 and was caught seven times—good for an 80.5 percent success rate, seven points higher than the team average without him. "I was running, running, running—and he enjoyed me running," Rickey said. Rickey led the team in doubles with 13. In those games, Treblehorn learned something he may not have suspected earlier: Rickey was one of the best hitters on the team. He hit .336, was always on base, and walked more than he struck out. And facing him in that unorthodox crouch, pitchers were finding out it was hell to throw him a strike—or even to get one called.

Treblehorn joined Rickey in Modesto for 1977, and that's when the two went to work. Finley promoted the two to A ball, so Rickey did not have to adjust to a new manager. Treblehorn unleashed Rickey and gave the entire team—including Woodard, who could fly—a mandate to run opponents off the field. Woodard was from Los Angeles, Bell High School, one of the LA destinations in the Great Migration. Born in Wilmar, Arkansas, Woodard was two years older than Rickey. Parts of Woodard's approach made him look faster and even more polished on the basepaths than Rickey—and maybe he was, but it didn't matter. When Rickey told Jim Guinn he wanted to be the greatest base stealer of all time, he had already made a deal with himself: he was going to put in the sweat.

And the thing about Treblehorn was that he wanted to know which players were willing to put their hands in the dirt, till the soil, and turn themselves into ballplayers. Rickey would ask for help, and Treblehorn would tell him they were going to do extra work. So Rickey would show up and grab a bat—then be surprised when Treblehorn told him to put it down, for there was no hitting involved in the extra drills he had in mind.

For someone as successful on the basepaths as he was, Treblehorn couldn't believe how bad Rickey's leads were. He was just a teenager, and his obvious raw potential was limitless. His burst of speed toward second was remarkable, and his ability to reach top speed within a step or two compensated for his poor jumps. With his speed, the jump was less important than getting the advantage on the catcher by stealing off the pitcher. If Rickey's jumps improved even slightly, Treblehorn figured out, he'd be unstoppable.

On the back fields, Treblehorn began working with Rickey on reading pitchers. He'd show Rickey how to spot the little things that made a base stealer great, like noticing how the pitcher fumbled around with the ball in his glove. Too much movement meant he was trying to locate his curveball grip. Curveballs were great pitches to run on because they were slower to the plate and had spin on them, which made it more difficult for the catcher to get the ball out of his glove and make a clean throw. Curveballs also presented a good running opportunity because they were difficult to control. No way was any catcher lunging for a curveball in the dirt going to catch Rickey—that just wasn't going to happen.

And if the pitcher had to worry about finding the right grip on the ball—a life-and-death proposition should he throw a hanger—he also had to worry about throwing a meatball to the plate.

"He took me to the field every day to work on pitchers' moves and jumps," Rickey recalled. "I wanted to go hit. I'd say, 'Extra hitting.' He'd say, 'Extra work,' and take me straight to the bases. He's the one who drilled that into my head. And the best thing about it was he was willing to work with me. His wife used to say, 'Why are you always going out there for extra hitting? Why do you have to go out there to do extra work all the time?' He'd say, 'I'm going out there with Rickey.' She came to me one day and said, 'Can you stop going out there and let my husband stay home for a little bit?' I said, 'He's the one getting *me* out there!'"

Modesto was a season-long track meet. Woodard hit leadoff. Rickey, wearing number 24 for Willie Mays, hit third. Rickey stole 40 bases in his first 45 attempts. Woodard stole 37 bases in a row. The *Modesto Bee* even ran a "crime report" in the paper to follow both the California League team record of stolen bases in a season (372 in a 140-game season) and Modesto's

single-season record (90). On July 20, 1977, before the A's took on the Lodi
Dodgers, that carnival barker Finley even had his speedster race a horse.
In the "Man vs. Beast" extravaganza, Rickey was scheduled to race both
Dodgers outfielder Rudy Law (who was from Richmond, a few towns north
of Oakland) and Clabber, a local quarterhorse saddled by Vicki Phillips, a
high school rodeo rider. Fifty yards for 50 bucks, 20 to place, 10 to show.
When Law pulled out with a hamstring injury, Lodi center fielder Marv
Garrison replaced him. In the end, Rickey and the humans predictably lost.
Rickey came in second and took his 20 bucks, but Clabber had beaten him
by 10 lengths—and the physicists saw their universe set back in order. Rickey
couldn't really outrun a thrown ball, and two legs still couldn't beat four.

In Modesto, Rickey made the All-Star team for the first time as a professional (after being snubbed in Boise). He and Woodard, who also made
the All-Star team, were running side by side through the California League,
with Rickey always holding a slight edge. On August 23, against the Salinas
Angels, and one away from the record, Rickey reached base on an error and
immediately took off for second and the record. Salinas pitched out, and
the Salinas catcher, Joe Maddon, erased Rickey at second. Later that night,
Rickey stole third off Maddon and had the record. He finished with a league-
record 95 steals in 134 games. The A's were demolished for all of 1977—last
place, Charlie Brown–bad—but Rickey tore the league apart: .345 average,
120 runs in 134 games, 104 walks, and even 11 homers. Rickey was so dominant that he walked away with the league MVP, even though his team was
in last place.

In two professional seasons, Rickey had hit .336 and .345. Joe Maddon, the
Salinas catcher who 40 years later would go on to lead the hopeless Chicago
Cubs to a World Series championship as their manager, immediately saw
Rickey's speed and power as elite—even miles away from the big leagues at
A ball.

There was the afternoon in the altitude up in Reno against the Silver Sox
in front of 339 clearly committed souls. Rickey didn't even do much that
game—going 0-for-3, with a run scored—but he and his pals were stealing
at will (Modesto stole seven bases that day), so eventually he had to expect a
response. Whether it was just wildness or frustration (pitchers always said it
just *slipped*), somebody was going to put him on his ass. That day they tried
Rickey. Two different pitchers hit him, and he got shaved a couple of other
times—fastballs right under his chin—but it didn't matter. Rickey just stood

right back in the batter's box, got real low in that crouch, and went back to business.

"The guy is impossible to pitch to. His strike zone is about 10 inches deep. He drives me crazy, and the umpires too. And when you do come in with a strike—Boom, he rips it," recalled Frank Quintero, who pitched for Visalia against Rickey in 1977. Quintero tried to put Rickey on his ass one night too. "I was getting fed up, looking at him all curled over, so I came in tight. I nicked him, but at least I got him to stand up for a minute so I could see him." Even in the California League, Rickey was pouring concrete early to lay a foundation: if you knocked him on his ass, it didn't matter. Rickey would dust himself off and get back to work—no histrionics, no mound charging. If you hit him, he'd see you at second base—and maybe again at third. He was fearless.

Charlie Finley promoted Rickey to Double-A for the 1978 season, which meant facing better competition that would match his edge, better pitching to test that .345 batting average, and better catching to challenge those 95 stolen bases. It was another step toward the big leagues, and Rickey would have to move across the country for the first time, to the East Coast and the A's new affiliate in Jersey City, New Jersey. In an understatement, the experience was a total disaster.

Rickey would have wound up in Chattanooga, Tennessee, but after the 1977 season Oakland and Cleveland swapped Double-A affiliates. The Jersey City team kept the same name, however, and that was how Rickey Henderson, Oakland A's prospect, found himself playing for the Jersey City Indians. The franchise also kept the same uniforms, and so Charlie Finley's Kelly green–and-gold A's were playing in the red-and-white colors of the Cleveland Indians. The Indians had been in Jersey City for only that one year. Before that, no team had played in Jersey City since 1956, when the Dodgers played a couple of home games in Jersey City to pressure Robert Moses into building a new stadium for Walter O'Malley in Brooklyn. (Spoiler alert: It didn't work.)

Three thousand miles from Oakland, Rickey was taking another step toward the solo baseball life. He was by himself as a teenager in Boise, but that was for 46 games—two months, tops. Modesto was only 90 minutes from Oakland, so Bobbie and Pamela (Bobbie agreed to be Pamela's guardian so that her parents would let her visit Rickey) and his boys could make visits when he got homesick. But Jersey City was another universe altogether.

He was away now, less able to rely on the old day-to-day relationships. His Oakland people were his bedrock—but they were on the other side of the country. Rickey was increasingly becoming part of the traveling professional baseball life, with its slew of temporary friends, available women, changing backdrops—and distance.

There were some familiar faces. Darrell Woodard, Rickey's base-stealing partner, was also promoted to Jersey City. Woodard had stolen 90 bases to Rickey's 95, and Treblehorn thought he might have been able to steal even more bases than Rickey if he could only hit like Rickey. But Woodard had spent four years at the A-ball level and only cracked .300 once—in 1974 as a 17-year-old in his first year of pro ball at Lewiston.

Rickey's new home ballpark in Jersey City was old Roosevelt Stadium, where on April 18, 1946, Jackie Robinson made his famous debut for the Montreal Royals, integrating the sport (at least the white-run professional ranks) for the first time since the end of Reconstruction. Other great players, like Willie Mays, Monte Irvin, and Don Newcombe, had played at Roosevelt, so the place carried a certain significance to the history of Black baseball.

Roosevelt may have had a legendary history, but in 1978 the ballpark was a dump. "That was the shithole of America," recalled Buck Showalter, who was a Double-A infielder in the Yankee system and frequented Roosevelt as a visiting player with the New Haven Yankees. "Five lights on a pole, but the place was cavernous. It held like 40,000 people, and you couldn't see shit. It was like playing in the dark. You couldn't see the spin on a breaking ball."

Charlie Finley had his team playing in hand-me-down uniforms in a pit of a stadium—another corner-cutting move in Finley's desperate hustle against a sport that was outpricing him by the hour. He was willing to subject fans to bargain-basement baseball, and by taking the A's to Jersey City he showed he was willing to subject his players to a ratty old yard that couldn't even guarantee that the home clubhouse would have running water.

Finley specifically instructed the Jersey City staff to take care of three players—Darrell Woodard, Ray Cosey, and Rickey, or "Charlie's Boys," as the staff called them. Soon that season a fourth player would be added—Mike Norris, whom Rickey knew from the A's clubhouse when Lewis Burrell got them clubhouse access. Mike made his major league debut when Rickey was in the 11th grade, in 1975. He had appeared in 44 games in Oakland and started 34 of them. He was a mini-celebrity, having already been where these kids wanted to be.

When Norris arrived in Jersey City and unpacked his suitcase as Rickey's roommate, he was there to get his game right. That didn't totally explain, though, how a big leaguer wound up in Double-A; guys trying to put more snap on their curveball usually got sent down one rung, to Triple-A. The real reason he wound up in Jersey City was that the A's thought he had gotten too big for himself. His game didn't need minor adjustments. His career was slipping, and Charlie told Norris he needed some humbling.

"Charlie sent me down there and said, 'You need to smell some bus fumes,'" Norris recalled. "That was my white daddy. I loved that mother-fucker."

The man charged with catering to Charlie's Boys was Jim Hague, a towering 19-year-old college sophomore from Seton Hall who served as the Jersey City public address announcer, official scorer, and traveling secretary, among several other titles. In fact, Hague wasn't a man at all. He had lied about his age. He wasn't a 19-year-old college sophomore, but a six-foot-eight 17-year-old high school junior whose job it was to make sure Charlie's Boys had the right stats, arrived at the ballpark on time, and returned home safely. "Unlike the other 21 guys on the team," Hague recalled, "Finley made sure those guys were treated better. I got a 'special services' deal with Finley, and all I had to do was clue him in on what was happening and I got an extra 100 bucks a month. That year was the best year of my life for making money.

"I was getting paid from all over the place. The Howe News Bureau paid me 11 bucks a game as official scorer. The city paid me 8 bucks to be the PA announcer. My salary was $175 a week to be the stat guy, PR guy, and I was getting another hundred from Charlie. I'm like, 'Wow, this is cool. I'm 17 years old!' The only problem was my school was cool with it as long as I made up the work, but my mother didn't want me going on road trips. I had to get the GM to write a letter to my mommy to let me go."

Fulfilling his deal with Finley, every day Hague would pick up Rickey, Norris, Woodard, and Cosey and bring them to the ballpark in his 1976 AMC Pacer, a space-age-looking little matchbox of a hatchback with a windshield that looked like a bubble. Hague would pick Rickey up from his apartment on Duncan Avenue in what Rickey called "the bubble car."

Hague immediately noticed two things about 19-year-old Rickey. "The first was that he was cheap," Hague said. "The second was that he cheated at cards." Rickey fleecing teammates at cards would become a half-century-long tradition. The game of choice in the Indians' clubhouse was acey-deucey: the player pulls two cards and bets the third card will fall between the previous two numerically. "One of Rickey's classic moves was knowing full well he was playing against kids from these Podunk towns. Bob Grandas, he went to the University of Central Michigan, so you'd think he'd have been more worldly. Nope." Hague saw Rickey was pulling his third card from the bottom of the deck. "So, yeah, I called Rickey Henderson out. He got up and stormed off because we accused him of cheating."

The Eastern League was different than the California League. The weather was raw and cold early before it turned roasting in the summer, and the California kids used to freeze their asses off—a hardship made worse playing at crumbling Roosevelt, which contained more leaks than a gossip column. The ballpark was awful, the East Coast weather was brutal, and Rickey was 3,000 miles from his girlfriend and the family, but neither the distance nor the conditions nor the ballpark could compare to what really made Jersey City a hell for Rickey: the manager.

The Jersey City manager was John Edward Kennedy, who played in the big leagues for a dozen years, mostly with the Washington Senators and the Red Sox. He had the distinction of sharing the first and last name and birthday of President John F. Kennedy, but had no relation to that famous family. Kennedy had been an all-effort, low-talent player at the big league level, getting by on the determination to make a living as a baseball player. Now he immediately zeroed in on Rickey and gave the young player coming east for the first time a master class in prejudice in the most basic sense of the word: Rickey sensed that Kennedy did not like him, sight unseen.

The two had no previous history, which left Rickey (and other Black players who entered similar environments in baseball at the time) to conclude that Kennedy was one of those baseball lifers resentful of the rising number of Black players in the game, their style, their mannerisms, and their backgrounds.

Kennedy reached the big leagues in 1962, by which time every team in the league had integrated. Most of the players of that era, however, were from the generation where black players did not draw attention to themselves—except, of course, for the great Willie Mays, whose on-field charisma couldn't be contained. But off the field even Mays conformed to white cultural sensibilities. Rickey's generation represented the television generation, the civil rights generation, and the old baseball men were confounded, envious of the great Black talents of the sport but unwilling to accept the culture and style they brought to the game.

"I encouraged my players to go all out, all the time," Kennedy told the Society for American Baseball Research in 2010. "Not everyone is going to play in the big leagues, but if you give your best effort every day, you can have peace of mind. If you don't, you take the what-ifs to your grave."

Rickey had been lucky playing in California. For the most part, the entrenched class divisions weren't as pronounced there as in other parts of the country, even if the segregation was equally rigid. He was lucky because the white men in Oakland who were prominent figures in his baseball world were generally nurturing to the kids. He was incredibly lucky that his first manager was a man like Tom Treblehorn, who loved the energy and style that Black players brought to the sport. When Rickey entered baseball, he was allowed to play the game as he enjoyed it. Now, in Kennedy, he'd encountered the first manager who was offended by him.

Kennedy was one of those baseball men (and his kind far outnumbered the Treblehorns of the world) who expected his players to adapt to the pre-integration, pre–civil rights, pre-television culture and style of the sport. To protect the white, segregated roots of the game, they punished originality, flamboyance, and anything that challenged the humility demanded by a game of failure. All of which guaranteed that Kennedy and Rickey were destined for conflict—and destiny did not disappoint.

As a player, Kennedy had prided himself on his hustle, grit, grind, and hard play to compensate for his lack of skills. Besides his superior raw ability, Rickey had all of these qualities as well—his speed game of daring and aggression always left him with the dirtiest uniform on the team—but the optics translated differently. Rickey sensed early that Kennedy was one of those baseball men convinced that Black players weren't as driven, weren't as hungry, weren't as committed to greatness—or to winning—as white players.

"Kennedy was a redneck. One of *them*. A *real* redneck," Rickey recalled. "He was on us for everything, and you know, being Black, you already had to be three times better than everybody else. We knew there was no equality. We already knew how they felt about us. You had to be great. No Blacks on the bench. No Blacks backing guys up. You had to be a star.

"Kennedy told us we were going to run through the bag to first base at all times. He had all these rules. One time, I rip a bullet, a line drive right to first base . . . *Pow!* . . . off my bat, into the glove. I hit it so hard. I took two steps toward first base and I was already out, so I walk back to the dugout. The inning is over, I go to center field, and *right* before the pitcher throws his first pitch, Kennedy calls time and pulls me out of the game! He could have made the switch before the inning started, but no, he wanted to show me up, teach me a lesson."

For the first time on a ball field, Rickey was faced with hostile coaching, with a manager who seemed more interested in making him play his way— the "right way"—than in helping Rickey become a better baseball player. To baseball men like Kennedy, playing the game his way *was* intended to make Rickey a better player—but Rickey needed to be broken first. It was likely the first time Rickey's talent wasn't enough to keep a manager from focusing on his persona. It was one thing for him to feel undervalued in the draft—Rickey had heard all that before. Once the game started, however, and Rickey stepped on the field, everyone knew he was a star, a top player whose abilities made assessing him uncomplicated. No one had ever stood in the way of that.

Kennedy rode Rickey relentlessly, determined to take the natural improvisation out of his game, but the manager had a problem even bigger than Rickey: Mike Norris.

"Redneck-ass John Kennedy. He was the second-worst manager I ever had. Harry Bright was a drunk who played for the New York Yankees who I had the misfortune of playing for in Birmingham—he was the worst. He was a racist and an Indian too, which we could never understand," Norris recalled. "They were really the only openly racist managers I ever had. I just don't think that came from Mr. Finley, because we had a great relationship. Maybe he was putting the finishing touches on me, but Kennedy didn't like Blacks. He was a 'neck. His job was to bury me—and the shit nearly worked. Charlie wanted to know if I was gonna quit. I locked myself in the Holiday Inn overlooking Roosevelt Stadium, that raggedy-ass stadium. Kennedy fined me for insubordination."

Rickey doesn't remember the exact date, nor does Norris, but they both remember when it at all came to a head, and where.

It was in Roosevelt Stadium, and Mike Norris was getting lit up. He was out of pitching shape and Kennedy was fuming, watching Norris on the mound, who didn't seem to care. A big leaguer with massive talent getting lit up by Double-A hitters. Watching Norris offended a man of Kennedy's sensibilities. (*Not everyone is going to play in the big leagues, but if you give your best effort every day, you can have peace of mind. If you don't, you take the what-ifs to your grave.*) Norris shouldn't have even been on his team. He was wasting his talent.

"Mike almost killed him. Mike was in the big leagues, and we were all rookies, and I had known him because he was from the Bay," Rickey remembered. "Mike was down there just trying to work on stuff, and boom, he might get hit, but he was down there working on stuff—splitters, sliders, he was working. And Kennedy got mad at him. Came down and said, 'You act like you ain't trying, and you ain't trying to get anybody out. You just working on things.' And Mike said, 'That's what I'm *down here* for. I'm a big leaguer.' Next thing you know, bang, bang. Took Mike out of the game.

"Mike told the clubhouse kid, 'Get me a six-pack. I'm going into the sauna, have a beer, and sweat this out'—and here comes Kennedy to talk to him. We had this sauna, and Kennedy came to keep yelling at him, and Mike almost choked him to death. We had to pull him up off of him."

Calling it a sauna was generous, Jim Hague recalled. It was just a rickety old shower that barely worked, but the confrontation between Norris and Kennedy further solidified Rickey's belief that Jersey City was a nightmare. Later that summer there was another indignity. After a road trip against the Reading Phillies, Rickey came home and found his door open—somebody had broken into his apartment, stolen all his clothes, his stereo, turntable, everything. Rickey made a decision: he was done. Done with the A's. Done with Kennedy. Done with baseball. He called Bobbie, told her Kennedy had taken the joy out of the game for him and it was time to go back to his first love: football. Having made up his mind to quit baseball, Rickey told his mother he already had a contingency plan worked out: he was still only 19, and there was plenty of time to switch gears, go to college, and get back on the football field. He even had a contact at Arizona State who might be able to make something happen quickly.

Before putting the contingency plan into action, though, he made another call home—but not to Oakland. Rickey called Chicago, the city of his birth, and the business offices of one Mr. Charles O. Finley, owner of the Oakland Athletics American League Baseball Club.

"I called Charlie O. Finley, and I tell him, 'You need to either send me *back* down from Double-A or bump me up to Triple-A because I cannot take this anymore. I quit.' Charlie says to me, 'Rickey, I can't put you up to

Triple-A, because it's a numbers game, and I can't put you back in A ball, because you're too good. I'm going to make a phone call. You concentrate on baseball. You're my number-one prospect—no football.'" Now Rickey was nervous. He knew exactly where Finley was going with that call. He was going to call Kennedy, which would subject him to the maximum of Kennedy's wrath. Why? Because Rickey had just made a power move: a 19-year-old kid who had never played a minute in the big leagues (or Triple-A, for that matter) went over the head of his manager and *called the owner of the franchise? Where did he get the balls?*

Rickey spent that morning alternately sweating and rehearsing what he would say when Kennedy blasted him. He didn't know what Kennedy was going to say. He didn't know what *he* was going to say. All he knew was that confrontation was imminent. Rickey recalled the confrontation nearly a half-century later: "The next day Kennedy calls me into his office, and now I'm waiting for it. I don't know *what's* going to happen. Kennedy looks at me and says, 'I heard you talked to the owner.' I said, 'Yes, I'm not making it here.' Then he says, 'The owner tells me my instructions are to leave you alone.'

"It changed everything. Changed my whole career. I was ready to quit, and it wasn't no threat. I was quitting baseball."

After calling Charlie O., Rickey took off. Everybody had an understanding. Rickey knew Finley valued him enough not to let Kennedy hurt him, and Kennedy knew if he messed with Rickey, Rickey would call Charlie and Charlie would be on his ass the very next day.

That didn't mean Rickey could cruise. That didn't mean every at-bat didn't count. There was the game against Reading when Rickey dropped a bunt down the third-base line. Mike Cash, the Phillies' third baseman, fielded the ball cleanly, then chucked it into the fifth row. Rickey rolled into second. Jim Hague, that night's official scorer, called the play: error, third baseman.

Standing on second base, Rickey gestured at the press box with both hands like he was trying to land a plane. "He was looking at me, saying 'E-5?'" Hague recalled. "He was like, 'E-5? What are you doing?'

"So I'm the official scorer, the PA guy, *and* manning the phones. Later on, the phone rings, and it's from an outside line, from outside the ballpark.

Like, the AP or one of the papers calling to get a score update or something.
I pick up the phone and I hear:

"'Jimmy, the fuck you doing to me?'

"'Who *is* this? *RICKEY?*'

"'Yeah. Fuck are you doing?'

"'The game's going on. Where are you calling me from?'

"'I'm in Kennedy's office. You gotta give me a hit right now! *Right now!*'

"'Rickey, I'm not changing it!'

"'*RIGHT NOW!*'

"They're in the field now, and Kennedy's office is not right next door from
the dugout. It was a good distance, down the stairs and about 650 feet in the
depths of the stadium," Hague recalled. "So, after the game, I decide to ask
both managers about my scoring. The Reading manager is Lee Elia, Lee Elia
from the greatest rant in baseball fame.* He says to me, 'Home game, close
play. Everywhere else, that's a hit, no questions. Just you asking, I give you
credit.' I asked Kennedy. He said, 'Hit,' and so I changed it. I tell Henderson,
and he says, 'Man, fuck you. It shoulda been a hit already.' For him to take
the time to call was incredible. That's how badly he wanted a hit. Every hit."

Without feeling Kennedy over his shoulder, Rickey's batting average crept
up and he would finish over .300, at .310. "He couldn't hit the ball out of the
infield, but he could bunt the ball like a motherfucker," Showalter recalled.
"He wouldn't often bunt to third but would push the ball down on the first-
base side and you had no chance." The stolen-base percentage didn't recover
from the early season, when, in his words, "I was messed up," but Rickey still
finished with 81 steals in 109 attempts, or 74 percent. He was tearing up the
Eastern League the same way he had ripped through Boise and Modesto.

Rickey knew people were talking about him. The reporters, even at the
Double-A level, took an interest in him, and he was all over the write-ups

---

* Lee Elia was the manager of the Chicago Cubs in 1983 when he criticized the home fans
at Wrigley Field for booing his struggling club with a classic three-minute screed that
contained the immortal, "I'll tell you one fucking thing: I hope we get fucking hotter than
shit just to stuff it up them three thousand fucking people that show up every fucking
day, because if they're the real Chicago fucking fans they can kiss my fucking ass right
downtown . . . The motherfuckers don't even work. That's why they're at the fucking
game . . . Eighty-five percent of the world is working. The other 15 come out here—it's a
fucking playground for the cocksuckers." Elia was fired at the end of the season.

in the paper, but there was one issue with the attention—Rickey wasn't sure exactly what they were saying about him.

Rickey would look at a newspaper, see his name, and quietly ask Mike Norris to read the write-up. At first it appeared to Norris that Rickey just wanted to be feted, to bask in the glory of what he had done that game by having it read to him, as if he were being fed grapes. Then one night, while writing Pamela a letter, Rickey asked Norris how to spell so many basic words—articles and prepositions—that Mike got suspicious. Soon his conclusions were confirmed: if Rickey could read, it wasn't well enough to read newspaper articles, which were generally written at a sixth-grade reading level.

"He said, 'Mike, I'm writing Pam a letter. How do you spell "they"?' And I said, 'How does it sound, Rickey?' And he said, 'T-H-A-Y.' As this went on, I said to myself, *He can't read what he's done in the newspaper.* And I would say to him, 'Who you gonna talk to if I ain't around? You have to be able to read for yourself what they're saying about you.'

"But let me tell you how smart Rickey is, how competitive and driven: within three weeks, Rickey taught himself how to read. We sat there with the newspaper before games every day. Every. Single. Day. And he sat there and he got it. He put the words together. When people make you feel inadequate or stupid, you try to hide what you don't know, and that's what Rickey was doing. And we were all in the same boat because of our athletic ability. The schools, they pushed us all through."

That Rickey sat with Mike that summer and concentrated on grammar as much as he did on his running technique spoke to Pamela about the closeness between the two of them, because Rickey rarely let himself be that vulnerable with anyone besides Bobbie, her, and probably Fred Atkins. Being 3,000 miles from home and unable to communicate the way he wanted to, Rickey reflected differently on the times back at Tech, when he thought he and his friends had gotten away with not doing homework assignments and escaped academic responsibility. Now he was trapped far from home and could barely read a newspaper.

At around the same time Mike Norris and Rickey were reading the newspaper together to improve Rickey's literacy, Lloyd Moseby, the batboy who was cut from Rickey's Babe Ruth team, was drafted second overall in the June 1978 draft by the Toronto Blue Jays. Moseby had known where the lack of emphasis on school would lead. It was the reason he transferred from

Oakland Tech to Oakland High. He would see the ruinous pattern repeat itself a hundredfold with young Black kids. "I enrolled in Tech. I went there because all these guys were going there. My brothers went there as well, but I found out that I couldn't go to Tech. I wasn't going to make it. It was the kind of school where cutting was cool. If you weren't cutting, something was wrong. So they got me out of there, but Rick and me, we stayed in contact. We did everything together."

Rickey was always comfortable with math, actually enjoyed it, and excelled with numbers—which was why he was such a dangerous card player. Words, though, had always been a jumble, and this was a truth he could not outrun, even if his personal charisma and ability to run kickoffs back for touchdowns or to steal bases at will allowed him to feel as if he had emerged unharmed. Rickey knew sentence structures and pronunciation were difficult for him, a frustrating kaleidoscope. Nobody in those days was particularly eager to address reading disabilities, preferring to tell students to better apply themselves. Rickey said he was never diagnosed with dyslexia or given any special attention for a reading disability, and he kept everything he didn't know about reading a secret. "Because of the athlete I was, I played football, basketball, baseball, I knew I was that guy," he remembered. "And I'd be in school, man, and they'd say, 'Don't even worry about it. We're passing you,' and *boom!* You passed. Just go out there and play. We were pushed through. I knew I didn't even have to go to class good and could come out of there with a passing grade—because I know I didn't learn shit."

Mike Norris had a theory as to what made his desire to improve his literacy possible: he wanted to be his best for Pamela. "Rickey was so far from home that you could see the puppy love between those two. You could see he wanted to *impress* her," Norris said. "It's hard for us to think about, because we spend so much time talking about what players can do, but you gotta remember, the brother was only 19 years old."

Watching Rickey struggle writing to Pamela sent Norris inward to reflect on his own sense of loss and melancholy, which manifested one day when Jersey City went up north to New Haven, Connecticut, to play the West Haven Yankees. Before the game, Norris decided to take a walk around Yale's campus. He was immediately struck by the aura of the Ivy League—the confidence of the students, who walked as if they owned the future, and the imposing old brick buildings, which were *actually* covered in ivy. He had always been smart, mentally quick, and intellectually curious, but standing at the epicenter of the American educational elite, Norris began to wonder whether, if his life had been different, he himself could have been one of these intellectual elites. Could he have handled the coursework? Would he have had the discipline? Could he have gone as far using his brain as he'd done with his athletic abilities?

"The right word wasn't 'envious,' but I felt shortchanged," Norris recalled. "I would have loved to have done that. I was in accelerated classes in middle school. And there were these three Asian kids, two were Japanese, one was Chinese. And I tried like hell to keep up with them and I couldn't. The Chinese kid ended up working at Lawrence Livermore Labs. He went to work with a briefcase connected to handcuffs and a revolver. He was on some real top-secret shit. One of the Japanese kids ended up being a big-time lawyer, and I think the other one was a professor at Cal. I don't want to be stereotypical, but they came there for an education. They weren't bullshitting with them books, and I always wondered about what I could have been in the classroom.

"I saw Bob Gibson pitch in the 1964 World Series on TV. I loved Giants-Dodgers. I loved school, debate club, history. I got more into sports and stopped going to class after the eighth grade," he said. "I had weed, girls, and I could play baseball—and I was in accelerated classes. They passed me through, the same way as Rickey. It was like two lives: You're hiding from Mom, cutting class. That was crazy. Then you go to sixth period, and then you go to practice fucked up. And I learned I could pitch fucked up. In the 11th grade, I was pitching drunk. I think I always wanted people to like me, and I found I could buy people to like me, I tried to drink people into liking me."

Being at Yale for just one afternoon carried Norris back to distant, lost possibilities, his own demons, and the possible explanations for them. On November 4, 1962, his father, Elmer Hall, age 40, was stabbed to death by his estranged wife Bobbie Hall, 25 years old, in San Francisco's Panhandle District. According to the *San Francisco Chronicle*, Bobbie Hall told police that Elmer arrived at 258 Central Avenue, where she was staying with a friend, to reconcile. A fight ensued. Elmer slapped her, she told them, and she stabbed him with a pocketknife. He bled to death on the sidewalk, and she was arrested on suspicion of murder. The reason for the altercation was listed by San Francisco Police as a domestic argument. Mike was seven years old.

Mike Norris would grow up, in his words, "afraid of horror movies,

funerals—anything that had to do with death." He immersed himself in baseball, and during his early school years, at Benjamin Franklin Junior High,
Mike found himself as enthralled by school as by baseball. But he was also
seduced by the streets, the women, the flamboyance, and the faster lanes.
That led him to believe that his future career-altering bouts with drugs and
alcohol were preordained, that he was his father's child and, in his words,
"proof that the apple didn't fall far from the tree."

While Rickey regrouped, free now that John Kennedy couldn't touch him,
his confidence rose. He always knew he could play for one simple reason:
every game he played, he always discovered he was the best player on the
field. Different from other players? Sure. Did some have more power? Sure.
But were they *better*? No. It was true at Bushrod. It was true at Tech (even
though they tried to stick him on the junior varsity). It was true in Boise
(even though Syd Thrift let him fall to the fourth round), Modesto, and now
Jersey City. Whatever team Rickey was on, he was a headliner. "I've known it
probably since the eighth grade," he said. "I was born to be an athlete." That
emboldened him. He was wasn't just one-name Rickey to his teammates—he
was Rickey to himself.

Maybe he had always talked to himself when he went to the plate and
now he was just talking a little louder. Or maybe as he neared the big leagues
more people were paying attention to this peculiarity of his. Opposing
catchers started hearing it, and umpires did too. Mike Norris began hearing
Rickey's monologue in the dugout:

Come on, Rickey . . .
Aww, you know Rickey don't play that shit . . .
All right, Rickey, you know that fastball can't beat you . . .
Oh no, no, no, Rickey. That's not the one . . . you know better.

Rickey was talking to himself—in the third person.

"I don't believe any of it was on purpose," Norris said. "It was totally spontaneous. He was in the moment and that's how it came out."

It was in Jersey City where another change took place. Rickey started sliding into second base headfirst. There were debates that would turn scientific
about whether sliding feetfirst or headfirst got the base stealer to the bag
faster, but the merits of this debate had little to do with Rickey's motivation.
He was scared of sliding in hard to the base and breaking his ankle. There
was one time when he came in headfirst and reached second covered in

blood—his belt buckle had gotten caught underneath him and lacerated his abdomen. His uniform looked like a crime scene. The key, he said later, was to land on his chest so it hit the ground before his belly—unless he wanted to cut his stomach open again.

Rickey was free finally. His personality got bigger, and his drive sharpened, so much so that he knew there was only one place he belonged—the major leagues. With the big club. The action was in the big leagues, not playing in some crumbling relic taking the bus everywhere. Rickey discovered that being in the minors might even be detrimental to him because he was playing with so many guys who didn't have big league ability.

Jim Hague remembered how the players would drink, but not Rickey. Norris might regale the guys with real big league stories (he was the only guy who'd actually *been* to the majors)—like the time he went tripping on LSD with Dock Ellis—but Rickey was unimpressed. No drugs. "'I'm not messing this up,'" Hague recalled Rickey saying one day. "He used to have all these training techniques working the forearms, wrists. He used to take a 50-pound weight and tie it to a broken bat handle and just curl the weight to strengthen his wrists. He never did anything to his body. He used to point at his body and say, 'This is my castle. This is my museum.'"

It was time to say goodbye to the minor leagues forever, just as baseball would to Jersey City. After the A's left at the end of the season, no big league team would ever choose Jersey City again as a minor league home. The next year the light tower blew over at the old stadium and that was it. In 1985, the city demolished Roosevelt Stadium. The ballpark made famous by Jackie Robinson's debut in 1946 saw its final game in 1978 with Rickey on the field.

The minor league apprenticeship, Rickey decided, was over. There was another reason he was convinced of this fact: Finley promoted Darrell Woodard to the majors (skipping Triple-A entirely) for the final 33 games of the 1978 season when Woodard had hit just .254 and stolen nearly 40 fewer bases than the previous year. (Rickey, by comparison, stole only 14 fewer bases in Jersey City than Modesto.) So one guy (Woodard) was in the big leagues and he wasn't, and another (Norris) wasn't in the big leagues but should have been except that he was drinking, out of shape, and getting lit up by B league hitters. Tired of watching Norris underachieve, Rickey gave his roommate the works.

"One day, Rickey told me, 'Norris, you used to be great, and now you're garbage,'" Norris recalled. "And I'm like, this little son of a bitch is in

Double-A and talking to *me* like that? Then I had to look in the mirror, and Rickey was right: I *was* garbage because that's why I was down there. You could see it building in him. Jersey City? It sucked, but with Rickey you could see it. He had that competition in him—love of the game and a desire to be the best. He was ready."

There was one person who did not believe Rickey was ready—Mal Fichman, the Jersey City general manager. The Indians lost a ton of ball games in 1978: they were 54-83 overall. One afternoon Fichman was watching the game with Hague—another day, another loss. Staring at the field, Fichman said, "There's nobody out there that has an ounce of talent on this field."

"Not even Henderson?" Hague replied.

"Meh . . . if he makes it, it'll be as a pinch-runner."

"He denies it, but I will go to my grave knowing that he said that," Hague recalled. "If there was one thing that stood out about that year, it was Rickey. Of *course* he had talent. Stevie Wonder coulda seen that."

4

I T WAS 84 DEGREES in Boston on July 24, 1979, and three teams were
playing .600 ball in the American League East while keeping a wary eye
on a fourth, the mighty two-time defending champ Yankees. The Red Sox
were chasing red-hot Baltimore, while trying to keep surging Milwaukee off
their tail, and Milwaukee was trying to keep the Yankees off of *theirs*. Nor-
mally, you could write a eulogy for a fourth-place team, but they were still
the Yankees—a year earlier they had come back on Boston from a 13-game
deficit.

On this particular Tuesday night, Oakland had come to Fenway Park for
a three-game set. The A's? The A's were dead last in the AL West, castaways
so lost they couldn't even see land, so bad they were more games out of
first place (31) than they had wins (26). Oakland was so deep in last place
that they were 16 games behind *second*-to-last-place Seattle. The AL East
was for killers only—three teams in that division were going to win at least
90 games—and the Orioles, Yankees, and Red Sox spent the weeks before
and after the All-Star Break killing the A's. Over nearly a month's stretch, the
A's had played 18 games against the three on both coasts and won a grand
total of three games. Just two weeks earlier, the former Red Sox wizard Luis
Tiant (now pitching for the Yankees, to the embitterment of the entire 617
area code) had thrown a one-hitter at the A's, a fourth-inning liner by Rickey
being the only Oakland hit of the day. Five days later, Steve Renko, the un-
distinguished Red Sox starter, was tossing another no-hitter at the A's—until
Rickey singled to break it up with one out in the ninth.

Now Oakland showed up in Boston and, not surprisingly, no one in
the Fens was particularly excited about their arrival. In its regular-season

preview, the *Boston Globe* had predicted that the A's would be "worse than last year," and under the column headed "Destined for Stardom," the *Globe* enthusiastically told its readers, "Henderson—maybe." Still, it was Boston in the summer, the Red Sox were in a pennant race, and that had brought 30,393 fans trudging up Brookline Avenue. The team's job that day was obvious: stomp on a last-place patsy and stay focused on Baltimore, where the action was. No suspense and no drama, with one exception—Rickey was making his debut in hallowed Fenway Park, one of the gems of the sport (though from the outside it looked more like a storage warehouse than a ballpark).

He had been in the big leagues exactly one month, but it was on this road trip that he experienced baseball royalty—Yankee Stadium and its trellises and history, Fenway Park and its lyricism, mystery, and nearly 40-foot-high left-field wall that turned home runs into loud singles. No more Roosevelt Stadium or pregame betting on quarter horses for 50 bucks.

Rickey led off the game against Dennis Eckersley. Eck knew Oakland style because he'd played against those city kids for years. ("Those guys fucking let you *know* they were good," he would say.) Eckersley knew that if you were going to make it in the big leagues, you had to believe in what you brought to the mound. No backing down. All confidence. Show no fear. Let 'em know. And Eck *had* let 'em know: on May 30, 1977, against the California Angels, he'd thrown a no-hitter—as a 22-year-old. He didn't just know Oakland from reputation; he was born there, at the old Oak Knoll Naval Hospital off Mountain Boulevard, and he'd been taught by Oakland. His first manager in the big leagues coming up with the Cleveland Indians in 1975 was none other than Frank Robinson, who was in his first year managing—the first Black manager in the history of Major League Baseball. (Seven years later, he'd be hired by the Giants, becoming the first Black manager in the history of the National League too.)

Eck thought he'd seen it all, until Rickey stepped in to lead off the game. The balls on this kid! Rickey sauntered into the batter's box, taking his time, putting the pitcher on his schedule. Rickey looked up and down his bat, giving it a couple of taps, before getting into a crouch that turned the strike zone microscopic. Behind the plate, the Boston catcher and legendary tough-ass Carlton Fisk looked up at Rickey taking his time (an irony of ironies because Fisk himself took so much time in the box you needed to shave by the time he was done). Was this kid a rookie or did he own the place?

"Rickey came up in 1979, and by that time I was already fucking dealing, and my first reaction was, '*Look* at *this* motherfucker! Who . . . is . . . THIS?'" Eckersley recalled. The first two at-bats, Eck cranked up the gas, delivering a couple of grade A, "This Ain't Modesto" fastballs to see if the kid could catch up. He couldn't. Rickey was late and grounded to first twice. Third time up, Rickey ripped a two-out single to center, then introduced himself to the future Hall of Famer Fisk by stealing second.

Eck-Rickey, round four: in a 3–3 game, Rickey on first, so he stole second on Fisk again—but he really stole off Eckersley, whose big windup took a month to get the ball to the plate. Fisk had no chance. "I knew it. I'd known it my whole career. Big leg kick," Eckersley said. "Frank Robinson used to get on my ass for being so slow to the plate. They'd try to speed me up, but if you do that, you make a mistake to the hitter. Do you want me to keep the fucking ball in the park or what? I tried to speed up my delivery over the years, but with Rickey on first? What's the use? Fuck it. Take the base."

The final act came with two outs in top of the ninth, after Carl Yastrzemski, another Hall of Fame–bound guy playing that night, broke the game open earlier with his 400th career home run. Eckersley was an out away from a complete-game 7–3 win. With a runner on second, Rickey tried to extend the game—but Eckersley struck him out to end it.

Over the next two nights, Eckersley watched Rickey and saw the raw ability. He watched Rickey on the basepaths—20 years old, fearless, he was completely convinced there wasn't a catcher in the world who could touch him. By that point, Carlton Fisk had already made the All-Star team six times, but Rickey didn't care. No backing down. Let 'em have it. The crouch made pitchers throw the ball damned near down the middle—if they wanted to get a call. Two things made his zone even smaller: Rickey's eye (he never swung at strikes) and Rickey's mouth. Even as a rookie he'd let the umps know *he* knew a strike better than *they* did—and they'd better get with the program.

"He wasn't in that complete crouch yet, but he was small. You had to throw it right to him, you had to center-cut the motherfucker," Eckersley recalled. "I remember one time, sunny day up in Boston, he takes ball four and just *walks* to first looking down, staring at his own shadow. He hadn't done shit in the league yet. Didn't take him long before he became a fucking star."

The fact was, Rickey wasn't even that happy about being in the big leagues for a month. He believed he should have been with the big club to start the season. He was arguably the best player in the spring, and to him there was no question that he should have skipped Ogden, the A's Triple-A affiliate. He was the prospect with the most promise for a team that was in a deep rebuilding phase—if that was even the right phrase for it. The 1979 A's were forecast to be bad—historically bad. Rickey was the best young player in the minor leagues and with the big club, the player with the biggest upside and the fewest complications, so there was no reason to leave him in the minors.

Finley had suspended Mitchell Page, who hit 17 homers and was the team's best player the year before, because he wanted more money. He had another promising outfielder, a free-swinging Venezuelan named Tony Armas, but so far Armas could never stay healthy long enough to be counted on. During spring training, Miguel Dilone beat Rickey out for the last spot in the outfield—but Rickey knew Dilone couldn't run or hit with him. Dilone swiped 50 bags while Rickey was in Jersey City, but he got caught a league-leading 23 times—a measly 68.5 percent success rate. The A's also had Glenn Burke, the Berkeley High and Bushrod legend who had come over from the Dodgers the year before but struggled in three big league seasons, unable to become a regular.

Then there were the growing rumors that Finley himself was done. Free agency had exploded salaries, and his days of holding a big league team together with chewing gum and guile were just about over. He would become a legend for naming his batboy Stanley Burrell a vice president on the company masthead—but running a major league ball club like a cheap motel wasn't cute for those who had to play for it. "It is evident," Ross Newhan wrote in the *Los Angeles Times*, "that Finley has no intention of returning the A's to its championship status. Not, at least, if it costs money."

Finley was ready to kill the Oakland experiment right then and there after only 10 years—not even as long a time as the 14 seasons the A's had spent in Kansas City—by selling the team to Colorado moneyman Marvin Davis, who would then relocate the team to Denver. The Coliseum Authority accused Finley of willfully not marketing his team and sued him for $11 million. After Reggie and Catfish, Vida and Blue Moon Odom and three straight titles, the whole thing was coming apart. "He deserves everything he gets," Glenn Burke said. "Anything that will get his ass out of here is fine with me." Finley had also been negotiating with none other than Sam Bercovich, lover of youth sports, kids, and Oakland, but would conclude that the Oakland furniture magnate didn't have the cash to buy into baseball. In 1978, when the A's came to Comiskey for a series with the White Sox, Finley told his players, "Bercovich doesn't have any more money than Mike Norris."

A week before the season started, new A's manager Jim Marshall explained to Rickey that, with the outfield so crowded, getting playing time in Ogden was better for a young player than sitting on the bench watching what was expected to be a terrible team. Rickey found Marshall's rationale to be nonsensical. If the A's were going to be so horrible, there was nobody on the team who should be playing ahead of him. "I shouldn't have been on the bench watching," Rickey recalled. "I should have been out there playing." Nevertheless, on March 30, 1979, Rickey was shipped out.

A'S SEND DOWN RABBIT HENDERSON
Rickey Henderson could be just what Charlie Finley has been waiting for, a "rabbit" who can hit as well as he runs.
    Unfortunately, the Oakland A's decided to send Henderson down to their triple-A team Friday as they cut their squad down to 27 players.

Feeling salty, Rickey went to Ogden, Utah, to the Pacific Coast League. The manager was Jose Pagan, the old Giants and Pirates infielder. Rickey lasted 71 games, stole 44 bags in 53 tries, and hit .309. On June 21, against the Phoenix Giants, Rickey knocked three hits and stole four bases. Three days later, with the A's living up to the prediction that they would be the worst team in baseball by racking up 50 losses before it was even July, three calls were made: Finley purchased Rickey's contract from Ogden and called him up to Oakland (starting salary $17,500), and Rickey called Bobbie and Pamela and told them both the same thing: he was never going back.

• • •

Billy Martin always knew. Billy Martin wasn't no real big fan of the colored or nothing. Could take 'em or leave 'em. Said he grew up around 'em in Berkeley, in that uncomfortable way people have of trying to prove that they know how to treat you by telling you who they have met before. Billy was pretty cruel to Glenn Burke, a man who had preceded Rick in left field for the A's, way back when. Glenn Burke and Rickey Henderson were two of the most perfectly built baseball players I ever saw. Billy cut Burke loose in favor of Rick. Turned out Glenn, the inventor of the high-five, was gay. Later, he died of AIDS. It turned out Billy was right. Not because of that. Because of Rick.

—*Ralph Wiley*

Ralph Wiley, another whose career was launched in Oakland, would become a legend in his own right: one of the first Black writers at the august *Sports Illustrated*, he became one of the first premier Black feature writers in the country. He was hired by the *Oakland Tribune* as a copy boy who handed the daily budgets to the different departments, got coffee for whoever needed it, and opened the volumes of mail that came to the sports department. His talent was so immense that it wasn't long (less than 36 months) before Wiley was promoted by the great *Tribune* sports editor Bob Valli and went from gopher to columnist; in less than another 36 months, he was writing cover stories for the biggest sports magazine in the country at a time when Black writers were virtually nonexistent in mainstream newspaper commentary and long-form magazine writing. Wiley never forgot Valli's fairness and disinterest in the existing racial hierarchies that prevented Black writers across the country from getting a shot. Wiley would call Valli a "great man, who didn't care about the paint job."

Wiley could spin a yarn—make you feel like you were sitting right next to him. His writing could be lyrical, abstract, direct, and beautiful—usually all in the same piece. He was there with Rickey for his debut. It could be said Ralph and Rickey made their big league debuts together, as Valli made Wiley a columnist in 1979, the same year Rickey was called up from Ogden. The year 1979 was pivotal for the *Oakland Tribune* too, for that was the year Robert C. Maynard purchased the paper from Gannett, making the *Tribune* the first mainstream daily owned by a Black man. (Two decades into the 21st century, there hasn't yet been a second.)

As entertaining as it was, the only problem with this particular Wiley yarn was that it wasn't exactly true. Some of it certainly was: Billy Martin was known throughout the game for being terribly racist, especially against Latino players, whom he would routinely refer to as "dogs" (a term also liberally applied to Black players accused of lazy play). But when Rickey made his major league debut on June 24, 1979, Billy wasn't even the manager. That distinction went to Jim Marshall, who was in the process of losing a boatload of games and his team.

Just before the first pitch of a doubleheader against the Texas Rangers, Rickey, playing left field and leading off, Marshall, and outfielder Miguel Dilone got into it. As the shouting escalated, Dilone pulled a bat out of the bat rack and started swinging in the direction of his manager. (Dilone was in the midst of an 0-for-16 slump, so perhaps Marshall was in less danger than it appeared.) The A's third-base coach, Jim Saul, and Mitchell Page stood between Dilone and Marshall. Security was called, and they would sit on the bench for the entirety of the doubleheader (the A's losing both games). Dilone was soon shipped out, demoted to Triple-A Ogden, and then bounced to the White Sox.

Watching from across the diamond was John Henry Johnson, the Rangers' starting pitcher whom Finley had just traded to Texas a little over a week earlier. "I saw what happened and just laughed." Afterward Mitchell Page said, "I tell you, every day it gets tougher to get up to play here."

Burke had let Dilone have it weeks earlier for not greeting a teammate after a home run. The A's were in total dysfunction. As Burke once told the *Berkeley Gazette,* it was common for the A's to settle matters with a fistfight. When such toxic incidents were brought to Marshall's attention, Burke told the newspaper, the manager would respond, "Quit whining and play baseball." Three weeks before Rickey's debut, Burke quit the team.

Glenn Burke was excited to learn that before the 1980 season Finley brought Billy Martin in as manager. Billy was one of them—a Berkeley guy who played at Bushrod and grew up on the same fields he did. Burke told the papers that Martin was one of the biggest reasons he had chosen to come back to the game—but the word went out quickly that Billy protested loudly and graphically against having a gay player on his roster. Even their common Berkeley roots did not protect Glenn Burke from Billy's cruelty. The whole world in general was cruel to Burke, and the baseball world in particular was chock-full of the Y-chromosome triple play of religion, fear, and rage that created an industry-deep homophobia greater even than that of an already viciously homophobic nation.

In the off-season, Burke played a pickup basketball game with Robert Parish and a few other players from the Golden State Warriors and injured his left knee, an injury that delayed his comeback. Wiley was incorrect in saying Billy chose Rickey over Burke because Rickey had already proven the year before that he was going to be a starter—but he wasn't wrong that, Berkeley-raised or not, Billy Martin was not going to field a gay player.

Glenn Burke played 25 games for Triple-A Ogden in 1980 and then never played professional baseball again.

The 1979 A's lost 108 games. Attendance for the entire season was 306,763—an average of 3,787 fans per game. On two occasions—April 17 against Seattle and September 18 against Texas (their 100th loss of the year)—fewer than 800 fans showed up. More people had come to watch Rickey run back kickoffs against Skyline.

Steve Vucinich, the A's assistant clubhouse man, had been with the team since the first day it arrived in Oakland for the 1968 season. Finley hired Vucinich when he was a 15-year-old sophomore at St. Joseph's High School in Alameda. Like so many Oakland kids, Vucinich played baseball for Bercovich Furniture in Pony League, and he remembered the old days against a previous generation of Porta House kids. ("We used to kick their ass—until Rickey got there.") Vucinich and Frank Cymczyk, the head clubhouse man, knew Rickey from Oakland, from the Burrell boys bringing him into the clubhouse, and they knew of his exploits on the football field. When Rickey got the call-up, they decided that even though he was now a professional baseball player, he needed a football number, a running back number. They gave him number 39—a fullback's number.

That first afternoon against Texas, in his first at-bat, Rickey doubled off John Henry Johnson, then ended the inning when Oscar Gamble gunned him down at the plate trying to score on a sac fly. Jim Sundberg put the tag on him—so Rickey stole his first base off of him after singling in his next at-bat.

A week later in Arlington against the Rangers, Rickey notched his first four-hit game. It was a wild one—15 innings, with the teams combining for 50 hits. Rickey went 4-for-8. After that game he switched his jersey to number 35. On September 17, again against Texas, Rickey stepped in to lead off the bottom of the first against Steve Comer, got into the crouch, recoiled—and launched one into the seats, his first career home run. When the season was done, Rickey had hit .274, with one home run. He stole 33 bases in 89 games, getting caught 11 times. It wasn't so much what he'd done that first season in the majors, but how he'd done it. He was a player to watch, and potentially a player to fear—for his production, for his speed, for the electricity he brought to the game, and all, it should be noted, while playing on a dead-ass team.

"Rickey Henderson has been showing he would have been a Rookie of the Year candidate, had he been up all season," wrote Tom Weir in *The Sporting News*. "Henderson, after just 80 games, had stolen 29 bases and raised his average to .277. Included among his steals were five swipes of third base in a 12-game period."

The A's came to Baltimore in late July, and that was where Rickey met Walt McCreary, a 16-year-old kid working at Sports World, his family's sporting goods store in Glen Burnie, Maryland. Rickey and Walt met through A's second baseman Mike Edwards and immediately hit it off. When the A's were in town, Walt would come over to the Cross Keys Hotel, where he and Rickey bonded over their mutual love of the Raiders. Walt was just a teenager, but he knew his town. He was also working for a local band, The Ravyns, and introduced Rickey to the Baltimore music scene. "Rickey loved music, so whenever he was around I would get him out to the clubs," McCreary recalled. "No matter when he was in town, we would get together. No one ever expected Rickey to be walking around there, and I used to hear people walk by saying, 'Hey, that guy looks just like Rickey Henderson.'"

When the Rookie of the Year voting was released, John Castino (drafted a round ahead of Rickey by the Twins in the 1976 draft) and Toronto's Alfredo Griffin shared the honors. As a June call-up, Rickey didn't crack the top five in the voting. When the season ended, he knew he had belonged in the running, and said so. There was something else he noticed: even at the big league level, with no higher league to be promoted to, he felt that one thing in baseball was still holding him back—his own team.

HENDERSON SEEKS A'S GREEN LIGHT

Rickey Henderson's life with the Oakland A's has been like prison.

No, the rookie isn't part of that majority of Oakland players that wants to go to another team. Henderson merely wants to get the shackles off his legs. At least the [*sic*] 21-year-old felt shackled every time he got aboard base last season. Unlike many previous A's teams, the leading base stealers didn't have the green light to steal at will in 1979. For Henderson, that was a first.

"I think with this team we need to run more. We need to make things happen. We need to run early and get ahead. Once we get behind, it's tough to come back, because we aren't that big-hitting a ball club."

Henderson hoped for a change in philosophy next year, whether
the A's are in Oakland, Denver, or wherever.

During the season, Marshall had two signs for Rickey: one when he wanted
Rickey to run, another when Rickey wanted to run. Marshall wouldn't give
Rickey permission to run. The first sign Marshall barely flashed, and the second he wouldn't let Rickey use. Rickey, who by this time had begun referring
to his legs as "his jets," was stuck. This time it wouldn't have done any good
to call Charlie, because Finley had emotionally checked out on his ball club.

When Rickey got frustrated, he would vent to Mike Norris. Norris was
back after smelling enough bus fumes in the minors to Charlie Finley's satisfaction to get called back up to the big time. Norris would listen, unsure
if Rickey really could back up his unbending belief that he was an impact
player, but convinced that Rickey's fearlessness was something he hadn't
seen in a 20-year-old, maybe ever.

"'If they took the brakes off, if they let me use my jets,'" Norris recalled
Rickey saying to him, "'there's no telling what I could do.'"

5

BILLY MARTIN LOOMED over the Oakland A's the way the *Tribune Tower* loomed over downtown Oakland. There was no corner of the franchise where the presence of Billy could not be felt. He would manage the A's just once, for a mere three seasons, but during those three years he was so omnipresent, and those years he helmed the club were so pivotal to A's history, that it would be like he was always there.

There was one sense in which this was indisputably true: Billy Martin was one of those players who was Oakland before the A's. From South Berkeley, he was one of the kid legends of Bushrod in the 1930s and '40s and starred at Berkeley High just as the Migration was kicking into gear and changing the city. Billy played for Casey Stengel with the Oakland Oaks in the late 1940s before becoming part of that very special clique: an Italian who played for the Yankees. Born Alfred Manuel Pesano Jr. (his mother later changed the family name to Martin), Billy even had a nickname with Italian roots: his grandmother used to call him "Belli" and that turned into "Billy." The Yankees were the only team during those years that Italian-Americans wanted their guys to play for. The legend went back to the 1920s, with Tony Lazzeri, then Frank Crosetti and Joe DiMaggio in the 1930s. And just like Crow and DiMag, Billy was from the Bay too. The Yankees were Italian America's team, and being a part of that, well, that made you legend.

As personalities go, Billy Martin was part hurricane, part tornado—the former because his volatility could be predicted for days in advance, the latter because his rages could devastate a narrow swath of his clubhouse with very little notice, destroying his targets while leaving the rest of the landscape relatively intact. With carnage in his blood, Billy was a fighter.

He got that from his mother Joan. It was Joan who was so embittered by the breakup with her philandering husband, Billy's father Alfred, that she never again called him by name, even to her kids, but always referred to him as "that jackass." When Finley hired Billy, the A's invited 78-year-old Joan to throw out the first pitch of the 1980 season. She told the *Oakland Tribune* that it would be the first time in her life she'd thrown a baseball. "I just threw my fists at the kids," she said.

Fighting was a reflex for Billy, just as it was for a lot of kids born during Depression-era America who came from bare-knuckle towns, where challenge was constant. You had to fight, and if you didn't, if you ran, everybody in the neighborhood smelled weakness. They'd take what little you had and keep taking until there was nothing left. The minute you ran, your destiny was set: you'd be running for the rest of your life.

In this, Billy was not unique. Many a reluctant warrior living in a hard place has had to throw down. Just to keep order there's often no other choice. Where Billy was different was in *liking* to fight. Détente, conflict resolution, conflict avoidance, compromise—these were not options in Billy's tool kit. He was a unique character: an aggressor and the bully who liked to fight, but also the underdog who threw himself into the ring when the odds were decidedly against him.

Anyone who witnessed Billy's street fighting streak would say he had a Napoleonic complex, but at five-foot-eleven, he wasn't a small man—he just wasn't big either. Billy would make it his life's work to fight every man in existence who stood over six feet tall. Six-five? Even better. "Billy had short man's complex," Rickey would say. "If you were his height or smaller, he'd leave you alone. But if you were a big guy? Oooh, boy, Billy couldn't wait to start something. You see Billy talking to someone, they're over there, boom-boom-boom . . . next thing you know—*POW!* It was on. I can't count the number of times I watched Billy get his butt whupped."

Everything about Billy was big and boisterous, combative and reckless, noisy and violent—and drunk—but Billy Martin was a winner, with a winner's demands, and that was something Oakland hadn't had in half a decade. The first thing Billy had to do was find out who could play.

When the A's convened for spring training in Scottsdale, Arizona, Billy brought in 100 players. He inherited a team that had lost 299 games over the previous three seasons and played like losers. Creating belief was essential. "Part of Billy's strategy was to win spring training games to build a winning

atmosphere," recalled Mike Davis, whose father came from Mississippi and
who grew up in West Oakland and was on the McClymonds basketball team
with Bill Russell and Frank Robinson. "Spring games would go and the other
teams would be taking their starters out after three, four innings. Our guys
would still be in there in the seventh inning. He wanted us to get a feel for
what winning felt like." Billy wanted the A's to play every game as if it were
Game 7 of the World Series—even games that didn't count. He wanted to
win everything: B games, intrasquads, exhibitions against Little Leaguers,
college teams, spring training games—that was the only way to flush the
loser's mentality.

The California Angels had won the American League West in 1979, finishing 34 games ahead of the A's. After beating the Angels *in March,* and raising the A's spring training record to 4-1, Billy took out the white glove and
slapped the Angels across the face, telling the Associated Press, "I'm going
after a pennant. I'm not rebuilding anything. You may not believe it now, but
the Oakland A's will beat out the California Angels this year."

Ralph Wiley also had something else right: the A's *were* different. In look.
In feel. In attitude. They were so different that Wiley gave the Billy Martin A's
a nickname that would forever define the Martin era—Billyball.

The arrival of Billy Martin meant change in Oakland, for the franchise
and for Rickey. The Marvin Davis sale collapsed, and Finley was forced in
the summer of 1980 to sell the team locally, to Levi's blue jeans magnate
Walter Haas. As history would have it, Charlie Finley's last major act as
owner of the Oakland A's was to put Billy and Rickey together.

Rickey signed for $30,000 in 1980, and for the first time in his career
he entered spring training on a big league roster instead of trying to make
one. He was in, and now he prepared for spring training not with the goal
of staying on the roster, but with the goal of letting everyone know he was
someone to fear. There was a symmetry that season in his goal of being
the greatest base stealer in the history of the game: Lou Brock, the all-time
record holder and Cardinals future Hall of Famer, had retired the year before, just as Rickey completed his rookie season. In 18 seasons, Brock had
stolen 938 bases, all in the National League. The American League record
belonged to none other than Ty Cobb, with 892, a record Brock had broken
in 1977. When he retired, Lou Brock was regarded as the best base stealer
in baseball (at the very least the most prolific), and reaching Brock was
Rickey's long-term target as well as his short-term target. Brock also held

the single-season record of 118, set in 1974. Only two players in the modern era had ever stolen 100 bases in a season, Brock and Maury Wills of the Dodgers, back in 1962. In the American League? No one had ever done that. The AL record for a single season was 96, set by Cobb in 1915. Willie Wilson had come close in 1979, with 83, enough to lead the league—and that put him on Rickey's radar. "Rickey wanted to be the best, but at that time, so did I," Wilson recalled.

The fact was that, in the American League, the Kansas City Royals set the standard as the speed team. Wilson was the reigning speed standard in the American League. He was big, six-foot-three, like an Olympic hurdler, and an admirer of another leadoff flyer, Bobby Bonds. He would lead the league in triples five times in his career. The Royals were also the best team in the AL West, and that combination explained why Rickey was so aware of Kansas City—he knew who needed to be watched on that team. While Wilson was chasing Cobb, Rickey was chasing Wilson—five of his 33 steals as a rookie came against the Royals. "If there was one thing Rickey knew," Mike Norris said, "it was who was in front of him. He knew who he had to catch."

The A's already knew what Rickey could do because, after a little more than half a season, there had been too many nights when he was obviously the best player on the field for it to be a coincidence. The only real question for Rickey was where he was going to play. He wasn't a right fielder—the arm just wasn't strong enough—and besides, the A's had Tony Armas in right. He preferred center field, but another young star, Dwayne Murphy, roamed center with authority and seniority. Rickey had led off and played center field in 1979 because Murphy was injured—but Murphy would be back in 1980. Defensively, only left field remained. Rickey had played left before, but center was his natural position.

No matter which players were returning for 1980, Rickey's 1979 season did make one thing clear: he was going to bat leadoff. Murphy had been there, but what Rickey brought to the leadoff spot, even after just five months as a big leaguer, wasn't just better than anything else the A's had on the roster, but possibly better than anything anyone in the game could bring. That was a bold statement, bordering on reckless, considering that the American League alone had Willie Wilson; the Tigers' Ron LeFlore (who switched over to the National League with Montreal in 1980); the hit machine in Milwaukee, Paul Molitor; and New York's Mickey Rivers, who could always cause trouble. Nevertheless, the projections weren't hyperbole—Rickey had proven himself a talent.

With Armas, Murphy, and Mike Davis, they had the makings of an out-field. The games didn't count, and many a spring legend evaporated once the regular season played for keeps, but even if nobody else believed it, Billy was convinced that the A's would surprise some teams.

They opened at home with Minnesota, and as promised, there was Joan—dressed in a green satin A's warm-up jacket and sporting jewel-encrusted earrings in the shape of a "J"—to throw out the first ball. The *Santa Cruz Sentinel* described Joan as "four-foot, 60 pounds." The A's lost a wild 9–7 game in 12 innings, but they didn't roll over at the first sign of trouble: down 5–0, the A's scored all of their runs in the seventh inning. For the first opening night of his career, Rickey introduced himself with a three-run bomb off Mike Marshall. "The style, the styling, the flair. It was always there, even when we were kids," said Dave Stewart. "When the game started, Rickey was going to let you know who he was."

It took but four games for Billy to get tossed, for kicking some dirt on the first-base umpire Larry McCoy in a game against Seattle. Rickey was hitting .176 with three steals, but then the lights came on.

It was April 20, the second game of a doubleheader with the Angels, who were already Billy's designated targets. The lefty Frank Tanana was on the hill. Rickey dragged a bunt past him for an infield single. Billy ordered Murphy to drop *another* bunt to get Rickey over to second, but as soon as Murphy made contact, Rickey took off for second—*and third!* Tanana threw the death glare at impudent Rickey, Eckersley style. (*Look at this motherfucker!*) One batter away from escaping the inning, Tanana threw his next pitch—just after Rickey broke for home. Bad news: Brian Downing, the Angels catcher, had no chance to get Rickey, who had just stolen home to start the game. Worse news: Rickey slid so hard into the plate that he broke Downing's ankle.

Tanana didn't last three innings, and Rickey smashed a two-run triple later in the game. Then, just to let Tanana know it was nothing personal, Rickey went on to torment the rest of the American League. Within a week his average went up 100 points.

May 19–22, Kansas City: The Rangers, Royals, and A's were bunched at the top of the division, all trailing the White Sox by half a game, but Billy knew the White Sox weren't going to stick around. The Royals were the team to beat—and Rickey knew Willie Wilson was on the other side of the field. In the four games, the Royals were better, taking three of the four, and they wouldn't look back for the rest of the year. But Rickey sent a message. Whether or not Wilson was even *thinking* about a rivalry with Rickey was immaterial to the fact that Rickey was definitely thinking about *him*. It wasn't that Rickey had anything against Willie. It wasn't personal—Rickey just had to have the crown. Not that Wilson didn't sense a challenge. Over four games the two put on a show on the basepaths, with this round going to Wilson and the Royals. Willie went 6-for-21, scored four runs, and stole two bases in the four games, while Rickey went 6-for-19, scored two runs, and stole five bases.

Rickey was in the middle of a streak—he would steal 13 straight bases— and leading the AL in steals. Now they were all talking about Rickey, trying to explain what he was doing to opponents as he stole bases by the bushel. Ralph Wiley weighed in again, coining a term for what he was doing. Wiley called it the Rickey Run: walk, steal second, either steal third or reach it on a grounder, then come in on a fly ball. With Rickey, the A's could score without even getting a hit.

He was in his first full season, 21 years old, and already had a style of play named after him. But it wouldn't be hyperbole to say that Rickey was being undersold, because while he was letting Willie Wilson and every other base stealer in the league know there was a new force to contend with, he was scorching the ball at the plate. The Rickey Run was a testament to how dangerous an offensive player he could be, but Rickey wasn't a bunt-and-run-for-your-life type of leadoff hitter.

When the A's left Kansas City on May 22, Rickey was hitting .258. Three weeks later, he was over .300. That got him the call to his first All-Star Game, held at Dodger Stadium. He called 17-year-old Walt McCreary, who flew to LA from Baltimore to hang out with Rickey—after he got permission from his parents to travel and a note from his mother authorizing him to use her credit card. Using his local connections, Walt scored some seats courtesy of the AL skipper, Baltimore's Earl Weaver. Rickey didn't start the game— which began with pitcher J. R. Richard of Houston going up against Baltimore's Steve Stone—and mostly watched, until he entered the game in the bottom of the eighth inning. In the ninth, he hit a grounder to third in his first All-Star Game at-bat, against the Cardinals closer Bruce Sutter. Not much to see, but Rickey was on the field with the 50 best players in the game.

Before the break, Rickey had been a blur, and so it continued after the break, as evidenced, for instance, by the afternoon of July 27, 1980. In game 2 of a doubleheader against Detroit, the Tigers manager, the legendary George "Sparky" Anderson, was already in a rage toward the A's, toward Billy, and toward his own team because of the events of May 3, when the A's had stolen home twice in consecutive innings. On the second steal, Dwayne Murphy stole home on the front end of a *triple* steal. Sparky fined his future Hall of Fame pitcher Jack Morris $50 for "defying orders" (Sparky had told him to pitch out of the stretch, but Morris chose the windup) and then laid a $200 hit on his catcher, Lance Parrish, who was so pissed the A's had run all over him that he came into the dugout and destroyed the water cooler.

The Tigers had taken game 1, but in game 2 Rickey went wild on the Tigers backup catcher, John Wockenfuss. Rickey swiped *four* bases, the final one in the ninth inning to add insurance to what became a 4–0 win. It was his 50th steal of the year.

It wasn't just what Rickey was doing, but how. There had been blazers before—Willie Wilson was one in his own division—but nobody ran the bases like Rickey. Talking about him through the prism of mere baserunning didn't begin to describe it. It was his aggressiveness that was different—the way he attacked base stealing and made the confrontation between pitcher and catcher and base stealer personal. Rickey made himself be seen—in the outfield, at the plate, on the basepaths—and the papers were starting to take notice.

ONE-MAN SHOW
HENDERSON IS TOO MUCH, TWO WAYS

Rickey Henderson is the compelling force of the Oakland A's. On offense and defense, he constantly harasses the enemy. He keeps squeezing until something gives.

"I try to make the pitcher look at me and concentrate on me," he said. "It gives the batter an edge. When they make a mistake, I'll be gone."

It wasn't just the base stealing either, but the whole Rickey experience. First, it was the body. He was the Football Kid—built like a tank—playing baseball. The players noticed the strides toward first base, the way one push toward second could morph into full speed, and the havoc he could wreak without even getting a good jump. There was that violent headfirst slide leap. Pete Rose often slid in headfirst—but not every time. Rose ran the bases hard, but this kid was a base stealer who literally put his nose on the base. In later years, Jeff Idelson, the president of the Baseball Hall of Fame, would ask Rickey about his particular style. How did he develop that unique habit of sliding so low, so late? Idelson recalled Rickey responding by giving him a primer in aerodynamics.

"You ever been in an airplane?" Rickey said.

"Yeah."

"You see how an airplane lands?"

"Yeah."

"That's me. I'm like an airplane."

By September, while Rickey was tearing through the American League, the *Boston Globe* ran a "Top 3" poll of various baseball categories, such as "Best Stadiums for Girl Watching." ("1. The Big A in Anaheim. 2. Arlington Stadium, Texas. 3. Fenway Park.") Rickey was voted second in "Takes the Longest to Get into the Box," behind Mike Hargrove (the legendary "Human Rain Delay"). He was only 21, but in his first full year Rickey was ranked third as the "Biggest Hot Dog"—baseball parlance for being a world-class show-off in a sport that demanded modesty and reinforced it by throwing at anyone who didn't comply. Kansas City's Clint Hurdle came in second, behind winner "Disco" Danny Ford of the Angels.

Rickey was also rated second in "Best Eye" (again behind Hargrove), an asset that made him even more of a force. Willie Wilson was having an MVP-level season, but he never walked. Rickey walked more in a month than Willie Wilson did all season. When Rickey went 4-for-4 against the Indians on June 3, his on-base percentage was .411—and would stay over .400 all season. Rickey wore pitchers out at the plate—even managers were complaining about the crouch—and he wore catchers out when he got on base.

The one curiosity of the *Boston Globe* poll was less about where he showed up and more about where he didn't. In the category of "Most Intimidating Speed," Rickey didn't even show. That went to Willie Wilson, Mickey Rivers of the Rangers, and Rickey's former bat-wielding teammate, Miguel Dilone, who was now with the Indians.

There was a reason he was overlooked: for most of the season, Rickey was just another fast guy in a league full of fast guys. He led the American League in steals, but the National League had Omar Moreno and Ron LeFlore, both of whom had numbers beyond Rickey's. On August 17, LeFlore had 77 steals, and Moreno 67, to Rickey's 61. That year everyone was running, and the big league record of 3,403 stolen bases set in 1911 was in danger of falling. (It didn't.)

It wasn't that Rickey wasn't special, but that he didn't yet stand out from his peers with more experience. There was a number, though, that could change that—100. LeFlore told the Associated Press that he couldn't beat Brock's record of 118—that wasn't happening—but he wanted to reach 100 steals. "That's a lot of steals and a lot of running, but it's not impossible," he said. "Brock stole that year even when his team was 10 runs ahead. I don't play that way. That's why I don't think about 118. But I would like to steal 100 because I'd be only the third man to ever do it."

LeFlore had something else to worry about—winning. The Expos were in a pennant race—every run counted. Game situations would cut into his steal attempts, and it was important to break records the right way (lest the wrath of the baseball gods be summoned for violating the unwritten rules). The A's, meanwhile, were as good as they'd been in four years, but in the standings they trailed the Royals by double digits.

On September 1, LeFlore had 86 stolen bases to lead the National League. In the American, Rickey had 66 steals and led Willie Wilson by eight. Rickey's percentage was also respectable—he had been caught 20 times for a 76 percent success rate—but the talk of the league was LeFlore and Moreno. Rickey was very good—he was 30 steals away from Ty Cobb's AL record with 30 games remaining—but LeFlore needed only 14 more to reach 100 with 31 games left.

Plus, Rickey had stolen his bases under the strict direction of Billy Martin. Billy told all of his players when they would go—and when they would not. He took credit for the A's daring steal of home, just as he took credit back in 1969 when he was managing the Twins and Rod Carew tied a big league record by stealing home seven times in a single season. Billy would tell everyone that, sure, the players were fast and talented, but *he* was the secret ingredient to successful base stealing. For record-breaking base stealing, the action was in the National League.

Billy was right. The White Sox didn't stay in the race—they lost 90 games that year. He also was right about the defending AL West champion Angels: they lost 95. The Royals dusted everyone and swept the Yankees three straight in the American League Championship Series, but lost to the Phillies in the World Series. Billy was right about something else as well: his A's were actually pretty good.

The three straight 90-loss seasons were history. Billy's spring training strategy of winning every game had created the belief in themselves that young teams need, and their surprising 83-win season was a huge success. The winning required some heavy lifting. Rick Langford, Mike Norris, and Matt Keough were 1-2-3 in the league in complete games, their arms held together with masking tape, grimaces, and the very cagey ability to expertly doctor the ball. Jim Hague recalled meeting the A's on a road trip to Milwaukee and over drinks and laughs in the hotel bar the guys were explaining how they wet the ball. None of that nonsense with Vaseline behind the ear or on the bill of the cap—that was for amateurs. The inseam of the pant leg was the proper spot—the player just looked like he was adjusting his cup. No ump ever saw anything suspicious in that.

Norris—the guy Rickey once said was garbage and wasting his talent in Double-A Jersey City—won 22 games. A 20-game winner for the first time in his career, Norris was forever now a member of the Black Aces, that exclusive group of American-born, English-speaking Black pitchers who had won 20 games in a season. (Canadian-born, English-speaking Ferguson Jenkins, who won 20 seven times, was also issued entry into the club—clearly on a work visa.) Everyone was talking about the potential of the A's outfield, and now they delivered. Armas hit 35 homers and drove in 109. Nobody at the beginning of the season was comparing Murphy to Gary Maddox—the great Phillies human vacuum in center—but the way he chased down everything? Now they were. The A's were still 12th out of 14 teams in attendance, but the number of fans swinging through the turnstiles nearly tripled. The reign of Charlie Finley was officially over, and Billy was good that year—maybe his best year ever managing. He should have won Manager of the Year, but alas, the award didn't yet exist.*

For a man in complete control, there was one thing Billy was unsure about, and that was Rickey. Billy was the big man in Oakland. He was home. His team was playing in his combative, aggressive image, and Ralph Wiley had given his team the nickname that stuck: the A's didn't even make the playoffs, but Billyball would be remembered throughout the decades as

---

* The Manager of the Year Award was introduced in 1983.

surely as the Gashouse Gang and the Big Red Machine. The A's were winning, winning Billy's way. Billy hung out with his players—the ones he liked
at least—and he got on well with Mike Norris, who was his sounding board
whenever there was a clubhouse issue, especially with the Black guys. Norris
and Billy, along with Billy's trusty deputy, pitching coach Art Fowler, would
have a drink on the road. No matter what team he was managing, Billy always felt that he had a rapport with his players (except with Reggie, but that
was another story). Billy felt that he could connect with the Black players
too—but Rickey? Nothing.

Billy lived up to his rep as volatile, but when it came to baseball, he lived
up to the other part of his rep—he didn't miss a single strategic opportunity.
He was as shrewd as they came. That shrewdness would explain how on
September 1, with 30 games left in the season, Rickey had 66 stolen bases
but would finish the season with 100, breaking Ty Cobb's AL record, which
had stood for 65 years. Rickey stole 34 bases in his final 31 games, including 31 in 27 games in September. In the process he shattered the A's single-
season stolen-base record of 75, set by Billy North in 1976. For the entire
1980 season, Rickey had not stolen more than 18 bases in any one month,
and because Billy tightly controlled the running game, there could be but
one explanation for Rickey's final-month explosion: Billy knew he needed
Rickey to trust him, and he knew the only way to do that was to be an ally in
helping him achieve his personal goals.

On September 4, the A's killed Baltimore, 7–1, and Rickey stole three bases
off Rick Dempsey and forced him into an error. Two of those steals came
with the A's up by six runs. Rickey would steal 13 straight bases over the next
nine games. Twice in the month Rickey stole four bases, once against the
Royals and again on September 27 against Milwaukee. That was the night
he came to the ballpark with 92 steals on the season and then tied Cobb,
swiping second and third with a four-run lead in the sixth inning. Rickey
grabbed the record three nights later against the White Sox when he hit a
single in the sixth off Dewey Robinson and then stole second off catcher
Marv Foley.

In the penultimate game of the season, up in Milwaukee, Rickey reached
on a fielder's choice, stole second for number 99, and then third for
number 100. He finished the season hitting .303, scoring 111 runs, stealing
100 bases, walking 117 times, and even clearing the fence nine times.

Everyone was watching, but that wasn't necessarily a good thing. Conspiring with his manager to get to 100 steals had not gone unnoticed around the league. Playing for the record was considered bush league (according to the stone tablets of baseball's unwritten rules), but stealing more bases in September than there were games was an example of Rickey's drive to be an impact player and his competitive spirit, which Billy loved. Nevertheless, stealing bases the way Rickey and Billy did was silently criticized (and sometimes not so silently). Stealing a record number of bases, like going for any other record, could be seen as a selfish pursuit, something done for the sake of the record, not to win games or to help the team.

In his kick to reach 100, Rickey stole 34 bases and was caught only six times—an 85 percent success rate. Besides breaking the record, he also let the game's best base stealers know they now had a rival, whether they wanted one or not. It wasn't a coincidence that Rickey stole the most against Kansas City, home of Willie Wilson, former defending AL stolen-base *champeen*. Rickey stole 17 bases against the Royals, getting caught only twice. Willie would finish fourth in the AL MVP balloting that year, and Rickey would receive his first top-10 finish.

Even more importantly, for the first time in his professional career, Rickey finished a season with a winning record. In Boise and Modesto, Jersey City and Ogden, Rickey had lit up the box score, but his teams got mashed. The Royals ran away with the West, but Rickey was finally enjoying a season of playing important baseball. He was an All-Star. He'd had a taste of winning now—and he wanted more.

6

BILLY HAD DONE Rickey a solid by giving him the "go" sign all month and allowing him to win his coveted first stolen-base title. By unleashing Rickey as a weapon—unlike Jim Marshall, who had put the brakes on him—Billy helped his player make history. Rickey's top-10 MVP season netted him a big raise from new ownership, an increase from the $30,000 he was making as a rookie to $185,000. It also netted him his first endorsement: the little-known Japanese sports equipment company Mizuno offered free gloves, free shoes, free gear—and the princely sum of $1,000.

Rickey would credit Billy (and himself) for their growing bond, but for all Billy thought he'd done for Rickey, what did it get him? Nothing—or so it seemed. Rickey confounded Billy. Even as a young player, Rickey was already considered something of an enigma. There was no question about his drive—he burned to be great—but Rickey was often a singular character, someone set apart from the rest. As much as he loved being in the clubhouse, he wasn't always exactly one of the guys, and he showed none of that puppy dog deference to the veterans. He hung out with some teammates, especially when Mike Davis got called up, but he wasn't filled with the stardust and fantasy so many players bring when they've just reached the big leagues.

His lack of reverence, of course, was very possibly a by-product of baseball not being his first choice of sport—Rickey's stardust was reserved for football. Another reason was Rickey's ironclad belief in his own ability. He did not walk into the clubhouse in awe of everything baseball. A third reason was that Rickey never forgot draft day: he believed he was a $100,000 player who signed for $10,000. The A's had not invested a great deal in him, and he'd never forgotten that. The team had ignored Jim Guinn's recommendation that he be drafted no later than the third round, and instead they had taken three players ahead of him—which Rickey *also* never forgot. That made him aware not only of his own worth but of everyone else's. If he had been shorted, everyone else damned well better carry their own weight.

His draft experience may have explained, at least in part, one of the A's early dustups with Rickey: he didn't want to pay his clubhouse dues. Dues in baseball were as common as tobacco. The clubbies did the laundry, collected the jockstraps, scrubbed the spikes, got the mail. Off the books, they also did all the other stuff—moving cars and setting up the premium perks for players, like getting their cars washed and detailed. They ran out to McDonald's when a player needed something, anything, to eat. They did all the grunt work, all the odd jobs that made the big leagues "the Big Leagues," and so the players forked over some cash for their services. Big leaguers were supposed to tip like big leaguers too. No matter—Rickey still didn't want to pay. His reason: they didn't do anything, he claimed. It was a weird move, because the clubbies were mostly kids who idolized baseball, the players, and him especially. "He can be the most gracious, engaging guy," the Mizuno representative at the time, Jim Darby, recalled, "and then go 180 degrees in the other direction."

The team tried to talk to Rickey, to no avail. When it got to be a problem, they called Jim Guinn. "I think Rickey trusted me because he knew I didn't ask him for anything," Guinn recalled. "He also knew I could talk to Bobbie if Rickey really procrastinated, but mostly I thought I could say whatever I wanted because [Bobbie and Rickey] knew it was about helping them more than anything. I didn't want anything in return from them.

"So we went into the weight room and we talked. He was like, 'Why should I pay them? They don't do nothing!'" Guinn recalled. "Ultimately, we got it solved because I just tried to tell him he was going to be a big star in the game. I told him everybody loved him and these were the kind of things that could give a player a bad reputation, and this just wasn't a big enough issue to be fighting the team over."

For all of the excitement he created on the field and the overabundance of swagger and style that made opposing players wonder just how much they liked the new guy, Rickey did not spend a lot of time talking about himself to the writers. He was not the guy in the room the writers went to when they needed to fill their notebooks—that role belonged to Mitchell Page. In his first full season, Rickey did not make the writers' jobs particularly easy, but he wasn't hostile to them—unlike the guys with a fearsome rep, like Dave Kingman, Jim Rice, or that switch-hitting brooder Eddie Murray. For a guy gaining a reputation as a showman, he was no Reggie Jackson talking about himself as a superman—letting everyone know (and reminding those who may have forgotten) that he was a somebody. "Sometimes," Reggie once said, "I underestimate the magnitude of me."

The ultimate Reggie story took place at a celebrity golf tournament in New York. The sportswriter Johnette Howard was covering it and brought along a blond, exotic girlfriend who was visiting from Scandinavia and knew nothing about American sports, its stars, or its culture. Throughout the afternoon, Reggie stole glimpses at Howard's stunning friend, and when the two finally made eye contact, Reggie looked at her and said, "Yeah, it's me."

None of which is to say that Rickey was oblivious to the ladies. He wasn't—far from it—and as his visibility increased so did the attention in that area. Nor was he above letting people know how good he was, but Rickey expressed himself by the stolen base, not by giving the newspapers gold-plated paragraphs by the dozen. Rickey may have shared a laugh with teammates, but he also made it clear he saw a line between the writers and the players—his humor, quirkiness, and flamboyance didn't translate into a great interview. The writers weren't allowed to be in on the joke. That was between the players. In later years, when his aloofness did not square with a hilarious story that became part of his legend—when Rickey *stories* had become more engaging than Rickey *interviews*—the writers weren't always so enamored by him. Many would just dismiss him as being on "Planet Rickey."

Pamela thought what people interpreted as distance in Rickey was actually his inherent defensiveness about his education—the Arkansas in him that remained from childhood. Rickey was nervous about being the butt of the joke and unsure about using the right word—certainly when he was around people, like writers, whom he assumed to be more literate than him. While Reggie reminded everyone that he possessed an IQ of 160, Rickey wasn't a wordsmith, so certain interviews put him at a disadvantage.

Rickey had charisma, but unlike the Boomer—the Boston slugger George Scott—he was not going to invite the newspapers to turn him into a clown because of his lack of formal education. Scott was a genial South Carolinian who referred to his home runs as "taters." Once, when Elrod Hendricks of the Baltimore Orioles asked Scott what he thought of Biafra, the breakaway republic whose secession from Nigeria prompted the Nigerian civil war, Scott reportedly replied, "I've never faced the muddafukka, but by the third time up, I'll hit a tater off him." All the writers laughed because ole Boomer was harmless and hilarious—but they also all laughed when *Boston Globe* writer Clif Keane referred to Scott as "an old bush nigger."

When it came to the newspapermen, Rickey's guard was always up. Unsure whether he was being laughed with or laughed at, he assumed—and not incorrectly—that the default would always be the latter.

Mike Davis and Rickey would play cards, dominoes, everything. Another game they played, the strategy game Pente, had a board that resembled the board game Othello. Games like Pente that required counting, memorizing, strategizing—those were Rickey's games. "Rickey was a true competitor. I thought he and I were really tight. In the hotels and stuff, we'd play Pente and mancala," Mike Davis recalled. "We were competing all the time. You had to think, study, and do all those things. We'd set up the board and play on five-hour East Coast flights. Murph, too, would come back after the game, and just keep playing."

Mike Davis and Rickey grew close quickly. Rickey and Mike Norris were already close from the Jersey City days, when Rickey had even lived in one of Norris's apartments. It seemed like everyone was getting a little closer to Rickey—except for Billy. People were now talking about the A's no longer being a nice little story, but maybe the team to beat in the AL West in 1981, and maybe the A's could even challenge New York and Milwaukee in the AL East—but Billy could get nowhere with his star player.

Billy decided to use a new strategy to reach Rickey: he employed Mike Norris as an emissary. "Billy used to love him, and me and Mike was tight," Rickey would say of Norris. "Billy used to come up to Mike and say, 'Mike, can you tell Rickey to come over here and talk to me, cuz, you know, I want to get to know him, and I want to do things with him,' and Mike says to me, 'Billy wants you to talk to him.' And I said, 'Listen here, the way I learned, I can *not* get close to a manager. If something happened and they release me, I be wanting to kill him.'"

Yet Rickey slowly relented, and it would be Mike Norris, acting as the bridge, who finally connected Rickey and Billy. Norris vouched for Billy, and it wasn't long before Rickey found himself out with Billy, hanging with Billy, and drinking with Billy (or more accurately after a certain point, watching

Billy drink). Soon Billy became closer to Rickey than he was with Mike. Rickey would be Billy's guy, and it didn't take a genius to see that it was in Billy's best interest to cultivate Rickey. For all of his volatility, Billy was considered a baseball genius. When it came to strategy, bullpens, the rulebook— both all the writtens and all the voluminous, byzantine unwrittens—Billy knew it all. What Billy didn't have was a great player who embodied him. All the greats he had managed before—like Rod Carew and Al Kaline—were already great before they knew Billy. With the Yankees, Billy could have molded a young Willie Randolph, but the two weren't close. And his greatest player, Reggie Jackson, not only was already a legend but also hated his guts. Rickey could be his masterpiece.

Rickey also had a need for Billy that went back to the absence of John Henley and Paul Henderson and all the adult men who were supposed to provide a solid presence in his life but didn't. Billy was the boss, and Rickey was reluctant to get close to someone who possessed professional control over him. Billy was also wild and unpredictable. But Billy did something the adult men in Rickey's life scarcely did—he took an interest. He stuck around. The other A's players saw it too: Rickey was getting the preferential treatment, and history was repeating itself. Billy was once Casey Stengel's boy, and Billy now liked to think of Rickey as his own protégé.

"Now, me and Billy started doing things. I remember one Saturday. We were out here partying up a storm, having a good old time," Rickey remembered. "I partied with Billy. We partied all day. One time, when we got back to the hotel, he left a note in everybody's locker that we had to be at the ballpark at 7:30. We just got *in!* Ain't nobody got time to get up to get something to eat. Figured we'd get a peanut butter and jelly sandwich, they'd put something together for us when we got to the ballpark. We came there, that Mother Hubbard didn't have *nothing* for us to eat. We're all back there starving and half-drunk, and he's up there kicking it. And I'm pissed off."

"Kicking it" was a serious understatement, for in the annals of baseball, no manager ever ate better than Billy Martin. When he managed, Billy had a personal chef. He knew all the owners of the best restaurants in Oakland and the rest of the Bay, and Billy *always* made sure he and his coaches feasted. He knew so many people that all he had to do was make a phone call, at any time of the day, and somewhere, someone in the restaurant game was willing to do Billy a favor—and that included the legendary Berkeley landmark, Chez Panisse. Billy always ordered from the top shelf: Lobster. Shrimp. Crab claws. The best pastas, the thickest steaks—and the good scotch. He even had food brought over from San Francisco, from Fisherman's Wharf—a hold-over from his Yankee days playing with DiMaggio. He and his coaches—Lee Walls, Art Fowler, Clete Boyer—would have a feast. That was Billy.

"Billy always had the perfect caterers. He had people cooking for his coaches," Rickey said. "We're back there smelling food and everybody's mad. About halfway through the meeting he says, '*Rickey!*' I'm pissed off and say, '*What?*'"

That was the moment when Billy took his shot. In his sweetest, most sug-ary voice, Billy responded to Rickey's broadside, not with a sledgehammer of his own, but with a disarming, "Do you want something to eat?" That was the moment when the two would be forever linked, when Rickey became the favored son. "He said, 'Come on up here and get something.' The whole rest of the team, he didn't give nobody else *nothing* to eat," Rickey recalled. "They were yelling at me, saying 'That's your daddy.' I said, 'What you want me to do? I'm starving. You want me to turn it down? I ain't turning it down.' And he pissed off *everybody*. And he kept doing certain things like that—and that was how we got close. He took me quail hunting. He did everything with me, and I began to see him like a man, not a manager. And he treated me like his son. And after that I couldn't do anything wrong. That man did everything for me. He was like a father to me."

Of course, Rickey *could* have used his newfound access to the manager to bring his teammates some food, but that might have severed his connection. Besides, the game was competitive—every inch, every advantage, had to be earned—and Rickey embodied that ethos. Competition wasn't just against the boys in the other dugout. It was against everybody—same uniform be damned. If there was one lobster claw to be had, Rickey was going to get it.

All of which left Mike Norris, the once-invaluable intermediary, sud-denly on the outside, holding the silver medal. "I thought *I* was the closest to him," Norris recalled, "until I found out Rickey was getting first-class meals. Rickey was eating good as hell. We're in the back, and Rickey's up with Billy eating crab legs . . . but he was deserving of it."

In 1981, with Billy and Rickey now understanding each other, Rickey took off. Andy Dolich, brought in by the Haas family and the A's, began the ardu-ous rebuild of Finley's threadbare front office. Old Man Finley hadn't spent a penny on promotion, so Dolich also took on the long-overdue promotion of the A's to the city of Oakland. They had become a team that was actually trying to win—on the field and in the community—and the new front office built an ad campaign around Rickey.

The A's started the season 11-0, then soon were 17-1. Rickey scored a run in 10 straight games. Their season began with an eight-game road trip, and when the A's came home for the home opener against the Mariners, 50,255 fans were in attendance (a home-opener record) to watch them win their ninth straight game. The game was wild, a 16–1 rout. Putting on a show for Mariners manager Maury Wills, himself a member of baseball's three-man 100-stolen-bases club, Rickey went 3-for-6, with three runs scored, three more batted in, a stolen base, and his first homer of the season.

Two of Oakland's hits that day came off the bat of second baseman Shooty Babitt. When Shooty made his big league debut on opening night, April 9, 1981, against the Twins, another one of Jim Guinn's signees had reached the big leagues. First had been Claudell Washington (who in 1981 signed as a free agent with Atlanta), then Rickey, and now Shooty, who represented yet another kid who played at Bushrod making it to the majors. When the A's signed Shooty in the 25th round of the 1977 draft, Jim Guinn would call Shooty his best signing—not because he had the raw talent of Claudell or Rickey, but because the signing reflected his own personal code. It was how scouting was supposed to work. "I knew his father, and Shooty had an offer to play at UCLA. His father asked me directly, 'What would you advise him to do if he were *your* son?' And I told him I'd go to UCLA, and that was when Shooty interjected and said, because of his low draft status, he wasn't sure he was going to get another opportunity to play and wanted to sign. Shooty made that decision on his own."

To Billy, Rickey could do no wrong, and to Rickey, that made Billy a great man. By contrast, the full force of Billy's tornado would be directed at Shooty Babitt, whom he brought to spring camp in 1981 as a nonroster invitee. "Shooty was one of my best friends," Mike Davis recalled. "Billy liked me, but he hated Shooty's guts. It was difficult for all the young second basemen, because it was Billy's position. They were all his whipping boys, and he stayed on those guys extra hard, especially if you were a rookie. For some reason, Shooty ended up underneath his skin. Whenever someone got injured, Billy would try to find someone he could bring up that could replace Shooty. He tried to get Shooty released and out of the game of baseball. He treated Shooty as badly as any player I ever saw, and in those days, you couldn't do anything about it because you may never, *ever* see the field again if you upset a manager. They could make it their goal to keep you out of the game."

No one knew for certain exactly why or how Shooty fell under the death gaze of Billy Martin. On its face, Shooty should have been the kind of player Billy would champion, and Jim Guinn believed that at one point that had been the case. "Billy was the one who brought Shooty into camp. He was supposed to take him under his wing," Guinn said. Billy and Shooty were both from Berkeley. They played on the same fields at San Pablo Park and Bushrod, though a generation apart. They were both second basemen, both attended Berkeley High, and both starred on the baseball team. Shooty was only five-foot-eight, so he wasn't one of the privileged big guys Billy couldn't wait to punch in the face as soon as he got drunk enough. Shooty was an underdog, just like Billy. It didn't make sense, and it didn't have to, because the A's deferred to Billy on personnel decisions, as did the new A's GM and president, Roy Eisenhardt.

"Billy was an arrogant, punk motherfucker, and they gave him full rein," Shooty Babitt recalled. "He was in total control, and he walked around like he was God. I could never be myself with that man. It was sometimes like he was reliving his career through me—always moving me, repositioning me no matter where I was set up—because we played the same position. I remember a doubleheader and we had a poor showing in the first game, and he was hoping the second game got rained out. By the third inning, Billy is cursing God. Can you believe that? This motherfucker is actually cursing God, like it's all about him. To come from the Yankees, with the rep he had, it was like in his mind he was too big for it. He came up with the weirdest stuff—and some of it worked. If he loved you, he loved you, but if he didn't, he buried you."

Jackie Moore was one of Billy's coaches. He would spend 57 years in the game, 37 of them at the big league level, and he'd seen it all. "Billy wanted to win," Moore recalled. "Shooty was a hard worker. Didn't have the most talent, and Billy really didn't have a lot of patience for those types of players. Billy paid most attention to his stars, to the guys he thought could most help him win games." Billy liked Mike Davis, and so Mike had few if any problems with Billy. Billy loved Rickey, but to Shooty that was a no-brainer. "Rickey?" he said. "Of *course* he loved Rickey. You gonna mess with your meal ticket?"

The word among the Black players was that Billy was as racist as the day was long. Billy hired several Black coaches, but what did that really mean? It was entirely possible, if not probable, that both things were true—that Billy could hire Black coaches and behave in positive ways, like drinking with Mike Norris and treating Rickey like his own son, and at the same time rage more harshly at Black and brown players. It was well established among the Latino players that Billy thought they were lazy—well established because he would often say it to their faces and follow up with all the requisite racial stereotypes. The Dominicans couldn't be trusted, he said, because they were only motivated to get away from the poverty of the island; once they got their money, they wouldn't play as hard. Called them *dogs,* he did. "Anybody who would have to ask the question of Billy being a racist, to even phrase it as a question, has the gift of being ignorant," Reggie Jackson said. "And by 'ignorant,' I'm being kind."

For Jim Guinn, it wasn't so simple. When Finley had dumped his scouts in favor of allowing the newly formed Major League Scouting Bureau to do the legwork for him, Guinn had been left out of a job. "When Billy took over and was in control, he called me and brought me back," Guinn recalled. "He asked me how much I made as a part-time scout, and when I told him the small amount, he immediately added $10,000 to it. I've heard a lot of bad things about him, but I can't say too much bad about him because nobody else would have done it."

In Billy, Shooty Babitt simply saw a man possessed by a kaleidoscope of destructive impulses, a man of racist impulses, substance abuse, pettiness, and rage who also played favorites to his benefit. "Tom Underwood and Bo McLaughlin were two of our relievers. I can't even remember the others because we never saw them," Shooty said. "The way he talked to people. Lee Walls, one of the coaches, was a great guy, and Billy treated him like shit. The ones he thought he could benefit from he was nice to, but it was just the way he talked to people. I mean, seriously, fuck that dude."

Mike Norris beat the Angels, 6–4, and the A's were 18-3 at the end of the April. By now the league was starting to believe. The national writers, including *Sports Illustrated,* were traveling with the team. *SI* wanted to put Rickey on the cover and also feature Jim Guinn, the Berkeley policeman who signed the hottest base stealer in the game. The magazine had a theme and all. "They wanted to call it 'Cop Catches a Thief,'" Guinn recalled. The scout declined to participate in the article because *SI* wanted only Rickey on the cover and he didn't like the implication that he was now riding Rickey's coattails when he was on the verge of superstardom, and that his other signings now weren't as important. *Sports Illustrated* remained undeterred—the A's were the hot story and would appear on the cover. On April 27, 1981, they went with the pitching: Steve McCatty, Rick Langford, Brian Kingman, Matt Keough, and Norris were all on the cover with the headline, "The Amazin' A's—And Their Five Aces."

The A's had a World Series–winning manager in Billy, a top-10 MVP candidate in Rickey, the best young outfield in baseball, and a pitching staff that always pitched nine innings and couldn't lose. But then the A's did just that: they started losing, a bad May wiping out the magic of April. (Maybe April *was* a fluke!) The team was still in first place, but just by a hair. On May 29, Norris was holding a three-run lead with two outs in the bottom of the eighth in Toronto when John Mayberry took him deep for a three-run homer that tied the game. The next batter was none other than Lloyd Moseby, another Bushrod kid, the one who kept getting cut as a 10-year-old and was Rickey's old running mate. Toronto had selected him with the second overall pick in the draft the year before. Moseby took Norris deep for *another* homer and a 6–5 Toronto win. "Better me than him," Moseby would later recall. "Mike was *nasty*."

By the end of May, Rickey was hitting .330, led the league in stolen bases, was second in the league in hits and walks—but the volatility was constant. The first problem was Billy.

"I was in the doghouse with him, but one night he closed down the bar and he's screaming in the hallway outside Cliff Johnson's door," Shooty Babitt recalled. "He's out there at the top of his lungs, just *beating* on Cliff's door, wanting to fight—"COME OUT! COME ON OUT, YOU MOTHERFUCKER!"—and Cliff wouldn't come out. Cliff's room was next to my room, and I peep out my door and look into the hallway, and I'm thinking to myself, *Come on out, Cliff. Come on out and whip this motherfucker's ass.* Billy had his coaches always trying to calm him down. Art Fowler, Lee Walls, Clete Boyer. Billy would just get drunk and we always knew he would sucker punch guys, but I *wish* Cliff would have beat his ass, that little hotheaded motherfucker."

The second problem was the labor situation in baseball. The players had already struck for the final nine games of spring training in 1980, avoiding the loss of regular-season games, but the owners were still mad over losing the reserve clause five years before and wanted revenge on the players. They wanted to turn free agency into an oxymoron: when a team signed a free agent, the team losing the player demanded compensation for the loss, which meant there was nothing *free* about free agency. Being forced to give up a player when they signed as a free agent made teams reluctant to sign free agents. After all, it was baseball, whose first proposal to the players in 1975 when the reserve clause was finally destroyed was to allow them to become eligible for free agency after *ten* years—when the average career lasted less than three.

On June 10, 1981, the players walked.

Rickey was having his best all-around year, challenging for the batting title and the lead in walks, while also leading the league in steals and runs. He was battling for the league lead in on-base percentage as well, but there were some concerns. Rickey was leading the league in stolen bases with 33 but had been caught 15 times, for just a 68.7 percent rate. That didn't bother Rickey, though, because most of those 15 times were pickoffs. The rulebook might have considered a pickoff a "caught stealing," but he didn't. "Why is getting picked off a 'caught stealing'?" Rickey would say. "I haven't even left yet!"

Additionally, there was this other kid, a switch-hitting rookie outfielder from Sanford, Florida, now with Montreal, who came from a football background (just like Rickey), who hit leadoff (just like Rickey), who was built like Rickey, and who was tearing his league apart (just like Rickey). His name was Tim Raines, and if all that wasn't enough, there was the fact that Raines was currently stealing *better* than Rickey. When the game shut down, Raines had 15 more steals than Rickey and had been caught only 10 times— 48-for-58, a shining 85.2 percent. After beating out Willie Wilson to be the game's premier base-stealing threat, Rickey had worn the crown for less than a year and already someone was coming to take it.

It all happened so fast that it was nearly impossible to determine whether the foundation was built on sand or concrete, but this much was real: on October 6, 1981, the Oakland A's, losers of 108 games two years earlier, hosted the defending AL champs, the Kansas City Royals, in the American League Division Series.

The 1981 Division Series wasn't a regular event back then, but rather an emergency remedy concocted for a season devastated by the nearly two-month player strike that lasted 50 days and wiped out 712 games. As part of the resolution to resume play, baseball decided that the winners of each division in the first half of the season, before the strike, would play the winners of the second half in a best-of-five Division Series. The A's were terrific in the first half but only passable after the players returned on August 10—they were just 27-22 in the second half. The vaunted Royals made the playoffs by winning the second half, but they were 20-30 in the first half; that made them the first team in a century of baseball to make the playoffs with a losing record, even though they finished behind the White Sox and Rangers. Even worse, Cincinnati had the best overall record in all of baseball in 1981, but because they finished second in both halves of the season, the Reds didn't make the playoffs at all.

The season resumed in Cleveland at the All-Star Game. Mike Norris had been named to the team, his first All-Star appearance, but even though Rickey was increasingly being called the best leadoff hitter in the game, he was not among the best players in the game in attendance. Not making the All-Star team was an affront to Rickey, and it created a minor outrage, but on August 27, a news story hit the wires out of Boston, written by Peter Gammons of the *Boston Globe,* with a historical comparison that elevated Rickey to the very top shelf of the game.

THE NEW MAYS
RICKEY HENDERSON HAS ALL THE TOOLS;
WINS A'S FANS OVER WITH MAGIC FLAIR

In less than two full seasons, Henderson has done away with the need for comparisons. At 22, he has one teammate, pitcher Matt Keough, saying "he is the most valuable player in the American League," another, Jim Spencer, claiming "he might be the best player in baseball."

It may be premature for these superlatives, especially the museum case next to Mays, but, as Keough says, "look at the skills."

". . . He can hit home runs," says Martin, "but he's more valuable hitting the way he hits now. It's hard to imagine a better offensive player. Also, when he breaks records, it will be to help this team. Of his 100 stolen bases last year, I'd bet 95 of them meant something."

Now, that last bit was a hefty scoop of exaggeration from Billy, designed preemptively to steer Gammons away from any criticism of Rickey's hunt for the record the year before. Betting that 95 percent of Rickey's stolen bases "meant something" was a bet that Martin would have lost. He knew better, because he was the one who set Rickey loose to specifically break the AL steals record when the A's were already out of it. Nevertheless, Gammons's feature on Rickey served the requisite purpose of setting him up as the very best player at his position and maybe even the "New Mays" in the historical pantheon: it was no longer hyperbole to include Rickey as potentially one of the very best players who ever played the game whose gold standard was Willie Mays.

The Division Series went by quickly. Norris was dominant in an opening-game 3–1 win. The Royals would score two runs in three games and be swept out of the picture. Rickey didn't do much in the series—just a buck-82 in the three games—but his numbers were deceiving. He was 0-for-9 in the first two games of the series, but in the clinching 4–1 win, he was 2-for-2 with two walks and three runs scored.

Making fast work of the Royals set up the main event: the A's and the Yankees in the AL Championship Series, the winner of which would punch a ticket to the World Series. All kinds of intrigue surrounded the ALCS. Billy Martin facing the Yankees. Reggie Jackson facing the A's. Billy and Reggie facing each other in the playoffs for the first time since Reggie left the A's. Rickey and Reggie facing each other as big leaguers more than a decade after A's superstar Reggie stiffed adolescent Rickey for an autograph. Reggie's expected successor, Dave Winfield, playing in his first Championship Series. The A's needing to prove they were ready for prime time. Billy versus George Steinbrenner.

Before the series began, Billy proclaimed that his A's were neither "awed" by nor "scared" of the Yankees. Steinbrenner reignited a season-long feud with the A's by accusing Norris of throwing spitballs (which might have been true). By the time the ALCS ended, the A's had been swept out of the playoffs in three straight by the Yankees and had not led after a full inning in any of the three games. Rickey hit .364, including two doubles and a triple, but didn't score a run in the series. In the finale against rookie left-hander Dave Righetti, Rickey fouled a ball off his left wrist. (Dwayne Murphy had already gone down in the first with back spasms.) Righetti tossed a 4–0 shutout, and that was that.

Nevertheless, the debut of the A's under Walter Haas had only made Charlie Finley's departure that much more welcome, and the predictions for the future were encouraging. "It'll be even better," A's pitcher Steve McCatty said, "because Finley won't be around." The A's had rebuilt their front office—someone actually answered the phone now when fans called wanting tickets. That they'd finished only one tough series away from reaching the World Series eased the sting of knowing the franchise hadn't been that far from moving to Denver. The more popular team across the bay, the Giants, had to be watching the A's revival with more than a little bit of envy.

Despite the shortened, scorched season, Rickey was a star. In 1981, he led the league in runs, hits, and stolen bases. In his two full seasons, he was hitting .310 with a .415 on-base percentage. He had stolen 156 bases and hit 40 doubles, 11 triples, and 15 home runs. He backed up his 1980 stolen-base title with another one for his 56 steals in 78 attempts—not up to his standard, but the crown did not leave his head. In the National League, though, the kid Raines (he was really just a year younger than Rickey, but 1981 was his first full season) blew Rickey out of the water—71 steals and only caught 11 times. *The Sporting News* named Raines the NL's Rookie of the Year, but the writers gave it to the Mexican tour de force, the Dodgers' sensation Fernando Valenzuela.

A force offensively, Rickey was being called the best defensive left fielder in the game too. That year he won both his first Silver Slugger Award as the best offensive left fielder in the league and his first Gold Glove as the best defender at his position. With two weeks left in the season, the handicappers saw two front-runners for the AL MVP, and they happened to play in the same outfield: Rickey in left and Tony Armas in right. In late September, Billy weighed in on the race by stating unequivocally, "Rickey Henderson is the best player in baseball." The votes were tallied, the envelopes were opened, and as Billy predicted, Rickey was pronounced . . . the second-best player in baseball. In one of the closest votes in recent memory, the AL MVP went to a *pitcher*. To a *relief* pitcher. That year's AL MVP was Rollie Fingers, the bullpen rock of the old A's dynasty, now of the Brewers. Fingers saved 28 games that year. Rickey finished second.

The fine print made losing the MVP even worse, because while Fingers shouldn't have even been on the ballot with Rickey, what likely cost Rickey the MVP was the one first-place vote that Armas received.

Rickey was furious. *Pitchers had their own awards!* That was what the Cy Young Award was for—and by the way, Fingers won that too. In Oakland, Mike Norris recalled that some of the starters had a nickname for Fingers:

they called him "the Vulture" because he'd blow a save for the starter and then pick up a win for himself. It was, in Rickey's words, "a disgrace." "Fingers was a relief pitcher who showed up every couple of games for one or two innings. Sometimes, he'd come in and get one or two outs. For him to win the MVP was embarrassing to everyday players who go nine innings of every game. Give me a break on that one."

Rickey had established himself over two full seasons as a frontline, All-Star-level player—but now he was counting the slights. It had happened in the draft when he went in the fourth round; thus far, no one drafted ahead of him was a better player. Floyd Bannister had gotten 10 times the money Rickey got. Bannister reached the big leagues within a year, had already been traded by the Astros to the Mariners, and had yet to post a winning record in spite of being in the league for five years. Bannister got the money, and Rickey never even had a chance to win Rookie of the Year—starting his first season in Ogden cost him his shot. And now he was the engine that turned a team of losers into World Series contenders and he'd been stiffed out of the MVP. Not only that but, for everything Billy had done for him, Rickey *still* couldn't run on his own. He still needed Billy's permission to steal a base, something he did better than anyone.

The examples were piling up, coalescing into one increasingly bitter lesson: no one in the game was going to look out for him the way he needed to look out for himself. From then on, the only side he was going to be on was his own.

Book Two

"THEY PAY. I PLAY."

THE A'S DEFENSE of their 1981 AL West title lasted a grand total of one day into the new season. On opening night, April 6, 1982, 51,513 in the house saw the A's beat California 3–2 in 11 innings, a victory that allowed Billy to continue taunting the Angels. After saying that the A's would finish ahead of the Angels in 1980, then taking the division in 1981 and going to the ALCS, Billy had challenged them to a fistfight—in spring training.

Billy immediately boasted that the 1982 A's were going to leave the Angels in the dust again. They were going to the World Series, he said, and now he'd gotten the Angels again in the first game of the season. Taunting the Angels anew was an especially delicious prospect for Billy considering that Gene Autry's shiny new free-agent acquisition was none other than Billy's sworn enemy, the great Reggie Jackson himself, signed away from the Yankees.

As it turned out, though, the 1982 A's would see the World Series only if they were watching on TV. At no point did the A's hold sole possession of first place, nor did they ever seriously threaten for the division. The A's did not post a winning record over any calendar month in 1982. They lost 94 games (the worst team ever for a Billy-managed club) and finished 25 games out of the money. Worst of all for Billy, when the champagne flowed, it was none other than Reggie and the Angels popping the corks, celebrating their AL West title right in Billy's face.

The A's crashed to earth, and yet for the entirety of the 1982 season Oakland led the evening news and was on the sports front of newspapers across the country for one reason—Rickey.

Rickey had one objective in mind for 1982—to break Lou Brock's all-time single-season stolen-base record of 118 steals. He already owned the

American League record. The number he wanted was 120. One-twenty had
a nice ring to it—round, distant, impossible. From Rickey's point of view, it
was only right that he would own the all-time single-season record. In his
first full season he had knocked Cobb from the top spot of the American
League stolen-base list. The strike was the only reason, Rickey felt, that he
didn't beat Brock in 1981. Big people held the big records, and Rickey came
to the majors with the intention of being big—the best base stealer ever.
Now, with the strike behind them, there was nothing standing in the way of
Rickey beating Brock—or so he thought. In fact, there was one major obsta-
cle standing between Rickey and his goals.

A'S HENDERSON AIMS FOR 120 THEFTS

PHOENIX (AP)—Rickey Henderson can think of several reasons why
he should reach his goal of 120 stolen bases this season. One reason
he may not is Oakland A's Manager Billy Martin, whose signals tell
baserunners when to go and when to stay put.

"There are no green lights on this team. The last green light here
was about five years ago," says Martin, alluding to a free-running 1976
A's team managed by Chuck Tanner.

"Rickey always tries to talk me into letting him run on his own. He
hasn't asked yet this year, but if he does, I'll just explain again why I
don't want him to," Martin said at the A's spring training camp.

"My goal is 120, the same as it was last year . . . I want my freedom.
I don't know when it's going to come, but when it does, I'll be unreal.
If I was on my own, I'd steal third base a lot more. I could almost do it
walking sometimes."

Billy said this to the newspapermen, to the local beat writers, Glenn
Schwarz of the *San Francisco Examiner* and Kit Stier of the *Oakland Tribune*.
He said it to the local columnists, like Art Spander of the *Examiner*. He said
it to the national guys, Bill Conlin in Philadelphia and Peter Gammons in
Boston: *There are no green lights on this team.*

Over the previous two years, Rickey had been circumventing Billy's di-
rectives by just playing dumb, going on his own under the philosophy that
it was better to ask for forgiveness than for permission. In later retellings,
Rickey would recall a typical exchange with Billy:

"When I went out there, he let me steal but never gave me the green light.

I knew I could steal. I knew I could take the base. I went out there, they used to give me signs. I used to miss the signs and steal anyhow. He used to pull me into the office and say, 'Do you know the signs?'

"'Yes, I think I know the signs.'

"'Did you get the steal sign yesterday?'

"'I thought he gave me the steal sign.'

"He said, 'No! They wouldn't *give* you the steal sign. I'm gonna *tell* you when you can go.' And then he said, 'If you're gonna steal like that without getting the steal sign, well, you better make it every time.' I said, 'You ain't gotta worry about that. And I stole out of fear too. Gotta make it every time.' Stole about 10 in a row once."

Constrained by Billy, Rickey felt that with more freedom he'd be making more money. So when Eisenhardt sent Rickey's contract for 1982, which called for him to be paid $350,000—a figure slightly less than double the $185,000 Rickey earned in 1981—Rickey sent it back. He wanted a long-term deal. Eisenhardt had just signed Tony Armas to a four-year, $3.3 million deal, but Armas was five years older than Rickey. The A's were firm in their policy—one-year contracts only for young players. The A's also offered Dwayne Murphy $350,000, the same offer they made to Rickey. "Usually," Eisenhardt said, "we think in terms of a multiyear deal when a player is at or near his peak."

The alternative for both players if they did not want to sign at the A's figure was salary arbitration, the underrated but critically important measure that Marvin Miller and the Players Association gained in 1976. In salary arbitration—which first became available to third-year players—a player chose the figure he believed he was worth, the team countered with its offer, and an independent arbiter decided which figure it would be.

Murphy did not want the grief that came from salary arbitration, nor did he want to risk bad blood with the A's if he beat them, or his own hard feelings if he didn't. Money could drive a wedge between player and team, so Murphy accepted the A's one-year offer of $350,000 and was philosophical about it. "There's always next year," Murphy said, alluding to a potential multiyear contract.

Rickey took a different route. The A's wanted $350,000, but what Rickey wanted was . . . $535,000. For the first time in his career, Rickey and the A's would be locked in a salary dispute. Sandy Alderson, the former Marine and Ivy League lawyer hired by Eisenhardt when the Haas family bought the club from Charlie Finley, handled the A's arbitration cases. When Alderson presented his case, he wound up looking like one of the dozens of helpless catchers victimized by Rickey on the basepaths. Rickey won his case, and now his earnings had nearly quadrupled. He received a letter from Eisenhardt, which read, "Congratulations. I expect you to buy me dinner." The old guard, which had forced the strike over controlling player movement and money, fumed at Eisenhardt's amiability.

Rickey had his money, and Rickey had his goals. He knew where he wanted to go, but what he didn't have was the pathway to get there, not with Billy in the way. In the spring, Billy told the writers that everything was going according to plan and that Rickey should be able to steal around 100 bases. That frosted Rickey even more. One hundred wasn't a big enough number. *Rickey wanted 120.*

One day near the end of camp, Rickey was sitting in the dugout and Billy sidled over to him and said, "We're going to break the record."

"I said, 'What do you mean *we? I* gotta go out there and do it. *We're* gonna break the record?'" Rickey recalled. "And he said, 'That's right—"we."' I said, 'How you gonna help me break the record?' And he said, 'I'm a pitcher's manager. I know pitchers. I know when they're going to throw a breaking ball, and all I want you to do when I feel they're gonna throw you a breaking ball, is take off running.' I'm like, '*What?* From now on, I'm on first base, and I'm *gone.*'"

What occurred over the summer of 1982 was a complete and total obliteration of a highly respected record, fueled by Rickey's obsession with greatness. As far as he saw it, the record was *his.* After 32 games, Rickey had stolen 35 bases. In the first 50 games of the season, Rickey had stolen 49. By late May, Billy had not only made good on his offer but pushed his chips—not freebies from the house but his own personal stash—across the table. Earlier in the month, Billy told the writers, "I'm going to make it a priority to see that Rickey breaks the record."

In the first half of the season, Rickey met every benchmark he saw as vital to breaking the record. His roaring start didn't discourage him into thinking his pace would slow in the second half. He wasn't just stealing bases for the purpose of swiping a bag—he was trying to score runs too. But the truth was that Rickey had charted a course toward the record when he was still in the minors. By the time 1982 arrived, in just his third full season (if the strike-shortened 1981 season could even be called a full roster), Rickey already knew there was no one in the sport who could run with him.

"He would literally tell me he needed to steal this many bases this month, and then go out and do the shit," Mike Norris recalled. "It got to a point where I couldn't remember him getting thrown out. You would watch him and he would just glide. You know how you'd go to the lake and throw the rocks that would bounce off the surface? That was Rickey. He was like a rock skipping off water, and it looked like he was accelerating. When Rickey took off, he literally looked like he was hydroplaning. It was the craziest shit I've ever seen."

His goal was to average a stolen base per game, and he was ahead of the pace. When he stole twice off Rich Gedman in Boston on June 1, he had stolen 50 bases faster than any player had ever done it—in only 50 games. When Brock broke Maury Wills's record in 1974, steal number 50 had come in his 69th game.

The American League was receiving the full Rickey offensive experience. A hitter with a good eye for the strike zone will generate enough walks to have an on-base percentage roughly 60 to 70 points higher than his batting average. At one point in April, Rickey's on-base percentage was *200 points* higher than his batting average. In the third game of the season, the Angels walked Rickey five times. At the end of the month, Rickey was in a slump, hitting just .228, but his on-base percentage was .445. These were the kind of walk numbers the power hitters put up because of pitchers' abject fear of them grooving one that would create far more damage than just a base on balls. Pitchers were walking Rickey as if he were Reggie, even though he didn't hit his second home run until May 18.

After one game against the Angels when Rickey went wild—3-for-4, three runs scored, a walk, a double, a homer, two stolen bases, including a straight steal of home, the only straight steal of home of his career—Reggie Jackson, who was on the field that day, said, "Rickey is probably the most feared offensive force in the game. I was leading the league in homers, but I'd fear him more than me. With him, if he gets on base, it's a triple. Lou Brock, Billy North, Campaneris were a double. This guy's a triple. I wish I could be around him every day. I'd keep him pumped up for every game."

By mid-June, Rickey had seven games of three or more walks, and 16 games of two or more stolen bases. Leading the league in walks, stolen bases, runs, and on-base percentage, he was an offensive machine without hitting the ball over the fence. "As Rickey Henderson dashes to a 175-stolen base, 200-walk pace, it's nice to see him give credit to his manager, whether he is allowed to run on his own or not. 'I'm lucky to be playing for Billy Martin,'" Henderson said, as quoted by Peter Gammons in his *Sporting News* column. "'The aggressiveness I have is the aggressiveness Billy has. I'm told Billy played the way I do, he just didn't have my speed. Between his style and my speed, we can make things happen.'"

Now everyone was getting pissed. For 30 years, Billy had been getting under everyone's skin, and now his prized disciple was continuing the tradition. Opposing managers complained to the umpires that the crouch gave Rickey an unfair strike zone. The pitchers complained too—but they had been complaining about the crouch since Rickey was in the minors. The difference was that nobody thought Rickey would hit big league pitching well enough and be enough of a threat for his quirky batting style to be much of an issue. Even Jim Guinn, one of Rickey's biggest advocates, was always skeptical that Rickey could be a successful hitter in the big leagues hitting from such an exaggerated crouch. For his *Sporting News* column, Gammons consulted Dennis Eckersley, who said, "The thing that drives pitchers nuttiest about the A's Rickey Henderson is his strike zone. What irks them is that Henderson recoils, so that he has a totally different strike zone at the point that he hits." Two guys who knew, the Tigers' Jack Morris and Eckersley, thought that while Rickey's minuscule strike zone gave him an advantage, the real advantage to the crouch was that it forced pitchers to throw directly into his power.

It wasn't as if guys hadn't hit in a crouch before. Pete Rose had been scrunching down in the box since the boy Rickey was living in Pine Bluff. Oscar Gamble did the same thing. Cecil Cooper, the Brewers' first baseman, scrunched down *and* leaned back toward the catcher to gain a little extra time to see the ball. So did the great Carew. The difference lay in Rickey's strength from the leadoff spot, in his selectivity, and in what he was going to do once he got on base. He was becoming the complete threat. Rose took his walks and slapped the ball all over the ballpark. He might steal, but Rose on his best day couldn't run with Rickey. Gamble and Cooper were power hitters—and they never walked anyway. Cooper enjoyed an illustrious 16-year career, and Gamble played 17, but neither ever walked 60 times in a single season.

The catchers were complaining about Rickey, but what they were really pissed about was Rickey Style, which made them look bad—and making them look bad was part of what made him look good. As he swiped second and third with impunity, with that Oakland combination of flash and style, they wanted to punch him in the mouth. Take, for example, the moment in April 1981 when the A's were demolishing the Angels and the new catcher, Ed Ott, who had come over from the Pirates, had simply had enough of Rickey's act. In his next at-bat, Ott stood up and got in Rickey's face. Ott told Rickey "to get out of his crouch and hit like a man." Then he told Rickey to stop working the umps and complaining on every call. That cleared the benches. "If he doesn't learn to button his lip," Ott said after, "he's gonna get punched out."

There was a fearlessness to Rickey on the basepaths and a single-mindedness in the pursuit of the record, professional qualities that might have been universally admired if they'd been wrapped in a different package. The guys in the other dugout were, of course, in awe of Rickey's skill, but that didn't mean they loved how he approached his business. Baseball is the one sport—because the defense has the ball—in which the opposition has the power to police the game. Step out of line and expect a fastball in the back. Step out of line by violating the codes of the sport and even your teammates can't always be expected to mount a robust defense. Nevertheless, for every salty catcher upset that Rickey had won yet another duel, Rickey was the player the fans couldn't take their eyes off of—at home or away, no matter what the score.

In Texas, the All-Star catcher Jim Sundberg couldn't stand Rickey, and when Rickey Style was in full flight, Sundberg's teammates egged him on in the dugout like eighth-graders ("Kick his ass, Sunny! Kick his *ASS!*"). The Rangers players implored Sundberg to order a knockdown pitch or just bide his time, waiting for Rickey to slide into home, and then *POW!*—Sundberg could nail him once and for all.

Those were delicious revenge moments for the all-grunt, no-glory catchers, a chance to send a little payback. Stealing bases looked glamorous, especially when the syndicated weekly show *This Week in Baseball* would show the speed guys running wild between the dirt cutouts of the AstroTurf, but stealing was hard-hat grunt work too. Rickey would take a lead. Dive back to the bag. A sweaty first baseman would slap some leather on him with the tag.

Again. Then again. Rickey would often get rapped three or four times with the glove before even attempting to steal—anything to slow him down. First basemen would just delight in beating the hell out of him.

And the catchers? They couldn't wait for a blazer to come round third if there was a play at the plate. Lee Mazzilli remembered the great Pirates catcher Manny Sanguillen tagging a base runner and then just *leaning* his entire body on him. "Sangy would just sit on you, he's fucking breaking your leg, and then when you got up in fuckin' agony, he'd give you this big smile and sound concerned about your health. He'd look at you and say, 'You all right, man?'"

July 2, 1982, Oakland—Sundberg got his chance. The knuckleballer Charlie Hough was spinning a gem—a two-hit, two-walk shutout so far—and the game was a laugher, 7–0 Rangers. Rickey already had a stolen base in the game, his 74th on the season. In the bottom of the ninth, Rickey led off with a walk and advanced to second on Dwayne Murphy's groundout—then he took off for third. Swiped it for his 75th steal of the year. Sundberg couldn't believe it. *Nobody* could believe it. Billy Sample, who played center field that night, recalled the Rangers sharing a collective sentiment. *Did that sonofabitch just steal THIRD? In the NINTH INNING? Down by SEVEN RUNS?* "Rickey was about Rickey," Willie Wilson recalled. "I really don't think he meant anything by it. I just don't think Rickey knew any better. He was on his plan. A lot of us, like Sunny, we were from the old school and you just didn't do that. You stole bases to win ball games. Rickey stole bases to break records."

There was one guy in the game, however, who happily accepted Rickey as the ultimate challenge. That was Bob Boone, the Angels' catcher. Boone was part of a baseball family that dated back into the 1940s. His father, Ray Boone, was a two-time All-Star over a 12-year career and a member of the 1948 Cleveland Indians, the last year that team won a World Series. Bob Boone would win a World Series with the 1980 Phillies, and his sons Aaron and Bret would also play in the big leagues.

Rickey had his way with everyone in the game—but not with Bob Boone. Rickey would steal off of the rest of the league at nearly 80 percent, but Boone nailed him half the time. That was unheard of. Boone was a catcher's catcher—cerebral, attentive, stubborn—and he quickly became Rickey's nemesis. "I had good help with pitchers when I was with California. Gene Mauch's guys got it to me, and when they do that, as a catcher you never have to rush and you get in a real good groove," Boone recalled. "I had gotten run out of Philly, traded, it was because they didn't think I could throw. And when I got there, I threw out 60 percent of runners. It was me, but it was also Gene Mauch's pitching staff who really got the ball to me. When you do that, you're really comfortable. It's like, 'That's plenty of time.'

"But I could read [Rickey] really good. I could read him and see him. I went in and I went, 'I know, I know, Rickey's probably had the green light his whole life, but Billy Martin's the manager. I know Billy Martin, and I know there's no way Billy Martin's letting anyone do it on his own.' And I also watched Rickey. He wasn't getting the sign from third. Rickey would look into the dugout. And I can't remember which way it was, but if Rickey looked at Billy and Billy looked away, Rickey was on his own to run. If he looked at him, [he wasn't] running . . . I had him down cold."

The many components of Rickey's style also increased the annoyance quotient. The first was just getting the at-bat started. Rickey took 10 years to step into the batter's box. For somebody so fast, nobody walked that slow. Mike Hargrove of the Indians took his sweet time once he was *in* the box, but nobody took more time than Rickey just to get there. Second were the tics. Rickey would tap his bat a few times, chip at the dirt in his spikes (digging in was already an offense that could get a hitter dusted). Finally, he'd create a running dialogue on every pitch. *Come on, Rickey. He can't beat you with that . . . Is that all he's got? . . . He better hope it isn't. Oooohhh, he better HOPE it isn't.*

Then there was that time Rickey was just having a little fun. Orioles catcher Rick Dempsey had taken a walk out to talk to his pitcher, on the grass just in front of the mound, only to see Rickey standing there, listening in. Dempsey, who wasn't in the mood for that bullshit, turned around and let Rickey have it, and it only took an umpire and a couple of coaches to get between Rickey and Dempsey. "That was the only thing I disliked about Rickey," Dempsey recalled. "And I told him, 'If you wanna fuck around, fuck around on your own time, but if you pull that shit again, I'm gonna knock you the fuck out.' He got his feathers ruffled and we had some words, and then it was over."

Then there were the umpires. When Rickey was up, they knew they were being watched, especially from the opposing dugout, to see if they were going to call the game—or let Rickey call it for them.

"Obviously, he was a very, very difficult player to call balls and strikes on," recalled Richie Garcia, a former Marine who umpired in the league from 1975 to 1999. Garcia worked four World Series. "Talking about myself, I had the same issue with really big guys, like Cal Ripken Jr., who stood straight up. They were so tall, I tended to call the low pitch. We didn't call high strikes. Not only was Rickey smaller, but he also had a crouch and stood pretty close to the plate. He'd complain. A lot of times he didn't like a pitch around the knees, and I'd say, 'Well, *something's* gotta be a strike.' Rickey basically had his own strike zone. I know how important that at-bat was for the team because he really was a one-man rally. Any time he got on, he could be at third base in two pitches.

"But I didn't feel intimidated by him. I was very conscious of his strike zone, and I always tried to do the best I could. He had a very, very small target. When you have all that attention on one guy, it creates a situation for umpires. If you call it a ball, they're gonna yell. If you call it a strike, *he's* gonna yell. He would complain if you let him. He'd say, 'That ball's low!' I'd say, 'Okay, let's go.' Sometimes Rickey would keep talking and I used to say, 'Hey, you wanna stay in the game? Cuz if you don't, I can take care of that.'"

The antics were getting the attention, but the numbers were immutable. He'd stolen 94 bases in 99 games. Rickey stole his 100th base on August 2 off Rick Sweet in Seattle. "He was perfectly willing to embarrass you," Buck Martinez, the Blue Jays catcher, recalled, but as much as he was competing against any individual catcher, he was competing against the record book.

Then there was Rickey's propensity to either forget names—like the Babe, who would call everyone "Kid"—or never learn them in the first place. Because of its slow speed, baseball has a certain formality. It's a tight circle for anyone on a major league team—same city, same staff, same umpires three games in a row. It's not the NBA, with teams flying in and out the next day. But even though Rickey played a game with plenty of time for manners, he just never took the time to remember names.

When he first came up to bat, he often avoided the common courtesy of treating the umpires as people. He'd step into the batter's box, look at the catcher and the umpire, and maybe give them a nod. But he never addressed them by their first names—because he never knew them. When he did talk, he'd ask the umpire a question and then answer it himself.

Umpire: "Rickey."

Rickey: "Hey now. How you doing? Goodgoodgoodgood."

He would refer to the umpires as "Blue," the universal term from slow-pitch softball to Little League to the Yankee Stadium bleachers for "umpire." "He didn't know anybody's name, so he called me 'Blue,'" Richie Garcia recalled. "Early on, he would say, 'Hey, Blue, gimme time.' I took it a couple of times. One day I'm working second base in Oakland, and Rickey slides in and says, 'Hey, Blue, gimme time.' While he was still on the ground, I knelt down and said into his ear, 'Rickey, you can call me "Rich." You can call me "Richie." You can call me "Mister Umpire," or "Mister Garcia." But don't. Ever. Call. Me. Blue.'"

Rickey was named by *Sports Illustrated* the biggest hot dog in the American League. "There isn't enough mustard to put on that hot dog," the Red Sox pitcher Dennis Eckersley told Peter Gammons. Of course, ironically, this was the same Eckersley, never lacking for style himself, who would strike out a batter, point at his vanquished foe, and yell, "*Get your fucking ass back in the dugout!*"

The moment finally came, on August 27, 1982, in Milwaukee. Rickey took the record with a flourish—a four-steal night. That set him apart. It put him at 122 stolen bases. It was a Rickey night, full of Rickey Runs: he didn't even get a hit—three walks led to four stolen bases and two runs scored. "He didn't just break the record," Davey Lopes said. "He shattered it."

Jim Gantner, the Brewers' second baseman, shook Rickey's hand. They stopped the game. Brock was there, not just because he was one of the great gentlemen in the game but because the A's had called and asked him to attend. Rickey was gracious, saying it was a "joy" to be in Brock's company. He thanked Dwayne Murphy for giving up pitches to give him a chance to steal.

Outside of Gantner, nary a Brewer offered Rickey congratulations. Milwaukee would win the 1982 AL pennant that year, and their postgame comments reflected their exasperation with Rickey as they sent a message to the A's and their star left fielder. Rickey may have stolen a ton of bases—from last place—but Milwaukee had won the first two games of the series. "We weren't thinking about Rickey Henderson," Milwaukee manager Harvey Kuenn said. "We treated Rickey as if he had no stolen bases." The Brewers' young shortstop Robin Yount parroted his manager, almost word for word. "We didn't care about Rickey Henderson. We cared about winning."

Rickey had the record. He'd reached his magic number, 120 steals, and then some. Stealing 122 bases—in 127 games no less—gave him an idea for *another* number: 140. Billy was into this idea too—140 was huge. Nobody would ever break that number—until Rickey jammed his shoulder sliding into second base a couple days later. He stole only eight more bases the rest of the year. Nevertheless, Brock's record was already his. The final tally was 130. To commemorate the achievement, Rickey bought a gold chain with a gold medallion the size of a sundial. Etched into the center of the gold disc was the number *130*. He'd wear that chain for the rest of his career.

While history was being made, Jackie Moore, the A's first-base coach, was the intermediary who would get lost in the retelling. There was Billy, who made sure everyone knew it was he who gave Rickey the green light ("*We're gonna break the record*"). There was Rickey who, of course, physically stole all the bases. There was Dwayne Murphy, whose selflessness in taking pitches from the two-spot gave Rickey a shot at his glory. But everybody forgot Jackie.

"Rickey had a habit—he always took off on the first pitch. He would just take off, and the other clubs realized it. The opposing manager saw it, and he'd pitch out," Moore recalled. "So, knowing this, Billy said to Rickey, 'I'm going to give you the sign.' We'd get the sign. Rickey knew if I winked at him, he was supposed to steal on the next pitch. So that year Rickey broke the stolen-base record and I broke the record for number of times winking at a ballplayer."

Throughout most of the season, Rickey had pretty much everything, but there was one thing he did not have—a nickname. That arrived on August 29, 1982, courtesy of the great Jim Murray of the *Los Angeles Times* in his syndicated column.

WHAT MAKES RICKEY RUN

What makes Rickey run? Sheer speed? That's not enough. That's like saying black gloves make you a burglar. There may be a dozen guys as fast as Rickey in the game. And they don't have half as many steals.

Rickey Henderson smiles slyly when asked his "secret." "Oh, I have my keys," he says, vaguely. The keys to the kingdom for Rickey proved to be amorphous things like the way a pitcher bends his knee, the way his shoulders point when he stretches.

Rickey Henderson may have Olympic speed and more keys than a night watchman. But that's not what makes him the greatest thief since Bonnie and Clyde.

What makes Rickey the Man of Steal is runaway confidence, bordering on arrogance. He doesn't believe there's a pitcher alive who
can throw 60 feet, six inches when he's on base, and then have the
catcher throw 127 feet, three inches in the time that it takes him to
dash 90 feet.

When it was awards time, however, the electrifying season of the "Man
of Steal" did not translate. Rickey finished 10th in the MVP balloting, which
gnawed at him, even though his finish reflected more on a team that lost
94 games than on Rickey's importance. Either way, analysis did not soothe
his bitterness. That Yount ran away with the MVP made sense—the Brewers won their first-ever pennant. Only one other player—Reggie for his
39-homer comeback season—mustered a first-place vote. But what stung
Rickey even more was that his 10th-place finish was behind Dan Quisen-
berry of the Royals—*another relief pitcher!* The guys who finished higher hit
more home runs, but did any of them really have a better year than Rickey?
What was it going to take to be recognized?

Jim Darby and the executives at Mizuno, however, were thrilled. They
saw Rickey's value to the company. "He breaks the record and obviously, to
take advantage of his notoriety, we give him a vacation, he and Pam, with
all the accoutrements," Darby recalled. "I'm the bag carrier, and I had to get
him a visa to be able to go to Japan, so I need a birth certificate. When I get
his birth certificate from Bobbie, I see he was born in Chicago, but then I
look at the name, and I see two things. The first is that his last name wasn't
Henderson, but Henley. The second thing is the name: 'Boy Henley,' born
Christmas Day. The hospital processed the birth certificate before Bobbie
had named him. His birth certificate says 'Boy Henley.'

"Anyway, we arrive in Tokyo, and Mizuno wants to hold a press conference at the Imperial Hotel right across the street from the Imperial Palace.
It's a big deal. Rickey walks in, and there's also a lady Mizuno put in charge
to be his interpreter. Michiyo Shuto, Georgetown-educated, fluent in English. Rickey takes the first question, and you can only imagine Japanese
guys trying to understand a word Rickey is saying. You should have seen the
look of terror on her face trying to translate that. I'm watching, and I feel like
Barbara Billingsley in *Airplane*. I was like, 'I speak jive,' and so that was how
I ended up interpreting Rickey for the Japanese press."

They went to Japan during Thanksgiving week, and Pamela noticed that a sightseeing tour was scheduled on Thanksgiving Day. "I told her, 'Pam, we're in Japan. They don't celebrate Thanksgiving here.' She said, 'Well, we do.' I had to fly two turkey dinners in from Seattle. That was a very expensive turkey for Mizuno."

With Billy, Rickey had what any player could ever want from a manager— complete devotion to his development. Billy saw Rickey's ability in a way no manager had seen since Boise, when Tom Treblehorn spent more time on Rickey's game than he did with his own wife—and he had traveled light-years from John Kennedy in Jersey City. Few players possessed the tools required to be a Billy Martin type of player, but Rickey did—his game was perfect for what Billy wanted. Of course, it didn't really matter *who* the manager was when Rickey was cranking—as long as they got out of his way and let him play.

Billy wanted Rickey not to be great, but to be an all-time great. Rickey was Billy's spear of lightning—the player he could see himself through, the one who would implement his managing vision. In return Billy played favorites with Rickey as he did with few other players. The problem was that Billy's pattern as a manager had followed him to Oakland: the best Billy years were always the first two. Rickey was great, but the team collapsed, and the Haas family had grown completely tired of Billy's act.

There was an unwritten rule in the A's front office—Billy could never be left alone. The club always had to attach someone to him. He was too unpredictable. Usually, it was Billy's pitching coach, Art Fowler, who had to keep Billy in check. Other times it was the A's clubhouse man, Steve Vucinich. Vucinich loved Billy. All of Billy's guys did. Billy showed enormous loyalty to them, and they gave it back. They accepted Billy and all the unpredictability and volatility that came with him, and whenever there was a story about Billy's dark side, they made sure it was parried by another about Billy's generosity.

Monte Poole would recall that, as a young reporter with the *Oakland Tribune,* he ventured into the clubhouse to talk to Billy. The manager was brusque—until Poole told him that he wanted to ask him about Mike Norris, one of Billy's guys.

"From then on his whole demeanor changed, because he loved Mike," Poole recalled. "He gave me all the time I needed, and that was the thing about Billy. He was subjective. If he liked you, you could do no wrong with Billy. If he didn't, you couldn't do anything right."

Billy's guys understood everything that came with Billy—the hangovers, the rages, the potential that everyone just might end up in jail if the scotch hit Billy the wrong way. But they would laugh off the monsoon that was Billy Martin because in a matter of days (or minutes) they knew it would be sunny again. During a 94-loss season, however, there was a whole lot of darkness.

"Billy would get drunk, and then he'd wanna fight," Mike Norris recalled. "He tried to fight me on a bus one night. He didn't like people laughing if we lost, and I was in the back of the bus laughing, and Billy said, 'Shut up back there, boy.' And I said, 'Ain't this a bitch? Now, I'm a *boy*?' And here comes Billy. And here I come. And Cliff Johnson got in the middle of us and said, 'Billy, sit your little ass down.' But he was willing to fight, always willing to fight. And he first-punched motherfuckers, but I was ready for his ass. *I* was gonna first-punch *him*."

A's president and general manager Roy Eisenhardt was watching, and so was his protégé, Sandy Alderson. As the team spiraled, Alderson knew Martin's way was untenable. The Haas family—the family-friendly, committed-to-the-community new ownership—wasn't going to tolerate its manager getting pounded with his players one minute and wanting to punch it out with them the next. Billyball had been an important springboard for new ownership and a break from the malaise of the final Finley years, but a street-fighting manager was not a long-term option. Those days were over.

During the spring, the *Detroit Free Press* began its A's preview with a question that encapsulated the dilemma that the Eisenhardt-Alderson front office had with Billy: "How long before Billy Martin—and the team built in his image—self-destructs?" "I was still adjusting to baseball, to the culture, and that adjustment was made a little more complicated by the fact that Billy Martin was the manager and the lead baseball person," Alderson recalled. "Billy was opinionated. Hard drinker. Racist. Volatile. Capricious. All those things. I can remember thinking to myself, 'This is what baseball is?' It took a while, not a long time but a while, to recognize that this is idiosyncratic. This is unique. This is Billy Martin."

Shooty Babitt knew what life was like not being one of Billy's guys. He lasted 54 games under Billy, became the scapegoat in 1981 for the A's defensive problems in the infield. Shooty never escaped Billy's doghouse. The A's signed Davey Lopes for 1982 so Martin could rid himself of Shooty. There were all kinds of stories and theories as to why Shooty was dead to Billy. In one story, Shooty's father, exhausted by the manager trashing his kid, came at Billy with a bat in an Oakland bar. Shooty himself had another theory: he crossed Billy by committing the grave sin of attempting to speak to Billy directly instead of going through his coaches, an offense for which Billy bitched out his coaches and never spoke to Babitt again. "What kind of manager doesn't have an open-door policy?" Shooty would ask. "This guy, man, what a motherfucker."

"When Billy sent him to the minors, it didn't stop there," Jim Guinn recalled. "Shooty got sent down, back to Ogden, and he was hitting real well. Then Billy called the Triple-A manager and said to him about Shooty, 'Release him or I'm going to get you released,' and that was that. People always talk about needing talent to make the big leagues, but the thing you really need is for someone to like you."

Eisenhardt and Alderson had concluded that the A's of 1981 were something of a mirage. Taking another look at what he had been watching the previous two seasons, Eisenhardt decided that the A's really weren't that good. They were overachieving and now regressing back to the mean. Even though being the buzzkill wasn't the most fun job in the world, Eisenhardt began taking a forensic look at his team. As with any surprise team, things that usually went wrong had gone right for the A's in 1981. But the one-run games they were winning in 1981 were games they lost in 1982. The thrilling extra-inning victories that were a staple on the road to the ALCS were now losses that just happened to take longer than nine innings.

Eisenhardt also concluded that giving Billy Martin complete control over the A's may have served the franchise while he and Alderson, two baseball novices, learned the business and rhythms of the sport, but now they no longer needed him. After two seasons, Billy was demonstrating the law of diminishing returns—more Billy equaled less success. Everybody in baseball knew the Billy Martin pattern: win earlier than expected, and then burn out earlier than expected. With the A's, that was especially true of his starting pitchers, who couldn't lift their arms after the 1980 season. The A's threw 94 complete games on the season, 46 more than the Brewers, who came in second. Rickey was great, but no one else by 1982 had become a demonstrably better player under Billy. He had to go.

Alderson was aware of something else: the Yankees wanted Billy back, and
if Billy Martin was anything, he was a Yankee. So on October 22, Eisenhardt
fired him. It was the first move that had critical implications for Rickey, for
no matter who the A's hired to replace Billy, no manager would ever be a
bigger advocate for Rickey. The second move that would alter the arc of
Rickey's career occurred weeks later, when Eisenhardt named Alderson general manager.

According to Alderson, "That happened by chance. At the time I went
over to the A's, Billy Martin was the manager, and he was the putative general
manager, because Roy didn't know anything about the game at the time. I
certainly didn't know much about the game. We didn't have anybody like
Bill Rigney, who came along later as an adviser, so Billy Martin ran the show.
He wasn't the general manager, but he acted in that role. Most of the people that were in coaching or even on staff, like our scouting director, they
were all Billy Martin guys, so when things started to fall apart with Billy, we
weren't playing that well, the Yankees were beckoning anyway, we let Billy
go. I think it was something that he wanted. There was a vacuum, so I think
Roy decided, rather than hire someone he didn't know, someone he couldn't
evaluate, at least he knew me. He knew my character, my judgment, and he
had more confidence in someone that he felt he knew without experience
rather than someone with experience he didn't know. So I kind of fell into
the job."

Billyball was over, but Rickey was still the guy the fans paid to see, the one
they couldn't take their eyes off of, even playing for a team that was barely
winning once a week. Billy was gone, but Rickey still was electric. "What
people don't really seem to get, and I don't know why they don't get it,"
Shooty Babitt recalled, "is that Rickey didn't *need* Billy, but Billy *definitely*
needed Rickey." The A's offered Rickey $750,000 for 1983 but did not fight
when Rickey asked for $800,000, another jump from the $535,000 he earned
in 1982. This time the two sides agreed to a contract cleanly, so there was no
contract fight with management, no arbitration, no bitterness.

After breaking the stolen-base record, Rickey was now a star. As the face
of Mizuno, he was now doing ads and commercials with other stars from
other sports. As his fame increased, so too did his exposure to uncomfortable situations. Reading was still a challenge for him; the rumors went out

that when Rickey did a TV spot or ad shoot, he would refuse to use a script, saying he was more comfortable improvising. But his true fear was revealing his reading difficulties.

The record also solidified Rickey's reputation as the most flamboyant, stylistic player in the game, but that didn't mean Mizuno was comfortable with him. Jim Darby saw Rickey as an enigma whose moods could change as quickly as he could accelerate for second—especially if he felt taken advantage of. "Signing a deal with Rickey didn't mean Rickey would show up in your product, and that was always scary," Darby recalled. "A contract didn't always mean to Rickey what we think a contract means. You just never knew if one day he was going to show up in a pair of Adidas."

The people who knew Rickey knew he had to win—winning was central to his core. But in the big leagues he was primarily seen as a "hot dog," as arrogant, showy, exaggerated. His grade school friend Dave Stewart saw Rickey as the same person he'd always been, but big leaguers were supposed to be humbler. "Rickey has been styling since we were kids, but the audience changed. The people who were doing the writing changed. The people who were shaping the opinions changed. To us, he was just Rick. To them, he was challenging the conventions of how the game was played. To them, he was being disrespectful to the traditions, to how you were expected to play."

Rickey was the showstopper, someone who could dominate the tempo and pace of a game. Even though the writers didn't always see him that way, Rickey was the player everyone was watching, both the home fans waiting to be electrified by something Rickey did and the opposition. "What I loved about him," Reggie Jackson said, "was his love of the moment. Everyone in the world knew he was going—the manager, the pitcher, the catcher, and he went anyway. And they still couldn't stop him."

There were so many ways to captivate the crowd. Rickey was all legs and thrust and ferocity. He was a walking demand. Batting leadoff, a position in the order that was supposed to be largely inconspicuous, the table-setter for bigger things to happen, he demanded to be recognized. His play wasn't effortless—he'd never be mistaken for a latter-day DiMaggio, whose legendary demeanor was all about art and class and ease. That baseball came easy to DiMaggio was, of course, only legend, but that legend was shaped not just to provide color and character to his otherworldly deeds but also to serve the Italian immigrant population who basked in his success. His expensive tailored suits and peerless professionalism lifted ordinary Italians trying to make it in America, giving them a sheen of dignity they were not often afforded in everyday life. In a country that often treated them as beneath contempt, DiMaggio's athletic elegance contributed to making Italians feel *respectable*.

Still, DiMaggio's game was in fact exceptionally smooth. "Once he got out there he stayed out there. He did everything so easily. That's why they never appreciated him as much as they should," Yankee manager Joe McCarthy once said of him. "You never saw him make a great catch. You never saw him fall down or go diving for a ball. He didn't have to. He just knew where the ball was hit and he went and got it. That's what you're supposed to do. The idea is to catch the ball. The idea isn't to make exciting catches."

If DiMaggio, clean and sound, caught the ball fundamentally, without frills, what in the world would old Marse Joe have done with Rickey, for whom the idea was to do both—to catch the ball *and* let them talk about the way he caught it? Or worse, what would have happened to him and his teammates if McCarthy had been managing in the opposing dugout while Rickey made a spectacle out of a simple fucking fly ball? In McCarthy's day, when even scratching out a little dirt in the batter's box was seen as a sign of disrespect, the sight of Rickey—moving slow as molasses to the box, carrying out a ceremony of rituals, and getting every call—would undoubtedly have warranted a fastball to the ribs. Somebody would have gone down. Right. On. Their. Ass. Naturally, the world will never know for sure, for McCarthy last managed a big league game in 1950 and died 18 months before Rickey made his major league debut.

If Rickey was born with style, and the fans and the writers were going to call him a hot dog, well, he was going to lean into the role, but the truth was that he always resented the implication that he valued style above winning. Rickey valued style as a spoil of winning. The Black fans and players knew that pitting charisma against winning was a false, often racist choice—and a way to punish the Black players for playing with Black style. More than any other sport, baseball demanded that Black and brown players adapt to the old ways of playing the game, which was to say, the white ways. Crack a smile, get knocked out. Penalizing Black style was the clearest way the game reminded post-segregation Black players just who it was professional baseball belonged to. Black players could now take the field, but they were renters.

If the baseball world was going to call Rickey a showboat, well, they were going to get a show whenever they bought a ticket. It was a new world, made for television, a game of pictures and images, not the words and ink of McCarthy and Joe D's time. In 1983 Rickey gave them a new show when he added another 24-carat gold piece of flash to his game that no one watching him would ever forget.

Surely the legend wasn't true—that Rickey introduced his patented "snatch-catch" during a no-hitter? And yet it was. It was also true that Rickey didn't remember the name of the pitcher who threw it—even though they were teammates—but he was certain the snatch-catch started there.

"It started off in Oakland, just trying to be like Willie Mays. What was the pitcher's name? He pitched a no-hitter for us," Rickey recalled. "Last out of the no-hitter I snatched that ball out of the air and gave everybody in the stands a heart attack . . . ! There're a lot of people today trying to make something fun, trying to create fun, but it ain't natural. It wasn't nothing I created. I just had style."

The legend was indeed fact: September 29, 1983. Game 159, A's–White Sox at the Coliseum. The A's were done, no longer in the running, 24 games out at first pitch. The White Sox, playing out the string, were very much in it. The White Sox and their young manager, Tony La Russa, were heading to the playoffs. Chicago hadn't made the postseason since Rickey was in diapers and living in Chicago when the Go-Go Sox won the 1959 AL pennant. This 1983 team was a beast. Chicago would win the division by 20 games, the only team in the AL West with a winning record.

The pitcher whose name Rickey couldn't remember was Mike Warren, all of 22 years old, a rookie making his ninth start in the big leagues. Wearing number 43, Warren took the mound against Britt Burns, the White Sox left-hander.

Warren erased two future Hall of Famers in the first inning, striking out Carlton Fisk and retiring Harold Baines on a fly-out. Rickey immediately gave the A's the lead, singling and scoring in the bottom of the first. Warren walked two and lost his perfect game, but he hadn't given up a hit. Fisk threw Rickey out trying to steal in the third. By the eighth, the A's led, 3–0.

Rickey made five routine putouts, DiMaggio style. Two hands on the ball, in his patented shallow position, nothing fancy. Catch the ball, throw it back. Warren, a Southern California kid with blond hair flowing out of his cap, entered the ninth with his no-hitter.

Jerry Hairston, the veteran utility man, led off the inning with a walk. Greg Walker, a Bay Area kid and lefty power hitter, flied out to center for the first out. Speedster Rudy Law, another Bay Area kid from up the road in Richmond, was next. It was the same Rudy Law who pulled out of the race Rickey was supposed to run against Law and Clabber, the quarter horse of Finley's "Man vs. Beast" extravaganza in Modesto when Law was a Dodgers prospect with Lodi back in 1977. Warren struck out Law.

That left Fisk. Two hours and 20 minutes after the first pitch, with nothing but zeroes on the board, Warren flipped a meaty breaking ball low and over the plate. Fisk, looking fastball, lunged and popped up to left.

Rickey tracked the ball, made a little semicircle underneath it. And as he secured the final out of the greatest moment of Mike Warren's professional life, Rickey snatched the ball out of the air and swung his glove down to his side in one crescent-shaped motion, slapping his right hip with his glove.

So it was technically true that Rickey introduced the snatch-catch during a no-hitter, but the truth was even more outrageous. After making five putouts, Rickey unveiled the snatch-catch, the showiest of show-off moves, *on the final out.*

"That's where it started. I was so used to it, I kept it," Rickey recalled. "Most people think I was snatching it out of the air, but I caught it first. You think I was gonna risk that? They used to go, 'If you throw it away, we're gonna be talking about your ass all day!' You gotta understand, I can't be the guy saying all this trash and then *miss the ball!* Ball was coming at me and I'm waiting for it? *BAM!* I'm snatching it. But if I gotta go get it, make sure you catch it first and then *BAM-BAM,* slap it off the hip to make sure it was in my glove. *And . . .* it looked so good. That's that flavor."

It was an optical illusion, really, or at least the drama of it was. "I never swatted at the ball while trying to catch it. I snapped it after I had already caught it." The goal was always to catch the ball, but this was Rickey. Rickey had to make it exciting for an America that would soon replace words with video—television was on its way to ruling the country. People were watching, and those at the game had paid good money to see a show. So it now became a thing: Rickey would catch a routine fly, a can o' corn, and as soon as the ball was nestled securely in the webbing of his glove—*BAM!*—he snatched it. It became Rickey's signature, and Little League and high school coaches around the country went insane because now the kids, wanting a piece of Rickey's cool, were incorporating the snatch-catch into their game.

• • •

Rickey and DiMaggio overlapped not just geographically but also historically. They were both from the Bay. DiMaggio grew up in the North Beach
section of San Francisco. When the A's moved west from Kansas City and
DiMaggio was a coach for the A's during their first two seasons in 1968 and
1969, Rickey was just a kid, a 10-year-old carrying a football around a couple
of miles away from the Coliseum and stealing bases for a quarter a swipe.

DiMaggio made his big league debut as a 21-year-old in segregated 1936,
and he retired in 1951, four years before the Yankees made Elston Howard
the first Black player to wear the pinstripes. Rickey arrived in the big leagues
as a 20-year-old, after the Philadelphia A's of DiMaggio's day had already
moved twice—from Philadelphia to Kansas City, then from Kansas City to
Oakland. Billy played two seasons with Joe D. Rickey played for Billy for
three.

Grace versus flash. They were worlds apart generationally, and on its
face, outside of both growing up in the Bay, there was really no reason to
link the two, except for one important commonality: statesman or showman, snatch-catcher or two-hander, Italian or Black, Rickey and Joe both
found out early about the hard business side of baseball. The game was never
going to pay them what they were worth. Respect was not paid in words
but in dollars, and whether in pre–World War II baseball or 1980s baseball,
players had to scratch and claw and hold out and dominate just to get their
share—even if in Rickey's time a player's share in one season was bigger than
what DiMaggio earned over his entire storied career. The great DiMaggio,
who never made a mistake, according to legend, and was called the perfect
ballplayer so many times that it might as well have been his middle name,
always felt like he had to fight to get his money. DiMaggio had even held out
way back in 1937, and now Rickey, who arrived in the big leagues nearly a
half-century after Joe, was about to go the same route.

B ASEBALL PLAYERS WEREN'T regular guys, but in 1974 they earned only slightly more than three times what the average American family paying to watch them play brought home. That year, the same year Rickey turned 16, the median household income in the United States was $11,000. The average major league salary was $35,000. Hank Aaron was in the final year of a three-year, $600,000 contract that at signing had made him the highest-paid player in the history of the game at $200,000 per season. A year earlier, Willie Mays retired. Mays ended his spectacular 22-year career never making more than $180,000 a year. There were always the outliers—a few players who dwarfed what the average American worker brought home, like Babe Ruth, who earned $80,000 a year during the Great Depression years of 1930 and 1931. The outliers were the Mount Olympus guys, however, guys like Aaron and Mays, DiMaggio and Williams, who were the best to ever play baseball—and who made their biggest money near or at the very end of their career.

Even though the players were the game, they didn't share in the profits. The public was rarely sympathetic, however, because most fans would kill to be able to just once—*just once!*—hit a ball the way Reggie did at Tiger Stadium when he took Dock Ellis off the transformer at the 1971 All-Star Game, or to hear the crowd gasp for them the way it did for Rickey when his fingers waggled, his legs gave that predator's twitch . . . and . . . *bam!*—he was gone. The players got the fame, the girls, the cheers, and the whole world chanted their names. To the average Joe, the anonymous cog working in his miserable cubicle every day who literally had to beg just to get a lousy 25-buck-a-week raise, adulation was compensation enough. To the public, no matter what the salary, the players were always the lucky ones. It would enrage Marvin

Miller every time this position was reinforced when the multimillion-dollar business of baseball was referred to as a kid's game, and worse, every time the players themselves sank into that sugary, love-of-the-game bullcrap and told the world they loved baseball so much they would have played for free.

By opening day 1984, Rickey was 25 and the average American household income had increased two and a half times, to $26,430 . . . but the average big league salary? It was now *12 times* higher, at $329,000. The players had fought and won their freedom from the reserve clause that had bound them to one team for life, and with free agency—the dreaded free agency that even the players were brainwashed into believing would kill the game if realized— came the real money. It was the real money of a free market—the self-made, you're-worth-whatever-someone's-willing-to-pay-you kind of market that was now theirs. It was the kind of capitalism by which Americans always said they swore, and they *did* swear by it—until they saw just what these suits were willing to pay professional athletes (*to play a kid's game!*).

When he worked for the Major League Baseball Players Association under Miller, Dick Moss feared the changing perception of the athlete, and he was right: as the money grew, so too did the resentment. Moss feared that the more the players earned, the less human they would become to the public. As they earned more money, players were expected by fans to be perfect, and even the coaches and peers who should have known better—they had played or coached in the game and knew firsthand just how difficult it actually was—developed the same expectation. At that kind of money, guys should be hitting .600 every season, even though that wasn't how any of it worked. Whether a player's annual salary was $100,000 (ridiculous!), $1 million (to play *baseball?*) or $40 million (never *ever* gonna happen!), the basic arithmetic of the game was unchanging: the very best players in the game were going to get a hit 30 percent of the time, and the very best teams, whether their payroll was $10 million, $50 million, or $350 million, were going to win between 95 and 105 games. Teams had been playing baseball since the 1870s, and only six teams in history had ever won 110 or more games in a season. It was the nature of the sport, and no amount of free-agent money or pennant-buying owners could ever change that arithmetic.

It had always been about the money, but never so much as during Rickey's time. Salaries had broken the sound barrier of comprehension. (*He makes how much?*) The public was still bitter toward players after the strike, and instead of embracing the rising value of their teams, the owners plotted revenge. The public said it did not care who was at fault—yet always found a way to blame the players, remaining both angry and incredulous about each new record-breaking contract. It wasn't who was making the money. It was the money itself.

"The fans were fascinated by money. They loved the celebrity," Roy Eisenhardt recalled. "But now Casey doesn't just strike out. There's no joy in Mudville. It's 'You struck out—and you're a fucking asshole.'"

The rise in salaries was so sharp and so *public*. In the real world, the woman down the hall may have *suspected* how much more her male coworkers earned, but in sports everybody *knew*. Near the end of spring training, the Associated Press, *The Sporting News*, and later *USA Today* would print out the team payrolls and the individual salaries of every player. This information fascinated and enraged the fans, who now felt the unfairness of the capitalism they so deeply embraced, especially as they saw their own wages decline, failing to keep up, or worse, when their unions couldn't protect them and the layoffs were announced. The public also wanted the players to compare their salaries not to each other's, but to what fans made.

The A's offered Rickey $950,000 for the 1984 season. Rickey wanted $1.2 million. From his first contract five years earlier, Rickey's salary had risen more than 5,300 percent. At $1.2 million, the percentage increase from when he entered the league would have been more than 6,700 percent. From the very beginning of his baseball arc, when Tommie Wilkerson had to bribe him with a quarter for every base he stole just to get him to step onto the field, the percentage increase he was earning from playing baseball was *480 million percent*. In later years, when the public was confounded by squabbles over astronomical dollar figures, the player response would turn into a cliché. *It's not about the money,* they would say, and the fans would roll their eyes and vow never to watch baseball again—just before getting sucked into another pennant race.

In raw numbers, the $250,000 between the A's offer and what Rickey wanted was not an intractable, defining amount, but to Rickey the symbolism of the difference was cavernous. The million-dollar plateau held enormous value to him—it was what the superstars made. To be offered $950,000 by Alderson and Eisenhardt, just $50,000 short of that mark, was to him a way of saying that he was an *exciting* ballplayer, an *excellent* ballplayer, but not quite a *million-dollar* top-shelf ballplayer, not quite a star. The A's seemed to be saying he wasn't in the class of Jim Rice and Mike Schmidt, or that sensation Fernando Valenzuela, who a year earlier became the first player to receive a $1 million award in arbitration from the Dodgers, beating Rickey's earlier record for the most money earned in arbitration. To Rickey, what his employers were saying was that these other players were in a different class, a better class, than him. "Salaries are as much a part of baseball knowledge as anything," Roy Eisenhardt recalled. "It sets your value. It validates you. The player is thinking, 'Pay me whatever you want, as long as it's more than *that* guy.'"

Money used to be metaphorical, alive only in the excited dreams of scouts: "This guy has a million-dollar arm." "That guy is a million-dollar talent." Now money was literal. When Rickey entered the big leagues in 1979, the Astros made Nolan Ryan the first million-a-year player. The next winter Dave Winfield signed with the Yankees for 10 years and $23 million. Cal Ripken Jr., fresh off of winning the World Series and starting only his third full season, signed for four years and $4 million for 1984. Mike Schmidt, the Phillies' slugging third baseman, earned $1.9 million a year. Some players tried to avoid the wrath of the public by adopting that aww-shucks, "nobody's worth that kind of money" posture, as Cleveland pitcher Len Barker did when he signed a contract that didn't even reach a million per. A million a year was the new benchmark. It was what the great players made, and Rickey believed that he belonged with them.

Publicly, Rickey and the A's both said that they were working on a long-term contract that would keep him in Oakland, but Eisenhardt and Alderson both knew that wasn't going to happen. Murray Chass of the *New York Times* reported that Rickey in 1983 turned down a seven-year contract worth between $10 million and $12 million, but neither Eisenhardt nor Alderson recalled making such a bountiful offer. It was unlikely that the A's would have been so extravagant, and if they had been, given the importance Rickey placed on earning a million a year, it is unlikely that he would have turned it down.

He led the league in steals for the fourth straight season, which was remarkable considering he'd only been in the league four full years. Rickey stole 22 fewer bases in 1983 and never really threatened the record (no matter, it was already his), but he still stole 108 bases. Four full years in the big leagues, three 100-steal seasons—no one in the history of the league had ever done that. Not Cobb. Not Brock. Not Wills. And the one year Rickey didn't steal 100 was the shortened 1981 season, when the strike wiped out 53 games.

When he broke the record, he did at boom-or-bust volume—130 steals (the most ever), while getting caught stealing 42 times (also the most ever). His 108 steals were more than the team totals for half the teams in the American League. Tim Raines, his explosive National League counterpart, had been in the league three full years and had led the league each year, but he never stole 100—and he never would.

Rickey also already owned the single-season steals record. He led the 1983 team in runs, walks, on-base percentage, steals, hits, doubles, triples, and total bases. As impact players went, Rickey saw himself as the ultimate lead-off engine, the guy who could lead off a game and score a run without even getting a hit. Mike Schmidt might hit 40 bombs a year, but was he really $1.1 million more valuable than Rickey?

Even though the game compared him to Raines, Rickey didn't view himself in direct competition with any one player. He was in direct competition with *everyone*. As spring training neared, there would be no compromise contract figure between him and the A's, and for the second time in three years Rickey and the A's, ostensibly on the same team, would again be adversaries in arbitration. Where Rickey saw the numbers speaking for themselves, his salary would be decided in a conference room.

Rickey never engaged in that love-of-the-game schmaltz that galled Marvin Miller and his successor in the Players Association, Donald Fehr. You'd never hear Rickey say that he'd play baseball for free. He knew what he was worth, and he believed that money was being taken out of his pocket.

Roy Eisenhardt viewed arbitration as a necessary evil. The players had earned the right to negotiate their salaries. The criminal days of the past when even the best players were overmatched at the bargaining table—no agents, no salary information, no opportunity to leave or create leverage via free agency—were long over. In later years Eisenhardt would take an even dimmer view of the process.

"I hated it. It looked good on paper. Arbitration: a generic term," he recalled. "The notion that each side picks a number and you, the arbitrator, pick the lower or the higher, and not the one in the middle, undermined the relationship between the club and the player. A player like Rickey is the 95th percentile. The agent sets the high number and the club picks the low, so what do you do? You pick on the deficiencies. You pick on the 5 percent. That is destructive. Nobody knows why these incredible players are capable of playing at the skill level they are. You don't know if tomorrow that's going to stop, and they don't know. They need that confidence. So, it was really awful to have to dwell on the things he could do better, to focus on that 5 percent. But that's what the process required. I thought it was really destructive."

Rickey's arbitration hearing was set for late February—just as spring camps were opening—with Rickey's representatives on one side of the table and Sandy Alderson on the other. It was, in sports terms, a rematch of 1982, when Eisenhardt offered to nearly double Rickey's salary but Rickey wanted nearly triple—and won. Alderson, who had prepared that case, had not forgotten it. "Rickey beat me in 1982," he recalled. Another victory in arbitration would validate Rickey's self-worth—and top Fernando's arbitration record.

At the hearing, Rickey's team laid out the case for rewarding Rickey's 95th percentile excellence while Alderson focused on the flawed 5 percent. Was Rickey the most versatile and valuable player on the team? Absolutely, Alderson conceded, but he didn't hit enough home runs.

Rickey's team pointed out that he walked a league-leading 103 times (a harbinger of the heavily analytical value the game would one day place on walks, and a commodity Alderson coveted) and owned an on-base percentage (another valued Alderson category that would remake the game) nearly 60 points better than third baseman Carney Lansford, the next-highest A's regular, whom Oakland acquired from the Red Sox when they shipped Tony Armas to Boston. Rickey was the only player on the team with a .400 on-base percentage, which was second in the league behind Boston's hit machine, Wade Boggs. All that was also true, Alderson agreed—but Rickey didn't hit enough home runs.

Rickey's people pointed out that Rickey broke the all-time single-season record for stolen bases the year before and in 1983 still stole *another* 100 bases, at an even *higher* percentage: 108 out of 127, a ridiculous 85 percent, 10 percent better than when he broke the record. Rickey's people even swung for the fences, knocking the Argument to End All Arguments out of the park: Rickey stole more bases by himself than seven American League *teams*. Alderson agreed—but Rickey hit only nine home runs.

Rickey scored 105 runs, his team responded. The next closest teammate was Davey Lopes at 64. Rickey's 105 runs scored was fourth-best in the AL on a team that finished 10th out of 14 teams in runs scored. Yes, Alderson conceded, but only nine of those runs came when Rickey hit the ball over the fence.

When the convincing was complete, the A's convinced better. Alderson got his win, and Rickey would make $950,000 for 1984. He was furious. "Power guys like Dave Winfield and Mike Schmidt were getting the big money, and leadoff guys were way down the scale," Rickey recalled in *Off Base*. "The big guys were knocking in 100 runs, but I was scoring 100 runs. Isn't that the same thing? Not according to the A's case in arbitration. Not according to the arbitrator."

Mike Norris always took an easier, more philosophical view of arbitration. The structure of sitting across from one's employer may have felt adversarial, and indeed it was: the team was arguing against paying a player what he believed he was worth—a player who after the hearing was now expected to put on the uniform and bust his ass for the home team that had just argued he wasn't worth what he was asking. Norris, however, saw the silver lining of the situation: Rickey was not fighting a pay cut—teams could hit a player with up to a 25 percent slash—and in fact the A's were offering a $150,000 raise. Rickey was asking for an even bigger one.

"Arbitration never bothered me," Norris said. "Hey, no hard feelings. The way I saw it, I was either going to wake up rich—or richer."

Rickey was different. Arbitration was about respect. Every year he'd been in the big leagues, he felt he'd had to fight for his money, even when the numbers proved he had done exactly what was asked of him—and more. He had to fight just to *reach* the big leagues, when the A's wouldn't promote him directly out of spring training in 1979. Respect came through money. Money told him what the A's front office believed about him, but it also reflected where he stood with his peers—and to him what the A's thought of him demeaned his game.

The public often scoffed when an athlete would declare that their issue wasn't the money, and certainly while Rickey understood better than anyone that he was now making 54 times what he earned as a rookie just five years earlier, he wasn't comparing his salary to what he once made but to the going rate for star players. When he reported to Arizona spring training 1984, one message repeated in his mind: his own club was telling him he wasn't elite. He wasn't Jim Rice. He wasn't Mike Schmidt. He wasn't Cal Ripken Jr.

"We thought we could always handle it internally. You could not put the club's face on this temporarily adversarial relationship, but it didn't just stop," Eisenhardt recalled on arbitration. "You want them to succeed. You want everything for them. From a socioeconomic relationship standpoint, it was just very damaging."

No one offered Rickey sympathy cards. "And one to grow on: Rickey Henderson of the A's just lost his arbitration case with his club, so he'll make just $950,000," Tom Barnidge wrote sarcastically in *The Sporting News.* "That must be a bitter pill to swallow." Richie Bry, Rickey's agent, told Barnidge not to compare Rickey to the electrician down the street, but to the other people in the world who did what he did. And besides, Bry told Barnidge, Michael Jackson made *$50 million*—and nobody batted an eye.

When Rickey arrived in Phoenix he had a message for the writers too—no more Mister Nice Guy. They were getting the silent treatment. "Left fielder Rickey Henderson is taking the Steve Carlton route at least for the time being. Baseball's best base thief said he isn't talking to reporters," *Oakland Tribune* beat writer Kit Stier wrote in a freelance piece for *The Sporting News.* "I'm going to take the Steve Carlton role," Rickey said. "I'll have to call him up and ask him what makes him do it, how he concentrates on what he has to do. There was a lot of criticism of me in the paper last year I didn't like."

Rickey carried a list of grievances. First there was losing arbitration. Then there were the writers. Then there was the new manager. Steve Boros announced a new rule on the team: when players needed a day off, they were now required to come directly to him instead of one of the coaches. Stier intimated in the *Tribune* that the rule was aimed directly at Rickey, who apparently angered Boros by taking off too many day games that followed night games.

Unlike Carlton, Jim Rice, Eddie Murray, and his new teammate for 1984, the universally-known-as-a-bastard Dave Kingman, Rickey did not have a reputation for being hostile. But neither did he cultivate the writers, taking them into his confidence, treating them like an integral part of the baseball universe. No matter how many hours they spent on the field, in the clubhouse, or on the road, they were outsiders. It was not an uncommon position for a player to take, but players also at some point found some middle ground with reporters. Rickey did not.

Additionally, Rickey did not view the writers as benign as much as he saw them as at least partially responsible for shaping the reputation he was gaining for not punching the clock as frequently as his teammates. It didn't take much in a clubhouse for a reputation to stick, and the pinpricks about Rickey taking games off and choosing when he would give maximum effort were subtle. They appeared in the newspaper notes columns, were written without quotations, were said to be whispers "within the organization" that could be about one guy or everybody, and soon they were taken as fact.

While it certainly was fact that unnamed people within the A's organization believed that Rickey could have played more than the 145 games he logged in 1983, it was also true that baseball organizations were expert at using the media to send messages to the public—messages that could hurt a player's value to other teams as he approached free agency, or messages that could suppress his salary in arbitration. The A's were sending messages that might ease the public backlash should they be unable to keep Rickey when his contract expired at the end of 1985, messages that did not have to be true for everyone to believe them.

What was true was that the 1983 A's played 58 day games, and Rickey played in 51 of them. On the 28 occasions when the A's played a day game after a night game (minus the one week Rickey missed August 6–12 after coming up lame running out a double-play ball at Minnesota), Rickey started in 25 of those games, or 89 percent. Two that he missed came when the A's were long out of the race, in games 150 (September 18 at Kansas City) and 159 (against the White Sox). Virtually 9 of every 10 times the A's played a day game following a night game, Rickey was there in left field. Still, the reputation stuck.

And Rickey was a big reason why that reputation stuck. It was not uncommon to see the A's out there taking infield—minus Rickey. When the Angels came to town, Gary Pettis noticed that, during Oakland's pregame warm-ups, Dwayne Murphy would be in center, Armas would be in right—and Rickey would be in the clubhouse.

If Rickey was going to look after Rickey, his teammates were going to look out for themselves too. Dwayne Murphy, who hit second behind Rickey, went public and said he was too patient in 1983. Rickey had thanked Murphy for being an unselfish two hitter two years earlier, but now Murphy said he took too many pitches to give Rickey a chance to steal. He saw 1984, he added, as an opportunity to get some more offense for himself.

Murphy led the team in home runs and RBIs, but his totals were relatively modest—17 and 75. He also hit .227 while leading the team in strikeouts with 105—back when striking out still mattered. A hundred whiffs was both a massive number and a serious blemish on a hitter's ability. Murphy along with Tony Armas and Rickey had been part of the outfield on the rise when the team made the playoffs in 1981. Though Rickey was the headliner, Murphy was the team's highest-paid player and had seniority over Rickey. His words carried weight.

Boros seconded Murphy, saying that the A's needed to go back to the pre-Billy days. Though Boros didn't mention Martin by name, to Rickey the implication was clear: Billy felt that Rickey was the player to build around. His new manager didn't think so. Rickey interpreted Boros's comments in the harshest way possible: he, their best guy, was the one holding the offense back—and *that* infuriated him too.

All of which explains why Rickey started the 1984 season out for blood. In arbitration, Alderson said that he wasn't hitting the ball out of the ballpark enough, so Rickey led the A's in home runs during spring training. On opening night, April 3 at the Coliseum against Milwaukee, the A's were trailing 3–0 in the bottom of the sixth against Don Sutton—the same Don Sutton who was in the Dodgers' starting rotation with Sandy Koufax when they won the 1966 NL pennant and Rickey was in the third grade, and the same Sutton who would average 14 wins a year for a quarter-century and, like a Toyota with 300,000 miles on it, take 324 unspectacular career wins to the Hall of Fame.

It was against that Sutton that Rickey started a rally with the A's first home run of the season. Sutton wouldn't last the inning, but Rickey wasn't done: he capped off a four-run rally in the ninth to win it 6–5 by singling off Rollie Fingers (who beat him out for the 1981 MVP) and scoring the winning run when second baseman Jim Gantner chucked a double-play relay wide to end the game.

Three days later, with Boston in town, Rickey immediately set about tormenting that throwback character, pitcher Dennis "Oil Can" Boyd, and his receiver, Gary "Muggsy" Allenson, with a leadoff walk and a stolen base. The Can, looking for revenge, spun toward second for a pickoff and Rickey was dead—till Boyd threw the ball into center field.

One of the great baseball nicknames was not bequeathed to Dennis Boyd because of some prodigious feat on the diamonds growing up in Meridian, Mississippi. He earned the name because even as a teenager his ability to drink beer was so smooth that the suds went down easy, just like oil. Oil Can was part of the great lineage of Black baseball in the Deep South, and he loved Negro League history. At six-one, 155 pounds, he was built like a reed and as a prospect enjoyed the physical comparisons to the great Satchel Paige.

But now it was the Can who needed a beer. Flustered by Rickey, he walked Joe Morgan (playing in his final season in Oakland en route to the Hall of Fame) and then gave up back-to-back hits to go down 2–0. Oil Can handled the rest of the Oakland lineup and kept the Sox close at 2–0 until the bottom of the seventh, when he faced Rickey again, who had doubled off him in his previous at-bat.

With two out, a man on second, and Rickey in his crouch, Can fell behind 3–1, then threw a pedestrian, get-me-over fastball that Rickey tattooed for an RBI single—3–0, Oakland. Going immediately for the kill, Rickey stole second off Allenson. Can escaped the inning, but the A's won the game—and Rickey was the difference.

Two days later, in the Sunday finale, Rickey tore apart the kid Mike Brown, a rookie who retired all of one hitter. Rickey started off the game Rickey Style: he singled, stole second, advanced to third on a fly, and scored when Morgan singled him home. Before long the Boston skipper, Ralph Houk, was making the long walk to the mound. With Brown in the shower, Rickey led off the fourth with a long home run off Al Nipper. Now Rickey was hitting .378. Later that month, in Toronto, Rickey swiped a base off Ernie Whitt (the long history between these two was just beginning) and iced the game with an insurance bomb of a home run in the ninth off a talented rookie left-hander named Jimmy Key.

As Rickey destroyed the Red Sox, and then the Blue Jays, Peter Gammons, the *Boston Globe* baseball writer, was watching it all—and listening. The weekend series with Boston was an example of how Rickey could single-handedly just wreck a club. Boros said that Rickey might be the "strongest player in the American League, and for a leadoff hitter [he] could hit the ball nearly as far as Kingman or Jim Rice." That weekend, Boros told Gammons, had been an example of "how great and dominant a player Rickey can be."

The catchers had the best measure of Rickey. They were the ones with tire tracks on their backsides from Rickey running all over them. Rich Gedman gave Gammons a forensic detailing of Rickey the player, as if he were updating Jim Guinn's old scouting notes. Gedman told Gammons about the difficulties Rickey posed as an opponent, the ways he made life difficult.

"He's the most disruptive player in the league," Gedman said. "He's got the toughest strike zone in the league because he crouches, then ducks when he takes a pitch. Anything from his waist up is a ball, and he hits the low ball exceptionally well. Then, if he gets on base, it's an automatic double—or triple."

But Rickey? For all the bouquets Boros threw his way, Rickey had nothing to say to Gammons about his lead, his crouch, or his bat. He didn't want to talk about his impact. He wanted to talk about his contract. More specifically, he wanted to talk about losing in arbitration. Boros took the long view of Rickey's ability, saw the potential of what Rickey could be. "The 100 stolen bases are fine, but he can be a combination of speed and power—like Joe Morgan in his prime—unlike any player in the league."

Rickey saw it all differently. When Gammons's weekly column appeared in the April 23 *Sporting News,* it read like Rickey and Alderson trading postgame notes—not about the Red Sox, but about that time in arbitration when Rickey wanted $1.2 million a year and Sandy beat him at the bargaining table and he had to settle for $950,000.

HENDERSON MAY BE TRULY "DEVASTATING"

"I'm just swinging the bat. I'm not trying for home runs. The management here told me I'm not a good player because I don't hit home runs and drive in runs. They told me my game isn't good enough, that walks and stolen bases don't mean much. So I'm just doing what I'm told. I'm just a player. They pay. I play.

"They don't think what I do is important. Until I'm a free agent, they're the only ones who count. . ."

Henderson's ego was bothered in the contractual fight, both because the arbitration process usually requires an attack on a player's talents, and, Henderson said, "because I deserve to be a million-dollar player."

"What Rickey hasn't yet understood is that we're not telling him he isn't a tremendous player already, we're simply trying to tell him how to be a *great* player, which he can be," Eisenhardt said.

"Right now, that's difficult for him to understand," Boros said. "Look, when I took over as manager, I was obsessed with stolen bases from my time as a first-base coach and working with baserunners. But I realized my vision had to be narrowed . . . Rickey's gotten trapped in the same narrow perspective. We've told him that Dwayne Murphy's not going to take pitches all the time just for him. We've told him that we don't want him stealing third with none and one out all the time . . . When he broadens his vision, which he will when he appreciates how he can dominate a game with his hitting, walking, running and power, and how that takes him from the class of being an outstanding player to being a superstar, then he won't be thinking we don't appreciate him. Tim Raines understood it more clearly. Rickey hasn't yet."

In his column, Gammons also repeated the whispers about Rickey— unattributed, of course. Rickey had an "outstanding season" in 1983, but "in the second half of the season, he began sitting out day games after night games. He started asking out in the seventh inning of games. He often skipped batting practice, and teammates became critical of his attitude."

As a player nears free agency, these were the type of code words that could stick, and the implications were obvious. "Complaining about money" . . . "absorbed with his own stats" . . . "doesn't follow along with the other guys" . . . "begging out of games." The implication was that Rickey was difficult, selfish, and—the worst adjective of them all—*unprofessional*.

The whispers were not always backed up by statistics, but the anecdotal evidence and the optics of Rickey setting himself apart created a powerful, tactile narrative. In the second half of the 1983 season, Rickey played in 76 of 81 games, starting 67 of them, and he played nine innings in 94 percent of them, in 63 of the 67 games. He came out of the game in the seventh on August 13 against Minnesota, his first game coming back from injury, and again on August 19. On September 5, Boros removed half his starters while the A's were getting crushed 11–1 by the White Sox, and on September 11 in Toronto Rickey came out of the game when the A's were getting pounded 14–6.

Attitudinally, whoever was doing the whispering may not have liked Rickey, or may have believed that he should be playing more, or thought Rickey groused too much before trotting out to left, but statistically, Rickey was in the lineup. There were other code words and thoughts in the Gammons column that betrayed the simmering tensions on the club. "In Rickey's case, someone has to occasionally tell him 'no.'" That was Eisenhardt unmistakably taking a shot at the Billy-Rickey relationship in which Rickey could do no wrong and Billy never told him no—except when Rickey wanted to steal on his own. Even then, it was like he was giving himself the green light, since Billy was already sending him so many times. Rickey had been Billy's favorite. The other players saw it, and the organization saw it. Rickey was golden to Billy, and with Billy no longer there (he had managed the Yankees in 1983 and gotten himself fired), Rickey saw just how privileged he'd been with Billy protecting him. Now other players had Boros's ear. No more lobster claws for Billy's favorite.

And there was just one other thing: that crack about Raines. *Raines.* "*Tim Raines understood it more clearly. Rickey hasn't yet.*" Rickey didn't read the papers (at least he said he didn't), but no doubt his people relayed Boros's words to Gammons back to him. Mentioning Tim Raines in the same category as Rickey was no insult, and after all, Boros was close to Raines because he had coached him in Montreal. But if there was a manual detailing how to make an enemy out of Rickey, mentioning his greatest rival as an example he should aspire to would have likely been in the first paragraph.

In the early part of the 1980s, Rickey and Raines were linked inextricably as the two best leadoff men in baseball, one in each league. Rickey respected Raines. He was impressed with Raines's power and thought they had similar base-stealing styles. For someone who was a natural left-hander, Rickey appreciated that Raines was a switch hitter. They split the covers of magazines. They were even built similarly, two football players dominating baseball.

Rickey had nothing against Tim Raines, but he was Rickey, the best in the game, he believed, and his organization had better think so too. But to his mind, it didn't. Rickey's anger about his deal combined with his manager's intimation that Raines had a better understanding of the game than he did "was like putting red meat in front of a lion," Mike Norris recalled. "If there is one thing I know, it's that Rickey was *competitive.* He didn't want his name mentioned in the same sentence with *anyone* else."

Intentional or not, harmless or otherwise, management had tipped its hand. Rickey was done with Boros. Boros's comments suggested that perhaps the organization didn't pay Rickey his million because they truly believed Raines was better, and Rickey was already making more than Raines. Ironically, up north in Montreal, it was Raines who felt underappreciated at the bargaining table: at $790,000, he was making $160,000 less than Rickey, and he wanted the money Rickey considered an insult.

On May 12, Rickey's average dropped to a season-low .246 after taking an 0-for-4 collar at Baltimore. It was one thing to go hitless, but taking the collar against the Orioles—that was a shock. "I don't know why, but

I used to hit the Orioles. Always hit well in Baltimore," Rickey recalled. "Whenever I wasn't going right, I'd just wait for Baltimore and then I'd get right. They were that medicine." Across Rickey's first four seasons in the big leagues, 1980 through 1983, he played 48 games against Baltimore, hit .359, and was on base nearly half the time with an on-base percentage of .472. He stole 34 bases at a 76 percent success rate—low for Rickey but far above average.

Part of the reason Rickey loved facing the Orioles was the confidence he felt against their catcher, Rick Dempsey, who was always helpless when Rickey took off. "Rick Dempsey?" Rickey would perk up at the name. "Wore his ass out." Rickey actually felt a degree of sympathy for Rick Dempsey because he knew the truth: Baltimore pitchers were the ones doing Dempsey wrong because so many of them—from the great Jim Palmer and his elongated delivery to the Nicaraguan wizard "El Presidente" Dennis Martinez—held on to the ball for so long and were so slow to the plate that Dempsey was helpless against an elite base stealer like Rickey.

"If the pitchers don't get you the ball, you ain't throwing nobody out," Dempsey would say. "Rickey was the best of the best. I got Willie Wilson enough times to make it legit. I knew early on I had a better chance against Rickey, and then I paid for it for the rest of my career. I gave it my best shot and had a pretty damned good arm.

"With Rickey, it was all about the first two steps. The first two steps were so quick, and Rickey had no fear. [Tim] Raines, Wilson, they were hesitant on the first step. They were afraid I was going to pitch out. Rickey had no fear to speak of. And Earl would never pitch out because he didn't want to give the hitter the advantage, and he felt I could get the guys."

Rickey recalled his numerous battles with Dempsey, who was a kind of proxy between Rickey and the Baltimore pitchers. One particular exchange with the Orioles stuck out: Rickey was facing Scott McGregor, who, along with Mike Flanagan and Tippy Martinez—who had once gotten Rickey with the old hidden-ball trick—was one of the Orioles' trio of tough left-handers. McGregor could just stay on the corners all day, live out there, giving Rickey a choice: chase an outside pitch, hope that the home-plate ump wasn't giving McGregor the outside corner that day, or be patient enough to take a walk. Rickey got in the box and crouched. McGregor started nibbling on the outside corner.

Ball one.

Ball two.

Rickey called for time and turned to Dempsey. "Rick, I'll make a deal with you. If he throws me a strike, and I get a hit, I won't go. But if he walks me, I'm gone. If he walks me on four pitches, I'm taking second— *and third.*"

"When you had a Rickey, you had to anticipate you weren't gonna get him," Dempsey reflected. "And that kinda hurt my pride. I had no fear either. I threw better off the slider than the fastball, and no one was ever gonna out-run the ball, so it was a matter of the pitchers getting the ball to me. If you got me the ball, I could throw anybody out, but Rickey was better. He got a better lead than Willie Wilson, all of them, and as soon as he decided he was going, you had no chance."

The Orioles were the elixir for Rickey. In 1982, he hit .409 against them, and when he got to old Memorial Stadium that year, he was even deadlier, hitting .538—but not this time. The May 12 game was one of those good days for the A's, who raked 14 hits in a 12–2 laugher, but it was misery for Rickey. He entered the game 5 for his last 27, drew a walk against El Presidente, and was summarily thrown out trying for second by "the Honey Bear"—Floyd Rayford, one of the game's few Black catchers.

The rest of the day didn't get any better: he struck out twice while every-one else was crushing the ball and dancing around the bases. Even in a cruel and melancholy eighth inning, when the 38-year-old legend Jim Palmer (whom Rickey owned—.476 lifetime) gave up five hits, four earned runs, and a home run in two innings, Rickey was one of the only guys Palmer retired. Palmer was headed to the Hall of Fame—he beat Sandy Koufax with a four-hit complete-game shutout in Game 2 of the 1966 World Series, when Rickey was seven years old—but now he was being battered into retirement. Palmer got Mark Wagner to end the top of the ninth, retreated to the dug-out, and never pitched in the big leagues again.

Rickey, on the other hand, would be back: two days later, at Yankee Sta-dium, he hit a long home run off the veteran knuckleballer Phil Niekro (who made his big league debut in 1964, when Rickey was five).

The A's were in the middle of what would become a seven-game losing streak, and 12 days after they scored 12 runs off the Orioles, Eisenhardt fired Boros and installed the first-base coach, Jackie Moore, as manager. The A's were 20-24. The Boros experiment hadn't worked, and Boros knew the end was coming; he believed it had been on Eisenhardt's mind for months. "After Roy told me the news, one thing was evident. It struck me that he was very sure of himself," Boros told the *Tribune*. "When Roy looked at me with those hawk-like eyes of his, like he does when he is really bearing down on you, I just couldn't get out of that office fast enough." Boros continued to be stung by the criticism that he was a pushover, and, according to the *Oakland Tribune*, he didn't show one guy in particular who was boss: Rickey.

"Boros said there were several reasons that he was replaced, including his constant changing of the roles of the pitchers and that he wasn't tough enough on certain players, especially left fielder Rickey Henderson," Kit Stier wrote in the *Tribune*. Gammons piled on Rickey too, dropping a line in his *Sporting News* column that Rickey had undermined Boros by refusing to bat third in a game against the Yankees after agreeing to do so earlier because, according to Gammons, "his mother told him he was a natural lead-off hitter." Gammons cryptically added that there were "internal problems" in Oakland.

With Boros gone, Moore told Rickey to play like Rickey, told him to play as if Billy were there. "With Rickey's talent and speed and what he could bring to the table, there was nobody like him," Moore recalled. "Rickey had more raw talent than anyone I ever saw."

Moore talked to Rickey as if Billy were there, as if they were putting the band back together. Moore reminded Rickey of their greatest hits with Billy: *Remember that time you were in scoring position and we put on the bunt-and-run and you scored from second? Remember when I gave you the wink and you were gone?* Moore got Rickey excited again about the game— because Moore saw that the key to Rickey was unleashing him. "He could steal third base whenever he wanted. Rickey stole a lot off the pitchers and he stole a lot off the catchers," Moore said. "Neither one of them really had a chance. One step and Rickey was full speed. He was there for excitement. He wanted to be exciting, and to me, that's the way the game should be played."

Managed by Moore, Rickey went on a tear, highlighted by a 3-for-3, three runs, two RBIs, three-steal game at the Coliseum against the Yankees and their rookie right-hander, Jose Rijo. "I'm fast. Let me be fast," Rickey said afterward, a return volley at Boros and his season-long makeover. "That's my game. If I get a steal a day, mix in a hit, no matter how, with an infield hit or a bunt, then I can go and drive in runs. I mess up the other team's strategy."

Even the kid Rijo had to like it. "He hurt me," Rijo said, "but he is beautiful to see play."

Rickey appeared as a reserve in his third straight All-Star Game—and in between gave the ladies a thrill by doing a photo shoot for *Playgirl*. (George Brett, Dennis Eckersley, Jerry Remy, and Steve McCatty did too—the magazine called it the "Men of Summer Hot Nude Pictorial.") Surrounded by 17 other future Hall of Famers at the 1984 All-Star Game, Rickey went 0-for-2 and Goose Gossage of the Padres struck him out looking to end the game, but his season was long gone. Everything had been off and wasn't getting right. Rickey had been hacked off about money from the start. Murphy had been pissed about taking pitches for Rickey. The two new old guys, Morgan and Kingman, didn't like Rickey taking off for second during their at-bats. Before he was fired, Boros had been pissed that everyone thought he was a lightweight. He took the rap for not being tough enough on Rickey; Rickey thought Boros was trying to restrict him, yet *he* was the guy who saw exactly what Rickey could be better than anyone, including Rickey.

The 1984 team finished with 77 wins, seven games behind the Royals. After knocking Jim Palmer into retirement, they never reached .500 again for the rest of the season.

In the papers, Rickey's name had been coming up frequently in off-season trade talks. He was eligible for free agency the following year, and the A's needed players. Alderson couldn't let him walk for nothing at the end of 1985, and talk of a contract extension was always half-hearted, a gold coin for the fans to keep the faith. "The bottom line is that Rickey was too good for us," Roy Eisenhardt recalled. "He was the only real valuable trade chip we had. Everybody would have loved to keep him in Oakland, but my feeling was, 'Rickey's too good for our team right now. We can't afford to have that much talent invested in our team when we have so many areas we need to address.'"

The decision now made to trade Rickey, the question was: Where? The most interested teams were the big boys, the Dodgers and the Yankees. Alderson flew to Los Angeles to meet with the Dodgers GM, Al Campanis. The Dodgers made sense. Had Dick Hager not left after Rickey struck out that afternoon years ago against Skyline, he would already have been wearing Dodger Blue.

Here was a second chance. When Alderson arrived at Dodger Stadium, at the famous 1000 Elysian Park Way, he was met by the Dodgers' brass: Peter O'Malley, Tommy Lasorda—the legendary baseball names everyone knew—and a groaning Al Campanis, his foot elevated, suffering from the gout. "Lasorda was there, and all this famous Dodger front office personnel," Alderson recalled. "Here I am, a newbie and not quite sure what to do. And they kept talking about getting Rickey and that they had the best deal. They were really known back then for pumping up their prospects. They were always the best."

When Alderson returned to Oakland, Eisenhardt was equally dubious about the Dodgers. They were great salesmen of their minor leaguers, especially the ones who couldn't play, Eisenhardt thought, and if they were going to trade Rickey, the A's couldn't afford to get swindled. Eisenhardt was already wary of Dodger minor leaguers because their Triple-A affiliate was based in Albuquerque, where the air was thin and the altitude high; the ball just flew into the stratosphere, making it difficult to tell just how good their hitters would be under normal big league conditions.

Alderson and Campanis met again at the winter meetings in Houston, but by this time the Yankees were making their move. The Yankees were a disaster in center, where Ken Griffey was playing out of position and speedy, no-bat Omar Moreno had not been the answer. The papers said that Yankees GM Clyde King had the inside track, but Rickey remembered another Yankee secret weapon: Billy Martin. Steinbrenner had fired Martin after the 1983 season, but he kept Billy in the family, on the payroll as a special assistant. Billy had been in George's ear whispering that Rickey was the guy. Rickey recalled that Billy called Richie Bry and told him the Yankees were serious about making a deal. In an attempt to close the deal, Billy called Rickey himself and gave him the great New York sales pitch: *You're never going to be the big star you deserve to be, get the status that's been denied you, until you come to New York.*

On December 6, 1984, a blockbuster five-for-one deal was done: The A's traded Rickey to the Yankees for Jose Rijo, Stan Javier, Eric Plunk, Tim Birtsas, and Jay Howell. The A's also threw in pitcher Bert Bradley as a player to be named later. Bradley had appeared in eight innings over six games for the A's in the 1983 season and would never play in the big leagues again.

It was done. Rickey was now a Yankee. The two sides hammered out the contract details, and by the time Bry left the Hyatt Regency, Rickey was officially in the million-a-year club: he had signed a long-term deal, at five years,

$8.6 million, with a no-trade clause. He would switch back to his original position to play in the most famous, most expansive center field in baseball, once roamed by Mantle and DiMaggio, while leaving behind all direct links with the city of Oakland for the first time since Bobbie took the family out of Arkansas. With Rickey's signature on his Yankee contract, two eras were ending: he was beginning his second act as a big leaguer, and the original Charlie Finley A's faded further into history.

As Rickey prepared for New York, another element of the trade was added to the legend: Was it really true that Alderson made the biggest deal of his career by selecting the players he received for Rickey out of a magazine?

It was true.

Alderson went to Houston for the winter meetings without a deal with the Dodgers and with Texas now expressing interest. But the Rangers wouldn't give him what he wanted: a combination of infielder Jeff Kunkel and his choice of either Danny Darwin or, in what would have been a true Oakland moment, another Rangers pitcher—Dave Stewart. Texas was being especially stingy on Kunkel, who had been the number 3 overall pick in the 1983 draft (but would never pan out).

Alderson focused instead on the Yankees at the meetings, but as the time to tell them what he wanted in exchange for Rickey drew near, he had a major problem: he didn't trust his own people. So Alderson looked at the Yankees' top prospects as listed by *Baseball America,* a fledgling magazine that had ranked the Yankees' top farm prospects for 1985:

1. Jose Rijo, rhp
2. Stan Javier, of
3. Tim Birtsas, lhp
4. Keith Smith, ss
5. Eric Plunk, rhp
6. Dan Pasqua, of
7. Jim Deshaies, lhp
8. Rex Hudler, 2b
9. Orestes Destrade, 1b
10. Al Leiter, lhp

"The most interesting part of the deal from my standpoint was that I didn't really have a lot of confidence in our scouting department at the time,"

Alderson said. "There was this new publication that had just come out called *Baseball America.* Most people in baseball thought it was a rag and that there was a lot of information in it that was just bullshit. Nobody would give them good information, that it was all misinformation.

"But they printed these top-10 lists. Top-10 prospects in this league, top-10 prospects in this organization, and what have you. So we went to the Yankees and I just asked for the top five prospects in the organization according to *Baseball America,* and we ended up getting five guys for Rickey. I don't know if we got their 1–5, but all five were their top prospects, and four of the five ended up being really good players."

RICKEY'S MIND WAS clear. For the first time in years, money was not an issue when he reported for spring training. There would be no more arm wrestling with Eisenhardt and Alderson about his worth, no question marks about whether the team he played for truly valued what he could do, no comparisons with rivals or teammates. He was 26 and going into the prime of his career, mentally and physically.

Rickey was comforted knowing that he would be compensated at a level that proved it. Not only that but he would now be paid by the Yankees, the most successful, most famous team in North American professional sports, the team whose very name symbolized empire. And unlike the A's, Rickey believed the Yankees clearly wanted him. In January, for instance, Yankee vice president Woody Woodward had watched a highlight reel of Rickey and remarked, "I've never seen a guy look so fast in slow motion."

Rickey also had security, on his terms. The Yankees' agreement to the trade had come with the contingency that Rickey sign a long-term deal, but Rickey also received a coveted no-trade clause; he couldn't just be dumped off to Cleveland without his consent. Rickey preferred the long-term contract because he did not want to play in 1985 with the uncertainty of not knowing where he was playing in 1986.

When it was time to deal, Richie Bry went big, asking Steinbrenner for seven years and $18.2 million. Steinbrenner balked, and after the first day of negotiations the two sides were $13 million apart. The papers made it sound as if the gluttonous Steinbrenner had targeted the biggest bauble of the off-season because he was George, who had to have the biggest of everything. But the fact was that Steinbrenner didn't really want Rickey.

He thought Sandy Alderson's asking price of multiple players in the trade was already too high, and now Rickey wanted nearly $20 million. The man who thought Rickey was indispensable for New York wasn't The Boss. It was Billy.

Martin's fingerprints were all over the deal, and he made no secret about how much he valued Rickey. While Billy was secretly calling Rickey, telling him his destiny lay in New York, he was also telling George that Rickey needed to be in pinstripes. In his memoir *Billyball*, Billy recalled George's reaction to the proposed deal at the Yankees' organizational meeting in Tampa:

> "I'm not going to give up all these guys for Rickey Henderson," and he jumped up and walked out of the meeting.
>
> I had Rickey in Oakland and I was in favor of making the deal. So were several of the other people in the room, but everybody was afraid to say anything. After George left, Clyde King, the general manager, turned to me.
>
> "Billy," King said. "Can you talk to him?"
>
> "Yeah," I said. "I'll go talk to him."
>
> We were meeting in George's hotel in Tampa, the Bay Harbor Inn. He had a suite there and I went up and knocked on the door. Before I could even say anything, I hear George's voice say, "Come in, Billy."
>
> "How did you know it was me?"
>
> "I knew you'd be coming up here," he said.
>
> "Look, George," I said. "You have to make this deal. I know you're giving up Jay Howell and three young pitchers, but young pitchers are a dime a dozen. You can replace them. They come along all the time. A Rickey Henderson comes along once in a lifetime. Believe me, if you get Rickey Henderson, he's going to make the difference in this whole ball club. He'll make Willie Randolph better. He'll make Don Mattingly better. He'll make Dave Winfield better. He'll help everybody. Please, George. If I'm wrong, then fire me. I feel that strongly about this trade. I know this kid that well."
>
> "Well, if that's the way you feel," he said. "I'll do it. OK, call them down there and tell them to make the deal."

The deal wasn't a week old before the papers began speculating that Rickey was the key not just for the top of the Yankee lineup but for Billy getting his old job back for the fourth time. Dave Anderson at the *Times,* for example, believed in Martin's dual motive. George had fired Billy in 1983 after the Yankees won 91 games but not the division and replaced him with Yogi Berra, who then won 87—not that it mattered. Nobody was beating Sparky's '84 Tigers, who famously started the season 35-5 and that was a wrap. Now, with George impatient, the Yankees entering 1985 having not made the playoffs since 1981 (three years was afterglow for other teams but an ice age for Steinbrenner), and Billy staking George's money by vouching for Rickey, having Billy back in the dugout felt like a bad road trip away.

Besides, nobody knew Rickey better than Billy—a fact that Billy would repeat more than once in the company of Steinbrenner, stoking the speculation. No manager in the big leagues believed in Rickey like Billy did. In turn, Rickey performed for Billy like he did for no one else.

When the deal was announced, the New York writers saw Rickey as a spark plug—a top-of-the-order guy who slapped the ball around, set the table, and ran fast. He was dangerous, certainly, but dangerous *for a leadoff hitter.* A year earlier, while making the case for his $1.2 million arbitration request, Rickey had viewed himself as Billy did—as a transcendent, franchise-lifting talent, a guy who could change the course of a game, not just to start the game but in every inning. When Rickey arrived in New York, however, the writers compared him to . . . Mickey Rivers.

Mick the Quick! Rickey and Mickey Rivers were both seen in the baseball world as characters, as entertainers, and that was not always a compliment. Rivers was an exciting, often above-average player, but he was also the class clown; though an important player, he couldn't always be taken seriously, and for good reason. He led the league in triples in 1974, and in triples and stolen bases in 1975, but he was equally well known for his malapropisms, like the time he said his season goals were to "hit .300, score 100 runs, and stay injury-prone." Reggie Jackson once told Rivers he couldn't spell "cat" if he had been spotted the "c" and the "t," and Rivers once said of Reginald Martinez Jackson, "You've got a white first name, a Mexican middle name, and a Black last name. Man, you don't know *who* the fuck you are." In 1976, Rivers finished third in the MVP voting, when he hit .312 and had 184 hits as he led the Yankees to their first pennant since 1964, but the award went to his teammate, the Yankees' very serious leader, catcher Thurman Munson.

Were there similarities between Rickey and Mickey? Only in that they played at the top of the order, their names rhymed, and in the eyes of the sporting press they seemed to fit a particular Black stereotype: aloof, amusing, but not particularly bright—in fact, amusing *because* they weren't seen as particularly bright. It was true that Rickey did some bizarre things, but that didn't mean he was dumb. The people close to him would just shrug and dismiss Rickey's ways by saying, "Rickey's on his own program," which would eventually be condensed into a universal shorthand: "Rickey being Rickey."

In Oakland, a story persisted that early in his career Rickey framed one of his massive paychecks and pinned it right up on his wall—*without cashing it first.* The story felt apocryphal, an ingredient seamlessly blended into the mythical gumbo of Rickey's life. Rickey stories that were too good to be true were also too good to dismiss, too good to forget. Even if they never happened, they *could* have happened. The check story *was* true, however, and Rickey eventually cashed the check only because Alderson received a phone call from a panicked bean counter in the accounting office to tell him that the club's books were off by hundreds of thousands of dollars. Eventually the bookkeepers uncovered the discrepancy—a game check issued to Rickey had gone uncashed. Fred Atkins remembered the story too. "I asked him, 'Did you lose it? Did you cash it?' And he said, 'Nah, it's on the wall.'"

There was something at once adorable and triumphant about a kid from North Oakland being so proud of now being rich that he framed the check, a symbol that he had succeeded the American way—like the barkeep tacking that first dollar earned in his new tavern on the wall next to the cash register.

That was the cute story. The real story, or at least another part of it, was that Rickey Henderson did not easily part with his money—not cashing a check was a way to show financial discipline, to stretch out a dollar. "Rickey hadn't cashed the check. It went void in 90 days," Mike Norris recalled. "The front office called, saying, 'Rickey has a check he hasn't cashed that's gonna be voided.' See, Rickey saved money by not cashing his checks. And his meal money? Rickey saved that too. That nigga would eat McDonald's. I used to tell him, 'McDonald's? That ain't no kinda fuel. Might as well eat a hot dog before the game.' If I'm lying, I'm flying."

It was true: Rickey wouldn't spend his meal money either. "Murphy Money" it was called in baseball, after Boston lawyer Robert Murphy scored a per diem from the parsimonious owners while trying to unionize the players back in the 1940s. Rickey would take the cash and put it in a shoebox, wrapping each per diem in an elastic band. Over his career, his meal money would range from $60 to $100 per day and the shoebox would fill with dozens of individually wrapped rolls of cash—thousands of dollars in total. Whenever Rickey returned to North Oakland, he'd interrogate the kids from the old neighborhood and then open up the shoebox and toss a roll to the ones who were keeping their grades up.

It wasn't that the Yankees were purposely trying to insult Rickey with the comparisons to Rivers. You just had to understand their history. These were, after all, the *Bronx Bombers*. They weren't the '82 Cardinals, those Astroturf jackrabbits turning 12-hoppers into two-run doubles. The New York Yankees made their money by hitting the ball over the fence. The 1984 Yankees stole 62 bases. That year Rickey, running far less after feeling insulted by Boros and arbitration, still stole more bases all by himself—66—than the whole Yankees team. The Yankee single-season stolen-base record of 74 was set in 1914 by a forgotten third baseman named Fritz Maisel; that was the deadball era, when the baseball felt like a paperweight. The top three stolen-base totals in Yankee history were Maisel's, that racist Ben Chapman's 61 in 1931, and the 55 that Snuffy Stirnweiss swiped in the war year of 1944—numbers Rickey could put up before breakfast. When Joe Morgan retired at the end of the 1984 season, Rickey, at just 25, had 493 stolen bases, already more than any other active player. Willie Randolph could run, but Mickey Rivers was the last pure base stealer on the Yankees roster.

Rivers could ignite a club, but he was no Rickey. Rivers would be done by the end of the 1984 season, having stolen 267 bases in 15 big league seasons. Rickey had 493 in five and a half. Rivers never struck out, but he also never walked; he finished with a career on-base percentage of .327. Entering his first season with the Yankees, Rickey's *career* on-base percentage was .400. Rivers had never hit more than 12 home runs in a season. Rickey, stung by Alderson's emphasis in arbitration that he didn't slug enough, hit 16 in 1984. It wasn't as if Rickey was sneaking up on the Yankees. Several wise baseball people were already calling him, at 26, the best leadoff hitter in the game, maybe in history. One of those people was Billy.

Nor was Rickey a class clown who reveled in what he did not know. He was a ferociously competitive, goal-driven athlete. It never failed to upset his best friend Fred Atkins to see Rickey characterized as unintelligent just because he struggled with words. Rickey was genuinely funny, even when he didn't mean to be, like the time he explained to the writers that living in his Hoboken apartment gave him a panoramic view of the New York skyline: "From my window," he said, "I can see the EN-tire State Building."

The press wanted to have it both ways with Rickey: they wanted him to cultivate and trust them while they simultaneously mocked him. Perhaps one of the greatest signs of Rickey's intelligence, Fred Atkins thought, was refusing to engage with the writers except on his own terms. He was onto them.

"People who don't know Rickey hear him speak and they think he's stupid," Jim Darby said. "He's probably the most street-smart athlete I've ever been around. When we first signed him at Mizuno, Rickey negotiated my butt off. He knew what he wanted and how much it would take to get him. He also knew how much he was needed, and that we needed him more than he needed us, because he had a cutoff point and I didn't, so I would eventually be the one to say 'yes.' He taught me the art of negotiation one way—by tearing me apart."

Rickey got his money, but Rickey also arrived in the Bronx with the growing reputation of a guy who played when he wanted to. "Rickey's on his own program" was shorthand for "Rickey isn't a team guy." The players knew it when they were on the field for pregame stretch and Rickey wasn't. Kit Stier had written about Rickey this way, as did Peter Gammons. And now, when Murray Chass of the *Times* introduced Rickey to the New York market, he foreshadowed just how devastating a player Rickey could be when he took over a game but also why his relationships in Oakland were so frayed. The A's knew they were in for some lean rebuilding years, but they also didn't seem too broken up about their best player leaving town.

THIS IS RICKEY HENDERSON: SPEED THAT DAZZLES

This is Rickey Henderson: "He took off from second base with the pitch," Butch Wynegar related, recalling his most vivid memory of a Henderson escapade. "It was a fastball right down the middle that the hitter took. When I caught the ball, he was barely reaching halfway between second and third. When I came up to throw, I remember thinking to myself, 'I got him, I got him.' I made a perfect, chest-high throw

to Nettles, but by the time the ball got there, he was sliding in safe. I
swear he accelerated like I have never seen anyone accelerate. I stood
there bewildered. I was in awe."

Chass followed up a few paragraphs later:

As disruptive and as scintillating and as productive as Henderson can
be, though, there apparently is another side to him, a side that occasionally discloses a lack of motivation.

"It was more or less a day game after a night game," said Dwayne
Murphy, Henderson's outfield mate for five and a half years. "The thing
I don't think he liked was we played 12:15 games. But we were pretty
close and I could talk to him. If I thought he should be in the lineup, I
just talked to him. It usually worked. But I don't think they'll have any
problems like that. I think Rickey will play hard. He'll play every day.
There were just a lot of things he was unhappy about. But I think he'll
be pretty happy now and do what he has to do."

Baylor acknowledged that he was aware of Henderson's occasional
reluctance to play. "I talked to him a couple of times in '81, '82," Baylor
said. "I told him he's too good a player to get a reputation as a bad guy."

Henderson does not agree with the view that questions his desire.

"I hate sitting on the bench," he said. "I don't see how in the world
I would not want to play. When they give me a day's rest, I can't stand
it. I want to be out there. I don't feel there are certain days I don't want
to play. If I'm sick, a sick man can't help you."

Now that Rickey was an opponent, his former teammates didn't have to
hold back. They knew Rickey was different, but 1984 represented a breach in
several relationships, and his teammates made it clear that they were upset at
how he acted out in response to not getting as big a raise as he wanted. They
were unanimous in regard to his gifts—there was never any debate about
that—but at some level he had also lost a bit of their professional regard. "If
Rickey wants to put on a show in Yankee Stadium, he will," Clete Boyer, one
of Billy's old coaches and a former great Yankee third baseman, told Dave
Anderson of the *New York Times,* "but in Oakland, he didn't always work
at it."

Ron Fimrite, the San Francisco writer who was a fixture at *Sports Illustrated*, wrote of Rickey: "Henderson, for all his flair . . . underwent a sort of personality change for the worse last year, offending even his own teammates with his uncooperative attitude." When the feature writers profiling Rickey, the new Yankee, traveled to Arizona to the A's spring training camp, they found that his teammates still felt singed from being the collateral damage of Rickey's fight with the A's over money. "In Oakland," a feature story read, "Henderson developed a reputation for coming to the park not always wanting to play." Now that he was out the door, the catcher Mike Heath let Rickey have it.

"I don't want to play with a guy who shows up late, doesn't take batting practice, and doesn't want to play a day game after a night game," Heath said. "You know who I mean."

It was no illusion that something had in fact changed with Rickey. He'd always had a desire to be set apart, to be considered one of the best in the game and to be paid like it, and he had succeeded in achieving that. But Rickey had also shown his hand during 1984: upset with Boros and unhappy about his money, he was willing to withhold his best, and his teammates had witnessed his unwillingness to participate in the parts of the job that came with the territory, on both good days and bad. Jim Darby had already seen that side of Rickey as the merchandise rep at Mizuno. "He was a team player, except when he wasn't, and that's how he was with us," Darby recalled. "You have a contract and a relationship, but a contract wasn't exactly binding with Rickey. You never knew if he was going to screw you if he was upset with something. He was a paradox—but that was what also made him kinda cool."

Rickey was now being paid the way the home-run hitters were paid. He also had his no-trade clause, a critical layer of control that the Big Boys like Winfield and Reggie and Gary Carter had. He had lusted to be seen as the player he envisioned for himself, and now that he'd achieved that status, he would be vocal about it. "I think I'm a great ballplayer," Rickey told the *South Florida Sun-Sentinel*. "But what I did in Oakland is separate from coming to New York." Rickey was also signaling that he no longer saw himself as a rising talent or a prodigy, but as an established star unleashed. "Then, I was trying to prove I could play in the big leagues. I don't have to prove anything now," Henderson told *Newsday* columnist Steve Jacobson. "People know what Rickey Henderson can do."

He was also going to take ownership of the flamboyant persona he had established—which was authentic and not a creation. If the papers were going to call Rickey a hot dog, he was going to let everyone know that he always belonged on the marquee. "A disciple of Mays and protégé of Brock, Henderson admits there's as much showboat as there is ballplayer in him, that he's paid to entertain as well as perform," the *South Florida Sun-Sentinel* said of Rickey. "Now, instead of stealing bases for lunch money, he's stealing them for millions. 'People say I'm a showman because of the style I play,' Henderson says. 'I like to make the people happy. I like to give them their money's worth.'"

Rickey had let them know he was a star, but now the combination of his marquee-level style and his potential to go dark when he didn't get what he wanted created a certain toxicity. He now had a reputation through which his every move, action, and injury would be filtered. For all the talk about Rickey's disruptions on the basepaths and the numbers he had put up just through age 25, there was some skepticism on the part of the baseball people about his greatness as a player. Sandy Alderson articulated it when he considered Rickey's time in Oakland before making the deal. The coaches, players, managers, and executives there were all rooted in baseball culture and fixated on "how the game is supposed to be played," so they tended to view Rickey with a certain qualification, constantly attaching the dreaded "but" to his game. For example, he could change a game from the first at-bat . . . "but he took too many days off."

Bill Rigney, the sharp and venerable veteran who'd been around the game since the 1930s—he'd even managed Mays with the Giants—had been brought in by Alderson as his own baseball man to cleanse the A's of the smothering institutional influence of Billy Martin. Rigney told the story of how he once watched Rickey and just couldn't believe it—the unlimited range of what this astounding kid could do. There was nobody like Rickey. "I told him, 'Rickey, that's the best game I ever saw you play.' And then I told him, 'That was a great game you played, but that was the way number 24 played *every* day.'"

In Alderson's view, even the most astute baseball men not named Billy Martin seemed preoccupied with the Rickey optics—the delivery, the flash, the personality, the whispers, the moods. Their inability to see through all that thus diminished his obvious ability in their eyes, partly because of their own prejudices, and partly because Rickey made the optics impossible to ignore. Rickey was a great player but, because of his moods and temperament, he was not quite a leading man. When it came to Rickey, baseball men focused on what he wasn't often more than on what he was.

"When the trade was chronicled in *Sports Illustrated*," a profile of Rickey read, "it was reported that the Yankees may not be getting their money's worth, that Henderson dogged it at times, and of the 20 games he missed in 1984, half may have been for no apparent reason."

In Oakland, Rickey had listened to Billy telling him he should be a Yankee, and when he arrived in New York he was appropriately deferential in the right moments about the honor of playing in pinstripes, about the magic and mystique of the great Yankees and the great city of New York. But Rickey had never been particularly taken by New York. Playing for the Yankees was never a childhood dream—at least not a sustained one. Occasionally, Rickey would say that playing for the Yankees had been a lifelong ambition, but the fact was that, as a kid, Rickey had idolized O. J. Simpson. On the baseball diamond, he loved Willie Mays, but his idolatry of another athlete only went so far—Rickey only wanted to be Rickey.

As for fealty to a team, Rickey was an Oakland Raiders man. Rickey spent most of his time on the ball field not dreaming about being anyone else, but constructing a pathway to his own greatness. He believed he was that good, that early in his life. He did not dream of playing for any one team as much as he dreamed of teams wanting him to play for them.

New York, though, loves nothing better than a narrative with New York centered right in the middle of it, with the big town receiving its curtsies. As much as Rickey was his own person, it was here where he was most similar to Reggie when Reggie said, "I didn't come to New York to be a star. I brought my star with me." That wasn't exactly playing nice with how New York saw itself. Of *course* it was New York who made the stars, not the other way around. (There was even a song about it!)

For instance, when Rickey took the number 24—Willie's number, still the most famous 24 in all of New York sports history, the 24 of stickball in Harlem and "the Catch" at the Polo Grounds to a generation for whom he would always be the greatest ballplayer of them all—he immediately told the writers, "I didn't take 24 for Mays." He explained that the number he wanted, *his* number, 35, was already taken by the ancient knuckleballer Phil Niekro, so he'd reverted back to 24, his number in the minors—without mentioning that he wore 24 in the minors because it was Willie's number.

In New York, 24 already belonged to "the Count," pitcher John Montefusco, but the Count thought 24 was giving him bad luck so he happily donated it to Rickey.

Instead of falling under the spell of the legendary pinstripes and its interlocking "NY," Rickey actually had a problem with the Yankees uniform. In Oakland, the A's uniform was a pullover top and baseball pants with an elastic waistband. The Yankees uniform buttoned down in the front, and the pants were not elasticized at the waist and instead required an actual belt. Rickey was wary of both the buttons and the belt because of his headfirst slide: the buttons would be uncomfortable when they met the infield dirt, and the buckle on the Yankee uniform belt—remembering how he gashed his abdomen on his belt in Double-A—was a laceration waiting to happen. In his last year in Oakland, Rickey had talked about returning to the feet-first slide, and now the Yankee uniform pushed him even further in that direction.

Rickey had loved listening to Billy tell stories about the old days in New York and prophesize that Rickey would one day be in pinstripes. But when he arrived there, Rickey felt that the stuff about the magic and power of New York was for the fans and the papers. He did not appreciate the intense relationships between the team and the writers, between the writers and the city. And there were so many writers. If Rickey thought the Bay Area press corps was often too intrusive—mostly because Kit Stier annoyed him—New York was an entirely different universe. It was like being packed in on the D train before a night game—nine papers *traveled* with the team, and the outlets that didn't covered every home game.

The writers, especially the big ones like Dick Young of the *Daily News,* made it clear to the players that they could make or break a guy in the eyes of the fans. The papers expected the players to bask in the New York mythology the way they did, to show a deference to the Most Dominant Team, which played in the Greatest City in the World. The tabloid *Post* and *Daily News, Newsday* out on Long Island (and in the city), the two North Jersey papers, the *Star-Ledger* and *The Record,* the *Hartford Courant* in Connecticut (which, owing to its unique geography, traveled with both the Yankees and the Red Sox)—all these newspapers traveled every day with the Yankees. As the conduit to the rabid Yankee fans, the New York papers were critical to a dynamic unlike in any other city in baseball.

There was one other thing about Rickey that threw the writers off: for all the style on the field, Rickey wasn't Reggie, who could give as much as he got, who was quick and glib with a quote, who reveled in being seen around the city and *reminded* everybody that his IQ was 160. For Reggie, sparring with the writers was sport, but he also understood that in New York a relationship with them was necessary. Rickey viewed the writers warily and chose the perilous route of letting his play speak for him. He wouldn't cultivate any of the city papers the way George and Billy and Lou Piniella would, nor anyone else who carried a notepad. "Totally closed," Bob Klapisch, who covered baseball for the *Post* and the *Daily News,* recalled of Rickey. "I couldn't get to first base with that guy."

When Reggie solidified his legend with his epic 1977 World Series and his prediction that if he played in New York they'd name a candy bar after him came true, it was Catfish Hunter who reviewed the new Reggie Bar thusly: "When you open the wrapper, it tells you how good it is." Unlike Reggie, Rickey wasn't into the verbal banter with the writers, who expected him to be as verbally exciting as his play. Reggie had made sure the writers knew he could spar with them intellectually and verbally and win. Rickey never advertised that part of his game.

It wasn't just that the writers and the Yankees wanted Rickey, as the newest free agent, to be the face of the franchise—it was that they *needed* him to be. For over in Queens, the crosstown Mets, asleep since winning the 1973 pennant, were putting together a pretty good squad, and one with personality. Rickey, the Yankees' prize off-season acquisition, was pitted against Gary Carter, signed by the Mets over the winter. Nobody worked a room (or a microphone) like Gary Carter, and to win the hearts and minds of New York Rickey was supposed to outdo Gary Carter? It was probably the only time in Rickey's life he went up against a catcher and had no chance.

When Rickey arrived in the Yankees' clubhouse, Billy Sample, a backup outfielder who had come over from Texas, noticed how ripped Rickey was when he saw him with his shirt off. The Yankees players would hand out a makeshift belt—wrapped in aluminum foil and made to look like a World Wrestling Federation championship belt—to the player with the lowest body fat percentage, and Rickey, at 2.9 percent, would go on to win every year. Sample reminded Rickey of how badly the Rangers had wanted a piece of him because of his antics in 1982, when they implored Jim Sundberg to knock Rickey out for stealing bases regardless of the score. Teammates now, Rickey looked at Sample and said, "No hard feelings. I was just going for the record."

The Yankees were stacked going into 1985. The great Yogi Berra was the manager, and his lineup was fearsome. There was the big man, Dave Winfield, in the middle of the lineup; the fearless one, former MVP Don Baylor; and the consummate pro, outfielder Ken Griffey, who had already won championships with Cincinnati's famed Big Red Machine. There was the mainstay, Willie Randolph, who went back to the glory days of 1977 and '78, when the Yankees were champions. And finally, there was the home-grown kid out of Evansville, Indiana, 19th-round pick Don Mattingly, who'd had his breakout year in 1984, leading the league in doubles (44), hits (207), and hitting (.343) and beating out Winfield for the batting crown on the final day of the season. It had been an amazing race between teammates that Steinbrenner ruined by pitting his two stars, one white, one Black, against each other—a modern-day Mantle-Maris competition with a side order of racism.

There was another thing about Mattingly that made him DiMaggio-level: he never struck out. Take 1984: 23 homers, 110 batted in, and . . . 33 *strikeouts*. New York loved him. He'd been in town 20 minutes and already had a nickname—"Donnie Baseball." He'd been in the big leagues two full seasons, and Steinbrenner was already calling him a Hall of Famer. Adding Rickey to an offense that was fourth in the league was going to be lethal.

Which is not to say that there was no anger, arbitration, or insult. When Mattingly won the batting title—the first Yankee to do so since Mickey Mantle's Triple Crown year of 1956—he received virtually no raise from Steinbrenner. After 207 hits in one season, Mattingly said he felt disrespected.

A year earlier, Rickey had wanted to be a million-dollar guy, and now, in 1985, seven other players filed for arbitration seeking a million, one of whom was his opposite number in the National League, Tim Raines. Players were voicing their opinion, ever louder, that their free-agent markets should have been more bountiful than they were. The implication was that the owners, still angry about losing the Seitz decision a decade earlier, were secretly working together to kill the free-agent market by agreeing that no team would sign the available free agents. Such collusion, the reporters said far more often than not, was preposterous. Why, the owners couldn't agree on what to have for lunch, and now the public was expected to believe that they had a league-wide, clandestine gentlemen's agreement not to sign anyone? Not even a star player who could help them win? As the writers dismissed the possibility of collusion, the free-agent offers for players dried up and the offers from their current teams often included pay cuts.

On the field, though, the Yankees were going to be formidable. "Rickey Henderson, Willie Randolph and Don Mattingly are going to get on base 750–800 times in front of Dave Winfield and the big boys. The only team I've seen comparable in terms of a lineup were our '76 Reds, with Joe Morgan, Ken Griffey and Pete Rose. Randolph will have a great year," said Sparky Anderson, whose Tigers had rolled to the World Series the year before. The Yankees hadn't played a single inning in 1985, and Anderson was already comparing their lineup to his legends. "Henderson will do that for him. And they'll make life like a shooting gallery for opposing pitchers. What we don't know about is their starting pitching."

Up in Toronto, Pat Gillick, his Blue Jays inching closer to becoming a great team, understood what the acquisition of Rickey meant to the Yankees—but he also knew that the Rickey deal had made it possible for Oakland to let closer Bill Caudill go to Toronto, which lacked a finisher. "Our deficiency was in the bullpen, and with Caudill, we could be in pretty good shape. The Yankees had a good offense. Now they have an awesome offense. But you have to question how far their pitching will take them."

In the AL East, the Tigers were the defending champs. The Blue Jays, who had been in the big leagues only seven years since the expansion to Toronto and Seattle, believed that they were championship-ready. Meanwhile, in Boston everybody was talking about the 22-year-old horse Roger Clemens—but the Yankees had Rickey. And Winfield. And Mattingly. And the great Guidry, the other last link to the championship days.

In spring training, Berra watched his team prove human. Rickey sprained his ankle trying to avoid a throw into third against Boston. There was no throw, but Wade Boggs, the Boston third baseman, had deked Rickey but good, and Rickey, trying to transition away from sliding headfirst, did exactly what he had feared doing so much that he had switched to the headfirst slide in the first place—he jammed his ankle into the bag. On March 18, he ended up in a cast. Winfield, already suffering with a bruised instep, was admitted to the hospital on March 20 with an infected elbow. Mattingly and Griffey were both sidelined with right knee injuries, and the gruff third baseman, Mike Pagliarulo, hyperextended his right elbow.

In their season previews, the national writers did as Gillick instructed and questioned the Yankees' pitching; the general conclusion was that it wasn't good. In a loaded American League East, the Yankees were picked to finish fourth.

Underneath all the strategies, everyone knew there was a trick to beating the Yankees. All you had to do was wait for that one week during the season when George or Billy would go nuclear, derailing a loaded club, and the Yankees would beat themselves. History would later portray the Bronx Zoo as wild and dysfunctional, and Steinbrenner would attempt to rehabilitate himself as committed to victory by caring too much during his time with the club, but the Yankees team that Rickey joined was entrenched in something far worse than wildness or dysfunction or wanting to win at all costs: a poisonous and destructive work culture created by Steinbrenner that did serious and lasting damage to careers and reputations.

"It did not take long to realize what many Yankees, including Reggie and Tommy John, had learned the hard way," the Yankees' designated hitter Don Baylor would write in his book *Nothing but the Truth*. "Once you sign, you are no longer treated like a celebrity. You are treated like a piece of trash."

Rickey didn't start the season with the club. When the Yankees went north following spring training, Rickey stayed in Florida to rehab his ankle.

With Rickey out, the Yankees collapsed. They started the season in Boston, got dominated by that top-shelf trash-talker Oil Can Boyd in the opener, and then ate a three-game sweep. By the time Rickey was ready to make his debut, Steinbrenner had already told Lou Piniella that he might be managing the team very soon.

Rickey headed for New York for an April 22 workout before a three-game rematch with Boston. The flight was late, and when Rickey arrived in the Yankee Stadium clubhouse, the voluminous Yankee press corps was waiting for the off-season prize to arrive. His car, however, got to New York right on time, courtesy of Walt McCreary and Aaron Turner, part of Rickey's inner circle. Walt and Aaron had ordered 100 chicken wings for the drive north in the special-built Mercedes that Rickey had personally customized after he and Lewis Burrell flew to Germany to purchase it. They drove all day and all night to get Rickey's ride to the city. They hadn't finished all the wings by the time they got there, so those went to a homeless guy.

While the writers across town were already gushing over the always coop-
erative, always accommodating Gary Carter, whose team was winning over
the town, Rickey, late and in a hurry, grabbed his glove and blew through the
kingmakers with their tape recorders and pads and paragraphs with a line
that turned every pen into a shiv. "I don't need no press now, man." Mike
Lupica of the *New York Daily News* went first.

RICKEY DAY HITS HEIGHT OF YANK WIT

There was some question afterward where the opening line would
rank in Bartlett's Familiar Yankee Quotations. Would you put it between Gehrig's "Today I consider myself the luckiest man on the face
of the earth" and The Babe's "Baseball is the only real game"? Did you
like it better than "I'm the straw that stirs the drink?" How did it stack
up with Billy Martin's version of the Hamlet soliloquy, the one that
began "One's a born liar and the other's convicted?"

Maybe it doesn't matter all that much since everybody wants to see
Rickey Henderson hit and run, and run and run . . . but when Henderson finally showed up at Yankee Stadium yesterday afternoon for a
very optional workout, he dumped his gear in a locker near Thurman
Munson's empty locker and said to the assembled press, "I don't need
no press now, man."

Don't need no press now.

So Rickey Henderson finally showed up at Yankee Stadium. Late.
So he didn't want no press before his workout . . . Makes you long for
the next Mets homestand, man.

Rickey told the writers he would talk later, after the workout—and he
did—but it was too late. Second impressions don't erase the first one. Rickey
hadn't even had an official at-bat as a Yankee and was already positioned as
the opposite of what it meant to be Yankee. He lacked the poignance of a dying Lou Gehrig, the childlike joy for baseball of Ruth—true Yankees both—
and he lacked the media savvy of Gary Carter—a true professional, that one.

Lupica saw in Rickey a potentially fatal flaw to playing in New York: being
a great player doesn't make you a great leading man, of looking the part, of
being a magnanimous star who knows how to win with talent—and warmth.
"As the summer goes along, he will have plenty of time to understand that

while he might not need no press personally, the Yankees are going to need plenty," Lupica continued, "because there is plenty of glitz at Shea Stadium. On Gary Carter's first day with the Mets, he did everything except call the clubhouse and ask if he could bring the writers crullers."

The image Lupica crafted of Rickey dumping his stuff next to the empty locker of the late Thurman Munson—the hallowed quiet space memorializing a Yankee tragedy being interrupted by Rickey's gauche obliviousness—was a special dose of carbon monoxide. That same day, Rickey confirmed his lack of reverence for or interest in history, the Yankees, or playing the media game. Expecting the usual gauzy quotes about the privilege of playing for the lordly Yankees before his debut, Rickey said of the hallowed ghosts, "I don't care about them. I never saw DiMaggio and Mantle play. It's Rickey time." Alan Greenberg, the *Hartford Courant* columnist, would not forget the insult. Later in the season, Greenberg would say that "Steinbrenner couldn't have been more embarrassed if Rickey had shown up at Thanksgiving dinner and poured cranberry sauce on Joe DiMaggio's head," and that "history is irrelevant when you live, as Rickey Henderson does, in a vacuum."

When Rickey made his debut the next day at Yankee Stadium against the Red Sox, it was Oil Can on the mound again, still talking junk. Baylor had shut him up with a home run, but the Yankees lost in 11. Rickey had gone 1-for-6, grounded into a double play, and booted a ball in center for an error. When the Sox beat the Yankees the next night, they had beaten the Yankees all five times they'd played. The Yankees were 5-7. Now, in addition to telling Piniella he might be the next manager, Steinbrenner had also called the famed Baltimore manager Earl Weaver to coax him out of retirement.

BERRA COULD BE HISTORY BEFORE THE WEEKEND.

NEW YORK (UPI)—Yankees manager Yogi Berra might have found himself in a must-win situation Thursday night.

If New York drops Thursday night's game at Yankee Stadium to the Red Sox, Berra could be history before the weekend, a well-placed source told UPI. Boston, which swept an opening three-game set at Fenway Park from the Yankees, was in a position to complete a second "Boston Massacre" of the young season.

If Steinbrenner does fire Berra, it would be the 12th managerial change since the volatile owner took over the club in 1973.

The Yankees beat Boston that night, but then lost three straight to fall to 6-10. Rickey was hitting .133 and had yet to come up with a clutch hit. With 146 games remaining, Steinbrenner fired Yogi Berra. When he heard the news, Baylor kicked a trash can across the clubhouse. George didn't hire Piniella, and he didn't hire Earl Weaver. With a promise that he would manage the entire season, he rehired Billy.

Billy was back, and for kicking the trash can out of disappointment over Yogi's firing, Baylor was already on the Billy hit list—you were either on the bus with Billy or under it. Rickey publicly expressed disappointment in himself for not being healthy from the start of the season—maybe a better start from him would have saved Yogi's job. Rickey had nothing against Yogi, who had given him the "permanent green light" to steal, but while the rest of the team was mourning Yogi, he could barely hide his glee. Billy was on the cover of *Sports Illustrated* the next week ("Billy's Back!"), and Rickey had his guy in the dugout again.

The 1985 Yankees never held a share of first place, not even for a single day of the season. On two separate occasions, they spent a week trying to climb within a game and a half of the lead—and each time lost a pivotal game they needed to win. They endured one of their most tumultuous and self-destructive seasons, one that would expose just how toxic the presence of both George and Billy was. Through it all they won 97 games, and it took 161 games for Toronto to finally eliminate them from contention, which it did in the second-to-last game of the season. Billy took the Yankees from a 6-10 team under Yogi to a 91-54 team by the end of the season—which may have reflected a team finding its way more than Billy's managerial skills.

Meanwhile, Rickey put on one of the great offensive shows in baseball history. If he did not turn in his greatest season to date, 1985 was certainly the year when Rickey became both Rickey Henderson, future Hall of Famer, and Rickey Henderson, revolutionary leadoff threat.

It started with a 3-for-5 game on May 12 against Kansas City. Rickey doubled off the latest prodigy, 21-year-old Bret Saberhagen. That got his average up over .300 for the first time. He'd gone uncaught in his first 13 steal attempts, but of course the guy to break the streak, on May 29, was his nemesis—Bob Boone. And of course when Boone got ejected later in the fourth, it was for arguing about Rickey's strike zone with home-plate umpire Vic Voltaggio—which, Rickey's teammate Billy Sample conceded, was "the size of a matchbox."

Rickey's on-base percentage was 100 points higher than his batting average. Nine days later, he went wild in Seattle—3-for-5, three runs scored, four RBIs, a homer, and a double. A leadoff triple the next day off Matt Young pushed his slugging percentage over .500 and into Bobby Bonds territory, but without the bushels of strikeouts and the .260 average. "Rickey," Red Sox catcher Rich Gedman recalled, "was an on-base machine. He was more dangerous than the power hitters, because you could always walk those guys. You could expand the strike zone and get them to chase. Rickey never chased, and if you put him on, you had even bigger problems."

On Friday, May 24, the Yankees were in Oakland. In anticipation of his return home for the first time since being traded, Rickey had already told the writers that "two-thirds of the fans will be there to see Rickey, two-thirds to see Billy and two-thirds to see the Yankees." He also told the writers that his former teammates who tired of him in 1984, well, they weren't exactly prime-time players themselves. The *San Jose Mercury News*'s Steve Fainaru wrote the feature.

COMING HOME

After the trade, topics left unsaid were brought into the open by some of Henderson's former teammates. There were allegations he sometimes loafed, that he feigned sickness to take days off, or sat out due to common colds, including a crucial series against the Tigers last year.

A's centerfielder Dwayne Murphy, considered a close friend of Henderson's, questioned Henderson's motivation.

Henderson, in turn, is just as blunt.

"I carried the Oakland A's," he said. "Whenever they were in a slump, I picked them up. So, if they say I didn't hustle or didn't take batting practice, why didn't they just do what Rickey did then we'll all have success and win. I still love Oakland, but the things they say about me, I'd have to disagree with."

When Rickey broke Brock's single-season stolen base record, one of the first people he thanked on that field in Milwaukee three years earlier was Murphy, who sacrificed at-bats and power-hitting opportunities to give Rickey a chance to steal not just second but third too. Three years later,

Rickey had another thought for his old outfield teammate. Afterward he said he was just stating the obvious and couldn't figure out what the big deal was.

"Murph cannot carry a team. I was the man to do it over there and they got rid of me. They put all the eggs on his back and he cannot carry it. The pressure was on Rickey, and now it's on Murph. Can Murph deal with that pressure? No, Murph cannot deal with that pressure. Murph is a helper. He's not a carrier. He's not one of those guys who can be outstanding all the time. He's solid, but he's not one of the greatest."

Rickey scored six runs in the four games against Oakland. Murphy won the four-game finale for Oakland with a late, satisfying home run off Dave Righetti. As much as both Rickey and Murphy said that the moment was finished, Rickey's return to Oakland had been a cold one. He went by his old clubhouse, and Murphy said hello. That was it. Other players felt it too. Murphy said he wasn't even mad at Rickey for his comments about him not being able to carry the team because, he said, "That's just Rickey." Where, then, did Rickey chafe Murphy? It was when Rickey said he was a better center fielder than Murphy, who would win six straight Gold Gloves in center. The home run felt good, though. When the *San Francisco Examiner* headline writers were done for the night, the subhead of the game story underscored how frosty Rickey's first return to Oakland had been: "A's centerfielder homers to win game, get back at Henderson."

Rickey tore through the league. At the All-Star break, he led the league in runs and stolen bases. (Keeping the Bushrod-to-MLB pipeline alive, Gary Pettis of the Angels was second.) Rickey was second in hitting, at .357, behind George Brett's .358. He was third in on-base percentage and second in slugging. On July 16, at the Hubert H. Humphrey Metrodome in Minneapolis, Rickey played in his fifth All-Star Game, his first as a Yankee, his second as a starter. Dave Winfield was also a starter on the team, and Mattingly was a reserve behind Baltimore's Eddie Murray. Rickey opened the game with a Rickey Run (single, steal, grounder, score on a sac fly), but that was it for him and the Americans: the Nationals would batter the AL, 6–1.

On the field, Rickey was constantly accessorizing the elements of Rickey Style. The snatch-catch was now a staple of the wardrobe. So too was the 10-finger-waggle before he took off for second. Just to be like Rickey, kids across the country had been practicing their headfirst slide since Rickey stole 100 bags in his first full season. In 1985, Rickey added another piece to the wardrobe that Rickey partisans would delight in and opposing dugouts would absolutely loathe—the Pick.

In the long annals of the game, there have been all kinds of celebrations—Reggie would hit home runs and stand in the box for what felt like a month, admiring his handiwork as the ball sailed into the night sky. Glenn Burke was credited with inventing the high-five. Pete Rose would step on first base after recording the final out of an inning and spike the ball on the turf, making opponents (and teammates too) want to punch him in the chops. Players would stand on second base after a double, point to the heavens, and acknowledge God, the departed, or whoever saw to it they succeeded.

The Pick? The Pick had to be seen to be believed. Rickey would homer and then, while rounding the bases, he'd pick at the fabric of his jersey as if here were removing lint from his cashmere. The Pick was reserved for those Very Special Occasions when Rickey did something so amazing that it surprised even him. The Pick was reserved for one thing and one thing only: a supremely impressive Rickey Henderson home run.

Rickey couldn't remember the exact month he debuted the Pick, but it was likely mid-May 1985, when he started getting hot. Nobody could throw him out on the bases. Nobody could pitch to him without putting him on. Still, by the end of May, for all he'd done, Rickey possessed a grand total of three home runs.

Just three! In batting practice, Rickey had watched Winfield send balls into the Harlem River. Baylor, batting upright like a skyscraper, would launch balls into the batter's eye. Mattingly would crouch, almost like Rickey, uncoil, and just *kill* the ball into the upper tank. With that short right-field porch in Yankee Stadium, even guys who weren't traditional power hitters could put a charge into the ball—but not Rickey.

"Let me tell you how the Pick came," Rickey recalled. "Willie Horton taught me that. Let me say, Willie Horton *helped* me with that. He's the first-base coach with the Yankees. I'm hitting balls. I'm down there *crushing* balls—but my shit ain't going out. Don Mattingly . . . *POW!* . . . Baylor . . . *YAKK!* . . . Winfield . . . *BOOM!*—not my shit. Willie Horton said, 'Rick, come here. I know you're strong enough to hit home runs, but your ball is getting to the outfield flat, and that's why it's not going out.' I said, 'What you talking 'bout, man? I'm *crushing* the ball. The ball's not going out cuz . . .

cuz . . . I don't *know* what's wrong.' He said, 'Come down tomorrow, and I'mma show you why your ball isn't getting out.'"

When Billy replaced Yogi, he brought in Willie Horton on April 28 as an assistant hitting coach to Lou Piniella. Raised in the Detroit projects, Willie Horton had played 18 seasons in the big leagues—he even played for Billy with the Tigers in the early 1970s. Horton made four All-Star teams and won the World Series with the 1968 Tigers, but he was best known throughout his hometown for leaving Tiger Stadium during the deadly, nearly weeklong 12th Street riots of 1967 to try to maintain peace in the neighborhood. As National Guard tanks rolled through the Black community, Detroiters would never forget Willie Horton standing on a car *in his uniform* pleading with his fellow Black citizens to go home.

When Billy was fired to end the 1983 season, he was haggard. He was still Billy, still the best in-game manager in the business, but he had come completely apart. Billy's extravagant days of having chefs on speed dial to lavish gourmet meals on his staff in the clubhouse were gone, replaced by full-time drinking. "Billy was fascinating. He was a quick drunk. He was a mean drunk, and he was a fighting drunk, which was a really bad combination," recalled Claire Smith, who covered the Yankees for the *Hartford Courant* during much of the 1980s. "But over the years I covered him I began to expand my observations and see who he really was, and I concluded the man had an illness, and by bringing him back to the Yankees—and he had the Yankees in his blood—it was like George was feeding alcohol to an alcoholic. Billy's breakfast was beer, and his day often deteriorated from there. He would say, 'I'm not drinking anymore, all I drink is beer.'"

Assistant hitting coach was Willie Horton's job, but unofficially he was also Billy's "Tranquility Coach," tasked with maintaining peace in a clubhouse hostile to Yogi's firing. "A lot of it was to make sure Baylor didn't jump him," recalled Billy Sample. Beyond his duty to keep a close check on Billy, Horton had also been watching Rickey during his first weeks with the Yankees.

"'Now, we were always taught that when we swing, in the crouch, come straight through, like Rod Carew sorta style—and *BAM!* But I'm hitting it flat,'" Rickey recalled telling Horton. "I said, 'Yeah, that's how I hit.' He said, 'That's why you're not hitting it out.' I said, 'You crazy.'

"Then he asked me to get in my stance. He got in front of me, and then he said, 'Now hit me in the chest.' What? Man, I ain't gonna hit you in the chest. He said, 'I want you to hit me in the chest with your swing. No bat. Just [your] practice swing.' So I did it. And he looked at me and said, 'You can't knock a person out like that. That's your swing.'"

Rickey swung through in slow motion a few times and saw that Horton was right: his swing was leveling off below the letters. There was no uppercut to the swing that would get the ball out of the infield with an arc, into the jet stream, especially with Rickey in his pronounced crouch. Rickey's was a line-drive swing, straight and strong. Then Horton took Rickey's hands, tilted them slightly downward, and told Rickey to follow his swing path up toward the letters of Horton's uniform—right up near his heart.

"Now, he says, 'Give me this: same swing—and hit me in the chest,'" Rickey remembered. "Now I'm swinging up and—*BOOM! BOOM!* I gotta come straight through and *up.* Then he said, 'Now don't hit me no more and go up there and swing like that!'"

In later years, when the smart guys from the Ivies took over the game and acted like they'd invented it in an MIT lab, everybody would talk about what Willie was talking about that day with Rickey. Decades ahead of the Sloan Analytics Conference, they even gave the swing Willie Horton taught Rickey a catchy name to make it sound like their own creation. They called it *launch angle.* Launch angle was what Willie Horton gave Rickey that day—the small adjustment, the little bit of an uppercut, that turned him into a knockout puncher.

"I turned that bat up," Rickey said. "First, it didn't work for about three, four days, and he said, 'You got it now.' Fella threw me a cock shot, I mean fastball right down the middle of the plate. It was mine. And I went *WHOOOSH* . . . Bat was way out there. Missed the pitch. He was at first base. 'When it's down, hit that pitch.' Ball one, ball two. Next pitch, same spot, head down . . . *POWWWW!* I hit this ball. This ball shot UP! Up and OUT. Like it went out of Yankee Stadium. I hit the ball, I was like *OOOOH! WHOOO! WHOOOO! I DID IT!* I was so excited! I started hitting myself in the batting helmet. I started tugging at my jersey when I started running to go round the bases. That was Pick One. Pick Two . . . *OOOOOH!* . . . They thought I was crazy!"

From that moment on, Rickey would hit 21 homers, more homers in four months than he had ever hit in a single season of his career at any level. Rickey would finish 1985 with a career-high of 24 home runs, and the Pick would turn into a signature element of Rickey Style. Snatch-catch on defense, picks on offense. Rickey then started refining his home-run celebrations: the number of picks at his jersey would come to signify just how satisfied he was with a particular home run. A couple of picks? Nice homer—but not top-shelf. Four or five picks? A no-doubter, either by distance or in importance to the ball game. The true Rickey watchers would know, without even needing to know the score or see where the ball landed, that their man had launched a big one just by counting the number of picks Rickey gave his jersey during the trot.

Rickey was putting up an all-time masterpiece—until August, when word hit that the players had set a strike date. This one didn't look like it was going to be as bad as 1981, but announcing a strike date was no idle threat. Dave Winfield was the Yankees' player rep, and he had given the word to the team—the players were going to walk on Tuesday, August 6, but everybody needed to stay close because it could be settled very quickly. On the sixth, the players did strike—all 13 games canceled. The next day the players and owners reached tentative terms. The strike was over. Winfield called his teammates and told them that games would resume leaguewide with doubleheaders on Thursday, August 8.

As the Yankees prepared for a doubleheader at the Stadium against Cleveland, Joe Safety, the traveling secretary, received a phone call. It was Rickey.

"Do we have a game tonight?"

"No, we've got two."

"When do we have a game?"

"In three hours."

Rickey told Safety he was in California. Safety said, "I thought he was kidding."

Rickey missed not only the Wednesday workout but the Yankees' doubleheader sweep of Cleveland that day. He met the team in Boston for a weekend series with the Red Sox. It was there that he learned the Yankees had fined him three days' pay for missing Wednesday and two games—a $24,000 hit. Even the diplomatic Winfield didn't want to mention Rickey by name.

HENDERSON'S ATTITUDE HAS YANKEES PERTURBED

BOSTON—Rickey Henderson leads the Yankees in batting average, runs scored, stolen bases . . .

And immaturity.

> Well, three out of four ain't bad.
> Which is the reason Billy Martin and George Steinbrenner haven't
> snapped, crackled and popped Henderson's head. They ought to. He
> isn't using it, anyway.

When Rickey heard about the fine, he took the offensive, essentially telling the Yankees that affecting his mood would affect his play. Steinbrenner
used his favorite weapon to take his shots at Rickey—the papers. "The young
man has things slightly mixed up," Steinbrenner told Phil Pepe of the *Daily
News*. "I read where he said, 'If they fine me, I'll be ticked off, and they don't
want me ticked off.' He's got that wrong. He should be saying, 'If I miss three
days, I'll tick off the boss, and I don't want to tick off the boss.'"

For the first time, Rickey and Steinbrenner were at odds publicly. "Do you
think I'm going to let some guy come in from Oakland, where they have no
discipline, and do what he's doing," Steinbrenner told Pepe. "And if Henderson lays down on us because of the fine, he's going to have to deal with me,
and let me tell you, he's never had to deal with anything like me before."

On the second to last day of the season, Toronto finished off the Yankees,
but the season wasn't lost completely on the field. Billy had still been the best
in-game manager in the game—nobody saw baseball, what had happened,
what could happen as the game unfolded, the way he did—until he inexpli-
cably cost them the season. For maybe the first time in his managerial career,
he was the guy people thought had lost the pennant for his team.

The Yankees had won 11 straight and whittled a 9 1/2-game August deficit
down to a game and a half. Then, starting with the infamous September
16 makeup game in the Bronx against Cleveland, Billy imploded. He let a
rookie, Brian Fisher, give up six runs in the ninth inning when the Yankees had started the inning up 5–3 and with Righetti ready, hands on hips,
waiting for the call that never came. The Yankees lost that game 9–5, and it
would be the first loss of an eight-game losing streak that included Billy's
decision to have Mike Pagliarulo, the left-handed third baseman, switch-hit
as well as the infamous, bloody denouement in Baltimore on September 21:
Billy's 20-minute brawl at the Cross Keys Inn with his own pitcher, Ed Whitson, a fratricide all too symbolic of the Steinbrenner years.

Whitson broke Billy's arm, but not before kicking him in the nuts, tossing
him to the pavement on his head, and trading punches in a sprawling row
that spanned three separate areas of the hotel and finally ended on the third

floor—where tranquility coach Willie Horton and hitting coach Lou Piniella blocked each end of the hallway to keep Billy and Whitson from getting another shot at each other. Afterward, Steinbrenner sent Whitson home and Billy left the emergency room in a cast and sling.

Rickey was there that night, having a drink with Walt. "It started with a wedding. Rick and I are watching Billy talking to the wedding party, and they were all so excited because they were talking to Billy Martin and the Yankees. Billy asked to dance with the bride," Walt McCreary recalled. "Then he sent a bottle of champagne over to the groom. Everything was social, then Billy says to the groom, 'If anyone's gonna marry a fat girl like that, they *deserve* a bottle of champagne.'"

That started the first fight. When Billy's fight with Whitson spilled into the street, Rickey was there for that too. Rickey and Walt watched one of the bizarre scenes: Billy Martin in a public fistfight with one of his starting pitchers.

"I had a really good relationship with Ed Whitson," Claire Smith recalled. "Billy was a mess. I wasn't one of the boys, and sometimes I just wanted to be by myself. On that occasion, I was invited to dinner with the boys and I declined. There was a Bill Cosby and Sidney Poitier movie on that I'd never seen.

"There was a wedding. Billy had congratulated the groom and bride. I heard he danced with the bride, then put his hands where he shouldn't have. And that led to an altercation with the groom. I got a call from one of the writers, who said, 'You better get down here. Eddie is trying to kill Billy. No, Eddie is *trying to kill* Billy.' War was being waged across the Cross Keys Inn. It's like a hotel toppled to its side. All the teams knew that the Yankees were the best team, but there was going to be one week of chaos that doomed them. We saw Billy in his office one day, and he was trying, but was just unable, to put his shirt on. And finally, he just said quietly, 'I'm a mess.' And he was."

Billy believed that, had he been the manager from opening day, the Yankees wouldn't have started 6-10. Had Steinbrenner given him the job from the start, Billy believed, the Yankees could have overcome Toronto. They would have won. He also believed that Fisher's implosion was not nearly as damaging to his team as Steinbrenner's proclamation that the season was over after the Yankees had won the opener of a four-game September series against Toronto at the Stadium but lost the next three. That series had highlighted Oakland versus Oakland, Bushrod versus Bushrod: Rickey, though he swiped five of six bags in the series, was upstaged by Lloyd Moseby, who was spectacular in the series, going 8-for-18. Billy thought the eight-game losing streak was caused by Steinbrenner proclaiming the season was over before the final battles had been fought.

Rickey's debut season in New York proved Billy's prediction to Steinbrenner. He was spectacular, Broadway ready—a .314 average, 146 runs, 24 home runs, 80 stolen bases, .419 on-base percentage, and .516 slugging percentage. He won the stolen-base crown for the sixth straight year and was caught only 10 times—80 for 90. The 146 runs were the most by a Yankee since DiMaggio's 151 back in 1937. He left Fritz Maisel's single-season stolen-base record in the dust and did it at an 88.8 percent success rate. Those 146 runs came in just 143 games—everyone had forgotten that he'd missed the first 10 games of the season. Rickey had proven that New York was not too big for him. There was no moment he couldn't handle.

What he could not shake, however, was his relationship with the reporters, who never forgave him for blowing past them to start the season and for his lack of deference to the Yankee Legend—or the suspicion that his .243 average over the final five weeks of the season was not due to fatigue but to discontent over the Steinbrenner fine. "*Don't need no press now*" followed every misstep, and so did "*It's Rickey Time.*" When Steinbrenner fined Rickey after the strike fiasco, Alan Greenberg of the *Hartford Courant* remembered Rickey's April arrival and wrote, "'Rickey Time' is I-me-mine time." The writers did not forget, and in turn, neither did Rickey. Even in triumph, he would not bend.

When the Yankees demolished the Tigers 10–2 the afternoon of September 25, Rickey went 3-for-4, and his steal of second in the third inning gave him 75 for the season and the Yankees' single-season record, passing the long-dead Maisel. Instead of allowing the papers to revel in his feat and giving them a chance to bring him closer to their readers—letting New York do what New York did best, which would have been letting him bask in breaking a record that had stood since 1914— Rickey bolted out of the clubhouse with a two-sentence exit that let everyone know he wasn't going to play the hero game: "Can't talk now. I got a date."

As in 1981, Rickey would be stung that he didn't win the MVP, but this time it didn't go to a pitcher—it went to Mattingly. "Donnie deserved it, but I could have won it," Rickey said. He finished third, behind Mattingly, who ran away with 94 percent of the votes, and George Brett, who finished second. Having finished in the MVP top five twice in the last five years, he now had his sights set on finally winning the award.

It burned Mattingly and his teammates to see the Royals wind up being the last team standing as World Series champions; the Yankees had beaten the Royals seven of the 12 times they played and outscored them 63–47. Echoing Mattingly's sentiment, Rickey told people during the off-season that the Yankees were good enough to make the playoffs, and he was already planning to be even better in 1986. But he'd have to do it without Billy. On October 27, George fired Billy. Again.

10

I N 1986, THE YANKEES finished second—again, this time behind
Boston—but unlike 1985, when the Yankees had several opportunities
to change the tenor of the race if they could only have won a single, crucial
game, this one wasn't that close. The Yankees fell out of first place in mid-
May and hung around during the summer, but it wasn't really a race. On
September 11, the Red Sox were up by 10 games. Boston clinched on September 28, when Oil Can Boyd beat Toronto. Then the Red Sox lost five of
six (including four in a row to the Yankees to end the season) to make the
final margin only five and a half games, suggesting it had been a respectable
pennant race. It wasn't.

None of the particulars, of course, counted for much. In the ensuing telling and retellings of the year 1986, what mattered was that the baseball calendar belonged completely and entirely to . . . to . . . to the *Mets!* To Straw
and Nails, Keith, HoJo, and Doc. The Mets owned the city in 1986. They
made history by winning the World Series, bringing New York the delicious-
ness of humiliating Boston *again.*

But 1986 was significant for another reason: for the first time in modern
New York baseball history—since the Giants and the Dodgers took their
acts out west and the Mets arrived in 1962—the Yankees and Mets were both
contenders at the same time, and it was the Yankees who were the after-
thought. Even worse, they were the sour and bloated team next to the Mets,
who connected with the city, who were tough, blue-collar champions just
like New Yorkers (as the city saw itself). While Gary Carter's thousand-watt
affability delivered the ticker tape, the Yankees were rich and sullen and
detached—traits embodied, so the stories went, by Rickey.

• • •

Armed with all the tools and now the power—thanks to Willie Horton's adjustments that helped him to a 24-homer season the year before—Rickey hit .263 in 1986, the lowest average of his career. He struck out 81 times, the second-most of his career, and his average never reached .290 on any day in the season. He began the season 1-for-19, and as far as his average was concerned, he never recovered. During the season, Rickey, armed with a home-run swing, suffered long deaths at the plate . . . an 0-for-18 stretch . . . 0-for-17 . . . 2-for-36 . . . 9-for-67.

The average tumbled, and yet the impact was still there—Rickey was still being called the most complete force in the game. Even at .263, Rickey walked 89 times, which gave him an on-base percentage of .358, nearly 100 points higher than his average, and that allowed him to steal 87 bases—passing old Fritz Maisel on the Yankee all-time leaderboard again. Rickey had worn the pinstripes for two seasons and held the Yankees' top two all-time single-season stolen-base records. He played 153 games in 1986—the second-highest total of his career—and followed up his 146-run tear in 1985 with 130 runs scored to lead the league for the second straight year.

As for the power? Rickey banged 28 home runs, from the leadoff spot, becoming the only player in the century-old history of the game to hit 20 home runs and steal 50 bases not once, but twice—a distinction that separated him even from the great Mays, for Willie was a home-run hitter who could steal bases. Mays was the best of that category, but there were others; Henry Aaron and even a young Reggie Jackson could run too. Rickey, on the other hand, was a base stealer who had unusual power.

Across the game, the bouquets fell from the balconies. "He's the best leadoff hitter of all time, no question," said Tony Kubek, the old Yankee great who was broadcasting for NBC. "There's never been a leadoff hitter who matched his combination of on-base percentage, base-stealing ability, and power." Maybe Bobby Valentine, the manager of the Texas Rangers, could be effusive because Rickey hit only .190 against the Rangers: "Facing Henderson is a choice of a slow death or quick death. If you walk him, he'll torment you on the bases. If you give him a pitch, he can hit it out. Take your pick."

Then there was the Scooter, the great and excitable Yankee shortstop Phil Rizzuto, who won championships with DiMaggio and Mantle and was now the broadcast voice for a new generation of Yankee fans on WPIX, Channel 11. "Henderson is a phenomenon. That's the only word that applies. I've seen so many great ones, but Henderson is special. Sometimes he gets me so excited in the booth, I have to start worrying about my blood pressure. The things he does on the bases, Holy Cow! And did you see how far he hit that one the other night?"

Around the league, from partisans and rivals alike, the acknowledgment came, and how could it not? Even in a down year, Rickey still crossed the plate 130 times. Outside of Rickey himself the year before, no Yankee had scored that many runs in a quarter-century—not since Roger Maris scored 132 runs in his tortured year of 1961. Rickey was putting up the monster numbers, establishing himself in the thinnest of altitudes, in the place where the home fans wanted to know if you were going to wilt. He didn't.

Yet none of it really mattered now, not when the Yankees were looking up at Boston in the standings and across town at the Mets holding a World Series trophy. As the Yankees fell and the Mets rose, much of the focus in the press box wasn't on what Rickey was, but on everything he wasn't.

HENDERSON: A FRUSTRATING, COMPLEX STAR

Rickey Henderson is baseball's bad boy of the base paths, arguably the best all-around player in the game, certainly one of the most exciting. A hot dog? Maybe. A loner? Undoubtedly. Disliked and misunderstood by teammates? Quite often.

When he is going right, there's none better. When he's going wrong, there's few badder.

"I am a creator," he says, flashing a disarming grin. "I want to make things happen, and I want them to happen with style. I like to do things different."

"He's pretty close to being the best player in the game," said A's centerfielder Dwayne Murphy, a former teammate.

And he may be one of the most irritating . . .

"A lot of the guys didn't like the way Rickey did things," said Murphy, who first joined the A's in 1978, the year before Henderson broke in. "Some didn't mind—like me—as long as he got the job done, and he always did. He'd always be the last one to take the field. He'd walk out or walk in from the infield. That kind of stuff really bothered some guys. He wouldn't take infield, or he'd miss batting practice. He'd come to the park when he wanted to. Those were the things people were most displeased with Rickey about."

Yankees co-captain Willie Randolph says, "As an athlete, you have to admire him, but you also have to wonder if he's getting the most out of his talent. If he practiced more, would he be even better?"

"I was like, 2-for-43, and the press—you know the New York press—they were dogging me. I mean *dogging me*," Rickey recalled. "So here we go again. Go out there for batting practice every day and I can't take it. I'm pissed off. I know I can hit, but go out there, go 0-for-4. Go out there again, go 0-for-4. I went out there for about a week and a half, and I'm 0-for-4, 0-for-3 with a walk, or 0-for-4. Every day. So I said, 'I'm not going out there for batting practice. I'm not going to take extra hitting. It's not doing me no good,' because I was playing as hard as I could each and every day. Press is killing me. Ripping me up every day.

"Don Mattingly went to the press and said, 'There is no player out here working harder than Rickey and playing harder than Rickey, and running and stealing and busting his butt every day, and y'all dogging the hell out of him.' That shut the press down."

Then there were the umpires, who had grown tired of Rickey's imperiousness at the plate. Around the league, his opponents complained about Rickey intimidating umpires, though all the great hitters, from Ted Williams to this new kid Tony Gwynn who had just hit the scene two years earlier, were imperious about the zone too. It wasn't a strike until they said it was. But Rickey? Rickey had created a national emergency. When he played for the Rangers, Billy Sample—speaking for aggrieved hitters not named Rickey—would see umpires call close pitches or even obvious strikes in Rickey's favor: ball. Sample would then yell from the dugout, "HEY, UMP! THAT WAS A STRIKE ON ME!"

One umpire, Jim McKean, even went on the record to Peter Gammons at *Sports Illustrated* and said the umpires were no longer going to allow Rickey's strike zone to be affected by his crouch, which meant pitches at his eyes might now be called strikes.

Finally, The Boss had to get involved. After reading Gammons's story, Steinbrenner set up a meeting with Dr. Bobby Brown, the American League president, and Peter Ueberroth, the commissioner, and released a statement protecting Rickey from retaliation by the umpires: "There is no way," Stein-brenner said, "that the Yankees will allow Rickey Henderson to be selectively persecuted."

When the Yankees played the Red Sox, Gedman would encourage his pitchers not to lose focus because of Rickey's crouch. Whenever a Red Sox pitcher got a strike called on a borderline pitch, Gedman would yell out to his pitcher, "*Good pitch!*"

And Rickey would look back at Gedman and say, "That ball low."

"I wasn't talking to you."

"That ball still low."

Twins manager Ray Miller complained to *The Sporting News,* "Every time a strike is called on Rickey Henderson it becomes a 20-minute ordeal. He starts whining. The bench is screaming. It goes on and on. It's a joke. Bert Blyleven throws a curve ball over the heart of the plate. It's called a ball. And now, when my pitcher has to come back with a fastball, Henderson hits a home run."

There was a June series in Baltimore when Rickey just tormented the Orioles—he was back to his old habit of killing Baltimore, going 7-for-13 in the series, with two home runs, seven runs scored, five RBIs, and five sto-len bases—and Rickey Style lit up Memorial Stadium. "The basic problem," columnist Ken Stoddard wrote in the *Baltimore Sun,* "is the way Henderson plays the game."

> The Orioles are fed up with the exaggerated way he catches fly balls, that little flick of the wrist as the ball settles in the glove. They're sick of his home-run trots, which might be the slowest in major-league history—although Eddie Murray isn't Edwin Moses around the bases, either.
>
> They're sick of how long it takes Henderson to get settled in the batter's box, and the way he steps out of the box for an interminable period after each pitch . . . and they're not wild about that crouched batting stance of his.

"He's got awesome talent—but he dogs you a little too much for me," Orioles pitcher Ken Dixon said of the way Rickey would show him up. "He doesn't give you any respect. There's a lot of animosity building . . . people will be looking for vengeance if he keeps it up. He hits a home run and he trots around the bases staring at you. He's trying to show you up. OK, that's

Rickey Henderson, but it's like he's directing an insult at you. Hey, if you get me, you get me, but don't make a big deal out of it."

Earl Weaver, headmaster of the old school, skipped the preliminaries and said that frontier justice was imminent: Rickey was at risk of getting knocked on his keister. "Sooner or later," he said, "one of those pitchers might lose control out there."

Another umpire told Gammons that Rickey "ticks everybody off. We're all sick and tired of his showing us up and slowing down the game by stepping out on every pitch . . . No matter what he thinks, the game wasn't created for him."

Rickey may have offended some of his peers or the reporters or the business part of the game, but the fans loved him, both at home and on the road. His teammates may have bristled at the perception that his head wasn't in the game, but no matter what city the Yankees were in, whether it was Boston or Seattle, there was Rickey talking to fans in the outfield in between innings, making them part of the game.

Claire Smith recalled Rickey carrying on full conversations with fans. "Rickey loved the fans, and I loved watching him in the on-deck circle," she recalled. "He wasn't studying pitchers. He wasn't watching the game. He was talking to the fans. It didn't matter if it was Yankee Stadium or somewhere on the road where they booed him. He carried on conversations, animated and laughing, and I always felt, 'Why can't every player love this game and have this much fun with the fans?' When Rickey would score a run standing up, he'd cross home plate clapping his hands as if he found a pot of gold at the end of the rainbow."

The fans, especially the kids, would yell to Rickey in center field to do the snatch-catch. They wanted to breathe his air, as fans do with the star players, the ones who possess that special thing that Mays had, that overflow of charisma that makes people care about the game.

In the papers, Rickey received no such dispensation. They let him have it.

IS THIS YANKEE CLASS, GEORGE?

Isn't it about time someone took Rickey Henderson aside and told him his "snatch" catch is bush and to forget it?

Yankee announcers have continually compare [*sic*] Henderson's "snatch" catch to the "basket" catch popularized by Hall of Famer Willie Mays, which is utter nonsense.

> One of the greatest defensive centerfielders of the past 35 years, Mays used the "basket" catch to increase the speed in which to release his throws. He used it to be a better performer and not a "hot dog."
>
> Henderson uses the classless move to be a "hot dog" and not to improve his playing abilities.
>
> Maybe Rickey should spend more time in the batting cage trying to break his horrendous slump which has affected the whole club rather than fooling with that catch.
>
> Owner George Steinbrenner always preaches about Yankee class. It would be nice to hear him explain how the snatch catch fits in with Yankee class?

All of this criticism, of course, was revenge, not to mention ahistorical. In his day Mays took all kinds of grief for his style. He was criticized for being a showboat with the basket-catch just as much as Rickey was criticized for the snatch-catch. When guys around the league grew tired of the glittering Mays aura, they would pit the solid, *sans serif* excellence of Henry Aaron against Mays's more exuberant style. And the tone was familiar: "Henry does everything Willie does—only his hat doesn't fly off." Willie was moody too—no one wanted to catch him on one of his dark days—but Willie did something Rickey would not: he played nice in public, fulfilling the requirements of being a hero.

So when Rickey fell, and fell hard, as he did in 1987, everyone was waiting for him on the way down. Rickey hit five homers in five games in April. He was hitting .403, and the Yankees had won 14 of their first 19 games. After scoring 276 runs in his first two years in New York, Rickey started 1987 scorching—he scored 43 runs in 44 games. Then, on June 4 against Milwaukee, he pulled a hamstring and missed three weeks.

After he returned—too early, he would say—Rickey went down again and missed the entire month of August.

The hot start provided no protection, no proof against the whispers around the Yankees that turned into statements out loud: Rickey could have returned but chose not to play. In June, Steinbrenner threw Piniella under the bus by publicly stating that in a private conversation Piniella had said he wanted Rickey traded. Piniella, Steinbrenner said, believed that Rickey could have played through the hamstring injury and was now just "jaking it"—the dreaded baseball slang for a player milking an injury, not playing when healthy, letting the team down when he could be contributing. Some people said the term had been around for decades, while others insisted that Steinbrenner himself had invented the word—just for this context. Wherever the word came from, it finished Lou with Rickey—but it also finished Rickey with the writers and parts of the fan base.

Rickey had always maintained a unique relationship with the fans, but talk radio was now raising the temperature of the negativity surrounding him. "How badly was Rickey hurt?" was replaced with "Was Rickey really hurt?" And why would anyone even ask that question if there weren't some truth to it? Rickey saw the writers and the media—and to a large extent, the Yankees—turning the city against him. In July, Bill Madden of the *Daily News* voted Rickey the "Most Overrated" player in the American League. "Yes, Rickey always has the numbers, especially the stolen bases and the runs scored, but why is it you feel like you've been cheated watching him play so brilliantly for a couple of months straight and then tail off?"

On the sidelines, there was nothing he could do about it. At the same time, 1987 was the year when the New York experiment would break beyond repair. Everything was falling apart around Steinbrenner. The Mets owned the city, and even that needed to be rephrased: The *World Champion* Mets owned the city. The Canyon of Heroes. David Letterman. The whole bit. When people talked baseball in New York, they were talking about the *National League*. When they mentioned players, they were talking about Straw and Doc and Gary Carter, not Rickey and Winfield. The Yankees were the bloated, ugly sideshow that had once been tolerable because with the chaos came the pennant. But now, with the championship flag waving high on the other side of the Triboro, Steinbrenner was no longer the savior but the disease—and Rickey was positioned as the ever-present symptom.

So much of it was payback—for not playing ball initially with the writers, for "I don't need no press now, man." It was payback for breaking the Yankees' single-season stolen-base record in 1985 and responding to reporters eager to convey his words to a fan base that reveled in the Yankees legend with, "Can't talk now. I got a date." For some teammates, it was payback for separating himself from them, for being on his own program, and for somehow telegraphing that he would not play if he was upset. There was the time Rickey had agreed to attend a Yankees team cruise. Other Yankees players would be there, but Rickey was the headliner. At the last moment, Rickey ditched the cruise and Walt ended up on the boat by himself. It was payback for all the times he didn't take infield, arrived later at the ballpark than his teammates, didn't run sprints, didn't bring the requisite enthusiasm.

All of it, some felt, had contributed to his hamstring pull—even the injury, they believed, was a by-product of Rickey not being professionally prepared. The prevailing attitude in 1987 was that Rickey Henderson, he of the 2.9 percent body fat in 1987, was not sufficiently taking care of his body and thus had courted his injury.

It was payback for Rickey keeping the writers at a distance, and for flying to California when Winfield told everyone to remain in the area during the 1985 strike. Underneath the glibness of *Rickey being Rickey* was the belief that Rickey purposely went to California to give himself a rest, that he chose to ask for forgiveness instead of permission when things inevitably went south. He had few true allies who would get across more favorable perspectives on him. Writers carried the message, but they were not the source of the information. That came from the Yankees themselves. Several voices among the coaches, players, and front office believed that Rickey could have played, and that if he wasn't 100 percent, 60 percent of Rickey was better than 85 percent of anyone else in the league.

It all amounted to an unwillingness to accept what would have otherwise seemed obvious: a hamstring injury to the one player in baseball whose legs were central to every facet of his game was devastating. Rickey was the most physical offensive player in the game; only catchers, who got beat up behind the plate, had injuries more severe. When Rickey wasn't flinging himself headfirst into bases, he was covering one of the biggest center fields in baseball, and for every base he *didn't* steal, he was diving back to first, usually repeatedly. "I'm in that dirt all the time, and they didn't understand me," Rickey recalled.

Walt McCreary was there when Rickey finally cracked. "We were in the apartment in Jersey cooking chicken, and I look over and he's tearing up. He's in tears," McCreary recalled. "He was talking about how nobody believed he was hurt. His legs were so muscular. He didn't have normal hamstrings like the rest of us, but it was real. He was literally tearing up because for weeks he'd been getting his ass ripped."

Before the initial injury, Rickey looked like he did in 1985. Over the first two months of 1987, he had stolen 23 of 26 bases and was hitting .321. He'd stolen 17 bases in May alone, 18 for the rest of the season. Rickey was playing with something to prove: having already mapped out how many seasons he needed to break Lou Brock's all-time stolen-base record, he concluded that he would catch Brock in 1990.

The reaction to Rickey's injury wasn't just about Rickey. A widely held prejudice predating Rickey and having nothing to do with him individually was that, deep down, Black players were not as tough as white players, did not have the personal pride to play through injury, and, in a time of rising salaries, did not feel a professional responsibility to the paying customers. The templates for this prejudice were so obvious as to become clichéd, and they played out with special harshness along the Northeast corridor—Boston, New York, and Philadelphia.

Everyone loved Lenny Dykstra, the far less talented and often recklessly unprofessional center fielder playing crosstown for the Mets, and everyone delighted in his nickname, "Nails," because he played so hard. All the hard hats loved Lenny. He was one of them, whether with the Mets or with the Phillies after he was traded. Dykstra was an inspiration to the underpowered white kids (and their parents) who vowed that if they ever had Rickey's talent, they'd make more of it than he ever did. (It was a hypothetical no one needed to lose sleep over.) Dykstra was the gritty, overachieving cog in two championship runs—a World Series with the Mets and a pennant with the Phillies—but the Black players in the sport knew the true root of the dispensation: the overwhelmingly white ticket buyers identified with the supposedly hardworking white players and saw those talented, flamboyant Black players as wasting their ability. (*If only they cared more!*) Meanwhile, those pesky statistics always got in the way: Dykstra never played 150 games in a single season in his time with the Mets, did so but once in a 12-year career, drank himself out of shape after one big year with the Phillies, and was out of the league by age 33.

Then the Yankees team physician, John Bonamo, just doing his job, told Steinbrenner that Rickey could play. The job of a team physician was not to get a player healthy, but to get him healthy enough to play. Bill Madden wrote an item in *The Sporting News*.

HENDERSON FEELS UNDERCURRENT OF CRITICISM
Was he or wasn't he? Only Rickey Henderson knew for sure how hurt he was.

Henderson, disabled three weeks earlier with a slightly torn hamstring, was still a frequent scratch from the lineup after being activated June 29. And in the games he did play, it was clear he was not playing all out, prompting undercurrents of criticism from both the media and his teammates.

Madden's piece infuriated Rickey, as did the countless others that carried the same conclusion: Rickey might have been hurt, but he just didn't want to play. "Was he, or wasn't he?" suggested doubt as to the extent of his injury. "Only Rickey Henderson knew for sure" was another suggestion that his injury was more debate material than certainty. The phrase "slightly torn hamstring" undermined the severity of the injury, making it similar to a mild cold.

Far from convincing him to change his demeanor with the writers, the season-long suspicion that Rickey wasn't playing hard could only lead to war. When Rickey returned and went on a 10-game hitting streak, the writers went to find him in the locker room and were met by a perimeter of athletic tape around his locker. "I told them, 'Don't come past this line,'" Rickey said. "Then I get two hits. Next day two hits. Here comes the press. I said, 'Don't cross this perimeter. You dogged me. I don't want to talk about it. I have a good couple of days and now y'all want to come talk?' Next day, 4-for-4, three stolen bases, four runs scored. I yelled across the room to Donnie. 'Donnie! Come tell these press people what I did. Do Not Cross. Y'all kept saying I'm faking or jaking it or some bullcrap.'"

The hamstring defined the season, and the injury was a clear and convenient issue around which to coalesce—but one of the real forces behind the payback was none other than the Mets. The Mets could pitch. The Yankees couldn't. The Mets had a championship aura. The Yankees were a mess. The team had so many needs that there was only one way to fill them to immediately make them competitive: trade Rickey.

Maybe there was nothing to the rumor, which could have been just another press-box amateur GM session. Nevertheless, for his column in *The Sporting News,* Moss Klein tapped the keys and gave it oxygen—and it was a doozy:

> The Yankees' need for pitching apparently led to the rumor of the month: Rickey Henderson to the Dodgers for a package featuring Orel Hershiser and Ken Howell. The rumor may sound sensible, but don't

expect it to happen. From the Yankees standpoint, it would make sense
because they need pitchers and Raines has Henderson-type talent and
Don Mattingly–type work habits and intensity, which are far superior
to Henderson-type work habits and intensity. But the Dodgers, despite
their stated aversion to free agents, would be foolish to give up significant players for Henderson when they could simply sign Raines for
approximately the same salary that they'd have to pay Henderson.

The deal, of course, never happened, because there *was* no deal, because
baseball owners were secretly playing *another* game, a long game of crushing
the free-agent market by agreeing not to sign free agents. Maybe the Yankees
needed pitching so badly they wanted Rickey out, and maybe the Dodgers
wanted Tim Raines, but all 26 teams had one certainty: they were involved
in a conspiracy not to sign anyone from another team.

While the rest of the baseball world was caught up in debating Rickey's
strike zone or carping on how he spoke in the third person or took too long
to get in the box, there was one guy who had known all along that Rickey
was building a Hall of Fame monument. Even some of the sharpest baseball
minds couldn't see it, or wouldn't, because they were so hung up on Rickey's
demeanor, on his refusal to act, speak, or move the way they wanted him to.
But Billy knew exactly what he had in Rickey. While Lou Piniella sparred
with Steinbrenner and alienated Rickey (who apparently was alienating
some of his teammates), Billy collaborated with *Daily News* writer Phil Pepe
on his second autobiography, *Billyball.* In the final chapter, Billy lists the
greatest players he's ever seen. His all-time outfield? Willie Mays, Mickey
Mantle, and . . . Rickey. Billy writes:

> Rickey is a once-in-a-lifetime player. You see very few Rickey
> Hendersons. You might not see another one for fifty years. He
> has to be the greatest leadoff hitter in the history of baseball.
> There has never been another leadoff man like him, not with his
> power and speed. When I was playing, Eddie Yost of the Wash-
> ington Senators was the ideal leadoff man because he got on base
> so many times. He'd walk anywhere from 125 to 150 times a year.
> And he could hit. He'd hit 11, 12, 14 home runs a year. And he'd

get 150, 160 hits a year. One year, he led the league with 135 walks, had 145 hits, 21 homers, 61 RBIs and led the league with 115 runs scored. But he didn't steal bases like Rickey, less than 10 a season. How many leadoff men do you know that can bat .314, get 172 hits, score 146 runs, hit 24 homers, drive in 72 runs, get 99 walks and steal 80 bases? Only one. Rickey Henderson. And that's what he did for the Yankees in 1985.

That's why I wanted the Yankees to get him. That's why I say he's the greatest leadoff man in baseball history and the best player in the game today.

I know I left off some outstanding outfielders of my day. People like Al Kaline, Carl Yastrzemski, Frank Robinson and some National Leaguers that I never saw much of, Stan Musial, Roberto Clemente. Hank Aaron. All great ballplayers. But I don't have to apologize for the outfield I chose. I'll be more than satisfied to take my chances with an outfield of Mickey Mantle, Willie Mays and Rickey Henderson.

For a time the 1987 Yankees had been in first place. Three teams that year won 90 games. The Yankees finished fourth with 89. Late in the season, frustrated that the star-studded lineup did not have the accompanying arms to win, Rickey recalled a meeting with Steinbrenner. "We were great. Powerhouse lineup, but couldn't beat Detroit, Toronto, so me, Donnie and Winfield meet with Steinbrenner," Rickey said. "Donnie stands up in the meeting and says, 'If you get us pitching, We. Will. Win.' George looked us in the eye, told us he'd handle it—and came back with Jack Clark."

Moss Klein of the *Newark Star-Ledger,* however, believed that he had pinpointed the Yankees' problem and detailed it in an off-season *Sporting News* column:

> Unless Billy Martin returns as manager, a possibility that always exists in Owner George Steinbrenner's upside-down kingdom, the Yankees would be well-advised to trade outfielder Rickey Henderson. Martin has some effect on Henderson, but other managers don't. Despite Henderson's questionable work ethic and hefty contract (a total of $3.55 million for 1988 and 1989), there are a couple of teams willing to take him . . . if one had to choose between which player this season made the least of

his ability while receiving an astronomical salary, it would be a toss-up between Henderson and Orioles first baseman Eddie Murray.

As it turned out, George *did* bring back Billy to manage the Yankees for a fifth time. The return of Billy was akin to a show that has been running way past its prime, a sagging, codependent dance that started when Rickey was in high school. Billy would last only 60 games in 1988, taken down in a drunken spiral. Another hangover, another haze, another fight, this one at Lace, a topless bar in Texas where Billy got whomped by three dudes in a brawl that spilled into the men's bathroom. When the fists stopped flying, Billy needed 40 stitches.

Pamela never stayed with Rickey full-time in New York. She remained in California. Her position with Rickey was solidified by time but remained vague by definition. They had been together more than a decade, since she was a ninth-grader, but Rickey was still on his own program, still singular unto himself—when he wanted to be, that is. The baseball life was full of special friends—everybody knew that. Commitment was a fluid concept to Rickey, but it was not for Pamela. He was the one with whom she was going to invest her life, even if reciprocity was not always or easily a given.

New York was never her kind of place. "Too busy. Too noisy. Too dirty," she would say. Pamela protected Rickey against the energy of New York with hawklike intensity; her instincts told her that neither New York nor the Yankees, and especially Steinbrenner, were to be trusted. She read the papers, knew what they were saying about Rickey, and she could never quite understand why the commentaries always had to be so *personal.*

Certainly, the competition between a dozen news outlets was cutthroat—every sliver of information the competition did not have was a coup—but Pamela could never get comfortable with the sharp binaries of New York, where you were either a winner or a loser. To her, baseball in New York seemed to contradict the idea that sports brought people together. Oakland had its issues, and liberal San Francisco was sneakily a very racist place, but nothing in her background prepared Pamela for segregation on the East Coast, where the racial hostilities simmered and the slightest provocation threatened to ignite hostilities between neighborhoods—even between streets—that were decades in the making.

The New York that Rickey inhabited was a cauldron of racial tensions.

Eleanor Bumpurs's killing by police in the Bronx, the Bernie Goetz subway vigilante tabloid frenzy, the Central Park Five, the Tawana Brawley
rape case, the attacks and killings of Black youths in Howard Beach and
Bensonhurst—these were the incidents that made the headlines and were
covered obsessively by the tabloids (and now by the newest bottom-feeder,
tabloid television), but the racism and animosities between the races
hummed daily like a circuit breaker.

No one would have known that racial confrontation defined New York by
listening to the players, who did not utter a word about it. Winfield, Baylor,
and Rickey on the Yankees, Dwight Gooden, Darryl Strawberry, and Kevin
Mitchell on the Mets, Patrick Ewing and Bernard King on the Knicks, Lawrence Taylor on the Giants—the Black superstar players in the city were not
going to wade into the city's racial morass. Even players like Willie Randolph and Bernard King, who were *from* New York and were, as they liked
to say, "down by law," still knew better. "They were missing in action," recalled Rev. Al Sharpton. "When they were confronting racists in the South,
it was permitted to fight Archie Bunker. That's dumb, down-South rednecks.
But when we started fighting Howard Beach, the Northeastern crowd, now
you're attacking the cousins of the guys who own the team. Big difference."

Pamela could almost *feel* the marinating racism in the city, and that feeling manifested at the ballpark, where that boom-and-bust, hero-goat cycle
was particularly powerful. She would always be wary of New York and the
way it could turn on athletes and gleefully bury them. The Black Yankees
players always knew they would take the brunt of the city's anger if the team
did not perform.

Pamela most fondly recalled spending time with the Randolphs, Willie
and Gretchen, as a special place of refuge when she was in town. No one
knew the culture of the Yankees and the rhythms of the city better than
Willie Randolph. Willie was not only the elder statesman of the Yankees
and cocaptain of the team with Ron Guidry, but for incoming Black Yankees
in particular, he was Yankee royalty. He was Mr. Yankee and a native New
Yorker, having grown up in the Brownsville section of Brooklyn. Tough, serious, no nonsense, Willie was there for the revival.

Pamela came to rely on their dinners and gatherings with the families
of other Black Yankees as well, such as the Griffeys (who lived in the same
Hoboken high-rise as Rickey) and the Winfields, at the Randolphs' home in
New Jersey. Pamela recalled the hospitality of Gretchen and Willie Randolph

serving as a necessary counter to both the negativity of Rickey's miserable 1987 and the extreme virility that came with being around the Yankees. "The Yankees were definitely macho," Pamela recalled. "If there was anything the players needed, they definitely got it. The women were way in the back. We weren't really all that welcome." Willie Randolph remembered Pamela for her high, squeaky voice, without ever knowing that "Squeaky" had been her childhood nickname.

Pamela had paid especially close attention to Rickey in New York during the raw year of 1987 and sensed the contrast between how Rickey was treated in the newspapers, by the front office, and on the streets. New York might not have been her kind of city, but the energy was undeniable. In Oakland they would sometimes be noticed in public, but in New York fans always spotted Rickey. Pamela felt warmer about the New York fans, and closer to them.

Even including his injury-plagued 1987 season, Rickey in his first three seasons in New York averaged .288 with an on-base percentage of nearly .400 and a slugging percentage of nearly .500, as well as 23 home runs and 69 steals, but there were no numbers that could soothe the intense pressure of the biggest number: 0. That was the number of World Series the Yankees had won with Rickey in pinstripes, and in the free-agent, big-money era, there was no forgiveness for making all that money and not winning. The Yankees hadn't even made the playoffs with Rickey in uniform. It sometimes felt to Pamela that winning was not a shared sports experience between player, team, and city, but an obligation the player owed to the public.

What Pamela sensed personally during the time she spent in New York was part of a larger phenomenon. Like Reggie and Winfield before him, Rickey was in the first wave of multimillion-dollar free-agent Black players brought to an organization via trade or free agency to be the face of the franchise—and to play in what was uncharted, hostile territory. Reggie had done the impossible—three home runs in Game 6 of the 1977 World Series had returned the glory to New York after a 15-year winter of no championships and mostly bad baseball. But now Winfield, Rickey, and whoever else George signed to big money was expected to take on the impossible task of duplicating Reggie. Reggie had conquered New York by surviving it, however; at times he would tell the world how 1977 damned near broke him, and even if few people noticed, the most important part of the Reggie legend was that the experience did not break him.

The only salve for the daily humiliations of being a Black Yankee was Steinbrenner's money—and even that often wasn't enough. Don Baylor was aware that when Steinbrenner raged about the Yankees not playing well, he always seemed to focus on the Black players first. The Black players used to call the Yankee clubhouse "the ghetto," because their lockers were invariably bunched together in one concentrated area of the clubhouse. When Steinbrenner would zero in on Yankee outfielder Steve Kemp, for whom he'd traded and who had been a disappointment, the Black Yankees would often tease Kemp, telling him, "He must have mistaken you for being Black."

It was no accident—at least not to the Yankees' Black players—that the team's darkest period was forever symbolized by an unassuming Black player, a second baseman from the US Virgin Islands named Horace Clarke. Yankee fans would refer to the years 1965–1975 as "the Horace Clarke Yankees," or "the Horace Clarke years." Clarke was saddled with the decline of the Yankees as if he had been the can't-miss prospect who failed, bringing the franchise crashing down around his unmet expectations. The Black guy from the sorta foreign country with the funny name who wore glasses (and a batting helmet in the field) was too irresistible a target to not be scapegoated.

The Yankees of the 1960s had players they expected to carry them into a new era of glory, namely, the pitcher Mel Stottlemyre and the prized outfielder Bobby Murcer. Stottlemyre was a five-time All-Star who pitched for the Yankees in the 1964 World Series as a rookie. Murcer came to the Yankees in 1966 as a 19-year-old touted as "the next Mickey Mantle" (even as Mantle was still on the team). Murcer made the All-Star team four straight years. They were the best players on a bad team, and both Stottlemyre and Murcer would always be viewed fondly as True Yankees—a dispensation later bestowed upon Mattingly. Meanwhile, New York chose to define its worse period with Horace Clarke, a hardworking, unspectacular ballplayer who never deserved a moment of their scorn.

The Black players of the 1980s knew they would never receive such rehabilitative treatment, and they knew the equation: *When we win, it's our team. When we lose, its yours.* To be a Yankee who did not win a championship was to not be a true Yankee. Black Yankees never felt like True Yankees even when they won titles. Elston Howard was a 12-time All-Star and won four championships, but he never felt truly accepted. Roy White spent his entire 14-year career with the Yankees but was historically invisible—his name rarely came up as a True Yankee, despite winning the World Series in 1977 and 1978. Willie Randolph, the mainstay, won four pennants and two World Series championships as a player, six pennants and four World Series titles as a coach, played by all the rules, and never embarrassed the organization. Willie even risked his standing with the other Black players by appearing to undermine Winfield when Steinbrenner launched an all-out attempt to ruin his star player. But even Willie Randolph was never really a full part of the family.

The players were brought to New York to win. They were paid to win. Steinbrenner made it a point to remind his fan base how much he was paying his players to win, and he remarked more than once that he preferred the horses he raced to his players. (They were to him essentially the same thing.) "They have fat contracts and soft jobs," Steinbrenner said of his players after he fired Yogi. "If they don't like their lot in life they ought to try to be a cab driver or a policeman or firefighter in New York City and put their lives on the line every day."

As the salaries multiplied to heights that the average shoe salesman could never comprehend, so too did fans' resentment toward the players—resentment especially aimed at Black players they stereotyped as surly, overpaid, and ungrateful, as not realizing how good they had it. Steinbrenner's dog whistle to the ethnic whites who epitomized the city's idealized blue-collar self was never too far out of reach.

The players were well aware of this dynamic, which is why so many of the Black athletes held it all in, saying nothing because nothing good would come of airing their grievances. They knew all-white juries were not exactly sympathetic. They knew that, as 24/7 sports talk radio intensified, so would the scorn toward a ballplayer making 20 times the salary of fans stuck on the Major Deegan listening in their cars. In signing players, Steinbrenner was no Yawkey. He signed the best players, no matter their race. In brutalizing his players, Don Baylor would tell Claire Smith, George was "an equal-opportunity abuser." In a 1986 essay on the Yankees, the celebrated author David Halberstam would write, "If Tom Yawkey was flawed because he loved his players too much, Steinbrenner is flawed because he envies them their talent and youth and fame too much."

The Black players all knew the game treated them differently. They knew that at the two poles of a spectrum, a player who carried himself a bit too professionally was "uppity," and one who was a bit too carefree was a minstrel. Winfield was seen as the former. Rickey used to call Winfield "the businessman" for the way Winfield would walk into the clubhouse looking like a corporate lawyer or bond trader—tailored suit, silk tie, briefcase, newspaper under his arm.

Baylor would see what Pamela saw: the resentment toward a Black man who carried himself as if he were an executive, accomplished, peerless. Such people, when white, were called a success. Steinbrenner, already enraged by his own carelessness in negotiating Winfield's original contract, saw him as an affront and spent the majority of Winfield's Yankee career trying to discredit and ultimately destroy him.

When Winfield's memoir, *Winfield: A Player's Life*, hit the shelves in the summer of 1988, Steinbrenner demanded an apology. Winfield refused. Griffey stood by what Winfield said in the book—but he was now playing in Atlanta. Baylor did too, but by 1988 he was in Oakland, playing on what would be his third straight pennant winner. (Steinbrenner had traded him to Boston in 1986.) Randolph, the loyal, venerable Yankee, released a public statement that breached the tight relationship among the Black players in the Yankee clubhouse: Winfield, he said, had "betrayed his confidence."

"A lot of people are afraid of the truth. Ken Griffey is not. Neither am I. Grif and I knew that what Dave wrote was true. And we both publicly backed him," Baylor wrote in his 1989 book *Nothing but the Truth* with Claire Smith. "I did not side with Dave Winfield and against Willie Randolph. I think Willie probably shied away from the truth because of the pressures of just trying to survive."

For all of Reggie's bravado, he wanted to be accepted and respected for his intellect and his achievements. He especially wanted to be considered a True Yankee. He was, after all, the one who brought the franchise All the Way Back. The Yankees were timeless, and now, so too was he. The same was true for Winfield. The final paragraph of his book was telling:

> The fact is, if someone handed me the 1988 world championship today on a silver platter, I'd reach for it, hold back, and choose to play through it, experience it, all the disappointments, all the highs, play a major role. Only then will I have what I want: the continuing respect of the fans, and yes, even the begrudging respect of George Steinbrenner. I want it today for my accomplishments on the field, and down the line for what I accomplish afterwards. And I intend to accomplish a lot.

But Rickey? Outside of the 1985 strike incident, Rickey never carried on extensive feuds with Steinbrenner, the fans, or, in a larger sense, the media. And why? Because Rickey didn't *care* about a lifelong legacy with the New York Yankees, or about Steinbrenner's respect, begrudging or otherwise. Rickey wasn't defined by New York. His battle with Piniella and Steinbrenner stemmed from a specific grievance: the Yankees questioned his injury, which questioned his integrity. And the writers? They were entitled to his performance—not to him.

One of Rickey's teammates, left fielder Gary Ward, also known for drawing a sharp line between the public and the personal, saw similarities between Rickey and himself. "Rick's like me. He'll give you everything you need to know about him as a ballplayer, but do you need to know *everything* about him? Why do people need to know *everything* about the man, huh?"

No one could anoint Rickey. Only *he* could do that—by his play. As soon as the fans filed out of the stadium after the final out, the lights went out and the show was over. When the second part of Bryan Burwell's 1987 two-part profile of Rickey appeared in the *Daily News* on June 8 under the headline "Rickey's a Reggie on Field, Not Off," Rickey offered his insights into the limits of being known.

> Reggie was always the kind of guy who wanted to be noticed, loved being in the public eye at all times. He loves the bright lights, he digs being seen in the clubs, the bars, all that stuff. That's good for him, but I don't want the public eye when I leave the field. When you allow the public into your life too much, it's like they can't get enough. They start asking for a little bit here, then a lot there.

If Winfield was "the businessman" at the "uppity" end of the stereotype spectrum, Rickey trended toward the other pole—he was seen as the uneducated, streetwise, fast-walking, jive-talking con man, as evidenced by the suspicion surrounding his hamstring injury in 1987. Since entering the league, Rickey had never played fewer than 142 games in a full season, and yet the organization—and by extension the fans and the media—accepted the idea that a player as driven to succeed and break records as Rickey did not want to play.

After a season of insinuation, a second MRI in August revealed swelling in Rickey's right leg, confirming the hamstring injury he had been suffering from since late June. Even when exonerated by the team doctors—which was actually the story, considering that the organization had spent most of the season whispering that he was faking an important injury, which, besides throwing games, was the most serious charge that could be made against a player's integrity—Rickey was treated like a self-absorbed clown who refused to play hurt.

RICKEY WON'T PLAY UNTIL HE'S RICKEY AGAIN

Rickey Henderson came out of his shell Saturday and went on the disabled list. Laughing. He and his "hammy" are officially out until a week from Monday.

"Now everyone will realize there was something wrong with me," he said. "Now everyone will realize I wasn't dogging it or jaking it."

Now, Rickey Henderson, in a convoluted way is happy, even though his hamstring hurts because everyone else knows his hamstring hurts.

That's the Rickey Henderson way.

Watch him in the locker room or on the field. Everything has to be just so. Every curl of his hair has to be perfectly in place. His baseball pants and stirrup socks have to be just right . . . Rickey Henderson never *ever* wants to be seen as imperfect.

So, Rickey Henderson gets hurt. How badly he gets hurt only he truly knows.

Rickey Henderson loves talking about Rickey Henderson. Rickey Henderson loves being Rickey Henderson. On this sparkling afternoon, he felt like talking and being himself again because he could be sure of himself again. Most important, everyone else could be sure of him.

Rickey's ascension happened during a period of suffocating resentment toward ballplayers, and it wasn't just about money. A cultural anger was being expressed toward professional athletes who were shedding the infantile, boyhood fantasy trope of having always wanted to be a ballplayer in favor of behaving like businessmen—or like that word baseball people hated so much, an "entertainer." The public saw the players not as providing the service of entertainment as much as being lucky to be blessed with a body capable of throwing a baseball 60 feet, six inches, at 95 miles per hour, and not one stricken with a debilitating illness at birth. Much of the public believed that in exchange for that good fortune ballplayers were prohibited from complaining about anything—work conditions, salary, racism, everything.

Besides a public willing to pay to watch what ballplayers could do with their wonderful, healthy bodies, there was a cabal of rich, white men who were willing to underwrite the entire industry that allowed them to do it. There could be no mistaking the racial element of this thinking. The cabal comprised almost exclusively rich, white men, in every sport. With the exception of the Mets' Joan Payson and the notorious Marge Schott of Cincinnati, the women prominent in the owners' boxes in baseball had married into them, which was a purchase of a different sort. Marriage bought their way into the boys' club, whether they wanted to be in it or not. It was the white men, the sportsmen like Yawkey and Briggs and Griffith, family scions and later heads of corporations, who made it all possible.

The customs of this sports world were both quaint and uncomfortable. There was the understanding that sports owners were called "owners," even though in all other American businesses owners were called "chairmen" or "managing partners." There was the expectation that the players would refer to them as "mister," even though many of the players would one day become millionaires themselves dozens of times over. From "Mister" Steinbrenner to "Mister" O'Malley to "Mister" Yawkey, the owners reveled in being called owners—that is, until the players, most notably the Black ones, extended the ownership metaphor and reminded the public that if they were indeed "owned," then their place of business just might be a "plantation." One player in particular, West Oakland's Curt Flood, extended the metaphor even further: if ballplayers were on a plantation, then they were "slaves."

The public also believed that in exchange for the players' good fortune, the owners deserved deference from them—most notably and especially from the Black players. After all, they weren't likely to become stockbrokers, and so they should be grateful that an industry existed in America that could turn the generally useless ability to run really fast into a multimillion-dollar asset that pulled them out of the ghetto or rural poverty. As the money they earned just to hit a ball with a stick mushroomed into eight figures, the public's anger about this kind of money acquired an edge: if these liberated Black players appeared to act too entitled, the public would remind them, "We made you."

In one form or another, all Black players, whatever their background, heard so much about their good fortune in being admitted to the body-breaking grind of professional sports that they were often made to feel like nothing more than lucky recipients of the rich man's benevolence, rather than professionals who scratched and fought to become world-class at what they did.

When Burwell, who would become a nationally known columnist for the *St. Louis Post-Dispatch,* worked on his two-part Rickey profile for the *Daily News,* Rickey asked him to avoid the clichés that so many white writers had used to describe him. "Do me a favor," Rickey said. "Make sure folks understand this was not your typical 'Black kid from poor ghetto family is raised by his mother 'cause his father left,' okay?"

The Black players on the Yankees and throughout professional sports were all targets of the hostilities that Pamela saw being directed toward Rickey, for Rickey not only rose to prominence in a time of multimillion-dollar contracts but also represented the end of an era that sports executives and fans were not ready to see depart. If Ruth and Gehrig, Waner and DiMaggio represented the immigration era, a time when sports introduced a generation of European kids to America, and Joe Louis, Willie Mays, Jackie Robinson, and Bill Russell were the first Black athletes of the integration era to compete, as a group, with whites and bring about the end of Jim Crow America, then Reggie, Winfield, and Rickey—along with Joe Namath and Nolan Ryan and other star white athletes—represented the money era. The players were now on the path to becoming super-rich. The humble days of Willie Mays playing stickball in Harlem after a game were being replaced by millionaires fighting billionaires for a greater share of the television money.

Rickey did not arrive in New York hat in hand, happy to be there. He believed that he was free—free to talk back to the fans or the newspapers, free not to sign autographs if he wasn't in the mood or if some snotty fan acted like a little shit to him, free to yell at umpires, free to be polite or rude, and free to publicly demand to be compensated what he believed he was worth.

The image of the liberated, rich, and distant Black player of the 1980s was heavily complicated by the drug scandals that plagued baseball and basketball during the same period. If the owners were still secretly (and not so secretly) pining for the Great White Hope—the clean-cut Midwestern boy who could sell beer and tickets and cars to the overwhelmingly white paying customers—the drug trials in Pittsburgh of several high-profile ballplayers made owners even more unconvinced that Black players could sell tickets—a fear since Jackie Robinson first integrated the postwar game. Black players could not be trusted as the face of a ball club. Even without drug issues, baseball executives did not often believe the sport could be sold through black players—especially if they were going to be impolitic about the game's past as Rickey had been. Even the great Maury Wills, now the Seattle manager, lost parts of his career to drugs. Oil Can Boyd, briefly the ace of the Red Sox staff before Roger Clemens, would say that he had been capable of winning 150 games in the big leagues, but had done so much coke that he never got any sleep. When substance abuse took down big-name, All-Star Black players—Willie Wilson, Willie Aikens, Darryl Strawberry, Dwight Gooden, Dave Parker—suspicion about their reliability only deepened.

That some Black players were drug users heightened the potency of long-existing racist attitudes and was used to justify the racial hierarchies and double standards embedded in the sport. Rickey Style might be entertaining, and Rickey's athletic gifts staggering, but he would never easily be taken seriously as a professional. Alvin Dark, who won pennants with both Reggie Jackson and Willie Mays, said in 1964 that Blacks and Latinos weren't committed ballplayers the way white players were. "We have trouble because we have so many Negro and Spanish-speaking players on this team. They are just not able to perform up to the white ballplayers when it comes to mental alertness. You can't make most Negro and Spanish-speaking players have the pride in their team that you get from white players."

With their afros and flashy cars and suits and styles, Black players talking about what they were *owed* just landed differently—even if the difference was rarely addressed by anyone in the game as candidly as Alvin Dark did. The Black players—Winfield, Baylor, Rickey, Griffey—all knew that the stereotypes prevailed in the front office and the press boxes, in the row houses, at the concourses, and on the subway. "Dark would sit in the lobby and wait for the players to see which Black players would come into the hotel with white girls," Jim Guinn recalled. "We used to tell all the Black players not to be messing with those white girls. That would get you released. That was the only thing you couldn't rehab from."

Black players knew the drug scandals would stick to them as a group in a way that didn't happen with white players, even though cocaine was roaring through Hollywood, Wall Street, the white suburbs, and the white white-collars, tearing families apart as certainly as it was ravaging the Black underclass. It was those stereotypes that prevented Black players from becoming True Yankees. They knew that Rickey's lack of interest in giving a postgame interview would stick to him in a way that cocaine use by Keith Hernandez, Steve Howe, and Paul Molitor would not; that Mattingly's feud with Steinbrenner over money was not the equivalent of Reggie presenting the same grievance; that Winfield's aspirations as a businessman looked different to the public than Steinbrenner's; and that showing up to the team holiday party with a white woman in the 1980s would not be much more comfortable than it would have been in the 1950s.

Billy Sample recalled Steinbrenner reflecting the fear that drugs would destroy the Yankee name—and in those days the Yankees featured several star-level Black players. Steinbrenner had already raged to the Commissioner's Office that the Pittsburgh trials were killing the game and the sport needed to act unilaterally—drug-test all the players preemptively, George insisted. In response, Winfield, the Yankee player representative with the union, would stand up to Steinbrenner, who already saw him as uppity, in front of the entire team.

"Dave would come in with his briefcase, put it down, and go to work. He was an erudite kind of guy. When he would talk to the owners, I would tell him I had to look up a few of those words," Sample said. "George had gone crazy. He was yelling at us, 'People in Indiana don't ask about the Yankees anymore! They ask about drug testing!' You could cut the tension with a knife. George had it in his mind that he could force the players into what he wanted. Dave looked at him and said, 'We'll give you our answer as a group, as a union.' That was a big move. He showed me something there, talking to someone unused to being spoken back to, especially from a player. That wasn't easy to do."

Rickey was part of the first generation of Black players who came of age after the civil rights era and who expected freedom to be a given, not something granted. But any Black players and fans who thought the game had put prejudice in the past were disavowed of that notion in 1987, when Al Campanis said that Black people lacked the "necessities" to fill executive or managerial positions in baseball.

"They used to talk about uppity niggers all the time. Big talkers. You know, when Reggie said he was the straw that stirred the drink?" Rickey said. "Now we got all this money too? People didn't like that. They really, really didn't like that."

E ITHER THROUGH A front-office leak or public proclamation to the tabloids from The Boss himself, the Yankees sent a message to the other 25 teams arriving at the Marriott Marquis in Atlanta for the 1988 winter meetings: everyone was available. Jack Clark? Traded to San Diego after one season. Rick Rhoden, the guy for whom they traded young Doug Drabek, future 20-game winner, ace of the staff, and Cy Young winner Doug Drabek? Gone to Houston. Claudell Washington? Gone to the Angels when the Yankees told him 34 was too old for a multiyear contract. Even the captains, Willie Randolph and Ron Guidry, the last remaining links to the championship days? Gone and gone—Willie to the Dodgers, Guidry to retirement.

Steinbrenner's scorched-earth tour left no untouchables. None, not even the headliners. That included Mattingly, the great Donnie Baseball whose relationship with the New York fans was legendary, but with Steinbrenner was never exactly harmonious. Mattingly had won the MVP in 1985, played all 162 games and should have won it again in 1986, but when injuries limited him to 141 and 144 games, respectively, in 1987 and 1988, even Donnie Baseball was now on the trade block.

When Mattingly was under team control, Steinbrenner was never particularly willing to pay him, despite calling him a Hall of Famer in his second season, despite that 238-hit season, the MVP, the crazy eight-straight-game homer streak, and all the talk about Donnie being a True Yankee. When Mattingly signed to stay, to be the anchor, Steinbrenner was further emboldened to trash him. Mattingly grew tired of Steinbrenner undermining the players, calling favored reporters to criticize them, and relentlessly destabilizing a good team, one that had been close to winning. The previous

August, Mattingly, who only wanted to play baseball, had finally let Steinbrenner have it. "They give you money. That's it, not respect," Mattingly said.
"There's never been respect here and that's not going to change . . . If you
don't have any respect for me, I don't have any respect for you and I don't
want to play here. I'll have fun playing somewhere."

Over the last 15 years of his life, which saw the second Yankee rebirth
under his ownership, Steinbrenner would be recast with the warm patina
of nostalgia as the tough but uncompromising leader, committed only to
winning and the Yankees, no matter what the cost. Willing to spend to give
New York the victors the city deserved, he would be seen as the guy who put
his money where his mouth was instead of being a panhandler like Minnesota's Carl Pohlad or Oakland's Steve Schott, welfare queen owners who
were richer than him on paper but who cried poverty and wanted handouts
to run their baseball teams—and then pocketed baseball's new revenue-
sharing money once they got it. To an America beset by the greatest wealth
gap in the country's history, Steinbrenner came off heroically. The Boss was
no longer gauche: he was the grandpa with the old-school values who still
had some fire left. Anybody born before 1980 knew better—that the real
Steinbrenner, in his prime, had been brutal, and the greatest impediment to
winning faced by those Yankee teams.

The Yankees' new senior vice present was Syd Thrift—the same Syd
Thrift who, as Oakland's scouting director in 1976, had been too busy to take
Rickey seriously as a prospect, then fell out of a tree and landed on his feet
when Rickey lasted until the fourth round. Thrift was working on a deal to
send Mattingly to Texas, but Mattingly remained a Yankee after the Rangers
landed Rafael Palmeiro, a promising young first baseman, in a deal with the
Cubs.

Also on the trade block was Winfield, whom Steinbrenner was not only
trying to trade but to destroy. Steinbrenner never got past the 1980 negotiations surrounding Winfield's original contract, when he either overlooked
or misunderstood the cost-of-living escalator clause included in the deal
and blundered into signing a deal worth $23 million—more than double the
$11 million he believed to be the value of the contract. Steinbrenner vowed
revenge, and while he plotted, nothing Winfield did on the field could ever
be good enough to make things right.

Throughout the 1980s, in the words of Jack O'Connell, who covered
the team for the *Hartford Courant* and the other Gannett papers, Winfield

"busted his ass for this town." Winfield drove in 899 runs. Only Baltimore's Eddie Murray and Philadelphia's Mike Schmidt—two guys who would both hit 500 home runs and be enshrined in Cooperstown as first-ballot Hall of Famers—drove in more. Winfield scored 804 runs. Only Schmidt, Milwaukee's Robin Yount, and Rickey—all of them also future first-ballot Hall of Famers—scored more. Winfield ripped 1,441 hits. Only Kansas City Royals speedster Willie Wilson, Yount, and Murray hit more. Dave Winfield was durable, played great defense, and ran the bases. He did everything.

But George never liked Winfield—he wasn't Reggie. The Yankees didn't make the playoffs after Reggie left, which stung even more deeply when Mr. October took California to the ALCS the year after Steinbrenner let him walk and gave the dynasty's keys to Winfield. He was convinced that Winfield was a phony, that he was nothing close to his clean public image. He also did not believe that Winfield contained that winning mystique—that thing Reggie and all the winners had. Steinbrenner, who had been trying to trade Winfield at least since 1984, maybe earlier, had vowed to ruin him. To dig up dirt on his own player, undermine his reputation, and crush his life, Steinbrenner consorted with con men and lowlifes. Steinbrenner's obsession with Winfield ran so deep that his vendetta eventually got him suspended from baseball. His absence led to the revival of the Yankees in the mid-1990s.

Steinbrenner's willingness to trade the entire team also meant Rickey.

On Christmas Day 1988, two weeks after the winter meetings, Rickey celebrated his 30th birthday. He had just completed his 10th season in the big leagues. Billy had told him that he belonged in New York, and Rickey in turn had put together a formidable body of work there.

When he arrived in 1985, the club's single-season stolen-base record, Fritz Maisel's, had stood for 70 years. In four seasons, Rickey had broken it three times. The top three names on the Yankees' single-season stolen-base list? Rickey, Rickey, and Rickey. Ever since Jackie Robinson had integrated the 20th-century big leagues in 1947, compelling the great white players to compete with *all* the world's ballplayers, no Yankee would score more runs in a season than Rickey's 146 in 1985. In just four years, Rickey was already the Yankees' *career* stolen-base leader, a record that Derek Jeter, the Yankees' eventual career leader, would need 18 seasons to break. Rickey didn't just steal bases: he stole bases and rarely got caught. When Rickey's sore hamstrings opened the door for Harold Reynolds to break his streak of seven straight single-season stolen-base titles, Reynolds stole 60 bases but got caught 20 times—a 75 percent success rate. In his first four seasons in New York, Rickey had stolen 301 bases at an 86 percent success rate.

By leading the AL in steals in 1987 and breaking Rickey's seven-year stranglehold on the top spot, Reynolds experienced one of the most famous Rickey moments. After winning his first stolen-base title, Reynolds was home one day when the phone rang. He picked up and heard a voice. No hello. No identification. The voice, however, was unmistakable. It was Rickey.

"Sixty bases?" Rickey said to Reynolds. "Man, Rickey got 60 by the All-Star break." Then he hung up.

Rickey scored 1,009 runs in the 1980s, more runs than any player in baseball over the decade. He was also the only player with 1,000 runs scored, with 163 more—the equivalent of a run a game over the course of a season—than Yount, who was second.

Rickey was always a disruption, but in the New York years he became a uniquely devastating player, as his exiled old manager Steve Boros had prophesized he would years earlier. In Oakland, he had gotten everyone's attention, but in a home run game he didn't hit homers. The only thing Rickey couldn't do in Oakland was drive himself in. Bob Boone, Rickey's greatest catching nemesis, recalled his advice at pre-series team meetings before Angels-A's games. "If you stopped *him,* you stopped *them,*" Boone said. "That team really was a very different team when Rickey wasn't on base. They were nowhere near as dangerous."

But make a mistake throwing to Rickey in New York? After Willie Horton had taught him to launch the ball? Trouble. "Throw something in the wrong spot and—*BAM*—Rickey's gonna get you," he would say of himself with an assassin's smile, "and I'mma tell you, it's not gonna feel good."

Rickey had leadoff power but didn't chase. You had to come to him— "and when you did, he was taking your ass bridge," remembered Dennis Eckersley. New York was where it all happened—where Rickey became complete. Before Rickey arrived in New York, he'd hit 51 career home runs in six years. In his first two years with the Yankees, he hit 52. "Initially, you always knew he was going to run, but then the type of hitter he became? He could do anything he wanted," said Eckersley. "Took any base he wanted. Let you know about it. I'm one to talk so I can't say anything about it, but I loved that swagger. And he was from Oakland. That fucking guy let you *know* he was good."

Ten years in baseball is not merely a good round number to begin the historical assessment of a player; it is also the minimum service time required for a player to be considered for immortality—enshrinement in the Hall of Fame after being elected by the Baseball Writers' Association of America (BBWAA). Some observers don't wait that long, though. Moss Klein referred to Mattingly as "Hall of Fame–bound" in print long before Donnie Baseball had reached his 10 years of service. In January 1989, Klein reflected on Dwight Evans, the underrated Boston right fielder. Evans had been overshadowed early by the legend of the great Carl Yastrzemski, who owned the town when Evans arrived in 1972; then by Carlton Fisk, the New Englander who became a star in Boston; and then by the super rookies, the Gold Dust Twins, Jim Rice and Fred Lynn, with whom he shared the outfield. "Most people, even Red Sox fans, do not regard Evans as a Cooperstown candidate. They may be underestimating him again," Klein wrote. A few months earlier, before the winter meetings and after his salacious extramarital affair threatened the clubhouse to the point where the Red Sox considered trading Wade Boggs, Klein wrote in the November 28, 1988, issue of *The Sporting News,* "Another criticism leveled at Boggs is that he's a selfish player, that he's too aware of his statistics. Heck, with the kind of statistics he puts together, how could he not be aware of them? They're historical. Boggs is headed for the Hall of Fame, an automatic."

The New York writers did not view Rickey as a Hall of Fame "automatic," nor did they condone his awareness of his own place in the game and his numbers as the acceptable self-recognition of a great player, a dispensation Klein afforded Boggs. He was the fastest player in history to reach 400, 500, 600, and 700 stolen bases and was headed toward an absolute destruction of a record (in the American League) that had stood since before the Great Depression. Rickey was the most dangerous leadoff threat in the game, quite possibly of all time. His 794 stolen bases in 10 years put him already at fourth all-time. He was 103 steals behind Ty Cobb's American League record and 144 behind Lou Brock's all-time mark. Cobb had stolen 897 bases over 24 years and 3,034 games. Brock stole 938 bases over 19 years and 2,616 games. Rickey's 794 steals came in just 1,322 games, and he got most of them in New York, where he had added the Rickey Special, the leadoff home run—a run scored and RBI with one swing of the bat.

Most of the writers responded to Rickey's 10th year in the big leagues, however, with silence rather than retrospectives. When they talked about him, it was to telegraph to the public what the organization apparently was saying privately: the Yankees wanted him out.

The writers often pulled off a clever sleight of hand when it came to Rickey. They would talk about the great Yankees record when he was in the lineup, ostensibly as proof of their respect for his game and for how formidable and important a player he was. The compliments sometimes sounded backhanded, however: instead of noting the Yankees' mediocrity when he was out of the lineup because of injury, they expressed exasperation that he was taking more time to recover than they thought necessary, and they rarely commented on the seriousness of his injury. Whether the writers were exhibiting the old prejudices that questioned Black players' toughness and commitment to winning or were just tired of Rickey and his idiosyncrasies, one unshakable fact remained: they did not believe his injuries were legitimate, and the whispers around the organization empowered them to question the seriousness of his pain.

A year earlier, at the 1988 All-Star break, Klein used his column in *The Sporting News* to say as much. It wasn't that Klein didn't know a Hall of Fame talent when he saw one. It was that when it came to Rickey, he simply did not believe he was in the presence of an all-time great player:

> If the Yankees fade out in the AL East, don't be surprised if they try to trade Rickey Henderson. In fact, if it weren't for his dazzling potential and what his talent could mean in a pennant drive, some of the Yanks' decision-makers would like to trade him now. Henderson wouldn't be easy to trade because he has a no-trade clause, his salary for 1989 is $1.95 million, and he's eligible to become a free agent after next season. But many Yankees have grown tired of his prolonged absences for minor injuries. With all his talent, it's a shame he's not a better player.

You didn't have to be a Pinkerton to decipher the code words used here to talk about Rickey: he was one of the best in the game "when he wanted to play"; the Yankees were exasperated with his "prolonged absences for minor injuries"; and a "motivated" Henderson was a dangerous threat. Klein and the rest of the media had come to the same conclusion: Rickey wasn't giving his best effort.

While there was no question that members of the Yankees' front office wanted Rickey gone—whether it was George or Piniella or that combination of scouts and spies described as "sources within the organization"—there was also no question that who held the lens mattered. All 26 *Sporting News* baseball correspondents—freelancers who covered the teams full-time for local newspapers, the pens and the pads shaping the story for the public— were white men. So were the half-dozen big-time national columnists writing for the magazine, as were, with the exception of Ralph Wiley, all of the big-time national mag guys at *Sports Illustrated.* A Black writer would show up here and there, last for a cup of coffee, and either flame out or go cover the NBA.

The visibility of *The Sporting News* in those days was enormous, and its influence on opinion—with both millions of fans and the game's insiders— represented power within the industry. Boston's Peter Gammons in the AL and Philadelphia's Bill Conlin in the NL—along with Klein and Peter Pascarelli—were the names that Boston and Philadelphia fans knew from reading their local papers, but because of *The Sporting News,* fans around the country knew those names as well. These writers were the gatekeepers— many of them the same gatekeepers who, before his tragic and valiant death made him a martyr, had called the great Roberto Clemente a "hypochondriac." They told the fans who the players were—who was jaking it and who they should pay to see. After all, for decades *The Sporting News* had been called "the Baseball Bible." And who argues with the Bible?

What could the writers possibly know about Rickey? Writing down what someone says is worlds away from understanding them. Moreover, Rickey understood more about the press than the press gave him credit for. Rickey said he never read the papers (all the players said it), but he knew what they were writing and who they were writing *for;* they certainly weren't writing primarily for the Black baseball fans, so many of whom enjoyed his flair and did not automatically see his on-field style as a reflection of unprofessionalism. To many in the white baseball establishment, style made a player unserious, a "hot dog"—a term rarely used to describe white players.

Whether they were being malicious or putting the team's needs first because they had to navigate the occupational hazards of giving readers what they cared most about, the writers were already often in the club's hip pocket. They were certainly committed to the club's point of view on labor issues: unless they were pointing out how much money a player was earning, writers treated complex money issues like Kryptonite. Following the Seitz decision in 1975, the baseball world had changed overnight—and not just for the players. When Rickey arrived, virtually all of the big-time writers earned more money than he did. They not only drank with the players but often bought the rounds. And even as the racial composition of the game was quickly changing—baseball had turned Latin America into its own personal sweatshop—none of the writers spoke Spanish, and virtually none ever would.

If there was a writer who produced consistently thoughtful pieces about Rickey that in turn produced less guarded, more candid responses from him, it was Claire Smith of the *Hartford Courant*. As unique as Rickey might have appeared in baseball, there was no one in the game more unique than Smith. When the *Courant* put her on the Yankees beat in 1983, she was the game's first female beat writer in its 114-year history. That she was a Black woman covering baseball made her even more of a rarity—and put two strikes against her in the clubhouse.

When she arrived, Billy was the manager, and he would not acknowledge a woman. "Things started off really rough. Billy didn't trust anyone he didn't know, and I don't think he had ever been covered by a woman. I don't know if they were hazing me, but I remember asking the other writers what time the bus was for a spring training road trip, and when I got to the bus, I was the only writer there. I stepped onto the first bus with great trepidation. Billy and the coaches were hostile. Very hostile. I thought I was going to be physically thrown off the bus. Billy shouted, 'GET OUT! GET ON THE OTHER BUS!'

"I got on the second bus, turned to the window, and tried not to cry. I was just thrown off the bus by a manager I was supposed to cover and didn't know how I was going to because he was so hostile. Jeff Torborg was a person I really liked. He was a person I had a lot in common with. We didn't do bars, and he was just a gentleman to the nth degree. George had given Jeff a personal services contract, so Billy never trusted Jeff and always gave him a hard time. It was a five-, six-hour bus trip, and Jeff came over and offered me some food. I refused. He said, 'You're going to have to eat something,' and then he said, 'You're always welcome on our bus.'"

When it came to writing about Rickey, Smith did not use the offended language of her white male counterparts, perhaps because she was not concerned about Rickey upsetting the great, grand traditions of the sport (she was, by her very presence in the press box, upsetting them too), and in turn Rickey talked to her with a depth and candor he rarely shared with other writers. There was the one Black baseball writer around the country, Larry Whiteside in Boston, but Claire Smith was the only full-time Black baseball writer who had ever covered Rickey in his home city.

As the tensions between Rickey and the media increased, he had to finally confront the fact that he was paying for his distance. Over the decades there would be players who made impossible, impractical demands, like Boston's Jim Rice, only to be judged on their numbers. But the game was not played by computer. The baseball life was full of daily interactions with virtually no respite—45 straight days of spring training, then a game every day with travel days sprinkled throughout the 162-game calendar. Rickey was a difficult personality, at once private and outgoing. He failed to remember names not only because it was a difficult skill for him, but also because he was not always that interested in happenings or people around him. His single-mindedness was not uncommon among high-achieving athletes, and it explained to some degree how he was always able to perform, regardless of whatever was going on around him.

As much as the writers wanted to have it both ways—depicting Rickey as a sitcom clown yet not understanding why he wouldn't cultivate them—Rickey wanted it both ways too. "Rickey, he was a character," Dave Winfield would say, using a polite dodge to avoid criticizing a teammate.

Invariably a teammate's anecdotes about Rickey would involve Rickey initially not wanting to play in a given game but, after some psychological coaxing from the teammate, going out and giving a command performance. Winfield himself would recall the time in 1985 when the Yankees were surging and Rickey wasn't feeling great but still stole a ton of bases and had three hits—all because Winfield appealed to him. Like so many Rickey stories, these anecdotes seemed apocryphal and self-serving, but they all had one thing in common: his teammates routinely felt that they needed to convince Rickey to play. When the Yankees let Willie Randolph sign a free-agent deal with the Dodgers, he said on his way out the door, "Now that I'm gone, who's going to get Rickey to play?"

So many versions of the same story created an aura of authenticity that Rickey would fight for his entire career. There was a code of professionalism that Rickey flaunted, the story went, and if the other players could not do the same, they concluded, then he couldn't either. Not that he would ever change. When Rickey would show up late to spring training, he invariably produced the same explanation: his grandmother was sick. One year, after hearing it one time too often, Don Baylor asked Claire Smith, "How many grandmothers does Rickey have?"

When it came to baseball, Rickey had been writing his own rules since he was in middle school, when Hank Thomasson would drive to Rickey's house to be his personal alarm clock, assistant, and car service. There was the story that during 1987, while Rickey was recovering from his hamstring, the Yankees held a team meeting in which some players admonished Rickey. The Yankees were still in the race, they said, and felt that with him in the lineup the Yankees could win it. They told Rickey that because he was refusing to play hurt, he was "messing with their playoff money," to which Rickey replied, "If they want their money so bad, why don't *they* go out and steal 80 bases?"

Whatever the Yankees' shortcomings, or his own, and however frustrated the press corps was with him, Rickey was undeniably a superstar on a Hall of Fame trajectory. He had proven that he wouldn't wilt under the pressure of the Big Town and put up the biggest offensive numbers of his career—all while playing for the most dysfunctional owner in professional sports.

When Rickey arrived in Fort Lauderdale for spring training (on Rickey Time, of course), he was already in the crosshairs of Dallas Green, the new manager who replaced Piniella.

When Green was hired in the winter of 1988, Rickey had rolled out the welcome mat for his new skipper Rickey Style: "I don't have to adjust to him," he said. "He has to adjust to me." When camp opened (without Rickey), Green told the writers, "Rickey Henderson is not going to run the Yankees in 1989. Dallas Green is." Green told the players that he wanted them in camp on February 23. Mattingly was already there, and so was Winfield. Green said that the Yankees had sent Henderson two letters outlining when he was to report to camp. When Rickey was a no-show on the first day, Green told the writers, "Maybe Rickey can't read."

Rickey arrived two days later, on February 25. According to the *Times*, Rickey entered the clubhouse around 9:15 in the morning, "wearing shades and singing a tune to himself." He hadn't arrived on the 23rd, he said, because "I had business." Rickey went to Baltimore, Atlanta, and Miami and arrived in camp two days after the date Green stipulated but before the March 1 mandatory reporting date stated in the collective bargaining agreement. "My reporting date was when I finished my business. I finished, then I came," Rickey told the paper. "They say I'm two days late. I think I'm five days early."

The players blew it off. Rickey was being Rickey. Green was angry that he had an insubordinate left fielder who was immediately undermining his authority. The writers described Rickey as being "two days late," when in fact Rickey was correct: the mandatory reporting date was March 1. He faced no fines or official discipline since he had arrived before March 1, but despite the empowering voice of Marvin Miller, the strikes and the lockouts, the fights to free players from the game's paternalism, decades of conditioning affected the reactions of the players and the writers. "Voluntary" was viewed as "mandatory," and the writers treated Rickey just as Green hoped they would—as late to camp, as not a team player, as a problem.

"He wasn't late," Rick Rhoden, now in Houston, told the *Times.* "There were guys who showed up here the day before March 1. He didn't have to be there. They were invited to be there Feb. 23. What would they have done if no one showed up? It was his prerogative to be there Feb. 23 or March 1."

The new manager was an old hard-ass. In his first season as a major league manager, 45-year-old Dallas Green had led the 1980 Philadelphia Phillies to the World Series title (after 96 seasons—a century—of spectacular failure in which the Phillies finished in either last or second-to-last place 37 times, or 38 percent of the time). It was the Phillies' first championship since entering the National League in 1883 as the Philadelphia Quakers. (They finished last that year.) Green left the Phillies after the 1981 strike year to take a GM job with the Cubs, and he had yelled and screamed his way out of favor in Chicago by the time Steinbrenner called.

A six-foot-five hulk of a drill sergeant who got tough with the players, showing them who's in charge, Green looked the part. That played well to the hard hats who bought the tickets and consumed the sports talk radio and were tired of the rich and spoiled ballplayers and loved when the new manager put the flashy Black guys they didn't think were raised right in their place, especially the ones who thought they could show up whenever they wanted, no matter what union protections they had (usually the same union protections the talk-radio listeners wanted from *their* jobs). The writers loved ol' Dallas because he was a straight-talking East Coaster from blue-collar Delaware—and because he had no problem criticizing his players in print.

The morning of Rickey's arrival, he and Green went behind closed doors. The two emerged laughing, but underneath the humor was great unease. Green saw Rickey's two-day absence as undermining his authority. Rickey saw Green as another crewcut who thought the best way to get the most out of players was by stepping on their backs. If Steinbrenner wasn't bad enough, now the Yankees players had *two* guys on their asses.

"I think we all expected it to a degree, didn't we?" Green said of Rickey arriving after the voluntaries began. "It's Rickey just being Rickey. I think he recognizes that things are different with a new manager, new coaches, and new players, and I would think that as a leader on the team he would see fit to come in with the group."

After the meeting, Rickey and Green both said that they considered the issue resolved. Rickey was in camp, ready to go, but he hadn't appreciated Green's suggestion that he was not only illiterate but stupid. "I don't know if he's smart enough to know what he's really doing, whether it's spiteful, or if he doesn't know what's going on," Green told the writers. Before the two men had ever met, Green was taking a tough-guy approach with Rickey based on his reputation. He'd heard all about how Billy spoiled him—everyone in baseball knew that—and Green's response was that Rickey hadn't been yelled at in the right way. Rickey wouldn't forget that, and had no time for Dallas Green. "The manager has got to say what he feels," Rickey said upon arrival, "but as far as him saying that I can't read, he doesn't need to say that."

Nor did Rickey forget Green yukking it up with the writers at his expense with a little theory as to why he hadn't arrived on the 23rd: he was "getting lucky" with Margo Adams, the mistress of Red Sox third baseman Wade Boggs. "At least we found out where he is. He's over at Margo's getting a little luck," Green told the *Hartford Courant*. "I hope Margo does a good job on him. Maybe he'll get that elusive MVP he's been looking for."

Adams had spilled the beans about her tryst with Boggs to *Penthouse* magazine, also revealing Boggs's racial animus toward his Black teammates Jim Rice and Oil Can Boyd, and the scandal had hurt the Red Sox and Boggs so badly that Boggs, dutiful wife Debbie by his side, conducted a nationally televised mea culpa interview about the affair on ABC with Barbara Walters.

Years later, in *Off Base*, Rickey would say that Green was the kind of manager who spent more time tearing down his players than building them up.

Pamela was also aware of Green's little joke about Margo Adams. She would become great friends with Debbie Boggs, and neither woman was laughing.

Rickey had two issues on his mind in the early days of spring. The first was a new contract. Eligible to become a free agent at the end of the season, he told Thrift that he wanted to remain a Yankee. Rickey wasn't pleading, as in the past, but staking out a negotiating position. He owned a no-trade contract and could veto any potential deal the Yankees might be considering. The team needed his consent to move him, and that gave him leverage. He was earning $2.1 million, and any team interested in him would be confident that it could sign him to a long-term deal rather than risk acquiring him in midseason, giving up players and/or farm prospects, only to watch him leave as a free agent after a couple of months when the season ended.

Richie Bry told the Yankees—both Thrift and the GM Bob Quinn—that Rickey wanted to stay in New York, but also wanted a long-term deal in place by the All-Star break. Otherwise, Rickey was content to play the rest of the season with the Yankees and then become a free agent. If they wanted him then, Bly told the Yankees, they could compete with the other 25 teams for his services.

There was another issue Rickey discussed with Green during their closed-door meeting on the 25th. The 1988 Yankees were a good team, far better than their sputtering fifth-place finish. Rickey told Green that it wasn't Boston that had doomed them, but too many guys leaving their fastballs with the empty bottles of Wild Turkey and Coors Light.

HENDERSON: BOOZING COST YANKEES THE PENNANT

When Rickey Henderson arrived to spring training two days later than everyone else, his teammates didn't think much of it. "Rickey's just being Rickey" was the general response.

A couple days later, however, Henderson drew a far different response from the other Yankee players when he claimed that his teammates' excessive drinking had cost the Yankees the pennant in 1988.

"I saw too many people getting drunk," Henderson said. "How can you perform the next day? Liquor doesn't leave you overnight. You have to know when to party and when not to party."

Now *that* got everyone's attention. So did the back page of the *Post* when it dropped the headline "The Bronx Boozers." The stories said that Rickey had named names: Tim Stoddard, Bob Shirley, and Neil Allen, all pitchers. In one story, Rickey even said that he once had to carry a stone-cold wasted Allen off the dance floor.

The players were outraged. Rickey had committed at least three top-shelf violations of the Ballplayer Code. First, Rickey had talked out of school. What happens in the clubhouse or on the team plane (or on the dance floor) stays there. Second, Rickey had gone to the manager without confronting the offending players face-to-face. All three players were already gone from the Yankees and now had to face their new teams (and their families) with the accusation of being drunks during a pennant race.

And third, he was one of them! Rickey freely admitted that he joined the boys in the back of the plane and threw a few back. He liked his brown liquor, on the rocks. So who was he to talk? "People in glass houses shouldn't throw rocks," Righetti told Bill Madden of the *Daily News*. The difference, Rickey said, was that he excused himself from his own indictment. Sure, he drank—a little. He knew when to stop. They didn't.

That was nowhere near good enough for Righetti, who took particular issue with Rickey's comment that "liquor doesn't leave you overnight." Righetti countered, "Maybe that's why his leg blows out every year."

The players were pissed. "It was a dumb thing to say," Mike Pagliarulo said. In Houston, where he'd been traded, Rick Rhoden let Rickey have it. "If he thinks it was a problem, he should've gone to the front office," Rhoden told Murray Chass of the *Times*. "Unless you're a player who hasn't messed up in his career, it's not your place to talk about someone else's problems. The way he did it, you jeopardize someone's career who had nothing to do with it. But it's out now; it can't be changed. All I can say is I didn't notice anything different there than any other club I've played on. I don't think it had any bearing on the way the team played. We didn't win because we didn't play as well as other teams."

Green, ostensibly the adult in the room, essentially said that whatever went down in 1988 wasn't his problem because he wasn't managing the club. "If they're not happy, let them go kick the shit out of him."

The consensus was that Rickey "stuck his foot in his mouth." After standing firm, he eventually walked back his comments and met with Righetti on a peacemaking mission. Still, he wasn't exactly wrong. What the players were really mad about was the fact that he went public.

It finally came out that for the final six weeks of the 1988 season Piniella had banned hard liquor from the team plane. Only beer was available. While Piniella protected the code ("There were 10 reasons why we didn't win and drinking wasn't one of them"), the manager wouldn't have banned liquor unless he recognized a serious, pennant-affecting issue.

Another issue was the messenger himself. Had it been Mattingly who called out the team or Claudell Washington (who, Rickey said, also went to Piniella but who, in his new home with the Angels, wanted no part of the story), perhaps the message would have been received differently. But it came from Rickey, the supposed me-guy, the one who didn't care about winning, the one who was only piling up his own stats, the guy who didn't want to play. He explained later why he came forward: he wanted to win. "It catches up to you. It catches up to you in hot weather, because you get tired. They're mad, but I'm mad too because I don't have a championship ring."

The tent was collapsing. The Steinbrenner way of incessant turmoil and turnover and instability couldn't last. It had been going on now for 13 years, since Reggie and Billy first poured gasoline on the fire. Steinbrenner had morphed from the absentee owner he promised to be when he bought the team in 1973 into the Maximum Leader he'd become. Talent had always saved the Yankees, but if the 1987 and 1988 fourth- and fifth-place finishes were disappointments, the scope of the Yankees' demise would soon be recognizable to the entire league, and there were no excuses for it.

As camp broke, the 1989 Yankees were very much expected to be a bad team. Green had been counting on Winfield to be the consistent power bat he had been for nearly a decade, but Steinbrenner took a sadistic glee in the left-right-left punches that finally felled the big man. Steinbrenner's lawsuit alleging financial misdealing by Winfield's charitable foundation was in arbitration. Then came an ugly lawsuit by the mother of Winfield's child, who now sought half of Winfield's earnings dating back seven years. The knockout blow came before opening day even arrived, when a ruptured disc in his back took Winfield out of the lineup for the season.

The Yankees opened in Minnesota. The 46-year-old Tommy John, who had made his big league debut when Rickey was four years old, faced the Twins' lefty Frank Viola. Rickey had two hits and terrorized the Minnesota battery with three stolen bases, and the Yankees walked away with a 4–2 win. It was John's 287th and penultimate win in a 26-year career, and a bright way for Green to begin his tenure.

The Yankees then lost seven in a row. Rickey hit safely in 17 of his first

19 games and a 2-for-4 against Kansas City pushed his average over .300, to
.301—for the last time.

Everything was off. Hitting in front of Steve Sax, a free-swinging second
baseman, was a disaster. Sax wasn't Willie Randolph, and he wasn't Carney
Lansford. He didn't take pitches, which rarely gave Rickey a free shot to take
second. Rickey couldn't get into a rhythm to steal bases. After the Kansas
City game, he hit .184 for the next three weeks, dropping his average down
to .241, and attempted to steal only five times over the next 19 games. Rickey
was even upended in the clubhouse body-fat contest, losing the belt to third-
year infielder Randy Velarde, who won the title at a little over 3 percent.

Al Rosen, the Hall of Fame third baseman who was also the Yankees'
president when the Yankees won the 1978 Series, called Syd Thrift. Now the
general manager of the San Francisco Giants, Rosen wanted to inquire about
Rickey. The Giants had come close, in 1985 and 1987, but they hadn't reached
the World Series since 1962 and had never won it since leaving New York
after the 1957 season. These Giants were loaded—Will Clark, Matt Williams,
and Kevin Mitchell were killing the ball. Rickey would make a fearsome
offense unbeatable. Rosen made the call, offering the Yankees the starting
right-hander Scott Garrelts and outfielder Candy Maldonado.

The Yankees said yes. Rickey said no.

"The Giants wanted me to bat fifth and play right field. They already had
a leadoff hitter, Brett Butler, and a left fielder, Kevin Mitchell," Rickey recalled in *Off Base*.* "The move would have meant going back to the Bay
Area, but I had to shoot that down right away. I had never batted fifth. I had
never played right field, and I had never played in the National League. Were
they kidding me? I was putting up the worst stats of my career and now they
were talking about bringing me to Candlestick Park? That would have been
a goofy move and screwed me up even more."

Rickey told Thrift that he would waive the no-trade clause for only one
other team: the A's. Thrift responded that a trade to Oakland was unlikely
because the A's weren't willing to make an attractive enough offer. That told

---

* Brett Butler enjoyed a very productive 17-year big league career—.290 career average,
2,375 hits, an All-Star selection in 1991, 558 stolen bases—but was Al Rosen really willing
to acquire Rickey Henderson, the greatest leadoff hitter of all time, and bat him *fifth*?
If true, it would be quite certain by the end of the 1989 season that Rosen had made a
terrible mistake.

Rickey that his old team—now a league powerhouse—was interested. Six months earlier, at the winter meetings, the Yankees and A's were so far apart on a deal for Rickey that a second conversation between Thrift and Sandy Alderson never materialized. "Then," Rickey told Thrift, "I guess I'll stay in New York for the rest of the year."

On June 20, as the rumors intensified, Rickey posed for the team picture, then took his usual spot in left field that night against the White Sox and watched Richard Dotson get hammered by his former team, giving up a four-spot in the first inning. Rickey led off the bottom of the first, walked, and scored, and he later threw out his former teammate Dan Pasqua at the plate. Down 13–5 with one out in the ninth, Rickey hit an RBI single to score Roberto Kelly for the final run in a 13–6 loss. In the next day's *Hartford Courant*, Claire Smith wrote a column about the .247-hitting Rickey.

YANKEES TRYING TO UNDERSTAND
WHAT MAKES THEIR RICKEY TICK

NEW YORK—All season long, the rumblings have been, "What's wrong with Rickey Henderson?"

Why is it such a mystery? Henderson, of all the Yankees, is the one the team can least afford to have distracted. And heaven knows, he has been distracted all season by contract negotiations.

Henderson dipped into a funk early this season. And he's been there since.

Why? "A lot of little things," Henderson said. "But the contract and the trades have a lot to do with it. It's been weird. Are they basing what I do this year on me signing? I don't know what their plan is. It seems like they don't know. And for them not to know hurts. What about the heart and soul I gave for four years? It seems like they don't care."

Eight hours later, he was traded. To Oakland.

Rickey was returning home, and unlike four and a half years earlier, when the Yankees had dealt for him, the shoe was now on the other foot. In 1984, the rebuilding A's traded Rickey to a rising Yankees team that needed a final piece to an offensive machine. Now the Yankees, sporting a 33-35 record and spiraling downward, were sending Rickey back to the West Coast, to the defending American League champions, to a team already in first place. In return, the Yankees received outfielder Luis Polonia and two relievers, Greg

Cadaret and Eric Plunk. Plunk had already been traded once for Rickey, in the deal that had sent him to New York.

As reporters gathered string for the Rickey trade stories, they descended upon Righetti, who along with the injured Winfield and Pagliarulo was a senior member of the team. To this day Righetti is beloved in New York for no-hitting the Red Sox at Yankee Stadium on July 4, 1983. The *Village Voice* sent Rob Cohen to do the story, and as fate would have it, his first day in the clubhouse was the day Rickey was traded. He followed the pool of reporters to Righetti's locker. Righetti was not particularly sorry to see Rickey go; his sentiment, Cohen gathered, was a strong good riddance. Pagliarulo enthusiastically seconded Righetti.

"For two summers I was living on 110th Street in my old apartment. I had the Yankee beat for the *Voice*. Writing whenever I felt like, whenever I felt. It was so loose, and I had this magical blanket of invisibility," Cohen recalled. "It was a dream come true. I was a Yankee fan, born in 1957. My years as a kid in the mid-1960s were the horrible years, and by the time they were good I was in college and moved on.

"So it was a total lark, a total treat. Sitting in the press box and Roger Angell was sitting next to me. It had been my dream to sit next to Roger Angell more than it was to cover baseball. It was my very first night at a game, and I'd never been in the clubhouse. I'm not a sports reporter. I don't even know what the fuck to do. I'm just following the herd. I was a middle-class fiction writer. I was a fan. I loved these guys. Then when Pagliarulo asked what Rags said, the reporters repeated it—with glee, I might add."

Rickey postmortems all sounded alike: the Yankees had unloaded a problem, a moody, temperamental star who was losing a step. Rickey wasn't even the most dynamic guy in the game anymore. Vince Coleman of the Cardinals had been to two of the past four World Series and stolen 100 bases in his first three big league seasons. Even Rickey had never done that. There was even talk that Coleman might one day *surpass* Rickey—he was that good. People were talking about the game's Superman, Bo Jackson, who played baseball *and* football—with Rickey's Raiders no less. It wasn't just Bo. Rickey's teammate on the 1989 Yankees was another hybrid star, this kid Deion Sanders, whose brashness could make Rickey look as irreverent as Cal Ripken Jr. Deion was also playing football, commuting by helicopter from Yankees games to Atlanta Falcons' practices.

Not a single piece from a regular news outlet that covered the Yankees po-

sitioned the trade as the Yankees dealing a future Hall of Famer to a World
Series team. This was addition by subtraction—the Yankees, now free, could
finally breathe without Rickey. Nor did anyone appear to notice that the
winner in the deal might actually have been Rickey, who got himself out of
there and landed in a realm he had not inhabited much in New York—first
place. With Rickey's bags packed, Dave Anderson of the *Times* got the door
for him:

PINSTRIPES NEVER REALLY FIT RICKEY

There is no quarrel here with the Yankees trading Henderson, only
with what they got in return . . . Presumably that was the best deal
available to Syd Thrift, the senior executive vice president who arrived on a produce truck from Pittsburgh only three months ago. But
that's what happens when an overrated Henderson is in the final year
of his overpaid contract.

The Yankees franchise was about to collide head-on with an iceberg: the
inevitable consequences of nearly two decades of George Steinbrenner's
madness. It had all finally become too much. The rages, the volatility, the
impulsive firings and capricious rehirings, the punitive attacks on his players
when they didn't perform. Steinbrenner and his thundercloud circus had
finally killed the franchise. When the facade that the Yankees thrived under this degree of chaos collapsed, the exhausted body collapsed with it. In
Rickey's four and a half years in New York, Steinbrenner hired and fired six
GMs. Rickey played for six managers. Dallas Green leaked to his friend-
lies with the notepads that, with Rickey gone, the atmosphere immediately
improved—and then Steinbrenner fired him less than two months later.

For Rickey's entire tenure in New York, the Yankees had never gained a
share of first place during the month of September—not for even a day. In
Rickey's best year, 1985, when the Yankees won 97 games and were elimi-
nated by Toronto on the second-to-last day of the season, they hadn't been
in first place for a single minute of the season; wire-to-wire they were out
of the top spot. The miracle wasn't that a team with Winfield and Guidry,
Mattingly and Rickey, didn't win the big one. The miracle was that from 1976
to 1981 the Yankees were able to win two World Series and four pennants
with a maniac running the franchise and another one in the dugout. Rickey
would always be Billy Martin's biggest advocate, but even he knew that Billy

was a man out of time, that his street-fighting ways were too volatile, too untenable.

"It is not easy, in the age of free agency, to screw up owning a baseball team in the media capital of the world, but he has done it," David Halberstam wrote of Steinbrenner. "The team is a wonderful extension of him, overpaid, surly, disconnected; The quintessential Steinbrenner player is Rickey Henderson. I do not doubt his talent, indeed his brilliance, but he seems, whenever I watch, in a perpetual sulk, entirely within himself."

By the time Rickey was dealt, there was even a feeling that trading him wouldn't have a negative impact on the Yankees. "There is not a significant void with his loss," Michael Martinez wrote in the *Times*. "Dallas Green, the Yankee manager, put Steve Sax in the leadoff spot last night against the Chicago White Sox and can use either Polonia or Mel Hall in left. A bigger problem is making room for Plunk and Cadaret, who have started in the past but who will initially be put in the bullpen."

Dallas Green had to know better. He may not have liked Rickey's attitude, but he'd been around baseball long enough to know that two journeyman pitchers and a triumvirate of Steve Sax, Luis Polonia, and Mel Hall could never re-create the impact of a player like Rickey. The Yankees were about to spiral the drain, and Polonia and Hall would make them wish for the "trouble" of Rickey being grumpy about taking batting practice.

Two months after the trade, on August 17, Polonia was arrested in Milwaukee for sexual misconduct with a 15-year-old. "She told me she was 19," Polonia told the cops—but the word in the clubhouse was that he told his teammates the girl's mother called the hotel room and, panicked, he hung up the phone. Steinbrenner fired Green the same day. Polonia was convicted later that year and served a month of a 60-day jail sentence for statutory rape. Mel Hall bragged of his conquests. Hall even began an affair with a 15-year-old Yankee fan. He was even her date for her prom—the team published a photo of the two in the Yankees' fan magazine. Hall, it turned out, had a proclivity for underage girls; finally caught and convicted after three decades as a sexual predator, he would be handed a nearly 50-year prison sentence for numerous sexual assault convictions, including one against a 12-year-old girl.

Replacing Rickey with a platoon of sex offenders was a sordid, inevitable devolution on top of business as usual with the Yankees: Steinbrenner destroying himself through his obsession with Winfield and the writers chasing the perennial rumor—that, with Green fired, Billy might be coming back to manage for a sixth time.

The Steinbrenner Yankees were effectively dead. The 1980s Yankees would win more games that decade than any other team in baseball, but under Steinbrenner the players were honor students expected to perform in an abusive household. His philosophy of creative tension, bolstered by a belief that fear would produce results, turned horribly toxic. A less distracted team might have been more successful.

None of that was Rickey's problem. For the first time in nearly five years, he was returning to Oakland. In New York, he had put up numbers that placed him on a clear Hall of Fame track, and yet the New York years left him with as much to prove upon his return to Oakland as when he had left four and a half years earlier. Steinbrenner's destructiveness had stuck to Rickey. Winfield-Mattingly-Rickey was the only superstar trio in the Bronx since 1921 that didn't win. But all the Yankee teams won, so in the public narrative that followed, if Rickey couldn't win in New York—the Canyon of Heroes, the home of winners—maybe it was Rickey, for all of his gifts, who wasn't a winner.

THE A'S WERE playing the Tigers at the Coliseum the night the trade was announced: Rickey was back. One fan, 17-year-old Chris Sauceda, was in the stands, watching batting practice with his father Carl. The joint was crackling with electricity, the way places do when big news breaks, with snippets of info making heads turn—an eavesdropper's paradise. *Did you hear? We got RICKEY?* "The stadium was absolutely buzzing," Sauceda recalled. "You could hear pieces of the news everywhere, because people were listening to the pregame on their radios . . . *They got Rickey? . . .* The A's were already a powerhouse. They were rolling at the time, and now they were adding Rickey? Things were about to get crazy.

"I remember it really well. Back then, they would let you in and you could watch all of BP, and I just remember how excited people were. I remember being down the left-field line talking to a fan next to me, and he was ecstatic about Rickey. He was going on about how Rickey didn't really belong in New York, that everything was so negative. In New York, they criticized you for everything you did. You could never win with those people. The guy was like, 'This is where Rickey needs to be. He's coming *home.*'"

As singular as Rickey had always been, sure of his abilities, with the numbers and the memories to prove it, you could say Rickey and the A's needed each other. Rickey had something to prove. New York had made him a ton of money, but sports were full of rich guys who put up huge numbers and didn't win. While the rest of the baseball world had been caught up in the Rickey drama—whether or not he returned from injury fast enough, or whether he styled a home run or offended the long-dead ghosts of the game—Rickey was focused on winning a championship. A Rickey focused on a singular goal, on something he craved, was the most dangerous kind. Individually, he understood that the greatest players held the greatest records, but he also knew that the best players played for championships, and he had never played for one. Greatness was never measured from last place. His time in New York served him when he put up the monster numbers, then undermined him when the Yankees never played in October, where the legends were supposedly made.

In the Bay, New York had stuck to Rickey, but so too had his time with the A's. Bruce Jenkins of the *San Francisco Chronicle* said that the move could end with the A's printing World Series tickets, but he also believed that Rickey's reputation was not unfounded either.

A STEAL OF A DEAL FOR LOADED A'S

Rickey Henderson. The man. The child. The A's either won the division title by 15 games yesterday, or they blew the whole thing.

Manager Tony La Russa called the trade "a challenge—for Rickey and for us"—and that summed it up perfectly. Henderson, for all his accomplishments, has still to prove he can play for a winner. La Russa has to blend a singular, self-centered personality into the A's incredible team spirit.

New York had said that Rickey was electric. New York said he was captivating. New York said he was gifted. But New York never said he was a *winner*. If anything, without using the word outright, New York was doing everything it could to suggest he was a losing player. At 30, maybe Rickey was destined to join the list of guys who just weren't there when the lights came on—or worse, who were blamed, despite all the stats, as the reason their teams never popped the corks. Rickey saw firsthand what Steinbrenner did to Winfield, saddling him with that "Mr. May" rap that lasted his entire decade in New York. Rickey's rep was so damaged that both the local papers in San Francisco and the national mood suggested that the A's had taken on unnecessary risk because they traded a couple of guys in the bullpen.

A'S MAKE MOVE—BUT LET'S WAIT AND SEE

The A's bid goodbye to three young members of their 1988 American League title team and opened their brawny arms to Rickey Henderson. Go figure.

There are at least a half-dozen Rickey Hendersons currently prowl-ing the AL basepaths and outfields. One is the most fearsome lead-off man in baseball, a quick-strike missile who can instantly put you behind with his bat or his feet. Another only hit six home runs last season and made people think he has lost his punch.

One has 819 career stolen bases, including a record 130 in one sea-son. Another Rickey Henderson was spotted just last Sunday loafing after a ball hit to the wall.

Moody. Now there's a polite euphemism. Rickey Henderson is moody.

But why, it says here, should a team with proven chemistry like the Athletics even take the chance? What if the wrong Rickey comes home?

Risky. Now there's a polite euphemism.

Rickey had already proven that he wasn't one of those guys by being a difference-maker in 1981, but nobody remembered that. It was the strike year—a year everyone wanted to forget. And the playoffs ended quickly any-way. Getting swept by the Yankees wasn't exactly a résumé-builder. Besides, that was when he was a kid. He was a veteran now, and his recent history was of one of *those* guys: "Doesn't play hurt" . . . "Isn't a team player—doesn't know how to mingle with the guys" . . . "A loner." New York said that, unlike championship players, he didn't sacrifice himself, that he lacked this quality. New York applied to Rickey the old math reserved for baseball's most tal-ented pains in the ass: addition by subtraction. As Rickey arrived back on the West Coast, the message was as bright as the green-and-gold uniform he was about to don a second time—the Yankees were a better team, win or lose, without him.

When a return to Oakland began looking possible, Rickey called Dave Stewart, his childhood friend from Little League. Stewart told Rickey he needed to come home. The legends of Oakland would be reunited. Use your no-trade clause for anywhere else, Stewart told him, but *not* against Oak-land. That was where he needed to be. Rickey, Stewart told him, was the missing piece.

The A's that Rickey returned to embodied the spirit of Dave Stewart. On May 9, 1986, he had been facing the abyss: 30-35 lifetime record. No one exactly knocking down his door. He was 29 and had been released by the

Phillies after throwing just 16 2/3 innings over two seasons. Stewart had been drafted by the Dodgers in 1975 and made his big league debut in 1978. In that first game, he struck out a batter in two innings against the Padres—then got sent down and didn't reach the big leagues again until 1981. Stewart won a World Series with the Dodgers that year, but it never came together for him. He wasn't Rickey, the immediate star. When Tony La Russa, the A's manager, called, Dave Stewart was fighting for his professional life.

Stewart worked out for Wes Stock and Dave Duncan. He was signed two weeks after being released by the Phillies with low expectations and started only one game, June 1 at the Coliseum against the Yankees. (Rickey doubled and stole a base off of him.)

A month later, on July 6, the A's were in Boston and La Russa called Stewart's room. "You're starting tomorrow's game." Against the Red Sox. At Fenway Park. Against Roger Clemens. Clemens would win the Cy Young and the MVP that year and had already set a record by striking out 20 Mariners earlier in the season. He was 12-1 on the season and would finish 24-4. By October Clemens would pitch the Red Sox to the World Series. Where Roger Clemens was in his career the night they faced each other—in the middle of a legendary season—was the exact opposite of where Dave Stewart was in his.

In front of a nationally televised audience—back when ABC's *Monday Night Baseball* was a thing—Stewart beat Clemens, 6-4. It was one of only four losses Clemens would take on the season, and from that night the legend of Dave Stewart was born. He would win 20 games the next season, and the season after that, going on to four straight 20-win seasons in all. Heir to Gibson, the glowering Black Ace, Dave Stewart would burn with intensity on the mound, his cap pulled so deep over his head you could barely see his eyes. It was the competitiveness and the Oakland in him—the recognition of where he had come from and his willingness to accept the challenge.

Stewart accepted the responsibility of an ace pitcher. He not only won 20 games in four consecutive years but led the AL in starts in four straight years, in innings and complete games twice, and in wins and shutouts once. His job was to win games and to pitch innings—not to pitch deep in the game, but to complete it.

No one in the game focused Dave Stewart like Roger Clemens. He faced Clemens with the underdog's fury, the intensity of a man with a grievance, as if Clemens symbolized an entire industry whose attention Stewart needed to claim, whom he needed to tell was wrong about him. It did not matter that Clemens did not view Stewart as a rival in their first meeting. Going against Clemens was not only personal for Stewart but also a way to send the message to the Red Sox that when their best pitcher faced him, the best pitcher on the field would not be wearing a Red Sox uniform. If to Rickey respect was best shown through money, to Dave Stewart respect was gained through head-to-head competition, and there was only one way to get that respect—he had to beat the best.

"You want to start talking about him like he's the greatest thing since sliced bread? Fuck that. I'm kicking his ass every chance I get," Stewart would say of Clemens. "After a while, I didn't worry if I was *gonna* beat him. I *knew* I was gonna beat him. It was a matter of whether *he* was going to beat *me*. I made sure I gave us what we needed. If it was an 8–5 game, I made sure I only gave up five. I could pitch to the score, to the situation, but if it was 1–0, I'd make sure I didn't give up any runs. Why do you think I whipped Clemens's ass so many times?

"There's no doubt Roger made me better, but it wasn't just Roger. It was Jack Morris. It was Frank Viola. It was Chuck Finley. It was Dan Petry. Every time I took the mound, I was getting the other team's motherfucker. I didn't get no punks. I never faced the other team's punk. If I got one, I was appreciative, but every time I got the ball, it was against fucking Saberhagen. It was against Gubicza. Tony believed there was something in that challenge that was always going to bring out the best in me."

You could see hunger to be great everywhere in Oakland. You could see it in La Russa. This was the same Tony La Russa who had sparred with Rickey six years earlier, when La Russa was managing the White Sox and Rickey was snatch-catching the final out of Mike Warren's no-hitter against Chicago. Tony was as hotheaded as any player and even had a little Billy in him in that, on a night when the players didn't have it, he was convinced he could be the difference-maker in a ball game. La Russa, with his impeccable eye for detail and his innovative decision to convert Eckersley from flame-throwing but declining starter to unhittable, one-inning closer, was already being called a genius. Meanwhile, Eckersley, once as close to baseball's exit door as Stewart, was staring down hitters—and if he caught them glancing at him on the long walk back to the dugout following a strikeout, Eck would yell at them, "*Fuck you looking at?*"

After pounding a rookie-record 49 homers in 1987, Mark McGwire went to bat the next year with a target on his back, forced to hit while constantly being knocked on his ass. "They really weren't that intimidating until I told them what they were worth," recalled Dave Parker, the fearsome former National League MVP Alderson signed in 1989. "McGwire was getting hit every day, and he came to me, upset that they were taking shots at him. I told him, 'If you want that to stop, go out and shake one of them.' They weren't aware of what they were capable of. Sometimes you had to go out to the mound and let them know."

In his absence, Oakland had become what Rickey's Yankees were supposed to be when he went to New York—brash and brawny, feared, fearless, dominant. "I'll tell you one thing I took from Roger. Clemens threw at McGwire, right at the head," Stewart recalled. "And the next day I told them . . . I let them know. The Red Sox were taking BP, and I interrupted their BP. It was Wade Boggs, Mike Greenwell, Jim Rice. Those three guys. I told them, 'You tell Roger, if he hits one of my guys again, I'm having a two-for-one special: two of you three—Greenwell, Boggs, or Rice—for one of my guys.' And it stopped. Don't hit my fucking guys."

Then there was the kid from Havana, Jose Canseco, who used to shave the handles of his bats down to toothpick width to create greater bat speed, then hit balls into the next time zone. Canseco ran like a deer and in 1988 unanimously won the AL MVP with a colossal year—hitting .307 with 42 home runs, 120 runs scored, 124 batted in, and 40 stolen bases, he was the first player in history to hit 40 home runs and steal 40 bases. Even Willie Mays, inventor of the 30-30 mark that he achieved twice (including 20 triples in 1957), had never stolen 40 bases in a 40-homer year. That put Canseco at the center of a new paradigm—or did it? (Mays, who gave quarter to no one, rolled his eyes at what he saw as stat fetishizing. "If I knew 40-40 was such a big deal," Willie once snorted, "I would have done it years ago.")

Canseco was a Ruthian showman. He hit titanic home runs, blowing kisses to the fans who serenaded him by attributing his massive power and speed to the use of anabolic steroids (spoiler alert: it was). But there were problems with him from the start. The A's knew he was talented but immature. Alderson had signed both Don Baylor and Parker to have veterans in the clubhouse modeling the professionalism that big leaguers needed. But the A's saw Canseco as the future.

Yet for everything the A's had—pitching, defense, relief pitching, intimidation, bushels of power—they didn't have an explosive leadoff man. Stan

Javier was a nice player. Solid, knew the game. Legacy kid. His dad Julian played in the big leagues, even won a couple of World Series titles with Bob Gibson's Cardinals in the 1960s. Tony Phillips, who played with Rickey during his first tour in Oakland, was an invaluable utility man who could play six positions, and the speedy Polonia was, well . . . heading to jail.

These A's were the kick-your-ass-and-laugh-at-you kind of winners, the best bullies in the game. They took turns crushing moon shots during batting practice for the singular purpose of scaring the hell out of the other dugout. Early adopters of the advantages of weightlifting, the A's used to win games psychologically before the first pitch was even thrown. During home games, the players would record their bench press statistics on a whiteboard in the weight room—but they would pump up the numbers, embellishing their totals by 50 or 75 pounds each, to increase the intimidation quotient. Visiting teams would use the weight room, notice the outrageous bench press numbers on the whiteboard, and go back to the clubhouse beaten before the national anthem had even been played. (Canseco deadlifted *how much?*)

They took the 1988 AL flag with 104 wins, peacocked all summer as if they were unbeatable—and didn't win. In the World Series, the A's got their asses handed to them by a scrappy, tough Dodgers team. Canseco and McGwire? A 2-for-36 between them in the five games. Game 1, the famous Kirk Gibson game? Eckersley hadn't walked a batter since August, but he walked Mike Davis—former A's outfielder Mike Davis—which set up Gibson's famous home run. The A's hit .177 in the five games. The bully got punched in the face in Game 1, and after that and a dose of Orel Hershiser, well, they didn't want to fight anymore.

The story didn't seem real (when it came to Rickey nothing ever did), but it was during that World Series humiliation that Alderson knew he needed another weapon. A big weapon at the top of the order—the biggest weapon in the game at that position. What Alderson was looking for happened to be at Dodger Stadium that very night, and he wasn't even wearing a uniform. It was Rickey. He was at Game 1, sitting in comped seats, a guest of Mike Davis.

Rickey returned to Oakland on June 22 against the Blue Jays and embarked on one of the great two-year periods of dominance in the history of the sport.

In the 13-inning loss to Toronto, he briefly wore number 22 before switching to number 24, which he had worn in the minors and with the Yankees.

(His old number 35 now belonged to the pitcher Bobby Welch.) Rickey went 2-for-6, and Pat Borders threw him out trying to steal second, but three days later, in the four-game finale, he swiped three bases—a perfect 3-for-3 off Ernie Whitt—while going 3-for-3 at the plate.

He came to Oakland hitting .247 with the Yankees, but in his first month back he hit .365. The 11–3 bombing of Cleveland on July 2 started with Rickey taking John Farrell deep in the top of the first, a Rickey Special; he was 3-for-4 that day. On July 8 against the Rangers, A's down 2–1, Dave Stewart and the ornery right-hander Kevin Brown matched zeroes until the eighth, when Rickey banged a three-run homer off Rangers All-Star closer Jeff Russell. In a July 29 game in Seattle, the A's had no chance. Storm Davis gave up eight in the first and the A's got killed, 14–6, but Rickey scored four runs without notching an official at-bat after Randy Johnson walked him four times and Rickey thanked him for the free passes by stealing five bases.

"Rickey Henderson is the perfect addition for the A's, an offensive spark plug extraordinaire. And Oakland is the perfect place for Henderson, his home sweet home," wrote Moss Klein in *The Sporting News:*

> The move was worthwhile. The loss of Plunk and Cadaret from that splendid bullpen was an affordable price, especially for a player who can be a highlight reel when he's happy . . . from the Yankees' standpoint, the blockbuster trade was more complicated. The Yankees were faced with a difficult decision. The team's decision makers thought that Henderson, nearing 31, had lost a step and were hesitant to let him take their money and continue to run for them—especially because he wanted $8.1 million over three years to bypass free agency.
>
> The Yankees have more revenue than any team in baseball, but George Steinbrenner is trying to keep payroll within reasonable bounds. And he simply did not believe Henderson was worth the additional investment.

On it went. When the A's traded for Rickey, they were in first place, but only by two games—but they would win the division by 13. The Royals won 91 games, even got as close as a game and a half on September 1, but the A's closed the season by winning 11 of their final 14 games. For the second time in his career, Rickey was back in the playoffs.

Rickey was closing the chapter on the first decade of his career on the same field where it all began—with the same objectives in sight. In one sense, there was no doubting the miles he had traveled toward accomplishing that original goal—to be the greatest base stealer of all time. He had met that goal, no matter what the backbiters said, with relative ease. At just 30 years old, he was only 67 steals away from Lou Brock's all-time record of 938 stolen bases. By no sense had the road been easy, but Rickey had made it *look* easy. Returning to Oakland had allowed him to reflect on the decade in his familiar space where he had established himself as a superstar player and to refocus his efforts on what he had come into the game to do.

When Rickey was running through the league, leading the league in stolen bases and heading toward the playoffs, the legend of Oakland only stood taller. His old North Oakland neighbor Gary Pettis was in the standings chasing him, just as they had competed at Bushrod. Pettis had stolen 50 bases twice in the big leagues, and 35 bases a half-dozen times. He and Rickey had played in the same division, just as they had in Connie Mack. In the American League Championship Series, the A's would play Toronto, whose center fielder and leadoff hitter was none other than the Shaker, Lloyd Moseby. One of them was going to the World Series. Stewart, the King of St. Elizabeth's, was starting Game 1 for the A's. Miraculously, the legends of Oakland were all there, in the big leagues and now in the postseason. And of their group it was the Football Kid who was emerging as the best of them all.

When he was on—when his body was free of soreness and his mind was right—Rickey would walk into the clubhouse and announce to the entire room, "It's Rickey Time!" Some of the guys would roll their eyes and go back to getting their ankles taped, while others would laugh. But many of his teammates remembered something else: it wasn't just talk. "Rickey Time" was uncannily accompanied by a monster night.

Rickey knew the lights were on: they were on a championship course—no underdog stuff. Everyone was monument building. Stewart and Eckersley were renewed, climbing to the top spots in the game. Alderson was being called the best executive in the game. The A's were the model franchise, building from the draft and the free-agent market—none of that little brother guff from San Francisco. And La Russa was being called a genius, not as a baseball guy, but as a *thinker*. He was even being validated by the smart set. The Pulitzer Prize–winning columnist George Will was hanging around the ballpark every day, working on a baseball book, *Men at Work*. Rickey recognized Will from the morning talk shows, never remembered his name, but whenever he saw Will at the ballpark, he'd say, "Hey, it's the politics guy."

As the A's clinched and the tour to avenge the loss to the Dodgers commenced, Rickey began referring to himself the same way Dave Stewart did—he now called himself the "final piece to the puzzle." The Blue Jays were no patsies; they'd been knocking on the door of the World Series for nearly five years and still couldn't get there. When they struggled during the season, they fired their manager, Jimy Williams, and replaced him with Cito Gaston, former teammate of Henry Aaron, Willie McCovey, and Dave Winfield and only the third Black manager in the game's history. Gaston, a quiet and serious Texan, was always underestimated as a leader for not flipping over the spread when things went sour, but it was he who transformed the Blue Jays from a spiraling disappointment into division champs.

The series opener in Oakland featured the two underappreciated warhorses, Stewart and Toronto's Dave Stieb. Stewart trailed 3–1 early before the A's got to Stieb and wore down Toronto for a 7–3 win. McGwire homered, Dave Henderson homered, and Stewart went eight innings—but the story was Rickey. The box score didn't reveal much—he was 0-for-2 with a run scored—but he was on base three times, stole two bases, and made the play of the night.

One out, bottom of the sixth, 3–3 game, runners on second and third with a run already in. Gaston brought in Jim Acker, who hit Rickey on the left wrist to load the bases. Acker appeared to avoid catastrophe when Lansford hit an easy double-play ball to short that would end the inning and keep the game tied—except that Rickey blasted the Toronto second baseman Nelson Liriano with a takeout slide at second that sent Liriano reeling as he tried to leapfrog Rickey to avoid the collision. Liriano's throw flew wide, and two runs scored.

Two innings later, up two runs, Rickey walked, stole second, and forced a wild pitch that led to an insurance run in the eighth that salted away the ball game. Bob Costas and Tony Kubek were on the call for NBC, and as Rickey clapped while crossing home plate with the final run of the night, Kubek said to a nationwide audience, "Rickey sure has a way of being in the middle of a lot of things, doesn't he?" Kubek, who played on three World Series title teams with the Yankees in the 1950s and '60s, knew winning baseball when he saw it, and what he saw was Rickey making championship-level team

baseball plays that supposedly weren't part of his résumé—without even
having a hit on the night.

It was in the second game that Rickey took up permanent residence in
the collective heads of the Blue Jays. In the fourth inning the hothead Todd
Stottlemyre was up 1–0. Rickey walked, and then stared at Stottlemyre on
his entire 90-foot trip to first. Stottlemyre stared back, but he was already
cooked. Lansford was the batter, but Rickey was the problem. Stottlemyre
threw more pitches to first to start the at-bat than he did to home plate.
Rickey stole second anyway. Rickey stared in at Stottlemyre from second.
Stottlemyre started his delivery. Rickey took off.

Foul ball.

By swinging at the pitch, Lansford had already given it away. Everyone
knew Rickey was going, so what did Rickey do? He took off on Stottlemyre's
very next pitch. Rickey leapt into third, and Kelly Gruber, the Blue Jays' third
baseman, kicked Rickey in the face. Rickey called for time and threw two
fist pumps.

In the broadcast booth, Costas wasn't focused on the batter-pitcher confrontation, usually the central nervous system of baseball. He was focused on
Rickey, who was devouring the 23-year-old Stottlemyre on national television. "Henderson, one of the game's premier players for a decade, but no postseason play since '81 . . . you can tell how charged up he is for the series . . .
watch his reaction as he goes headfirst to third ahead of Gruber's tag."

Now Stottlemyre was staring at Rickey on third, as if Rickey were heading
for home too, but what he really wanted to do was punch Rickey in the face.
All this time, Lansford was still up. Distracted, Stottlemyre threw a cookie
that Lansford ripped for an RBI single—and there went Stottlemyre's lead,
and eventually the game. In the broadcast chair, Kubek let America know it
was watching a special performance—and it was only the fourth inning of
a tie game:

> There was so much going on with this play, and Rickey got kicked
> pretty good by Kelly Gruber. He's all charged up . . . Stottlemyre
> sped up his delivery and threw a ball . . . It was Rickey's slide yes-
> terday. Today, two stolen bases.

In the seventh, another youngster, the rubber-armed lefty David Wells,
was on the mound, and Rickey was at it again: he walked, stole second easily,

and then . . . *he slowed down* a few steps before reaching the bag and just *walked* into second. Two pitches later, Rickey took off for third. "Do you think," Costas said after Rickey swiped third again, "that Rickey Henderson is enjoying the spotlight?"

The A's won, 6–3, and were up 2–0 in the series. Two games. Two A's wins. Two dominant performances by Rickey. He had reached base in seven of his first nine plate appearances. He'd stolen six bases in two games, without being caught, and the four stolen bases in Game 2 alone marked a playoff record. In the Toronto clubhouse they wanted to beat his ass.

"Fuck Rickey Henderson," Whitt said after the game. "He's a great ballplayer, but fuck Rickey Henderson."

It wasn't just the results that chapped Whitt (he was helpless out there). It was Rickey Style. It was the way Rickey slowed up at second, even though Whitt had conceded the base by not making a throw. *What kind of bush league shit was that?* Whitt saw Rickey not only slowing up to the bag but taking a few stylish steps toward the outfield—sending a message that he had the entire Blue Jays squad at that moment right in his pocket. "No one likes to be shown up. As far as I'm concerned, Rickey tried to show us both up when he pulled up short at second. We conceded it to him, so just take it. Don't tiptoe around the base. That's bush. You don't see Carney Lansford doing that."

In the A's clubhouse, Rickey got dressed, heard Whitt's grievances in the postgame media scrum, and said, "If you think I'm showing you up, I'll just steal more bases. Anyway, I never run on the catcher. I run on the pitcher."

In the Blue Jays clubhouse, on the flight back to Toronto, at their homes and in their dreams, stopping Rickey was the top priority. He was beating them not just on the field but psychologically. His game was in their heads, and he was taunting them. He was *embarrassing* them. While Whitt appealed to the game's code of professionalism, even the hometown commentary wasn't too sympathetic, calling the Jays "whiners." In the Toronto team meeting before Game 3, the consensus opinion was to administer some frontier justice—Rickey needed to go down. Enough of this guy making them look like clowns. Put him on his ass. There was one dissenter on the team who argued against that strategy—Lloyd Moseby.

"That kind of stuff didn't bother Rick," Moseby recalled saying in the meeting. "Everybody thought I objected because we were tight, because we grew up together, because we were both from Oakland. They were like, 'That's your homeboy,' and I was like, 'Nah, you don't understand. You can't

intimidate Rickey by throwing at him.' He just wasn't that guy. The only effect putting him down was going to have on him was he was going to go at
you twice as hard—and we all saw what he was already doing."

Earlier in the year, back in spring training when Rickey was still with the
Yankees, Dwight Gooden threw a fastball under Rickey's chin that dropped
him to the dirt. Rickey had stepped into the box and then stepped out because his bat had inadvertently made contact with Mackey Sasser, the Mets
catcher—but Gooden thought Rickey was playing games in the box to upset
his timing. It was spring training, his first appearance of the *year,* and in
response Gooden fired a heater right at Rickey. Rickey spiraled into a cloud
of dirt, dusted himself off, stepped back in, and ripped a single. Then he
faked taking second and forced Gooden into a balk. Then he stole third and
scored—and the games didn't even count.

On the eve of Game 3 of the Championship Series, Rickey announced
it was Rickey Time—with a bullhorn. During a media session after the A's
workout, reporters asked him how Toronto could contain the Oakland running game, which meant Ernie Whitt stopping him. "I don't think he can
ever throw me out," Rickey said. "If they want to win, maybe they should put
someone else back there."

The Jays came home and made it a series. Jimmy Key rebounded from
a 3–0 deficit and held the line after the offense chased Storm Davis off, but
not before absorbing another Rickey insult. Rickey had gas that morning.
Whatever he ate, he was like walking methane, cutting nuclear farts in the
clubhouse. Even during the card game, Rickey stunk up the joint something
awful. Mike Zagaris, the A's team photographer, thought the place needed to
be fumigated. When Rickey stepped into the box to start Game 3, he broke
off one last chunk of wind—right in Ernie Whitt's face.

Later in the game, he stole third, but for once in the series Rickey didn't
have the last laugh. The Blue Jays won in a waltz, 7–3. The Canadians were
happy to christen SkyDome, their new ballpark with its fancy retractable
roof, with playoff baseball, but it was all just an oasis, merely an intermission
in the Rickey Show.

Rickey didn't steal a base in Game 4. He made an error in left. He even
got picked off first by the pitcher John Cerruti (no revenge for Ernie Whitt).
Canseco hit a ball that landed somewhere near the Arctic Circle that people
would talk about 30 years later, and yet the story was still Rickey.

Scoreless game. Third inning. One out. Runner on third. Rickey facing

Mike Flanagan, the lefty who was part of the Orioles pitching staff of the 1970s with Jim Palmer, Dennis Martinez, and Scott McGregor. Flanagan was 37 now, just like his catcher, Ernie Whitt. When Flanagan retired Rickey in the first, Toronto had gotten him out four straight times now. Maybe the storm had passed.

Flanagan tried to sneak a slow change on the outside corner past Rickey. Ready for it, Ernie Whitt reached out to snatch it off the edge of the plate. Rickey recognized the change of speed, readjusted his hips with a little hitch, and lifted the ball out to center. Lloyd Moseby turned and gave chase. On the NBC broadcast, Bob Costas told 50 million Americans that Rickey's fly was going to score a run—just a manageable sacrifice fly, a good baseball play—but the ball kept going . . . and going. Moseby suddenly stopped running—he was at the warning track. Broadcast pro that he was, Costas quickly recalibrated: This was no sac fly. This wasn't even just a home run. Rickey's ball cleared the center-field fence, then the back wall just beyond the fence, and landed in the black-covered section of seats—a quarter of the way up the batter's eye.

"This will get a run home, maybe more . . . Moseby going back . . . look up . . . and *outta* here into the black seats—the *hitting* background! There aren't many leadoff men who can launch one like that, into dead center field. About a 430-foot shot, two-nothing, Oakland," Costas said on the air.

On contact, even Rickey didn't think it was going to go where it went, but when it did, he began a medium trot around the bases, picking at the jersey. This one was a bomb, deserving of *all* the picks, all the style—three on the left shoulder, another chest-high, and another pick at the jersey as he rounded third. The Big Boys—six-foot-four Canseco, six-five McGwire, six-five Parker—all awaited him at the plate and in the dugout. At five-ten, Rickey was putting the ball in Home Run Derby territory.

In the fifth, again with a runner on and the A's leading 3–1, Flanagan tried to beat Rickey with a fastball. Rickey did not miss, turning a meatball into a missile with a straight pull job over the left-field fence. Back-to-back at-bats, back-to-back two-run homers. That was it, for the Blue Jays and the series. Toronto made the final two games close—each a one-run game at the end— but the A's were too good. They'd had at least a three-run lead in every game of the series, even in the one game they lost. It was too much Rickey, who, in the 4–3 pennant clincher won by Stewart, added a triple and a stolen base to his weeklong masterpiece.

The image of the ALCS was Toronto's utterly defeated third baseman Kelly Gruber sitting in the dirt, holding the baseball, while Rickey exhorted him. In a scene from Bushrod, Moseby homered off Stewart to start an unsuccessful comeback, but it wasn't enough. The A's had won the pennant for the second straight year—and Rickey was going to the World Series for the first time in his career.

Rickey was the unanimous MVP of the American League Championship Series. He hit .400, with a .609 on-base percentage. The slugging? 1.000. In five games, Rickey was on base 14 times. He led the team in runs scored (eight) and walks (seven) and never struck out. It was one of the greatest postseason performances the game had seen. Before Canseco dropped his upper-deck 500-footer, Costas and his color man Tony Kubek were devoting the rest of the third-inning commentary of Game 4 to Rickey—and running out of words for what they were witnessing.

> COSTAS: Lou Brock had a couple of years with good power numbers in the '60s. I think he hit 20 one year with the Cardinals. He was stronger, especially in his prime, than people would have thought . . . but all things considered, Rickey has had several years of 18, 20 home runs. You saw where he hit that one. I can't think of many, if any, leadoff hitters who have combined power with anything like his sort of speed . . . Is he, is it even worth questioning now, the greatest leadoff hitter of all time?
>
> KUBEK: Maybe in modern baseball, I dunno . . . I never seen any better than him . . . That well rounded in every area? High on-base percentage, decent slugging percentage . . . Get you a quick lead with all the home runs he hits leading off ball games . . . And gets into scoring position at will. It's a Rickey Henderson rally—walk, steal second, steal third. Sac fly . . . Without a hit you can get a run with Rickey. He's worth a run a game. I don't think there's any question.

It was a fast, bitter series that planted the seeds of a rivalry. Ernie Whitt couldn't stand Rickey—the style, the impunity—but he couldn't stop him either. He had to take it. Cito Gaston believed that La Russa and the A's bench were stealing signs. He thought Eckersley was doctoring the ball. Gaston was a reserved competitor, and his team had just been manhandled, so there was no value in firing at Oakland. Still, he thought the A's were cheaters.

"It wasn't just the winning. It was the way we won," Eckersley recalled. "Jose hitting that 500-foot home run. Rickey is having everyone's ass, taking what he wants, going bridge, and then Cito checked my glove. Called me half-a-woman. We didn't care. We were going to the World Series. See you later, motherfuckers."

The A's had the pennant. Rickey was the MVP—there was nothing Toronto could do with him. Oakland would play the Giants in the Series. An international audience had seen what he could do, but before the first all–Bay Area World Series, Mike Lupica brought out the sharp knives from New York to shank Rickey's bravura performance.

WILL THE REAL RICKEY PLEASE LIE DOWN?

Come Saturday night, Rickey Henderson will continue to run all over the month of October. The World Series, going in, will be about Rickey and Will Clark. Rickey will get more air time. He will get to first base and that will just be the overture. Clark is a swing of the bat. Rickey, he seems to be the whole inning. He will start out in Oakland and then try to steal San Francisco. And the rest of America will perhaps get the notion that he is this interested in baseball all the time. He is not.

Rickey's footprints were all over the American League Championship Series from the time he knocked someone named Liriano into Jack London Square in Game 1 . . . He did everything on the basepaths except moonwalk. Rickey looks pretty chipper these days. But then he ought to. April and May were fairly slow months for him in New York.

Rickey Henderson can start the first inning with a home run, make the strike zone seem the size of a dime, steal a base, get you a run a game, and look like the best leadoff man of them all. He also gets managers fired. He occasionally makes you wonder about his heart.

Dallas Green, unemployed and living on his farm, told Lupica, "I like Rickey, I really do. But he didn't seem alert or on top of his game the first part of this season. I understand he wanted around three million dollars a year for the next three years, and from what I saw, I wouldn't have given it to him." Unemployed Dallas Green, who in his short time with Rickey suggested that he couldn't read and that his teammates should "kick the shit out of him," and who insinuated for yuks that he was banging Margo Adams, then called him a "model citizen," positioned himself as the self-satisfied arbiter of professionalism. Lupica, in a final paragraph, wrote:

> The Yankees got two pretty good arms and Luis Polonia. Rickey got the World Series. He probably will leave his footprints all over the Series, too. It doesn't change the way he went out in New York. October doesn't mean May didn't happen. Sometime over the next week, just for old time's sake, I hope he lets one go through his legs and jogs after it like his name is Roseanne.

Lupica took his whacks. So did Dallas Green, but it was too late for either of them to land anything on Rickey. Lupica's line "October doesn't mean May didn't happen" was pretty cheeky for the place that supposedly only measured itself by Octobers, and proof that Rickey was beyond them. As shocking as it must have been to the collective ego of the 212/718 area code and its belief that the rest of the world must always answer to and revolve around it, New York was in Rickey's rearview. The big town didn't matter anymore.

The 1989 World Series will always be remembered for the Loma Prieta earthquake that shook the Bay at 5:04 p.m., right before Game 3 at Candlestick Park. The 7.1-Richter scale catastrophe killed an estimated 67 people and caused $7 billion in property damage. The quake collapsed the Cypress Structure in Oakland and a portion of the upper deck of the Bay Bridge. It would be remembered for the images of San Francisco's Marina District, and for Buck Helm, the 58-year-old longshoreman on the Oakland docks who was trapped in his car for 90 hours in the rubble of the mile-long collapsed section of the Nimitz Freeway before rescuers found him alive, his life at the mercy of luck and nature's force. Buck Helm was a national inspiration. They even made a TV movie about him (*Miracle on Interstate 880*). A month after being rescued, Helm died from his injuries.

The Series was delayed 10 days, with the A's leading two games to none, Stewart having shut out the Giants 5–0 on a five-hit complete game in the opener, and Mike Moore following up with seven innings in a 5–1 win. When it resumed, the A's closed out their inevitable championship with a couple of laughers. The title was the culmination of the legend of Oakland. The A's averaged eight runs in the four-game sweep. At the end of the fifth inning in each of the four games, the A's led 5–0, 5–1, 8–3, and 7–0.

Rickey? As gallows humor goes, the laughing to keep from crying, there was always Rickey. When the earth shook and everybody panicked and ran for their lives, Rickey was on the toilet.

"To tell you the truth, we were at, uh, San Francisco, getting ready for the game, and I was preparing myself for the game. I think, you know, you get butterflies or something," he recalled. "I think I had a bad stomach, and I think I went to the john. And you know, the earthquake came and shook. I thought it was the fans getting excited, so I didn't freak out that there was an earthquake. I think the security guy had to come in and tell me that, 'Hey, y'all, we just had an earthquake. Everybody's got to get out of the locker room and get on the field.' And that's where I realized. But at that time, I was in the john relaxing, trying to get myself prepared for the game."

Rickey destroyed Toronto and might have been even better against San Francisco. He could have won the World Series MVP trophy too—but that hardware went to Dave Stewart. Rickey hit .474 in the four games, including a moon shot to lead off the clincher against Don Robinson, accompanied by a single, a triple, and a steal of third. He hit 9-for-19 for the Series, four runs, two triples, a home run, a double, three stolen bases. Brett Butler was a fine leadoff hitter for San Francisco, though it could have been Rickey leading off for the Giants in the World Series against his former team, trying to beat his hometown. But Al Rosen had wanted him to bat fifth.

After the World Series came another go-round with Sandy Alderson, right before Rickey's 31st birthday, but this time it wasn't an arbitration case that needed to be settled, with the player having no leverage to change teams. This time Rickey was approaching free agency, and if the A's wanted him they had to negotiate with him on a level playing field. He was a playoff MVP, a World Series champion, the dominant postseason performer. He was at supernova. That laid the groundwork for the goal Rickey now always had in mind: to be the highest-paid player in the sport.

Claire Smith spent Christmas Day at her parents' house in Langhorne, Pennsylvania, just north of Philadelphia. While Rickey was on the West Coast celebrating his 31st birthday, Smith's mother was watching TV when she saw Billy Martin's face inserted in a graphic. She called Claire into the living room.

"It was turned on to CNN. I said, 'I have to work. Billy's dead,'" Smith recalled. "There was just no other reason for his face to be on television. As the details came in, it was somewhat ironic that he died in a drunk driving accident, because Billy never drove drunk. He always had someone else drive for him. He died in a drunk driving accident and wasn't even driving."

The details were sad and grisly. Billy and William Reedy, an old pal from Detroit, were driving on an icy road near Binghamton, New York. Reedy lost control of his truck, which skidded off the road and plunged 300 feet down an embankment. Neither was wearing a seat belt. Reedy was charged for driving under the influence. Martin, after all the fights and the bars and the championships, the good times with Mickey Mantle and Whitey Ford and all the booze that came with it, was dead at 61.

"By the time I covered him last, we had a really great relationship," Smith said. "I don't think he ever recovered from being the youngest of Mickey's boys and being blamed for getting Mickey in trouble, and the Yankees traded him for that."

"Alcohol was such a central part of his life. His coaches would close down bars with Billy. I didn't work for a New York paper. I wasn't one of the boys, so I didn't need to do Billy 24/7, but so much of it came back to Billy and George. Billy Martin was a man who needed help, but instead of putting out fires, George was really good at putting gasoline on them. It was a sad ending, but not a surprising one."

The Black version of Ellis Island: The violence and lack of opportunity in the Jim Crow South led Black people in Texas, Louisiana, and Arkansas to flee the South in record numbers. Many chose Oakland as a destination. *Russell Lee / Library of Congress*

In 1940, Oakland was 2.8 percent Black. By the end of the decade, the Black population would increase by nearly 2,000 percent, forever transforming the city. *African American Museum & Library at Oakland*

Known as "the Football Kid," Rickey was once placed on the Oakland Tech junior varsity baseball team—until he told the varsity coach, "You must not know who I am."
Oakland Technical High School

Senior Year, Oakland Technical High School, Class of 1976.
Oakland Technical High School

Mike Norris was a 22-game winner in 1980. Unlike Rickey, Norris was unfazed by the constant battles with A's ownership over money. He once said of salary arbitration, "I was going to either wake up rich—or richer." *Ron Riesterer*

No manager connected with Rickey like the explosive Billy Martin. Rickey called Martin a "father figure," and even in his first full season with Rickey, Martin was already calling him the greatest leadoff hitter of all time. *Ron Riesterer*

Unconvinced by their own scout's enthusiasm, the Oakland A's did not draft Rickey until the fourth round of the 1976 draft. The slight was magnified when none of the A's players drafted ahead of him ever reached the majors. *Michael Zagaris*

Coined by the writer Ralph Wiley, "the Rickey Run" became a feared part of Rickey's game: walk, steal second, steal third, and score on a fly ball without even getting a hit. *Michael Zagaris*

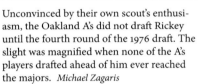

At the 1984 All-Star Game with Eddie Murray (left) and Chili Davis (right), Rickey was now a perennial All-Star—but fumed about not being paid as much as the game's home-run hitters. *Ron Riesterer*

Billy Martin told Rickey that his destiny was the bright lights of New York, where no trio of hitters would instill more fear than Dave Winfield (left), Don Mattingly (right), and Rickey. Their offense, however, could not produce a division title. *Keith Torrie / New York Daily News via Getty Images*

No two players embodied the speed and dynamism of 1980s baseball like Tim Raines and Rickey. Base-stealing rivals for a decade, both would wind up in the Baseball Hall of Fame. *Focus on Sport / Getty Images*

Rickey's 1985 was one of the greatest seasons in history, but despite four and a half years of dominant numbers, he left New York with a reputation as a player who did not play hard and was not a winner. *David Madison / Getty Images*

The relationship between Tony La Russa and Rickey was often tense, but Rickey's return in 1989 began a two-and-a-half-year run that was one of the greatest of any player ever—and brought a championship to Oakland. *Focus on Sport / Getty Images*

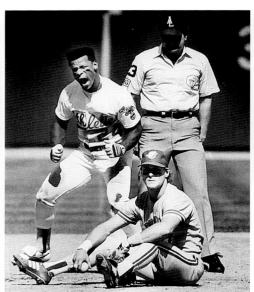

Rickey at supernova: The 1989 American League Championship Series. *Matthew J. Lee*

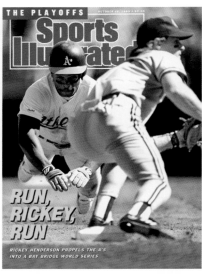

THE PLAYOFFS

Sports Illustrated

RUN, RICKEY, RUN

RICKEY HENDERSON PROPELS THE A'S INTO A BAY BRIDGE WORLD SERIES

Rickey would grace the cover of *Sports Illustrated* three times. His performances in the 1989 postseason removed any doubt that he could be a championship performer. *V.J. Lovero / Sports Illustrated via Getty Images*

No player instilled more fear in a pitcher starting a game than Rickey, who tortured pitchers with not only a keen eye but astounding power. He led off games with a home run a record 81 times. *Brad Mangin*

Rickey was nearly traded to the San Francisco Giants in the spring of 1989, but by fall he was hitting .474 against them in the World Series and capturing his first World Series title. *Ron Riesterer*

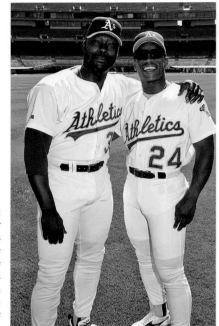

Two legends of Oakland: Dave Stewart and Rickey were childhood friends who played Little League together and would make the majors and win World Series titles together in Oakland and Toronto.
Michael Zagaris

Over 25 seasons Rickey would play for nine different teams—but Oakland would always be home. He would play for the A's on four separate occasions, for a total of 14 seasons.
Brad Mangin

Most all-time records are broken late in a career. On May 1, 1991, Rickey broke the all-time stolen-base record at 32 years old. In a feat virtually unheard of, he would hold the record as an active player for a decade. *Brad Mangin*

Rickey always credited his mother, Bobbie, with making him choose baseball. The legend was that he wanted to play football, but she believed he would be injured. *Brad Mangin*

Rickey and the 1990 American League All-Stars. *Michael Zagaris*

Dave Stewart would say that no player played the game more physically than Rickey, but the demands of stealing bases did not garner him sympathy from a sport and public that believed he should have played injured more often. Rickey would eventually be vindicated by his longevity—and staggering statistics. *Michael Zagaris*

Rickey would always be seen as a singular figure in his drive to be great. As teammate Terry Steinbach once said, "The things Rico could do, you had to see it to believe it." *Michael Zagaris*

Pamela (second from left) and Rickey began dating as high schoolers in the early 1970s. Being the wife of a famous baseball player was never easy, and she cherished the rare family times away from the ballpark. *Michael Zagaris*

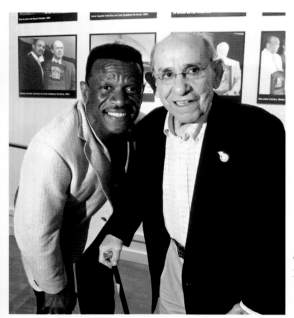

Two American philosophers:
Rickey Henderson and Yogi Berra.
Walt McCreary

As with Yogi, it would often be impossible to separate fact from fiction when it came to Rickey stories—none of them more famous than the legendary exchange with John Olerud that never happened. *Matt Campbell / AFP via Getty Images*

With the Padres for the second time, in 2001, Rickey broke Ty Cobb's all-time runs record by hitting a home run—and sliding into home plate. *Jon Soohoo / WireImage*

A 43-year-old Rickey, as a member of the Boston Red Sox, waves to the crowd on Rickey Henderson Day in 2002. But it was not a farewell: Rickey would join the Dodgers the following year. *Brita Meng Outzen*

Another day, more victims: Rickey at the card table with Ariel Prieto (center) and Yoenis Cespedes (right). *Michael Zagaris*

Rickey at Cooperstown: Flashing the number-one sign in front of Ty Cobb's plaque, having broken two of Cobb's hallowed records. *Walt McCreary*

Devoted superfan Kent Corser's homage to Rickey: The Man Cave of Steal. *Kent Corser*

Fearing the public's expectation that his 2009 Hall of Fame induction speech would be self-absorbed, Rickey took a college course to perfect it—and finally won over the public.
Milo J. Stewart / National Baseball Hall of Fame and Museum

"Today, I'm the greatest of all time!": Rickey shatters the all-time record. This statement would eventually be a fondly recalled part of his legend, but he was criticized at the time as classless for making it. "Once I said it," he said, "I knew I'd never live it down." *Michael Zagaris*

A S RELATIONSHIPS WENT, Rickey and his money were never far apart. In Oakland, the stories were legendary about how tight Rickey was with a dollar. In the Yankee clubhouse, only Dave Winfield was considered more frugal, but with the A's, Rickey was king. "I remember one time, and I think I was out of baseball at the time working a regular job, but we all went out to dinner one night, Mexican place," Shooty Babitt recalled. "The bill came, and Rickey was like, 'Separate checks.' Now, I'm a man, I don't need anybody buying me food, but typically, it's common practice if you're making four million dollars to, you know, maybe pick that one up? But Rickey was tight. Like 'capital T' tight."

Rickey was the epitome of pure competition, and adding a pot to the clubhouse card games only increased his intensity. If there was money on the table, it was going to be his. Whenever the rookies would show up in the A's clubhouse, they were warned: if you want to keep your shirt, your socks, your shoes, if you don't want to go home wearing a barrel, *don't play cards with Rickey.*

Rickey would laugh at the reputation that he was tight, partly because it was true—he was nobody's fool, who *wouldn't* want more money?—and also because he believed that, essentially, it wasn't true. As someone who never removed himself from his town, from his people, from where he came, he had long sponsored community programs in Oakland. He owned several properties and rented housing to friends and family at sharp discounts. It was why Monopoly was his favorite board game and everyone hated playing it with him because he was so relentlessly capitalist. Just as there was a difference between having fun and being reckless, there was a difference between being conservative with money and being cheap.

When it came to money, there was something deliciously counterintuitive about Rickey Henderson: he'd spent his career having his intelligence questioned, and the natural extension of that skepticism was that he was another Black athlete who burned through money. But Rickey knew exactly at all times where every dollar he ever earned had been spent. After being teammates with so many players and hearing all the stories about professional athletes losing everything, especially the Black ones, Rickey knew he was never going to be the guy who didn't know where his money was or how much he had. People would constantly ask, *Is Rickey broke?* It was a common, but incorrect, assumption made because of his flamboyance—anyone who invented the snatch-catch *must* have a hole in his pocket. But Rickey wasn't going to be one in the long list of players whose people had their hands out, expecting him to pay for them until there was nothing left.

Later in his career, Rickey was sitting at his locker reading the newspaper in the cramped visitors' clubhouse in Boston before a game at Fenway Park. When his teammates arrived and saw Rickey's nose in the newspaper, one said, "Catching up on the news, Rickey?"

"Nah," Rickey replied. "My portfolio."

Pamela would always describe Rickey and herself as grounded, as not ostentatious in their spending, even though Rickey's ride would always be clean. "He's a man," she said. "You know he needed his car." Rickey still loved his gambling and was always well known in Vegas. Pamela remembered the final weeks of the 1982 season, when Rickey had already broken Brock's single-season record but wanted to go for 140 steals—then jammed his collarbone. That moment was crucial, for it encapsulated the paradox of his supreme self-confidence being guided by his goal of security. "He knew with the style of play he had, all it could take was one injury for it to all be taken away," she said. People who thought Rickey was destined to be that guy— the athlete bankrupted by bad business investments, lots of diamonds, and quick-talking but underqualified financial advisers—all because he picked at his jersey after home runs, did not know who they were talking about.

Except for kids, Rickey did not just give people money. His personality was big, but it was also a performance, his part of a transaction: fans paid him to be entertained, and so he entertained them. Rickey wasn't Babe Ruth or Charles Barkley—walking into the joint and buying the entire town a round because he was all about the high times. That was the fastest way to go broke. He loaned money out to people routinely, but he wasn't *giving* anybody anything.

With Rickey, there was nothing complex about money: it was the currency that Americans most coveted; it made things happen; and it was the reason why some other things did not happen. Money was the American language. Rickey was aware of money because it was the barometer that measured his achievement of what he coveted the most: respect. "There have been so many times I've given people the shirt off my back," he would say. "If you're in trouble, I will always try to help you. But when you're not in trouble anymore, you have to make *some* effort to pay it back. And if you don't make *any* effort to pay me back, what you're really saying is, you don't have any respect for me. You have to give me back something. You have to at least try."

If you didn't make the effort to pay Rickey back, he might not have been completely done with you—he didn't cut off former intimates DiMaggio-style—but you could bet things would never be the same. Money could definitely come between a friend and Rickey. In 1986, when they were teammates with the Yankees, Claudell Washington was going through a rough marital stretch. Rickey loaned him $50,000. That's what friends do sometimes, especially when one is making nearly $2 million a year. That was one half of the story. The other half was that Rickey held Claudell's 1974 World Series championship trophy for the next three and a half decades—as either collateral or for "safekeeping," depending on one's perspective.

Money was a tricky area now. Rickey kept his circle tight and private, but as such, there was often an enormous financial imbalance between him and those in his group. Claudell was in a different category because he was a big leaguer too; it wasn't like $50,000 was an insurmountable amount of money for him.

In Rickey's world, money revealed character. "This was when he was coming up, but Rickey had asked me to work with him as an adviser, and I never went into business with him, because it was all about helping him and you don't want to come off like you've got your hand out, or that your counsel comes at a cost," Jim Guinn recalled. "If there was an issue, we would just go into the weight room and talk. And I could say what I wanted to, because it was about helping them more than anything. When Rickey started to become a real superstar, there were enough people he had to worry about having their hands out. He didn't have to worry about that with me."

Now a champion, it was time to cash in. Rickey had become a free agent a week after the World Series and was going to be the coveted player at the winter meetings—if testing the market was his objective. As the baseball world prepared to descend on the sprawling Opryland Hotel in Nashville, the word was that the Dodgers, having failed at it for coming up on two decades, were going to make another run at Rickey. Rickey wanted to stay in Oakland. "He wants more than one year," Sandy Alderson told the writers, "and he wants a sizable raise, which is not surprising."

On November 22, 1989, outfielder Kirby Puckett became the first player in baseball history to average a $3 million annual salary when he signed a three-year, $10 million deal with the Twins. Six days later, on November 28, Richie Bry and Alderson agreed on a whopper of a deal for Rickey: four years and $12 million—the highest contract in the game.

Announced with the deal was the news that Rickey was giving $100,000 back to the community—$50,000 to fund local programs for the youth of the city and $50,000 for Loma Prieta earthquake relief. Rickey referred to the deal as a "dream come true." He told the press that he had always preferred staying in Oakland, "no matter what the terms." He praised Alderson as "fair." After being doubted in New York, dominating the postseason, he had finally done it: Four years, $12 million. Guaranteed. A no-trade clause. The highest-paid guy in the game. That was ace-of-the-staff money. That was cleanup-hitter money. A leadoff hitter was leading the market. Nobody had done that before.

It might as well have lasted 30 seconds. Rickey was the game's highest player literally for 48 hours. Two days after his deal, the Angels signed a pitcher, the left-hander Mark Langston, to a five-year, *$16 million* contract. In the span of nine days, baseball had broken its record contract three times. One reason was that the owners had been busted for collusion—the conspiracy to destroy free agency when the owners secretly agreed not to sign free agents, the conspiracy that the writers said could never occur—and now they had to pay up. With the conspiracy agreement now broken, the owners had gone back to spending.

When Rickey made his debut in 1979, Nolan Ryan had become the game's first player earning $1 million per year. Entering the 1990 season, 152 players were earning at least $1 million annually. Rickey stayed silent, but inside he was burning. After Langston's deal, Dave Stewart wanted a contract extension—that was about respect too. During the first weeks of January, Eric Davis signed a three-year, $9.3 million deal with the Reds—topping Rickey's annual salary. That same week, the A's gave Stewart a two-year extension at $3.5 million per year—topping Rickey. A week later, the Giants gave Will Clark, their National League playoff MVP, a four-year, $15 million extension—topping Rickey.

A month after the final pitch of the season was thrown, Rickey was the highest-paid player in the game. A month before the first pitch of spring training, he was the third-highest-paid player in his area code. Rickey's contract was worth more, but Milwaukee's Robin Yount (who had just won the 1989 AL MVP) was earning $3.2 million for 1990—a full million more than Rickey.

As the sports pages headlined each new member of the $3 million a year club, Rickey—now signed and locked in with a figure that had been higher than ever but was being surpassed every day—was aware of the numbers down to the decimal point.

Rickey in 1990 was staring down the American League as a world champion and a postseason superstar who, like Reggie Jackson, had proven, when the lights went on, that his every boast was justified. All those articles about Rickey not being a winning ballplayer, well, they were just fish wrap now, yesterday's news.

Even in his boasting, Rickey had never compared himself to Reggie. He compared himself to Muhammad Ali. Rickey was staring down history in a way that was incomprehensible: he was 31 years old and only 68 stolen bases away from Lou Brock's all-time record. Brock's record of 938 career steals was set when he retired in 1979. He'd stolen his final base on September 23, at Shea against the Mets, when Rickey was in Oakland, navigating the final days of his rookie season and not doing much. Darrell Porter of the Royals threw him out that afternoon. Less than a dozen years later, Rickey was about to make sure Brock's all-time record didn't last even a decade.

The honor he really craved was the one most out of his control—Most Valuable Player. The way Rickey saw it, that trophy should have already been his. Dave Stewart felt similarly about the Cy Young Award, a prize Stewart coveted but believed he was never going to win. With Stewart the reasons he didn't win it shifted from year to year, but the BBWAA always found a reason

to give it to someone else. Rickey saw the MVP award, like money, usually going to home-run, middle-of-the-lineup hitters, or to pitchers. Leadoff
guys, defensive players, run scorers—they never won. Even Joe Morgan, the
great Little Joe who went back to back in 1975 and 1976 for Cincinnati, hit
third. "I cannot believe I lost the MVP to a relief pitcher," Rickey would say
often, but never to much comfort.

The A's were defending champions, and the goal was to get back to the
World Series and go back to back. Nobody had done that since Reggie's
Yankees. The A's had all the boxes checked, though they were a different
team than the previous year's champions. His work grooming Jose Canseco
supposedly done, Dave Parker left for Milwaukee, where another project
awaited: the organization thought a super-talented Black kid named Gary
Sheffield needed mentoring. Tony Phillips went to Detroit, Storm Davis to
Baltimore. Alderson replaced them with the laconic Harold Baines, who had
played for La Russa in Chicago, and Willie Randolph, Rickey's old Yankee
teammate, who came over from the Dodgers.

In personality, Baines was the polar opposite of the loud, bopping Parker,
who would tear an opposing pitcher to shreds and challenge his own teammates to bring it or risk his biting commentary. If a player talked too much
on the bus or in the clubhouse, Parkway would look up their stats, then let
the numbers decide who could talk. Randolph was still the same Willow, the
same serious, professional, all-business grown-up—and he was still carrying the underlying hurt of not being anointed an immortal by the Yankees,
as they had done for so many others.

In between, an old name from the old days had unfinished business with
the game of baseball. In 1990, Mike Norris attempted a comeback after years
of injury, drug use, and being something of a pariah during the "Just Say
No" 1980s and baseball's drug scandals. While Rickey was building his monument, Norris hadn't pitched in the big leagues since 1983, when they were
teammates. That night in '78, back in Jersey City when Rickey told him he
was garbage, gave Norris a lift that turned him into a 20-game winner, but
now he was fighting three enemies virtually every day: substances, himself,
and a body that could no longer do what he wanted it to do. Norris was
the living example of Billy Martin running his pitchers into the ground—
and evidence for why Rickey made sure he listened to his body more than
he did the managers, trainers, and team doctors who treated ballplayers so
disposably.

The more his body quit on him, the more Mike Norris depended on cocaine. Whoever was in the batter's box was a concern further off in the distance. Norris was one of the players named frequently during the Pittsburgh and Kansas City drug scandals, and as he attempted to recover his life, no matter where he went inside the game, he found he was never seen as just Mike Norris, former 20-game winner. He was always Mike Norris, former 20-game winner *and drug abuser*—the deadly (to his career at least) appositive that he couldn't shake off.

"They put us out on front street like that," Norris recalled. "And who is gonna want to touch you after that, even after baseball? But I'm not gonna lie—it was on me. I always wanted people to like me, and I found out I could buy people to like me—but that shit wasn't true either. You can't drink people into liking you."

When Alderson invited Norris back for a tryout, the love was still there. "Why? Because he was unemployed. Because he has a likable personality and goes way back with the organization," said Alderson in explaining why he offered Norris a comeback path. "And because he's the type of person you'd like to give a second chance. And a third. And a fourth."

Norris was one of the good guys, easygoing, never full of moods or rages, and in Oakland that created compassion for his demons—Mike Norris never flinched from the facts of his life. The fans remembered Mike from Billyball—good ol' Mike from the good old days when the A's surprised everybody, won a bunch of games, and wound up on the cover of *Sports Illustrated*. So people wanted Mike to succeed—who didn't love a good redemption story? Wes Stock, the former big leaguer who had been on the A's payroll as an adviser to Alderson, worked him out. Stock was central to helping Dave Stewart become a perennial 20-game winner, and he had been Norris's first pitching coach with the A's back in 1975.

After receiving a standing ovation from the Coliseum crowd when he made his season debut—proof, Rickey told the writers, of how special a place Oakland was—Norris would appear in 14 games in 1990. He even won a game—April 17, on the road, in Anaheim, his first win in seven years. Some of the fastballs popped just like they used to, but Norris knew what a fastball was supposed to sound like all the time, not just now and then. He didn't have much left.

"The game got too easy for me," Norris reflected. "Then you get ignorant, and you flaunt it, and you just keep going and push it, and you keep pushing it. 'Let's find out how high I can be and go out there,' or 'How much I can fuck and go out there.' I know it sounds crazy—and you don't realize how much you've got it until it's gone. Then, I'm trying to make a comeback and I'm throwing. Wes Stock, he was a good man, but we all knew the truth—I'm not half the player I was.

"When I grew up in San Francisco, I used to watch them all—Marichal, McCovey, Mays, Jim Ray Hart. I would dream I'd be in the dugout, and no one would talk to me. Then one day Willie McCovey said to me, 'Mike, when you gonna get a chance to pitch?' I said, 'I hope soon.' Then I'd wake up. And one day Willie McCovey and I ended on the same team in the big leagues. So when they say dreams come true, I'm a living example of that."

The A's were as fearsome as they were the year before when they went 8-1 in the playoffs, with one major exception: now they had Rickey for a full season. The same jabs from the same sources kept coming ("Now that Rickey has achieved his goal of a World Series ring and had a four-year, $12 million guarantee, will he go at full throttle?" wrote his old New York nemesis Moss Klein in his *Sporting News* column), but nothing could stop Rickey in 1990.

April 13, fourth game of the season, up in the Kingdome: the A's put up five in the first in a 15–7 rout of the Mariners, set off by Rickey with a leadoff bomb to start a 4-for-5 day, the 41st time in his career he'd opened a game by clearing the fence. Rickey's average would not drop below .320 for the rest of the season.

There was the opposition, there was the history, and there was the money—always the money. Across the country on opening day, April 9, the Yankees extended Don Mattingly's contract—five years, $19.3 million. Steinbrenner told Mattingly he deserved it—and he did. Nobody had survived the insanity of the Yankees quite like Mattingly. Baylor was long gone. Griffey was gone. Guidry and Randolph were gone. Rickey was gone. Mattingly upheld his professionalism in the face of a monsoon. A month after Mattingly signed his deal, Winfield was gone. Having finally waived his no-trade, George traded Winfield to California—a last Steinbrenner act before baseball sent George himself away.

Rickey loved Donnie and was happy for him. Nobody, including all the Black players, had backed Rickey in New York like Mattingly did. But now Donnie was at $3.86 million on average per season, topping Rickey, so Rickey dug in. April 21, three hits, two stolen bases against the Mariners. A two-homer game (including a ninth-inning blast off Eric Plunk, the guy he was traded for both leaving and returning to Oakland) in his return to Yankee Stadium. Ten days later, when the Yankees came to Oakland, clinging to a 1–0 lead, Rickey dug in even more—and had an all-time Rickey moment.

Stewart was on the mound, pitching a game and a half in front of a great crowd, 32,000-plus on a Wednesday afternoon. Stewart had won his first six starts, and now he was spinning his best game of the season—but he was losing. Stewart was ornery. The pitcher who would later measure his control by saying, "Man, I could hit the hair on a fly's ass," hit three guys that day, including Mattingly—drilled him right in the back and watched emotionless as Donnie writhed on the ground. Stewart wasn't having control issues that day. "If I hit that many, it was because I felt like it." Only weeks later did Stewart discover that Mattingly was recovering from back surgery. "I felt bad for a minute after I heard that—but it was only for a minute."

Now Stewart's 6-and-0 start was about to be ruined by a 1–0 loss to these going-nowhere Yankees. "I go into the clubhouse, salty as hell. Pitching my ass off and we're losing," Stewart recalled. "Rickey follows me in the clubhouse and says, 'Davey! . . . Davey! . . . I got you. I'll take care of it!'"

Bottom of the eighth, one out, Rickey hit a bullet to left for a double. Then Carney Lansford grounded to short, right in front of Rickey standing on second. Rickey took off for third, and Alvaro Espinoza, the Yankee shortstop, did the right thing by making the safe play, the sure out at first. *But Rickey kept on running*, blowing past third and turning on the jets for the plate like he's got a promise to keep. Mattingly, stunned, and maybe still smarting from Stewart drilling him in the back, wheeled and gunned home, but Rickey was a cloud of dust, already past the helpless Yankee catcher, Bob Geren, already popped up from his slide—already celebrating. Pumping his arms, he started dancing, right at home plate. Without assistance from a bobble or an error, Rickey scored from second on a ground ball out to short. Tie game.

Stewart didn't win the game, but thanks to Rickey, he didn't lose it either. The game went into the 11th, bases loaded for Rickey—and who was he facing? *Twice-traded-for-Rickey* Eric Plunk. *I-just-got-taken-deep-by-Rickey-10-days-ago* Eric Plunk. From the on-deck circle, Lansford told Rickey that Plunk was too rattled to throw him a strike. Plunk threw four pitches. None of them were in the zip code. Rickey walked, driving in the winning run. A's win.

When Rickey dug in, the records fell. May 26, fifth inning at the Coliseum against Cleveland, Rickey swiped third off the talented kid catcher Sandy Alomar for career stolen base number 892, tying Ty Cobb's American League record set 62 years earlier.

Cobb was done when he set that record, just finishing up a quarter-century career with the A's—the Philadelphia A's. He stole his last base on July 4, 1928, in the first game of a doubleheader at Shibe Park against the Red Sox. Cobb retired at the end of the 1928 season, but not before bitching that baseball only cared about the long ball, the big inning, that baseball had abandoned the art of base stealing. A rookie in 1905 with the Tigers, Cobb accomplished on the bases in 24 seasons what Rickey would do in less than 11. Cobb stole 892 bases (the stat guys would discover five more long after the Georgia Peach was dead and pad his total posthumously to 897) in 3,204 games. Rickey had barely played 1,500 games. A couple of weeks later, on June 12, Rickey stole two bags for 900. Only Brock remained.

Rickey was tearing up the league while the A's were fending off a surprise charge from the White Sox. October 1989 had been the crowning achievement—Dennis Eckersley would never forget Rickey's destruction of Toronto and San Francisco in succession—but now he was extending his level of play in that monthlong performance to every game of a 162-game season. Eckersley said that he had never seen, to this day, such a complete masterpiece of focus, competitiveness, and one player's ability to simply bend the sport—especially this sport, in which failure is so deeply embedded—to his will.

"When Rickey kept his nose in it—and I don't mean that bullshit of him wanting or not wanting to play, but kept his nose in it, no give, no fear—and he decided that outside corner was his, you couldn't stop him," Eckersley recalled. "When a hitter gives, you can get him out. But when a guy of Rickey's ability keeps his nose in there . . . You can't do it every single game all the time, because in the back of your mind you can get hurt, but when he did, and he was fearless? Forget it."

Before the All-Star break, Kim Boatman of the *San Jose Mercury* was one of the first reporters to begin mentioning Rickey as an early MVP favorite. He had been in the top 10 in 11 offensive categories for a team where each game mattered. The A's were defending world champions, and every team they played was giving it their best; beating the champs meant something even for teams that weren't going anywhere. Rickey was having his career year and carrying the team without a full complement of players, since Canseco and Willie Randolph had been injured. Then, on July 8, the Big One hit.

$23.5 MILLION FOR CANSECO HAS RICKEY DOWN IN THE WALLET

OAKLAND—To keep Jose Canseco in Oakland, the A's have made him baseball's first $5 million man.

Rickey Henderson isn't happy about the development.

On a day the A's fell out of first place for the first time since April 14, Canseco put his name on a contract extension that included a $3.5 million signing bonus, and will pay him $2.8 million in 1991, $3.6 million in 1992, $4.1 million in 1993, $4.4 million in 1994 and $5.1 million in 1995.

The contract is the richest ever signed by a baseball player. The deal Don Mattingly recently signed with the New York Yankees will pay the first baseman an average of $3.86 million for five years, while Canseco's will average $4.7 million.

This couldn't be happening. *Four. Point. Seven. MILLION?* Rickey bee-lined straight to La Russa, who told Rickey to just play his game, to be the great player he was and the organization would fix it. Rickey called Alderson, who said that he and Richie Bry would talk. Both Alderson and La Russa, Rickey said, promised him they would make things right, which to Rickey meant somehow—by contract renegotiation or extension, by knocking over a Wells Fargo, whatever—paying Rickey more. Neither Alderson nor La Russa saw it that way. Alderson explained that the contract "reflects Jose's ability as a player and a dramatic change in the marketplace that has oc-curred since last December."

That was one reason for paying Canseco so much, but another was that the A's were certainly more invested in and forgiving of Canseco than any-one had ever been with Rickey. The A's made Canseco a $5 million player though he had now been struggling with back issues for parts of two sea-sons. He was also busted carrying a loaded gun and got pinched by the cops for driving 125 miles an hour in a 55-mile-per-hour zone. Rickey had never landed in the police blotter. The worst thing anyone had ever said about him was that he didn't like day games after night games.

Before receiving his megadeal, Canseco had even called out baseball's racial double standards and the A's in particular for preferring that the face of the franchise be white, bright, and polite. Canseco criticized the contracts of Will Clark and Mark McGwire, the chosen ones, and pointed out that Black and Latin players were expected to put up machinelike numbers and then were vilified at the first sign that the numbers were slipping.

"It's a matter of politics," he said. "Will Clark gets a long-term contract with the Giants. Kevin Mitchell doesn't. Clark's white. Mitchell's Black. I'm Latin . . . Will Clark does not just represent himself. He represents America. Mark McGwire came up with the A's. He's the All-American boy from the All-American family. He's not just representing Mark McGwire anymore. He's representing the United States. If he fails, the US fails. If I fail, I'm just a Latin guy trying to make it in baseball, and I'll be buried. Nobody would let me forget the mistakes that I've made."

Canseco's words were dismissed as nonsense coming from a meathead. After he made this statement, the negative reactions from the mainstreamers, who were allowed to practice racism and then tell the public it didn't exist, were so strong that Canseco was eventually mocked into compliance. But he wasn't exactly wrong. Chris Sauceda, the kid who was at the Coliseum the night the Rickey trade was announced, was attending Cal State–Hayward (as it was called back then) and had landed a part-time job covering high school sports at the *Oakland Tribune*. "John Simmonds was the night sports editor, and I just remember him being so angry at Canseco's comments. He was at his desk, and just kept repeating, 'This is such bullshit . . . such . . . bullshit!'"

The fact was that, while everyone was dismissing Canseco's position, he knew how the game worked. Across the country, in Pittsburgh, the same dynamic was playing out: a nice player, Andy Van Slyke, was receiving a certain dispensation from the fans and the media, while the league's best player, Barry Bonds, was not. Bonds had taken to calling Van Slyke "Mr. Pittsburgh." It was not a compliment. While the white men who ran the sport and the white men who wrote about it ridiculed him, Canseco had actually hit the bull's-eye on a topic that was ripping the game apart. It wouldn't be the last time.

None of which was to say that the A's weren't frustrated by Canseco, privately tired of him, and possibly thinking that perhaps he wasn't worth all of the headaches. Still, being annoyed didn't prevent them from making Canseco the highest-paid player in the game.

Rickey was seething about the Canseco contract—and about the celebrity megastar treatment Jose was getting after being seen leaving Madonna's place in the wee hours during one road trip against the Yankees—but instead of erupting, Rickey dug in, put his nose in it. In the second half of the season, the A's had beaten back the White Sox and the Twins and the Royals, finishing off the division comfortably with a 103-win season. Rickey, who hit .352 in July and .313 in September, had never been on a team that won so many games, and he had been the consistent engine, from start to finish, to make that happen.

Rickey hit only .243 against the lowly Yankees for the season, but he also stuck it right to them—the A's cleaned their clocks all season, sweeping them 12–0 in the head-to-head and outscoring them 62–12. The Yankees, who dumped Rickey a year earlier as "addition by subtraction," lost 95 games, the most for a Yankee team since 1912. The A's were in the postseason again and facing a formidable challenge in a rematch with the Red Sox, who had won the East for the second time in three years. But the A's were seen as the team to beat. When the playoffs began, *The Sporting News* ran a feature on them headlined, "Can ANYONE Stop These Guys?"

When it was over and the A's had crashed out of the World Series, destroyed in a devastatingly comprehensive four-game sweep by a fearless and terribly underappreciated Cincinnati Reds squad (managed, by the way, by Lou Piniella), the numb feelings and recrimination sat heavy throughout the Oakland clubhouse. When the American League Championship Series was over, the A's had been invincible, having slapped around a strong Red Sox team in four straight, just as they did in the ALCS two years earlier.

"They were just so good," Ellis Burks, the Boston center fielder, recalled. "They were so intimidating. That lineup. And Dave Stewart always got up for Roger, always brought his A+-level game." It was true. Clemens—ejected for arguing with home-plate umpire Terry Cooney—couldn't even get out of the second inning of Game 4, a must-have elimination game, after giving up three runs, the only three runs Boston allowed in a 3–1 loss. The Red Sox scored four runs in four games.

Stewart had gotten to Clemens again, and again with the season on the line, but this time there was an added bonus—Clemens looked like a total

maniac, wearing eye black on the mound as if he were a football player, or
a center fielder. When the TV cameras caught him mouthing something to
Cooney to the effect of *Get your fucking ass back behind the plate*, Clemens
was in the shower before the fight even began. "That meltdown," Dave Stewart would say, "that's when you know you were in somebody's head."

In the ALCS opener against Boston, Clemens versus Stewart, the two
titans actually engaged in a real pitchers' duel, before Boston's bullpen gave
it up: the A's scored nine runs in the final two innings. In the World Series,
they scored eight—in four games. Eight runs in 37 innings will send a team
home in a flash. McGwire hit .214. Dave Henderson hit .231. Mike Moore
was ready in Game 3, but gave up six unearned runs. Stewart was bombed
in Game 1 but valiantly pitched a complete game in the finale, giving up one
earned run in a 2–1 loss as Cincinnati won the title at the Coliseum. Stewart
was outclassed by Jose Rijo, the Series MVP and one of the players the Yankees had traded to the A's for Rickey back in 1984.

Canseco hit .083 and took a casual jump on a Billy Hatcher drive in a
crucial Game 2 that sailed over his head for a game-tying triple. The A's
eventually lost that game, 5–4, in 10 innings. Canseco was benched in the
clincher, appearing meekly as a pinch hitter, and the season was lost. Tom
Barnidge of *The Sporting News* laid much of the loss at Canseco's feet, but he
wasn't being provocative. Everyone was in the know, whether wearing the
uniform, holding a tape recorder, or signing the checks:

> We'll never know if Canseco shared the same aching sense of empti-
> ness, if his stomach was tied up in knots, if he felt at all personally
> responsible for what had happened. After Game 4, Canseco was absent
> from the locker room, secluded only he knows where. Absent, just as
> he'd been throughout the Series. The question that the A's may ponder
> in the coming months is whether the Canseco who was once a unani-
> mous MVP candidate will ever reappear.

Then there was Rickey. He hit .333 in the four games, with a .444 on-
base percentage. He was 3-for-3 in steal attempts, but with the power outage
in the lineup, Rickey scored only two runs—and one of them came from
driving himself in with a home run in Game 3. He was described by the
newspapers as "numb," his features "frozen" sitting in the clubhouse afterward. "It went by too fast," Rickey said. Next to Rickey was Eckersley. "Some

people had some great years on this club," Barnidge quoted Eckersley. "We won a division and we won a pennant, but we'll be remembered for getting our ass kicked."

La Russa would blame the debacle on himself. "I feel it was my greatest failure as a manager. I remember during the workout some of our players were watching Cincinnati take batting practice, watching where their balls were going, and you could just feel they didn't have the sharp focus. They didn't have the kind of respect you needed to have for an opponent. They had just won their league. There are no pushovers at that point. I thought when we beat Boston in 1988, we were the superior team, but in 1990 they were a very, very good team when we beat them four straight and that made me fearful that maybe our guys were feeling themselves a little too much," La Russa recalled. "I did not have the right words to motivate them, and I was frustrated on why I didn't have the approach to get the team ready."

It didn't click for La Russa until a couple of decades later when he attended a banquet in Wisconsin honoring the old Green Bay Packers of the 1960s, so many of them long gone by then. All those autumns later, the Packers were still seen as timeless—because they won. Not because they were always the best team, but because they finished the job. Because they did not finish the job, a great A's team would be remembered only as a good team—as champions like so many others, certainly, but not as legends. They weren't timeless. They were now in the category of the two-pennant, one-title Milwaukee Braves of Aaron, Mathews, and Spahn who beat the Yankees in 1957 and had a 3–1 lead to beat them again but then lost. Or more accurately, the A's resembled the Earl Weaver Orioles of 1969–1971, who demolished the league, won 100 games in three straight years, and emerged, like Oakland, with but one title.

If he had spoken more to their vanity, their ego, to their sense of immortality, La Russa concluded, the A's might have found the necessary motivation to complete the quest. What he should have done, La Russa thought, was convince his team that if they could just win this last series, people would never forget this group, the way people never forgot the Packers. They would be remembered forever—they too would be timeless. Had he found those words to appeal to their greatness, La Russa concluded, the A's would have been ready.

"It wasn't the team. It was 'the one.' 'The one' was the difference in the clubhouse—Jose was a major distraction," Dave Stewart recalled. "Anytime Tony asked him to do something, Jose would do the opposite. He was the guy complaining. 'Why are we always in the playoffs? Why are we in the World Series? Why's the season so long?' I mean, who actually *says* this? So, on this, I disagree with Tony: the team was ready to play. The 'one' didn't want to play, and he was distracting for everyone."

Stewart did not suffer from faulty recall. Early in the series, after Cincinnati pierced their invincibility with a 7–0 Game 1 win over Stewart, Canseco walked into the trainers' room for treatment and groused to the medical staff, "Why do we have to play all these extra games?" Members of the training staff were aghast. One of the trainers responded, "*This* is *why* we go through spring training and 162 games of bullshit, to be *here, in the World Series,* to play these extra games."

After Game 2, when Canseco did not catch Hatcher's drive, Lansford didn't attack Canseco by name, but the team, which knew about what Canseco had said earlier in the trainers' room, didn't need him to. "We can't quit in a World Series," Lansford said. "And if someone here doesn't want to play in a World Series, I wish they'd go home right now."

Three weeks later, Rickey was named American League Most Valuable Player. He had missed out on his first batting title thanks to a furious second-half charge by George Brett (clinched by Brett choosing to skip the final four games of the season to protect his average, much to Rickey's annoyance), but he had hit a career high of .325. Besides hitting 28 home runs, he stole 65 bases and led the league in that category for the 10th time.

Rickey had become so strategic in his steals, however, that he didn't even conquer Lou Brock's all-time record but finished the season two shy of the all-time record. (That was quite a difference from 1982, when Billy sent him to steal regardless of the situation.) Rickey's on-base percentage was .439, he led the league with 119 runs scored, and he had an OPS (that newfangled stat that combined on-base and slugging percentage to emphasize a player's total offensive impact) of 1.016—from the leadoff spot. Rickey had also hit five homers to lead off games, bringing his lifetime total to 45, a record he already owned.

He had done over a full season nearly what he had done during his one electrifying month of playoff baseball the year before, but there was serious MVP competition from Cecil Fielder, the discarded slugger who had returned from the Japanese League and joined the Tigers, slugged 51 home runs, and driven in 132 runs for good measure. Nobody had hit 50 since 1977, when George Foster hit 52 homers for the Reds—and nobody had done it in the American League since the famed Mantle-Maris home-run chase in 1961, when Mantle hit 54 and New York hounded Roger until his hair fell out and his 61-homer season became the least enjoyable year of his life.

There were other candidates. Bob Welch won 27 games, and he would win the Cy Young—even though he wasn't even the best pitcher on his own team (that honor went to Stewart, who finished third). There was Clemens, who finished second in the Cy Young voting and logged a microscopic 1.93 ERA, and Dennis Eckersley, who saved 48 games and held an ERA of 0.61. But were the baseball writers really going to give the MVP to a pitcher again when Rickey was a front-runner, the best player on a 103-win team? In 1990, Rickey was in the middle of an 18-month streak of complete brilliance that not only solidified his place as the best at his position in the game, if not history, but made another case—for Cooperstown.

The great Willie Mays, who already resided there and was the original Bay Area number 24, was celebrating two of his most famous protégés—National League MVP Barry Bonds and Rickey. Both wore number 24, and both idolized Mays coming up. Mays was Barry Bonds's godfather. Both were from the Bay, and both had been named MVP in their league. "They're both my kids," Mays said.

Even his constant critic Moss Klein, writing in *The Sporting News,* could not argue with what Rickey had done:

RICKEY OVER FIELDER: RESULT IS RIGHT ON TARGET

The debate surrounding the American League's Most Valuable Player Award was whether Rickey Henderson's all-around excellence for a winning team merited the honor over Cecil Fielder's memorable slugging for a non-contender. The result of the voting was right on target—a strong showing by Fielder and a much-deserved award for Henderson.

Henderson is the most talented player in the game, and has been for years. The curse of so much talent is that it's virtually impossible to achieve other people's expectations. Henderson hasn't always made the constant, all-out effort he made for the A's this past season, and his occasional funks have created what is, for the most part, a bad rap.

Rickey had won 14 of the 28 first-place ballots. Fielder won 10. To Rickey's annoyance, two pitchers, Clemens and Eckersley, also received first-place votes.

Rickey was gracious in victory. He said the right things. ("I want to tip my hat to Cecil Fielder," the Associated Press reported him saying. "He had an outstanding year and he deserved to win this award, too. But I think because of all the things I did for my team I was able to edge him.") He said he was as happy as he'd been in baseball since breaking Lou Brock's single-season stolen-base record of 130.

Rickey was finally vindicated for his play—and even served as something of a hero to the little guys out there, even if his game was about power as much as it was about speed. Home-run hitters won MVP awards, not leadoff hitters. For that you had to go back to 1973, when Cincinnati's Pete Rose won it in the NL, and 1965, when Zoilo Versalles of the Twins took the AL MVP.

Winning the MVP also vindicated Rickey's game style, recognizing it not as complementary but as essential to winning, even if that recognition made the slugger Fielder feel robbed. "I did everything I could except fill out the ballots," he said, playing to his audience. The locals in Detroit couldn't be faulted either, even when they went so partisan they sounded ridiculous. ("Years from now, nobody will remember Henderson's season, not even in Oakland," Mitch Albom wrote in the *Detroit Free Press*. "It will be just another pile of statistics.") They weren't bad people, the Detroits. They just wanted their guy to win.

After winning the MVP, Rickey said that Brock's all-time record was the next big target for 1991—but that wasn't exactly true. Brock wasn't next. Brock was first. Lou Brock had *always* been the target. Rickey had 936 stolen bases, two away from tying the all-time record, three away from breaking it. Once the season started, Rickey could break the record in a single afternoon, which was hardly suspenseful. It was inevitable. After hoisting his MVP trophy (and receiving his contractual incentive of a $100,000 bonus for winning the MVP), and after watching his peers zoom past him on the salary scale, Rickey's next big target wasn't the all-time stolen-base record—it was for his salary to do what it had done a mere 13 months earlier: reflect that he was the best player in the game.

When Alderson and Richie Bry met, the meetings were productive, Alderson said. Bry said that he didn't want to renegotiate Rickey's contract, but only to extend Rickey's deal to bring it closer in line with a market that had mushroomed in the past year. No deal came of the talks. As the A's broke for spring training, Rickey was a no-show.

From the outside, it wasn't complicated. After winning the World Series, Rickey had chosen the security of a long-term deal and the ease of mind that comes from signing a contract early (thus eliminating the anxiety of an off-season of negotiation) as well as the prestige of setting the market as the highest-paid player in the game. He had known he wanted to remain in Oakland, to be home with his people, and the greater the uncertainty the greater the chance that something could go wrong, that life or fate or a changing market might undermine his wishes. The safe move had been to sign his deal where he wanted to be.

At the time Rickey and Richie Bry were also being practical: the worsening labor situation was tilting the game toward catastrophe, either a strike or a lockout. In addition, after the owners were finally busted for collusion—all 26 teams had in fact conspired to dry up the free-agent market and crush salaries during much of the 1980s by agreeing not to sign free agents—Rickey had another reason to be cautious. There was a chance, no matter how small, that the money might dry up, and after the electric postseason show Rickey had just put on, there was no way he was going to jeopardize the payday he had coming.

As extra insurance against labor uncertainty, Rickey joined a trend among major league players when he signed his contract by taking some of his salary in a signing bonus. Eric Davis, for instance, took $1.5 million of his new $3.1 million salary for 1990 up front. Dave Parker, now with Milwaukee, converted $400,000 of his new deal into a bonus. Hubie Brooks of the Expos did the same. When Rickey took the first $1 million of his $3 million salary in the form of a signing bonus, he and his team were protecting the money he knew he could command. Rickey wasn't alone in reading the market with a work stoppage in mind. Waiting constituted an unnecessary risk.

It almost worked. Bry's strategy was nearly perfect. The owners *did* lock the players out of the 1990 spring training for 32 days. But the lockout began in February, so there was no work stoppage during the regular season. With no lockout and no lost money, the cash didn't dry up after all. Instead, it flourished. For as legendary a gambler as Rickey was, this time the dice he tossed against the wall had come up snake eyes. The owners spent big money in 1990, but Rickey had played it safe and lost.

Rickey's situation was the best example of what Alderson called the "dra-

matic change in the marketplace since last December": by the time the A's
opened camp, Rickey had gone from being the highest-paid player in the
sport in December 1989 to the 36th-highest-paid player by January 1991, and
at the same time he had lost his leverage. When Bry told Alderson that he
did not want to renegotiate Rickey's contract but to extend it to bring Rickey
in alignment with the new realities of the market, Alderson told Bry that the
A's would do neither. Rickey had signed a four-year, $12 million contract,
and a deal was a deal.

"I knew when Rickey signed it he was gonna be leapfrogged," Dave Stewart recalled. "We knew whoever was the highest-paid guy on Monday, it was
gonna be different on Friday because the numbers kept changing so fast."

Everybody negotiating a contract was running on different fuel, but the
common ingredient was pride. "It's a pride thing," was Rickey's public response to Canseco's contract. That was what the game demanded, but pride
was also the sin the game mistook for another—greed. Stewart had won
20 games in four consecutive years, had not missed a start in three years,
and was the undisputed ace of a historical powerhouse. Stewart was a better
pitcher in 1990 than his teammate Bob Welch—he dusted Welch in every
important category except wins—yet he finished third in the Cy Young voting behind Welch and Clemens. In those four years, he would be named to
exactly one All-Star team.

"It was always said that people show you how good you are by how much
they pay you," Dave Stewart recalled. "For me, I was home. I was playing in
Oakland, and I looked at it like it wasn't going to be my last contract. The
Cy Youngs were getting by me, but I was winning 20. I wasn't even getting
selected to the All-Star Game, even by own manager. Roger Clemens was
the best thing since sliced bread, but I was putting a foot in his ass. I wasn't
getting anything else, so I figured, when I got my next contract, it was going
to be reflected there, that I was going to be paid as the best or one of the
best.

"Don't ever underestimate one thing with Rickey—it's always about the
money. Always. *Always*," Stewart recalled. "I wasn't playing for money. I
played to make sure people knew I played the game. I wanted my fucking
name known, that if you were going to let those other pitchers' names roll
off your tongue, don't forget mine. For what I did during those years and the
years I did it, people still don't recognize me as one of the best."

Alderson leaned on the volatile nature of the market to explain Rickey's discontent. He said that he empathized with Rickey and conceded that the system was not fair. "That's the sad part. You have all these guys making all this money and nobody's happy," he said during spring training. "Unless they signed within the past few days, players are second-guessing themselves."

Rickey was earning $3 million. So was Eck, and so was Stew, but the guy who really burned Rickey by making more than he was? Canseco, with the five mil he was getting. The players knew Alderson was not completely wrong in signing that contract with Canseco, but they also knew that if the A's handling of Canseco was infuriating to the rest of the club, it incensed Rickey. Alderson had either misread or disregarded an important element of Rickey's drive. It was one thing to attribute Rickey's anger about his contract to greed and selfishness (which the public and the writers immediately did), or to market forces out of his control (or to Rickey choosing the security and ending up getting lapped financially by a record spending spree, as some privately suspected), but it was another thing altogether to not understand that to a person with Rickey's sense of accomplishment and respect, the rise of Canseco was particularly galling.

The way Rickey saw it, the organization enabled and rewarded Canseco when it was an open secret in the clubhouse that Canseco was not exactly dedicated to the game of baseball. Canseco did not bleed to play baseball, and then Canseco backs up his megadeal with his abominable World Series, when he was benched in an elimination game. In later years, Canseco would be asked if he played the game because it lived in his veins or merely because he was good at it. He responded, "Where the fuck else am I gonna make seven million dollars?"

Competition was not the fuel that drove Canseco, and if La Russa, the coaches, and especially the medical staff did not say it publicly, they knew it in private. They also knew something else that wasn't public knowledge: Canseco was hounded by steroid use. How much of what he was as a ballplayer was even real if he was using steroids?

The A's knew Canseco did not grind. No matter how misguided, one reason why La Russa would be more sympathetic to McGwire's steroid use was that McGwire put in the work. La Russa knew Canseco was not a dedicated professional, knew he was disruptive, knew that lack of professionalism might one day cost them (it did), knew Canseco had a potentially serious back issue, *and* knew he was getting a boost from the needle—but *still* the

A's gave Canseco $23.5 million. To someone like Rickey, for whom money was the ultimate and only barometer of professional respect, the Canseco contract was a deep wound.

The public rolled its collective eyes at Rickey's perception of the club's disrespect. After all, millions were millions, and it was only baseball—a kid's game, not a business. The pile-on from columnists, like Lowell Cohn of the *San Francisco Chronicle,* from readers writing letters to the editor, and from the fans (Rickey was booed when he ultimately made his spring training debut) was quick.

HEY, RICKEY, YOU'RE WRONG

When you're around Rickey Henderson, you always expect to hear the sound of barking. He is the greatest player in the history of baseball also to have a reputation for being a dog.

Woof. It was one thing when he didn't report to camp early, although all the other A's were in Arizona. He was being faithful to the letter of the law, even if he was violating the spirit of the A's. But yesterday he missed the official reporting date, and that's a serious matter. Give Rickey the Latecomer, this year's Alpo Award for best impersonation of a canine by a millionaire ballplayer. Orchestrating his ridiculous delayed entrance may turn out to be the biggest mistake of Rickey's life. When a man has a bad reputation, he should do everything possible to make sure people don't get the wrong idea.

When he reported to camp, Rickey said that he deserved to be in the top five of the highest-paid players in the game. In New York, a news report on Rickey featured a man in the background wearing a T-shirt that read, RICKEY HENDERSON IS PROOF THE PRICE OF HOT DOGS GOES UP EVERY YEAR. When Rickey entered the clubhouse, a gift was waiting: a jar filled with cash, and with a note taped to its front that read, "The Rickey Henderson Appreciation Fund—not tax-deductible."

The gag was engineered by Reggie Jackson. Alderson had brought him back to Oakland as an adviser, the first and only time Rickey and Reggie were on the same team. Reggie was trying to lighten the mood, to bring Rickey back into the fold emotionally. When Rickey picked up the jar and kissed it, the photographers snapped the moment, and the picture of Rickey kissing his money would appear in newspapers across the country—a light moment of the olive branch being extended in the clubhouse now symbolizing him as greedy outside it.

For a day, the peace overture worked. Rickey was back, the cloud lifted, and he was back in business. But with a secret caveat: he was not going to allow the A's to coddle Canseco without coddling him. Every special favor Canseco got, every day off, every perk, he was going to get too.

The part that steamed Rickey and his people was that Rickey was on the receiving end of the criticisms that Canseco was able to elude. Not only was Canseco earning twice what Rickey made, but Rickey's injuries and work ethic were questioned as legitimate in a way that Canseco's were not. Rarely if ever was Rickey out of the lineup without some questioning of his effort and motivation, while Canseco's injuries—and the length of time he took to recover from them—were never seen as the by-product of his lack of dedication. "After he went 40-40 and won his Gold Glove, he got challenged by Dave Parker and me to be a better defender," Dave Stewart said. "But there was a strong decline after he got paid. Then again, they gave money to a guy that didn't like baseball."

A month after the World Series, Kit Stier of the *Oakland Tribune* wrote a sympathetic piece on Canseco's injuries and the lack of compassion he received from his teammates.

CANSECO TOOK THE HEAT, ALL A'S SHARED BLAME
OAKLAND—How quickly the good times are forgotten.

It is strange to reflect on the 1990 baseball season and realize that in its final hours, Jose Canseco, one of the game's superstars, and a unique and engaging personality, became a whipping boy of a frustrated Oakland club.

Did anyone pat Canseco on the back and praise him for staying out of traffic court the entire season? No.

Was much made of the fact that he gave most of the proceeds of his 900 telephone number to needy kids for a baseball camp? No.

Instead of giving credit, most persons waited until he was physically unable to perform up to par and then landed on him, talons bared.

This person asking that Canseco be praised for staying out of court, of course, was the same Kit Stier who, in a commentary criticizing Rickey for wanting to renegotiate a contract he'd signed just a year earlier, wrote:

"Rickey, I thought your mama raised you better." That nearly set off a fight in the clubhouse between the two men.

"Rickey was the guy that everyone just wanted to dog. The feeling Rickey Henderson gives you is that he couldn't give a shit what you have to say about him," Dave Stewart recalled. "Jose dealt with it better. I liked to say people ate up more of Jose's bullshit. He had more charisma, although he didn't care about the game. Rickey just did his thing and he was gone. If he thought you were a good person, he might give you a little bit of his time. If he thought you weren't, Rickey was more inclined to tell you to go fuck yourself and you wouldn't get any of it."

Rickey was still Rickey, and when the lights went on, Rickey was going to be there—the best money player in the business. The season had started on a sour note—Rickey started the season and then missed a couple of weeks—but the day inevitably arrived, and when it did, it came in a flash.

May 1, 1991, a Wednesday afternoon in Oakland against the Yankees. Good crowd—36,192 was the announced attendance. Just as they had done when he broke the single-season record in 1982, the A's flew in Lou Brock, a great ambassador of the game. Rickey had tied Brock's record a few days earlier against the Angels, and now, at 938, at home, it was time to cross the line. Rickey had already been thrown out in the first by Matt Nokes. In the fourth, he took off for third against Tim Leahy—stole off the pitcher. Nokes didn't have a play, and Rickey dove in headfirst, pulled the base out of the dirt, and raised it high above his head.

It was done. Rickey had stolen 939 bases. He had not broken the record. He had obliterated it. He was 32 years old and had taken down a career record—that never happened. All-time records don't get broken that early. There just isn't enough time. Babe Ruth had broken the all-time home-run record before his 30th birthday, but that was because baseball replaced the paperweight it used to use with a ball that had a live center and could be hit out of the park routinely 40 times a year. Ruth ushered in the modern game so completely that the first all-time home-run mark, for all intents and purposes, was his from the beginning.

The umpires stopped play for an in-game ceremony. Rickey took the microphone as a small crowd of family, friends, and A's and baseball officials stood behind him and addressed the crowd.

"It took a long time, huh? First of all, I'd like to thank God for giving me the opportunity . . . I'd like to thank the Haas family, the Oakland organization, the city of Oakland, and all you beautiful fans for supporting me . . . I'd like to thank my mom, family, friends, and loved ones for their support . . . I want to give my appreciation to Tom Treblehorn and the late Billy Martin. Billy Martin was a great manager, and he was a great friend to me . . . I love you, Billy. I wish you was here . . . Lou Brock was the symbol of great base stealing, but today, I am the greatest of all time."

With that, Rickey serenaded the crowd with both arms in the air as the crowd showered him with applause. The game resumed shortly after, and Rickey embarked on his new life as the all-time leader in steals by getting thrown out by Nokes again the next inning.

In the dugout, Carney Lansford smiled, proud of his teammate, but he also cringed, as they all did, for the speech was quintessentially Rickey. Carney Lansford knew immediately how it sounded, especially that crack about Brock, the poor guy who happened to be a first-ballot Hall of Famer and two-time World Series champion, and a gentleman for flying out to Oakland. *This is gonna be bad,* he thought. *Did he really say he was the greatest of all time? With Brock standing right next to him?*

Willie Wilson had the same thought. Wilson had joined the A's that year. Standing next to Dave Henderson, he was stunned. "I was thinking, 'He said *what?* He said he's the greatest of all time, but *Lou Brock is standing right next to you.* You have to insult the man, put it right in his face?' But I really don't think Rickey thought about those things. I don't think he meant anything by it until he thought about it later." Lansford, too, knew it was harmless, just exhibit A of Rickey being benign old Rickey, but a nation that already saw him as self-absorbed now possessed even more kindling.

The challengers to his throne did not go away quietly, but it was hard to take their words seriously. Vince Coleman acknowledged Rickey for breaking Brock's record—but only for getting there first. Coleman predicted that stealing 1,500 bases, Rickey's next mark, would not be enough to stop Coleman from eventually overtaking him.

If Rickey was the building everyone came to see, the stunning Art Deco wonder of design that adorned the covers of the glossy magazines and that tourists journeyed for miles to visit and snap pictures of, paying money so they could say they saw him up close, it was Pamela who provided the foundation for that fancy structure, who was the reason why it didn't topple. In

Rickey's private world, everybody knew it was Pamela who kept Rickey's life in balance. Need to get Rickey's attention? Talk to Pamela. Arranging schedules for the girls? Talk to Pamela. Got a business proposition that Rickey said he'd deal with but is procrastinating? Talk to Pamela. Need to get an urgent message to Rickey but he isn't picking up the phone? Talk to Pamela.

Rickey would do the same. When he needed to make a public appearance, he'd go to Pamela and she would get him ready. She knew just how to make Rickey sound and wrote virtually all of his prepared remarks. In later years, Rickey would rebuff the suggestion that he was a self-made creation who now stood above the thousands of baseball players who had worn the uniform since 1869. "Nobody does it alone," Rickey would say. "Everybody has help. Everybody has support." Yet in that moment, at the peak of Olympus, with third base pulled out of the infield and lifted high above his head, Rickey was singular, complete unto himself.

During the on-field ceremony, while Rickey spoke, Jeff Idelson, the future president of the Baseball Hall of Fame, was standing between Bobbie and Pamela (who was wearing a big coat because she was six months pregnant). A Yankee employee at the time, Idelson would become an expert at ceremony, the moments of historical acknowledgment. He would listen keenly to how players responded to completing the quest for baseball immortality—to what they said and to what they *didn't* say. On that sunny day in Oakland, he did not hear magnanimity. The longer Rickey spoke, the more Idelson winced inside with embarrassment because he was not hearing one name above all the rest: Pamela.

Idelson kept a stoic face that poker players would have admired, never revealing his embarrassment for Pamela that day. He assumed that she would have found it painful to listen to Rickey's speech, but Pamela herself would say that she wasn't overly bothered by it, because of where she and Rickey were in their relationship in 1991. "I was just the fiancée," she would say, adding that she knew Rickey at that time was not willing to release details about his private life and risk giving information to whatever female ears— "strays," Pamela would call them—might have been listening. Part of it, she understood, was part of the athlete's life, like the time she recalled the singer Olivia Newton-John throwing out the first pitch at an A's game wearing a Rickey jersey, and many of her friends asking afterward if Rickey was having an affair with her.

Idelson ached for Pamela, and for the fact that Rickey forgot—or refused—to thank the woman who had stood by him since she was a 14-year-old girl wearing his varsity jacket at Oakland Tech. To Idelson, it was, for the moment, a revealing omission.

The public would not judge Rickey for forgetting to mention Pamela, but only because they immediately had two other reasons to judge him. The first was that Lansford was right: his speech was taken by baseball fans and everyone inside the sport as a humiliation of Lou Brock, who was just the nicest guy in the world. *He flies to Oakland to be a statesman for the game and Rickey dunks on the poor guy?* "When he said that, I wanted to puke," Padres reliever Larry Andersen said. "Lou Brock should have slapped him. He should have hammered him."

The second came later that night, after Rickey had savored his moment. When Nolan Ryan threw his seventh career no-hitter, soaking up the headlines and more, he provided the contrast of humble greatness to Rickey's braggadocio and, in many people's opinion, put the spotlight back where it belonged.

Nevertheless, in the span of roughly two years, from the time the Yankees traded him back to Oakland to that May 1, 1991, afternoon at the Coliseum against them, Rickey had been in supernova. He was a playoff MVP, a World Series champion, the league MVP, and now the all-time leader of the stolen-base record—all while still in his prime. Brock played 19 years. That Rickey had not completed his 12th was a staggering achievement. His old teammate Mike Davis thought Rickey's accomplishment exemplified how he had always set enormous goals, beginning early in his life. He was reminded of what Rickey had told Jim Guinn as a 17-year-old: his goal was to be the greatest base stealer of all time.

Rickey's supporters still loved him—and now loved him even more—and his feats and numbers spoke for themselves. But once again the focus was more on what Rickey had said than on what he'd done. The criticism for appearing uncharitable to Lou Brock dampened his moment of triumph, as did the widespread view that the consummate professional Nolan Ryan throwing a no-hitter the same night self-absorbed Rickey broke the stolen-base record was poetic justice.

"After I said it," Rickey would recall years later, "I knew I'd never live it down."

14

JOHN SHEA HAD no idea why Rickey said yes. Everybody knew that Rickey had virtually no interest in the press. Shea knew Rickey was well known for not cultivating favorites among the writers or attempting to win them over. Even at home in the comparatively relaxed West Coast media environment of Oakland, Rickey and the media had a famously distant relationship. Even his teammates experienced that personal distance. "Rickey had other shit going on," Dennis Eckersley would say.

Rickey viewed most reporters with either indifference or disdain, and his being so terrible with names made the feeling mutual. It was hard to build a relationship with someone who talked to you every day for years and probably still did not know your first name. The one name he knew by heart was that of the *Oakland Tribune*'s Kit Stier—because he couldn't stand Stier. The rest? Invisible. No hard feelings. All the legends had a favorite inside the press box, a guy they could trust when they needed a solid. In the old days, Jackie Robinson had Roger Kahn. Joe DiMaggio was tight with Walter Winchell. Reggie could always call Lupica. On the West Coast, Willie Mays had Charlie Einstein. Not Rickey. Press just wasn't his thing.

Yet after Rickey won the 1990 AL MVP, Shea took his shot: he asked Rickey if he had thought about doing a book. If he had, Shea told Rickey, he'd love to be considered to work with him on it. To his great surprise, Rickey said he was interested.

Shea then worked a few channels. One of Rickey's representatives on the business side was Miles McAfee, once the coach of St. Mary's College over in Moraga in the East Bay. McAfee happened also to be an unknown legend in the Bay Area: in 1973 he had been the first Black Division I baseball coach in the country's history. In 1980 McAfee quit St. Mary's and became an agent, running his own shop, Golden Gate Sports Management. As clients, he had Wade Boggs and Eric Davis, Bip Roberts (the Skyline High kid who was now in the big leagues too) and Willie McGee—and Rickey.

The potential for disaster in collaborating on a memoir with a celebrity was always high—especially with a wild card like Rickey, who'd shown little interest in telling his story and was notorious for procrastination. Would Rickey even show? When Roy Johnson Sr. had teamed with Charles Barkley on his autobiography a few years earlier, Chuck said he was misquoted—in his own book! John Shea thought he had a couple of advantages that might make the experience a little easier. The first was that he was from Rickey's time: they were the same age, born just six months apart. Shea wasn't one of the old guys who couldn't get past the money the players made and were mad that players were more attracted to the power of the runaway television machine, which continued to devalue the influence of reporters. Since he wasn't carrying the generational baggage of the older writers, Shea knew he could be fair.

Shea's second advantage was being local, like Rickey, only from the other side of the Bay. Shea was from Mill Valley in Marin County, just north of the Golden Gate Bridge. As a baseball writer for the *Marin Independent Journal,* he covered the San Francisco Giants. That may have provided him with another advantage—he was from the area, but he wasn't one of the daily guys who covered Rickey on the A's.

With the all-time stolen-base record in sight, Shea thought he'd be collaborating on the memoir of a player who had reached the pinnacle of his ambitions and was now heading for the back nine. Rickey had always said his goal was to be the greatest base stealer who ever lived, and now that was exactly what he was about to become. "To be honest, one of the reasons why the book was appealing to me was because I thought Rickey was close to retiring. I thought it was going to be a book about someone wrapping up a record-breaking career where he could reflect," Shea recalled. "I had no idea I was writing a book about someone who was only halfway through his career. Rickey had a dozen years left."

Despite the book being his idea, Shea nevertheless feared the assignment. He worried about being stuck with an uncooperative subject, but during the off-season Rickey was diligent about meeting with Shea at a Holiday Inn off Route 101 in Redwood City, on the peninsula, not far from Rickey's house in

Hillsborough. Shea estimated that they spoke weekly for 10 sessions of about three hours each. For someone with a reputation for not being punctual, Rickey was not only engaged, Shea found, but rarely canceled.

The book, released in the spring of 1992, was titled *Off Base: Confessions of a Thief*. The promotion and the book itself focused on the reaction to Rickey—how baseball viewed his flamboyance, how he stood outside of convention, how baseball had cultural problems with his personality, how the sport called him a "hot dog" as often as it called him by name.

Rickey did not stray far from the biographical timeline he had been telling the newspapermen for years, but in the book he added details about his search to know and locate both his biological father, John Henley, and his stepfather, Paul Henderson. Rickey even expressed through the book a desire he rarely showed while playing: he wanted to be a better public figure, and more affable with the writers, the people who depicted him for the public. As an athlete, he was not a political figure in the mold of Jackie Robinson or Henry Aaron, whose autobiography *I Had a Hammer: The Hank Aaron Story* had been released a year earlier and filled up most of the player autobiography space, or fellow Oaklander Curt Flood, whose 1971 autobiography, *The Way It Is,* gave voice to the business of baseball and the weight of being Black in a sport reluctant to accept Black players.

Rickey had played his entire career to that point during the most tumultuous economic period in the game's history, and just two years after *Off Base* was published the game would shut down in the longest strike in North American professional sports history. Rickey did not frame his tome through the lens of the business of baseball, or of race, but he did contextualize his time with frequent mentions of the drug issues in Oakland and what the proliferation of drugs had done to the city's youth and promise. Although *Off Base* was written during the specter of the Reagan-era "War on Drugs" and baseball's cocaine scandals, Rickey did not advocate a political position regarding drug use so much as lament its costs and the damage it did.

Pamela recalled being generally pleased about the book—except for making sure that a few passages in which Rickey was critical of Mark McGwire were deleted from the finished manuscript. There was no reason to start a fire by ripping a popular teammate. Jose Canseco, a less popular teammate, wasn't so lucky. Many of the A's, including Rickey, had never forgiven Canseco for what they saw as his disinterested performance in the 1990 World Series against Cincinnati. Rickey went a step further and criticized

Canseco in the book not just for his critical misplay but for committing the cardinal sin of then loafing after the ball. When the A's season was spiraling down the drain, Canseco had just watched.

When the manuscript was complete, Pamela had one last issue: she didn't like the way Rickey referred to Bobbie as "Momma" throughout the book, even though that was what he had always called her. Pamela thought the word looked different on the printed page. It sounded affectionate when Rickey said it, but written down it read to Pamela as an opening for the public to criticize the way Rickey spoke, as a reflection of his education, as another opportunity for the public to condescend to him.

When it was published, the book caused very few waves. It was a relatively by-the-numbers baseball book in which Rickey kept most of his comments restricted to the field, not a barn burner like Dave Winfield's book, which infuriated Steinbrenner and caused a riff within the clubhouse when Rickey and Winfield were on the Yankees. The only real issue arose over what Rickey had to say about his nemesis Bob Boone, the four-time All-Star and seven-time Gold Glove catcher. Boone was pissed that Rickey accused him of reaching to catch a pitch before the batter had a chance to swing as a sly way of getting a better chance to throw Rickey out. When Boone read that passage, he wanted a piece of Rickey. Rickey was a great player, but what he said there, Boone said, that was just wrong. "I read that, where he said I was getting an edge. It was bullshit," Boone recalled. The only problem for the angry Boone was that he couldn't exact his revenge on Rickey on the field—he had retired the year before.

Shea heard nothing from Rickey about the book after it was published—because Rickey didn't read it. Rickey and words still weren't a great mix, and he was disinclined to read a book from cover to cover. It wasn't until the audiobook was released that Rickey grew enthusiastic about it. An audiobook that was all about him—that he would listen to. What changed Rickey's attitude toward the book wasn't just the audio format but also the voice of the reader, a 29-year-old emerging actor named Andre Braugher, who in 1990 had played Jackie Robinson in *The Court-Martial of Jackie Robinson*. Rickey loved Braugher's voice. "Nobody had ever heard of him," Shea recalled. "Rickey loved it. He said, 'I love that guy. He sounds like me!'"

During the publicity tour, Rickey said that he hoped the book showed a different, fuller side of him and could be a springboard to a better relationship with the press and the public. But if he thought that being a published author could soften the edges, well, even Rickey couldn't always get what he wanted, for one last fight loomed.

Rickey was a part of Oakland, and no matter where he wound up, Oakland was in his blood. What Oakland meant to him would never change, but he and the A's had never reconciled the best and worst moment of his career—that 1989 contract. It was 1993, the last year of his contract, and for the previous four years Rickey had been burning about his rapidly declining rank on baseball's salary scale. Now he was barely in the top 40 highest-paid players in the game, and salaries were moving so quickly that he would soon fall out of the top 50 best-paid players.

The A's were tired of fighting with Rickey over the same issue for four years, tired of how sour he was over money. Didn't he understand that he was the one who signed a contract that valued certainty over risk? After two years of Rickey threatening to withhold his services because he was still stung about the issue, Alderson threatened to suspend him. But now how much the A's paid him wasn't even the half of it for Rickey.

The talk around baseball wasn't just about the San Francisco Giants being rescued from relocation to St. Petersburg at the 11th hour, but about the six-year, $43 million deal that San Francisco made to land Barry Bonds. Playing in the same market, the ascending Bonds was making nearly three times what Rickey was earning. In a legendary broadside, Rickey whacked an innocent bystander, A's utility infielder Mike Gallego, to make a larger point. "If you're gonna pay me like Mike Gallego, I'm gonna play like Mike Gallego."

If you're gonna pay me like Mike Gallego, I'm gonna play like Mike Gallego. It was another all-time Rickeyism that would be repeated forever, but it was also an all-time threat. Did Rickey insinuate that he was going to play at the level of a player who didn't have a 10th of his talent? Yes, yes, he did. Did Rickey also suggest in advance when he wouldn't be able to play? Yes, yes, he did that too. When Rickey said he wanted to leave the team, Alderson put him on the trade block, further enraging Rickey. Perhaps to widen his appeal or perhaps because he actually meant it, Rickey even said that he'd go back to the Yankees and George Steinbrenner, who was back from a two-year suspension for trying to destroy Dave Winfield.

Some of the A's players were also running out of patience. There was that time A's hard-ass third baseman Carney Lansford finally got tired of Rickey and challenged him to a fistfight on the team plane. Lansford sat in the back of the plane waiting for Rickey, who had no interest in punching it out with Carney. So Rickey avoided the back of the plane that day. Carney had played with Rickey in Rickey's early years in the big leagues and then again when he returned to Oakland as a star. Sometimes Carney was amused by Rickey and sometimes he just wasn't in the mood—like the time he called Rickey "a cancer." Pamela never forgot that one.

Two local columnists, Glenn Dickey and Lowell Cohn, both of the *San Francisco Chronicle*, openly called Rickey a dog, and the headline writers couldn't help but assist ("Old Dog Up to Old Tricks" read the March 9, 1992, *Chronicle*). Dickey even wrote that the A's should "throw in a can of Alpo" to the team that acquired Rickey.

So much of it all came back to the Canseco contract, which beyond the money revealed the profound power of advocacy in the game. Canseco was Sandy Alderson's guy—the first player who put Sandy on the map as a rising force in the game. Canseco won Rookie of the Year in 1986, as did McGwire and Walter Weiss in the next two years. Alderson was seen as the mastermind behind the A's revival. He had put all the pieces together, hired a great manager, and was now known as a master in the draft room and at the winter meetings. Canseco was the prototype of a new kind of ballplayer—and he was Sandy's discovery.

Mark McGwire was Tony's perfect boy. Quiet, uncomplicated, uncontroversial. Put McGwire's name in the line and he'd play. McGwire could do no wrong with the manager, even when he hit .201—even when he could be dark and moody. La Russa would protect and support McGwire his entire career and beyond, rehabilitating him when McGwire's own steroid use eventually disgraced both himself and the game. La Russa was the best friend McGwire would have in the game.

Rickey? Rickey may have produced his greatest years under La Russa, but Tony and Rickey were a relationship of convenience and tolerance. La Russa respected Rickey's ability—it didn't take a genius to do that—but La Russa was no advocate for his leadoff man. The writers were not independently emboldened to attack Rickey. They had a quiet and often privately vocal supporter in the towering figure of La Russa. La Russa was not Billy, who accepted Rickey on talent alone and forgave his quirks, knowing that the best Rickey made them all look good. Tony wanted performance in a specific fashion; he loved Rickey's talent but not his wattage, a dichotomy common between the modern game of Black and brown style and the game's roots in a culture created by the white men who kept the game segregated. La Russa's favorite Black player was a guy like Harold Baines—laconic, uncontroversial, noncombative. Baines played for La Russa in Chicago, where he was seen and heard only with his bat.

"Tony tolerated Rickey. Tony tolerated Jose," Willie Wilson recalled. "They were flamboyant on the field and off. I don't think he minded the flamboyance as much off the field, but Tony's old school. He's trying to win ball games. Didn't want to see that flamboyance on the field. It took a lot to be able to see beyond it. Rick pissed a lot of people off. I'm from the old school too, but it didn't bother me that much because deep down I knew Rickey wanted to win. "

La Russa saw the business of baseball as separate from the three-hour mission of winning a ball game. With Rickey, performance and business were two sides of the same coin—the coin of respect. One could not come without the other, and as Rickey insisted on a certain level of disruption to leverage his points about respect, fairness, and his right to guard the limits of what his body could do, it wasn't long before Tony had concluded that, for all his immeasurable gifts, Rickey was an indisputable talent, but not a truly great player.

Periodically—and later more frequently as their relationship soured—Tony would volunteer his opinions, and in his moments of pique he would explain why Rickey was not a great player in the classic sense. Great players did not engage in the extracurricular circus. They did not withhold their best because they were pissed off about their contract, or because the other guy got a day off. They fought through pain because they knew at their worst they were still better than every other player in the game at his best. While Alderson would eventually conclude that Rickey was reacting to the real disruption that was Canseco, Tony was convinced that too often Rickey could have given more and chose not to. No truly great player ever had that said about him. When the columnists teed off on Rickey on these topics, they knew they were relatively safe, in spite of La Russa's legendary reputation for protecting his players. As much as he admired what Rickey could do, La Russa did not respect Rickey's choice to put his long-term health over Tony's (and the ball club's) immediate need—to win a ball game. Tonight. Whenever Rickey told Tony he couldn't play because of injury, Tony tacitly agreed with the withering critiques of Rickey that routinely appeared the next day.

From the day he stepped into the big leagues, Rickey only had one advocate—and it was Billy. Billy understood Rickey, allowed Rickey to play the game on his terms without the constant psychoanalysis and insistence that Rickey conform. Perhaps the most unique element of Billy Martin as a manager was his ability to see the value in the numbers Rickey put up over whatever disruptive, idiosyncratic path Rickey took to achieve them.

Enter . . . Toronto! The same hated Blue Jays whose tail feathers were still burning after Rickey obliterated them in 1989? The same Blue Jays who had that manager, Cito Gaston, who couldn't stand Tony La Russa, called Dennis Eckersley "half a woman," and was tired of the tough-guy A's kicking sand in everyone's face? The same Blue Jays who were serenaded by Eckersley after the 1989 ALCS with a hearty "See you later, motherfuckers, we're going to the World Series?" Yes, those Blue Jays.

The times had shifted. All those years when the Blue Jays came close, so tantalizingly close—well, those years were gone. These Blue Jays were the best team in baseball, and there were no caveats on their success because they were also defending World Series champions. Of the earlier days, Gaston recalled, "It was tough around here. Even going on caravans. You go to luncheons and they'd roll the video and we'd get up to the last day and we'd lose, like over in Detroit, when we had to win one game and we couldn't win it." In the five years from 1987 to 1991, the Blue Jays had either won the division or finished no worse than three games out—but they never won the pennant. They had won the division for the first time in 1985, then lost the pennant after blowing a 3–1 lead against Kansas City in the ALCS. They collapsed in 1987 against the Tigers, and then the A's slapped them around, winning three straight pennants. Blue Jays president Paul Beeston said, "It was starting to come together but was getting very frustrating because there was always a reason, like wait till next year."

Those same Blue Jays took their revenge on La Russa, Rickey, Stew, and Eck by beating the A's in six games in the 1992 ALCS. These A's won 96 games, a big number for a good team, but outside of Eckersley and Rickey, the team was more feisty than dominant. The swagger belonged to the Blue Jays, a highlight being David Cone's 3–1 win in Game 2 after the A's took the opener. Cone knew how dangerous Rickey was, especially on the first pitch of a big game. "I struck Rickey out on three pitches to start the game. First time I ever started the game with a first-pitch slider—because it was Rickey." Then, threatened in the fifth, he struck Rickey out again on four pitches in the clutch. Rickey was human this time—he made three errors in the series. In the deciding sixth game, Rickey dropped a fly ball that led to a two-run homer by Joe Carter. Cito Gaston got his revenge on La Russa.

"They did try to intimidate us, but I'm the kind of person who will go right back and try to intimidate them too," Gaston remembered. "Tony and I would stand and talk the whole batting practice, and the one thing I would say to Tony before I left was, 'Hey listen, we're gonna pitch inside, and if you guys wanna pitch inside, that's fine. And if you guys wanna fight, we'll be right here.' He shook his head and said, 'Okay. Got it.'"

Trailing 2–1 in games, the A's led 5–1 in Game 4, then took a left hook and never survived the 10-count. After Roberto Alomar hit a game-tying homer off Eckersley in the ninth, Toronto won it in 11, essentially finishing the series. The Blue Jays went on to earn their first World Series—Dave Winfield with the title-winning two-run double. "They got me back," Eckersley said of the Alomar homer that doused a season when he would win the AL Cy Young *and* the MVP. "Boy, did they ever get me back. That one hurt worse than Gibson." It was these Blue Jays who, fresh off that first World Series championship, punched the A's in the gut again by signing Stewart as a free agent in the winter of 1992. The same Blue Jays who had for years been putting the championship pieces together and now finally had secured the trophy. Those Blue Jays.

The reality, of course, was that the A's dynasty was dead anyway, weakened by age and the fatigue of holding on to so much resentment. The team would never again be as good as it was in 1990. It never recovered from giving Jose Canseco that mega-contract, with all its ripple effects, and never recovered from getting swept by the Reds in the 1990 World Series.

Canseco had back issues and was never the same player. Little came of coddling him because of his ability: Canseco never matured—or, in Stewart's mind, never liked baseball enough to be better at it when it was no longer easy for him. When Alderson and La Russa finally got tired of his act, La Russa dramatically pulled him in-game from the on-deck circle at the Coliseum and Alderson shipped him to Texas for the wonderful five-tool player Ruben Sierra. Although that didn't really work either. Sierra, trying to replace Canseco's power, transformed himself from a lithe and gorgeous, Clemente-esque athlete, a slashing hitter from both sides of the plate who could fly and had a lightning bolt for an arm, into a muscle-bound lump who tried to hit every ball to Hayward. La Russa and Sierra clashed so hard that the guy known for endlessly protecting his players famously referred to Ruben Sierra—in print—as "the village idiot."

And Rickey? Sierra was also making more than Rickey, so Rickey just replicated his Canseco protest with Sierra—if Ruben got a day off, Rickey wanted a day off too.

The Canseco trade ended two years of internecine warfare between Canseco and Rickey, who kept his promise to not tolerate the team treating Canseco like a protected member of the Royal Family. Pedro Gomez of the *Sacramento Bee* kept a running tally of when Canseco missed time owing to injury, and he found that when Jose missed games, Rickey soon did too. Take the stretch of May 23–28, 1992, when Canseco missed five games. When Jose returned May 29, Rickey was then out from May 29 to June 16. Two weeks later, on June 29, when Canseco was placed on the 15-day disabled list, Rickey landed on the DL on June 30. When Canseco returned July 15, Rickey returned July 16. Given Rickey's history and resentment over money and his treatment by the organization—not to mention Rickey essentially telling the world it would happen—Gomez was not willing to buy the possibility that Canseco and Rickey both missed time during the same period by cosmic coincidence.

"The team was known for coddling Jose, and you could just see how pissed Rickey was about it, so I kept track. When Jose was out of the lineup, the minute Jose came back, Rickey would be like, *Well, if you get time off during the season, motherfucker, I'M getting time off during the season,*" Gomez recalled. Everybody on the A's kept their traps shut while the Canseco-Rickey drama played out, but Gomez recalled that when he published his story, several exasperated team and staff members privately thanked him for exposing the childishness and unprofessionalism of both players.

In Toronto, GM Pat Gillick, Blue Jays president Paul Beeston, and Gaston brought a half-dozen players into Beeston's office and told them the news: the team had a chance to get Rickey. Were they interested? Dave Stewart had signed with the Blue Jays in the off-season. He called Rickey and told him that Toronto was a great place to land—they'd be teammates again too. Rickey would also be back in the pennant race, Stewart told him, with a shot at a second World Series ring—and some more playoff money.

"They said to us, 'Hey, we're thinking about getting Rickey, and what do you guys think?'" recalled Joe Carter. "We looked at each other and said, 'Get him over here quick,' because we knew what he brought."

Rickey recalled Alderson and La Russa giving him the same speech that Roy Eisenhardt had given him nearly a decade earlier—he was the most valuable trade piece. Alderson, Rickey recalled, also said that there was a sweetener in the deal, but Rickey had to trust him. If Rickey would do the organization the favor of agreeing to a trade, the A's would be aggressive in the free-agent market to bring him back to Oakland for a third time. Rickey agreed, but also told Alderson that he wanted a $50,000 incentive to take the deal. At the trade deadline, Alderson traded Rickey to Toronto for the young right-hander Steve Karsay.

Rickey was in the mix again, back in a pennant race on a team that was literally a Hall of Fame team. The magician Roberto Alomar was at second, Paul Molitor was the DH, and now Rickey was in left field—all three would one day wind up in Cooperstown. The ace of the staff was the hard thrower Juan Guzman, and the fourth and fifth starters were Dave Stewart and Jack Morris—two of the greatest competitors of their time. With the exception of the catcher, every Blue Jay in the starting lineup had made the All-Star team before.

Rickey had always been the sworn enemy. He unsuccessfully slugged it out with the Blue Jays during his monster 1985 with the Yankees, destroyed them in 1989, lost to them in 1992, and now here he was in Toronto, wearing the powder blues with the red maple leaf. At the time of the trade, the defending champs were sputtering. Tied with the revived Yankees for first place, they needed a spark. All of Canada braced for the arrival of the biggest personality in the sport, a player whom they had once booed lustily, but then came the international plot twist—they loved him up there.

"Rickey Henderson was somebody, when you played against him, he had this persona about him, and you just wanted to beat him, you wanted to beat that persona," recalled John Olerud. "And when he came to our team, I was expecting that persona that you saw on the field to be the same persona in the clubhouse—but he was a *great* teammate. Just down-to-earth guy, fun guy to be with. I don't know what I expected. I remembered that I was thinking, *The same guy I wanted to beat so bad is going to be the same in the clubhouse,* but I really liked Rickey."

Rickey didn't do much in Toronto. He injured his wrist and hit just .215 in 44 games, but he was still Rickey: the .215 came with a .356 on-base percentage. He also found a way for them to talk about him eternally in a way no .215 batting average had ever been talked about: Rickey would forever be the guy who developed frostbite in the middle of the summer when he fell asleep while icing his left ankle. That isn't a misprint: Rickey got frostbite. In August. He missed three games.

As he stole 22 bases in 24 tries (a 92 percent success rate), Rickey, by his presence alone, reminded the Blue Jays that they were still the champions— and so was he. When he arrived, Toronto was tied for first; from then on they remained in sole possession of first place for the rest of the season. "When he joined us, he just fit right in. It wasn't like it was someone we didn't know. He fit right in like he was one of the boys," Joe Carter recalled. "He was a character. There's never a dull moment. Even before the playoffs started, he's walking around, telling everyone, 'I'm gonna be the MVP!' And Stew was like, 'I'M gonna be the MVP.' And then I was like *I'm* gonna be the MVP. It was amongst ourselves that we had that competitiveness."

When the playoffs started, it was almost as if Rickey saw his alternate universe on the other side of the field. Toronto played the White Sox in the ALCS, and on that team was none other than his rival Tim Raines. Rickey and Raines had circled each other for years, and now in the postseason they would go head-to-head.

Rickey was also competing that postseason against Bo Jackson, the two-sport phenomenon whom Rickey would refer to as his successor. "I was Bo before Bo," he would say, referring to his own two-sport prowess, though he had abandoned football for baseball. Jackson had been making a comeback from the devastating hip injury that ended his football career and derailed one of the great athletic stories. Rickey saw himself in Bo—the Football Kid who could also do everything on the baseball diamond. In fact, it was the possibility of being injured like Bo that made Rickey choose baseball in the first place. Bo was so good, so electric, and (with the help of Nike) so ubiquitous in the popular culture that Rickey, nearly 30 years old and having not played football competitively since high school, was inspired to call Los Angeles Raiders owner Al Davis for a tryout. The two-sport guys were all over the place now—Bo, Deion Sanders, Brian Jordan—and over the years more would follow. Whenever Rickey wondered if he too could have dominated both sports, he immediately concluded that there was no doubt he would have.

The Blue Jays defended their pennant by beating Chicago in six tough games. Rickey had all the motivation, competing against Raines and Bo— but Dave Stewart was the ALCS MVP, winning two games, including the clincher at Comiskey. The World Series against Philadelphia—when Joe Carter's three-run homer ended the season and defended Toronto's championship.

Rickey only hit .170 in the Series, but he was where he needed to be—in the thick of a wild Game 4. The Blue Jays came back from a 14–9 deficit with six in the eighth, and a Rickey two-out, two-run single aided the victorious 15–14 comeback. In the clincher, with the Jays down 6–5, Rickey led off the ninth with a walk off Mitch Williams, setting up Carter to take center stage. Before Carter became a national hero, he thought it was Rickey who was going to be remembered for that inning. Carter was sure Rickey was going to try to steal second and maybe third, but instead Rickey didn't even take third when Molitor singled to keep the rally going. "He should have been on third base! Because Molitor gets the base hit, and Rickey goes from first to second that would have made my life a lot easier. I would have only needed a sacrifice fly to tie the game."

Toronto was the first back-to-back champion since the Yankees in 1977–1978. They had exorcised all their demons—and with the help of two of their prime tormentors.

"What they had was swagger," Beeston said of the A's. "The long hair. The way they walked. The way they talked. The way they took infield. The way they took batting practice. They were a juggernaut. One of those times where you knew you lost to a better team. They were just better. We knew we didn't lose to a good team. We lost to a great team.

"There was this arrogance about them. The fact of the matter was, they were very easy guys to dislike. That swagger. *How dare you get a hit off of us? How dare you win a game off of us?* But you know what? It worked for them. But it only worked for them once. You know what? *They only got one World Series.* WE REPEATED! Cito got us back in 1992 and 1993! And . . . we did it with Rickey and Stew!"

Rickey had won his second World Series championship, and then Alderson was as good as his word. Two months after the World Series, Rickey re-signed with the A's. He was going back to Oakland—for the third time.

"Rickey, I only wish I had him a few years longer," Gaston recalled. "He was really something special. You're talking about one of the best players who ever played this game. He could do everything. I used to joke with Pat Borders. 'How do you get Rickey when he's on first base?' I said, 'Throw the ball to third and cut him off at the pass, 'cuz he'll be there soon.' Or, 'Instead of putting him on first, just put him on third and save some time.'"

Over the years, Rickey had built for himself a fortress around his personal life, protecting it from his celebrity. He was not a magnet for the paparazzi; he didn't need to feed his ego by drawing attention to himself, letting everyone know his favorite haunts, and when he would be there. Even when he played in New York, the papers never tailed him the way they did all the other big New York guys—Ruth, DiMaggio, Mantle, Namath, Reggie Billy, from the 1920s to the '80s and beyond. Pamela could tell the difference, though, between playing in New York and playing in Oakland. "In Oakland, people might look at you, but you could go out for a nice dinner, even when Rickey came back the second time and he was a bigger star. In New York, the Yankee fans knew all their players. You couldn't go anywhere without a crowd around you. Once you went out, Yankees fans spotted you," she said.

Rickey had consistently told everyone that buying drinks and snapping pics with the fans when he was off the clock wasn't his way. Rickey Time provided a nine-inning spotlight for his abilities, and their money's worth for the fans, but after the final out he became as anonymous as a commuter. Rickey even constructed a moat around the fortress that protected his personal life when he bought a 26-acre compound in Coarsegold out by Yosemite. That wasn't a vanity purchase. Rickey preferred having space away from the glare produced by his dazzling abilities.

For 16 seasons Rickey had perfected the art of creating distance between his two worlds—but then an atom bomb was dropped right into his living room. During the first week of August 1994, his younger sister, Paula, told the *Oakland Tribune* in an exclusive that Rickey had raped her when he was 17 and she was 12. She told the *Tribune* that the sexual assaults might have begun when she was as young as eight, and that Rickey, as a teenager, was under the influence of marijuana and cocaine.

On August 5 at the Coliseum, with the A's in town against Texas, the *San Francisco Examiner* put three reporters on the story. "This is just an attempt by her to obtain money from me," Henderson told the paper. "I deny the charges and will fight them in court, if necessary." The A's put out a statement from Rickey denying the charges, and Sandy Alderson told reporters in the clubhouse that Rickey had the team's full support. "Our approach is very simple. Rickey is an employee. He's been with the Oakland A's a long time and he's denied the charge," Alderson was quoted as saying in the *Examiner*. "Until such time as the facts establish otherwise, we'll be fully supportive. We expect him to be exonerated. It's a difficult line to walk, but it's not our job within the system to be fact-finders."

Chris Mirzai of nearby Albany bought a ticket near the railing to the left of the A's dugout, close to the tunnel leading to the clubhouse. Mirzai wasn't there for an autograph. He was a process server sent to the ballpark by Daniel Horowitz, Paula's attorney, and he showed up at the game for a single purpose—to hand-deliver a complaint filed in Alameda County Superior Court that would soon become case number 739133-4: *Paula Henderson, Plaintiff, vs. Rickey Henderson, Defendant.*

Wearing a San Francisco Giants cap, Mirzai attempted before the game to lean over the rails and get Rickey's attention. Coliseum security attempted to have Mirzai removed, until he showed them his appropriately purchased ticket. He returned to his seat and later in the game served the summons to Rickey's attorney. That night, Rickey had a hit in a 5–4 win.

Over the next several weeks, Paula Henderson went public, graphically describing what she alleged Rickey had done to her for years of her childhood. Her attorneys said that Paula was extremely credible—she had twice passed a three-and-a-half-hour polygraph test. She said she hadn't come forward for publicity, and did so reluctantly, but she wanted Rickey in jail. "I think he needs to suffer," Paula told the *San Francisco Examiner*. "He hurt me. He took my virginity. I didn't have a normal childhood." Horowitz said he wanted a settlement of $3 million for his client. "That's three-quarters of a season," he said, doing the math from Rickey's $4.3 million annual salary, "in exchange for ruining Paula's life."

Rickey brought in heavy legal artillery: the attorney G. William Hunter, better known around Oakland as the formidable Billy Hunter, the defense lawyer who had represented the Black Panther Party for Self-Defense and the Hell's Angels—*and* who had defended Stanley Burrell, aka MC Hammer, a year earlier in a gang rape charge against his entourage in which Hammer was not accused. Billy Hunter was a fighter in the courtroom and out. A former athlete, he had even played in the NFL for a couple of years in the mid-1960s, as a kick returner for both Washington and the Dolphins. A story had gone around for years in legal circles that once, in a judge's chambers, a prosecutor called Hunter a "nigger" and Billy dropped him to the floor with a right. Staggering to his feet, the prosecutor said, "I deserved that." When

Hunter began representing Rickey, his response to Paula's charges was direct: she was extorting Rickey for money.

A week later, on August 12, 1994, the game shut down. The players went on strike, and a resolution would not be quick. A month after the strike, the owners canceled the remainder of the season, including the World Series, which was not held for the first time since 1904. The work stoppage insulated Rickey from what would have been daily bombardment by the media, inquiring about the case. Nevertheless, Paula's case against him went forward.

In mid-September, she appeared on the television tabloid show *Inside Edition*, where she repeated her story in front of the nation. Nor did she limit her charges to Rickey—she implicated the entire family. Two months after her original complaint, Paula Henderson amended her complaint with an allegation that her two brothers, Tyrone and Johnny, and a cousin, were pimps who assaulted prostitutes. The amended complaint also alleged that Bobbie was not only aware of what was happening but condoned the behavior because she benefited financially from the violence of the men in the house.

In November, Rickey countersued Paula for defamation. He also petitioned the court to seal the complaint. Both the *Oakland Tribune* and the *San Francisco Examiner* had dedicated staff to the case, and the constant reporting, he argued, was unfairly damaging his reputation. For a decade and a half the reporting on Rickey's personal life had barely included anything worse than a parking ticket. Paula's accusation that Rickey was using cocaine also undermined Rickey's longtime public reputation of not putting drugs into his body. "There is no way to explain to my three daughters why and how their aunt can say such vile lies about me," he said in his countercomplaint. Rickey also said that the allegations could ruin his endorsement opportunities and affect his chances of election into the Hall of Fame.

Lawyers from the *Oakland Tribune* challenged Rickey's petition. A week before Thanksgiving the court denied Rickey's motion to have the case sealed, on First Amendment grounds. The case, and all of its details, would remain public.

Publicly, Rickey said that he was devastated by the accusations, but privately he had known about them for months. Before Paula went public, she had gone to Rickey first. Paula told the press at one point that Rickey had agreed to go to counseling with her, but that never materialized. Between April and August, Paula told the court, she had asked Rickey to speak with her. After his continued refusals, both to meet with her and to negotiate with her lawyers, she went public. "I really tried to get him to come to the table and not file it. I didn't want to file it," Paula's attorney Daniel Horowitz recalled. "And it wouldn't have taken a huge amount of money to settle—but he was stubborn and brought it on himself. If he really honestly apologized, I don't think she would have ever come forward. I think all she wanted was an apology. There was no pot of gold at the end of the rainbow. He made a big mistake not settling."

In Paula's statement to the court following Rickey's countersuit, she told the court a story of a life devastated by trauma and disappointment, derailed by an abusive household in which Rickey, Bobbie's favorite from the start, received all of the dispensation and attention. Paula was unemployed at this time and had just had a child the year before. She described herself to the *San Francisco Examiner* as a recovered alcoholic. "I grew up in a family where women were not given a great deal of respect. Two of my brothers were pimps and in my household this was accepted. My mother never criticized my brothers for being a pimp or for being violent toward women. Ricky [sic] was the most important person in the family and I learned from an early age to accept what happened in my household without complaint."

For the better part of 18 months, the private wounds of an entire family would be annotated in the public record of court documents and depositions, suits and countersuits. Four years earlier, on October 10, 1990, the *Examiner* had published a profile on the close bond between Rickey and Bobbie in the glow of Rickey and the A's heading to another World Series. In that feature, Paula was quoted as saying Bobbie always favored Rickey. "It was always a comparison thing," she said. "We'd accuse her of doing this or that for Rickey."

Four years later, much of Paula's complaint argued that it was this same favoritism that exposed her to sexual assault. "Paula's mother would rarely attend any school function or athletic event for Paula or her other children," the complaint read. "However, the mother attended each and every game or event [for] Ricky [sic] Henderson. This created the impression with Paula Henderson that Ricky [sic] had a special place of importance in the family structure. The mother's identity and family identity revolved around a worship of Ricky [sic] Henderson."

Court documents submitted by Paula purported to reveal the extent to which the family relied on Rickey financially. He was the family engine. His two sisters, Paula and Glynnes, as well as Bobbie, lived in properties owned by Rickey in Oakland, while three of the boys, Alton, Tyrone, and Johnny, lived on a ranch Rickey owned in California. That meant, according to Paula's allegations, nearly everyone in the family was to some degree financially dependent on Rickey—that meant it was perilous to cross him. Paula claimed she filed the lawsuit only after Rickey stopped paying for her education when she was not performing academically. Paula accused Rickey of intimidating her into dropping the case by evicting her from Bobbie's house, which, she said, he owned. When Glynnes, Bobbie's youngest child, made statements supportive of Paula in the *Oakland Tribune,* Paula told the court that Rickey illegally raised her rent, refused to make repairs on her house, and had Glynnes evicted too.

There was another, unknown source of information secretly aiding Paula's case, a person who was not deposed and made no public statements, but who was in constant contact with Paula's counsel—Rickey's stepfather Paul Henderson. In *Off Base,* Rickey said he believed that Paul Henderson lived in Kansas City. Perhaps he did when the book was released, but in 1994 Paul Henderson was living in East Oakland, apparently unknown to Rickey—exposing another fissure of the family dynamic. Paula and Glynnes were his daughters.

"There was a lot of animosity toward Rickey from the people around him who felt like he wasn't sharing a lot of his wealth, that he wasn't giving them enough money. The people around him really treated him like a commodity," Horowitz recalled. "His father was giving us all this negative information. Paul Henderson. Smart guy. I don't know where he was coming from. I don't know if he was angry because he wasn't getting money from Rickey and was taking revenge. But he was a nice guy. He wasn't a weirdo. You could relate to him. I don't recall the things he was telling us being particularly helpful, but he was routinely in contact with us."

By the time the strike was settled in the spring of 1995 and the players went back to work, the lawyers haggled behind closed doors. Motions were filed, then amended. Paula backed off some of her claims about Bobbie, but she held firm in her accusations against Rickey. On November 17, 1995, after 15 months of litigation, Alameda County Superior Court judge John F. Kraetzer issued his final summary ruling in favor of Rickey:

IT IS HEREBY ORDERED that the motion of plaintiff be and it hereby is denied, except to as the Fourth Cause of Action as to which motion for summary judgment/adjudication is denied.

IT IS FURTHER ORDERED that the Court reconsiders and alters its ruling to become the granting of a motion for summary adjudication in favor of the defendant as to the First, Second, Third and Sixth Cause of Action.

The legalese translated simply to this: the case was over, and Rickey had won—if such a victory was possible given the disturbing accusations and the graphic, public airing of Paula's allegations and the emotional collateral damage of the case. As for Rickey, another chapter had closed in Oakland. He knew he wasn't returning to Oakland, and it would always be unclear how much impact the case had on the A's decision not to bring him back. Daniel Horowitz viewed Rickey as cold and uncompromising, seemingly able to detach from the catastrophic allegations against him, but the reality was that in 1994, aware that Paula might follow through on her threat and go public, Rickey had his worst year as a pro.

By 1995, the A's had sunk further into a rebuild. No matter how many shoving matches happened behind closed doors that Rickey and Tony emerged from smiling, it was over between Rickey and La Russa. The two had done their best work together, but the relationship had run its course. Rickey hit .300 in 1995 but wasn't the same explosive player. The hamstrings were sore. The wrist was sore. And the ego was bruised when he found out midseason that the A's were trying to trade him for the second straight season.

As the winter meetings concluded, Rickey was still unemployed. The White Sox had inquired, and so had Cincinnati, but Rickey said he wanted to stay on the West Coast. San Diego needed a leadoff hitter but lost out on Houston's Craig Biggio and Cincinnati's Ron Gant, their top targets, so they settled for their third choice—Rickey. Four days after his 37th birthday, Rickey signed a free-agent deal with the Padres—at a 50 percent pay cut. Instead of the two-year, $8.6 million deal he had signed two years earlier, he accepted two years and $4 million from San Diego. And after 16 years in the big leagues, Rickey was headed to the National League for the first time.

On each of the six original charges that Paula levied against him, the court had found in Rickey's favor, but it ruled that Paula's complaint of sexual assault and battery was dismissed because the statute of limitations had expired. There was, in the court's opinion, "no triable issue." A month later, on February 6, 1996, Rickey's attorney moved to deny the "Fourth Cause of Action"—that Rickey had used intimidation tactics to pressure Paula into dropping the case.

In April 1996, Paula filed a final appeal that the court dismissed two months later. Legally, Rickey had won. There were no charges, and he did not settle. But though he was exonerated, he did not emerge unscathed. Rickey had spent nearly 20 years of a professional career without being implicated in a scandal of any kind, but now Paula's lawsuit had been damaging to him, to Paula, and to the entire family. Rickey had always skillfully separated his public world as a baseball player from his private life, but the public nature of the lawsuit and the details of an alleged childhood sexual assault against a family member shattered those boundaries.

"We lost on everything," Horowitz recalled. "We lost on the statute of limitations, [so] on that basis the case didn't go forward. Paula was very brave. She grew up in a broken home. He was this revered figure in the neighborhood, who then went away. This situation, whatever went on between those two, is not as uncommon as we'd like to admit. He was coming from a wounded emotional place as well. Take away his incredible talent and financial success. I feel badly that this damaged him in any way because he could have come to the table.

"The same toughness that allowed him to get two hits* the night he was served did not serve him well in this," Horowitz recalled. "A little compassion would have avoided the lawsuit. I remember doing his deposition and you could see that toughness. You could not touch him emotionally."

Intimates who recalled that Rickey was heartbroken by Paula's allegations would conclude that the lawsuit was an example of him being victimized by a family member, that it was the cost of fame, and of being the one who made it but was now suffering the consequences of being an entire family's financial fulcrum. That fame, however, may have also provided Rickey with his greatest protections. Paula returned to her life, left to rebuild without the closure of victory and not much to show for her efforts. (The court at one point ordered Rickey to pay Paula $7,000 for legal fees.) Nor did Paula have the support and unyielding adulation of millions of fans as well as an em-

---

* Rickey actually got one hit that night.

ployer willing to protect her, as Rickey did. Meanwhile, the once-hungry *San Francisco Examiner* and *Oakland Tribune,* which had sued to retain access to the case, did no additional reporting—the case was closed.

Once the games resumed, the fans and the press were eager to reconcile with Rickey and get back to baseball and all that was good about the sport. While Paula returned to the anonymity of her life, the public, which had always loved Rickey, was eager to get back to loving Rickey. The strike was over, baseball was back, Rickey was in San Diego, and the matter would not be mentioned publicly again.

Book Three

"WHEN THE LEGEND
BECOMES FACT . . ."

O N APRIL 25, 2001, when the season was just three weeks old and the country was entering the final months of its pre-9/11 life, Rickey Nelson Henley Henderson, aged 42, took ball four to lead off the bottom of the ninth against Jose Mesa of the Phillies. It was the 2,063rd free pass of his career, and with it Rickey passed Babe Ruth as the all-time leader in walks.

Later that year, on October 4, 2001, in the bottom of the third inning against the Dodgers, Rickey stepped into the box at Qualcomm Stadium. (The big yard had once been named after the legendary San Diego sportswriter Jack Murphy, back before the corporations made stadium naming rights too lucrative to ignore.) Tie game, Rickey facing Luke Prokopec, born in 1978. The day before, the Dodgers had creamed the Padres, 12–5. There'd been nothing much to see there—except that when Rickey walked and scored in the third inning, the run tied him with Ty Cobb for the all-time lead. Now, a day later, again in the third, Prokopec tried to sneak a fastball past the old man. The crouch wasn't as deep as it used to be, but Rickey uncoiled and connected. Padres broadcasters Jerry Coleman and Ted Leitner were on the call:

> There's a high fly ball left field . . . that ball is to the wall, at the wall . . . There goes another home run and there goes a new all-time runs scoring record by Rickey Henderson! . . . WHOAAAA DOCTOR! . . . If you're gonna do it, do it with class and that's the way to do it. Score yourself. Hit a home run . . . He SLIDES into home plate and is surrounded by his teammates . . . Well Rickey didn't waste any time that time. He hit the home run, got

the run, got the base hit. He's two shy now of three thousand, and
he hasn't finished yet. He's got three games to go including this
one . . . Wow. Look at him. Happiest man in the United States.
Rickey Henderson.

Rickey rounded the bases, clapping his hands. When he approached
home, in a moment of Rickey Style, he did indeed motion to his teammates
surrounding home plate to make way and then he *slid,* feetfirst, into the
plate. The players smothered him when he came up. In the years following
the miserable 1994 strike, when the game lost the public, that was what baseball did now—it celebrated things. You could show a little flair and nobody
even got decked for it anymore. After Rickey's home run, they stopped the
game. The great Tony Gwynn, the eight-time batting champ—who had broken into the big leagues in 1982, the same year Rickey was breaking Brock's
single-season record, and who would retire that year—presented Rickey
with a solid gold-plated replica of home plate.

Three days later, on October 7, in Gwynn's final game, Rickey flipped a
bloop double to right against Colorado's John Thomson, a little dead fish
in his first at-bat on the first pitch he saw. It was hit number 3,000, making Rickey the 25th player in history to reach the sacred plateau. As they'd
done three days earlier when he homered to pass Cobb on the all-time runs
list, the Padres players raced out to mob him—this time at second base.

When Rickey slid into home plate after hitting his record-breaker over
the fence—who else but Rickey ever completed a home-run trot by *sliding*
into home?—he was still the Man of Steal. That was the nickname, forever
imprinted on the business card. He was the stolen-base standard, but stolen
bases were never what made him proudest. Steals were a means to an end.
The endgame was scoring.

"Of all the records Rickey cared about the most, it was the runs scored
record," Pamela recalled. "That one meant every time Rickey scored, he was
actually contributing to his team in the best possible way—he put a run on
the board. There was no more clear way to helping your team win than to
cross the plate." Since the first professional baseball game was recorded in
1869, no one crossed home plate more than the 2,246 times Rickey had.

Rickey had even done something that season that shouldn't have been
possible—and yet it was. From Rickey's big league debut on June 24, 1979,
to the end of the 2001 season, he had stolen 1,395 bases. During that same

period, the Boston Red Sox franchise had stolen 1,382 bases. Rickey hadn't just stolen more bases than any other player during his career—he had out-stolen an entire *team*.

The numbers were too big to ignore. The history he was now reaching back and touching, the names whose real estate he now shared. Rickey occu-pied the top shelf with Ruth . . . Cobb . . . Mays . . . Williams . . . Aaron. He was part of the 3,000 hits club—Williams and Ruth never got there. These players had become the bedrocks of the sport, and in 2001 Rickey, still an active player, had already been the all-time stolen-base king for a *decade*.

When Rickey's career finally ended, he was a Dodger, playing for the team that wanted him first as a 17-year-old but got him last, as a 44-year-old. By the time Rickey had ripped his 3,055th and final hit (on September 1, 2003, against the Astros), stolen his 1,406th and final base (on August 29, 2003, against Colorado), and hit his 297th and final home run (five weeks earlier on July 20, a leadoff homer off the Cardinals' Woody Williams, naturally, for a record 81st and final time), he had been transformed. As Bill James, the godfather of the statistical analysis revolution, once famously said after writing an essay on Rickey, "If you split Rickey Henderson in half, you'd have *two* Hall of Famers."

Rickey was vindicated by the numbers—he was a Made Guy now—so they told stories about him. He had become that most unique, most untouchable of characters—an American treasure and a living part of baseball folklore in the tradition of Satchel Paige and Yogi Berra. What had once made him frus-trating now made him a character—and everyone laughed together. He was no longer self-absorbed for not remembering names—he was just Rickey. The people who knew him told stories about him, and people who didn't repeated the stories they'd heard—they were too good not to be repeated. People who had never met Rickey spoke about him with a certainty that underscored his ubiquity. His legend was baseball's legend.

And now their eyes lit up when they heard his name. Rickey had always been special, a one-namer like Prince and Reggie—that was all it took for an entire generation to know automatically who you were talking about. It was the 2000s. He was playing in his fourth decade, and the name Rickey was now no longer a pejorative. Over the past 20 years, that had never happened before. Too many years of column inches had been devoted to everything he wasn't, to all that he could have been if he were just somebody else, if he were just more dedicated to the game. Yet here he was, still standing, and now associated with joy, nostalgia—and awe.

Remember when Vince Coleman said that 1,500 stolen bases wouldn't be "nearly enough" to keep him from passing Rickey? Well, Vince was long gone, retired in 1997 with 752 career steals. That was good for sixth on the all-time list, remarkable and highly respectable on its own, but it was light-years away from Rickey. Rickey knew that Coleman could never catch him for the simple fact that Coleman just didn't hit well enough. "You gotta *get* on base to *steal* a base," he would say. In the 1980s, Tim Raines and Rickey were side by side, the American and National League mirror images. Raines was still in the business too, playing into his forties. He'd retire in 2002 with 808 steals, good for fifth place all-time—but nearly *600* fewer stolen bases than Rickey.

Cobb's runs record had stood since the 2,245th and last time he touched home plate, on July 26, 1928, at Chicago's Comiskey Park on the South Side, not far from where Rickey would be born 30 years later. Cobb had become the all-time runs leader in 1925, when he passed Cap Anson—a notorious name that reached even further back in the game's history, to the late 1800s, when Anson famously championed and actively promoted the removal of all Black players from the sport. Babe Ruth's walks record had stood since May 29, 1935, when the Babe was at Baker Bowl, playing during the Great Depression for the Boston Braves against the Phillies; Rickey and Ruth both set their marks against Philadelphia. When the Babe walked for the second time that afternoon, it would be for the final time in his career. Ruth had been adding to his own record since 1930, when he passed Eddie Collins for the all-time lead.

This was the same Eddie Collins who, as general manager of the Boston Red Sox—the last team to integrate—said with a straight face in 1944 that the Red Sox were not segregated by choice. "I have been connected with the Red Sox for twelve years and during that time we have never had a single request for a tryout by a colored athlete. It is beyond my understanding how anyone could insinuate or believe that all ball players, regardless of race, color, or creed have not been treated in the American way so far as having an equal opportunity to play for the Red Sox."

A section of the Baseball Hall of Fame in Cooperstown is dedicated to the "first class," the inaugural inductees to the Hall in 1936. Babe Ruth and Ty Cobb were part of that class, the two best ever when the game was white.

The baseball legends of Ruth and Cobb became a part of the nation, part of its soul. There were only 25 players who had amassed 3,000 hits since Americans began playing baseball around the time Civil War hero Ulysses S. Grant was elected president. Of the players in baseball history who could say they had 3,000 hits, 2,000 runs, and 2,000 walks, however, there was just one, and it wasn't Ruth or Cobb, DiMaggio or Mantle, Mays or Aaron, or any of the other immortal gray ghosts of the sport. It was Rickey.

Leave it to Reggie to remind everyone that during the election process, not all Hall of Famers are created equal. There is no pass-fail, up-or-down vote that grants the worthy candidates equal access to consideration, even though, once elected, all the legends become members of the same fraternity with the same equity stake—you're either a Hall of Famer or you're not. Everybody knows, though, that there's a hierarchy to getting into the club, like it or not, and that's why baseball makes such a big deal about being *a first-ballot* Hall of Famer. That means you're the best of the very best—no debate, no doubt. None of this Veterans' Committee stuff where a player's contemporaries settle scores, or having to wait in the soup line every January with the rest of the hungry greats to beg the baseball writers for the immortality they stingily ladle out. It's why everyone was so concerned about vote totals and percentages (*would there ever be a unanimous choice?*).

But everybody knew who stood at the top of the record books. The record-holders are the foundations upon which the hallowed game stands, and it was their numbers that put them there. Rickey Henderson, the guy they all said didn't want to play, now resided in the uppermost regions of the sport. The numbers had exonerated him.

What could anyone say against the monument that Rickey had built? You had to look at Rickey's neighborhood now. He had moved uptown. The statistical arguments for his greatness were irrefutable, and in baseball it was the numbers that the old guard respected so much, the numbers that built the unbreakable records that Rickey was now breaking. The stats used to measure all players, past and future, were the same numbers that had so often been used against him to argue that he was not one of the greats—but now the numbers said he was. Cobb? Rickey had scored more runs. Ruth? Rickey had more walks. Steals? Everyone was already chasing Rickey. Aaron, Mays? Rickey had passed both in at least one important offensive category. There was no alternative. The critics were forced to relent.

When they did not, as Bob Ryan of the *Boston Globe* did not, they headed down the dubious path to argue that Rickey *still* underachieved: he could have been even better had he just left it all on the field. As Ryan saw it, teams knew that acquiring Rickey was like buying a quart of milk—good until a certain date before it soured.

HE CAN'T STEAL HEARTS

The following premise is inarguable: Rickey Henderson is the greatest leadoff man in the history of the game.

However . . . the following premise is widely held: Rickey Henderson is one of the biggest pains in the butt who has ever played. And as amazing as his career numbers are, most people who have come in direct contact with him say they could have been even better if Rickey weren't, well, Rickey.

As great as he is, no one ever seems particularly sorry to see him go. They seem to dwell more on the balls Rickey doesn't run out, the balls he no longer hustles to get (and in his properly motivated prime no one ever got to more), and the incessant, squeaky wheel complaints that he is underappreciated and underpaid. Sooner or later, a judgment is made that the bad is outdoing the good, and off Rickey goes. No matter what he has done in that uniform, the manager can't help thinking about the great "what if?" of Rickey Henderson.

Still, he'll be a first-ballot, 90 percent plurality Hall of Famer.

On its face, Ryan's position made some sense—except that Rickey's final career output refuted it. There was another column that wasn't often associated with Rickey that was immutable—his teams were better with him. Rickey led off a game with a home run 81 times—and when he did, his teams won 61.7 percent of the time. When he hit a lead-off homer in a tie game, Rickey's teams had a winning percentage of .716. "Don't forget to label Rickey a winner," Dave Winfield said. "Not just a star, not just a one-of-a-kind talent." Had Rickey handled himself better, been more accepting of the perceived slights, and been less public about being underpaid, it might have kept him from playing for as many of the nine uniforms he ultimately donned. It might have made him less of a target for the scribes, the drive-time radio, the front offices, managers, and teammates. It might have given him a better chance of sliding into the Ernie Banks–Lou Brock space of the player who loved baseball and was loved in turn by the public—which was really a way to be more attractive to the overwhelmingly white body of fans, coaches, teammates, and rivals who were always so quick to exaggerate the transgressions of Black athletes. There was also some magical and bizarre thinking at work: asking Rickey to be more like Ozzie Smith, Ernie Banks, Tony Gwynn, or any of the other more affable ballplayers would be to forfeit the Rickey who had just torn apart the record books—it was to want Rickey to be someone other than Rickey. It was to eliminate Rickey Style.

All of these arguments were valid—but to say that Rickey could have been even *better?* How much better was Rickey supposed to be? What seemed to confound the people who thought Rickey should have been better was the conviction that for a quarter-century they had been watching, say, around 80 percent of what Rickey Henderson could do on a baseball field, and that if Rickey had unleashed that volcanic 20 percent—as he did in the 18 months immediately following his trade away from the Yankees—the world would have seen a truly transcendent figure, without qualification or complication. To those men, even the numbers he amassed could not completely protect Rickey. Having spent their lives in the game, they believed that Rickey had withheld that 20 percent far too often, and for reasons that often detracted from his greatness.

How many career hits was he supposed to have? Four thousand? Five thousand? How many more stolen bases would a compliant Rickey have amassed? Two thousand? Three thousand? Rickey had 468 more stolen bases than second-place Lou Brock, and that difference alone, 468, still would have put Rickey in the all-time top 50. Rickey stole 612 bases after his 30th birthday, a number that by itself put him inside the top 20.

Rickey had been framed, shaped, and sold as an underachiever. (*Think of how much better he could have been . . .*) His career had been narrated as if his career totals would expose him—the consequence of his personality, of not playing as many games as the old traditions said a great player should, of not appearing to be as motivated as the thought-makers demanded he be, of always, *always,* being pissed off about money—but they didn't. The numbers gave him the last word—and he won two championships. What the opinion-makers were really saying was that they believed *their* words would ultimately overshadow *his* deeds. In the end, though, the numbers provided his greatest insulation.

The debate was over, but the work was just beginning, for Rickey *did* have relationships he needed to repair for all the years of being rude and unreliable, self-absorbed. Take, for example, the time Rickey and Walt McCreary were in Las Vegas and a rep from the MGM Grand came to their table and told Rickey that the legendary singer Tony Bennett wished to come to his table and say hello.

"Tony Bennett!" Walt recalled. "And Rickey said, 'Tell Tony Bennett Rickey would like to have him come over when Rickey has finished lunch.' It's Tony Bennett, but Rickey didn't know who Tony Bennett was. Rick's frame of reference was always sports. I'm sure he was offended because we went out to eat and never met with him."

Rickey was radioactive in the memorabilia market because of the old days, when the card shows feared that he'd agree to an appearance and then stiff them, or worse than a no-show, arrive and make an embarrassing scene on the show floor because he wanted more money—all the things he had done before. The cumulative effect could be felt in Rickey's baseball card market value. A Barry Bonds, Frank Thomas, or Ken Griffey Jr. card was worth twice a Rickey card.

"He had all the records in the world, but no one wanted Rickey," Walt McCreary recalled. "A big part of my job was customer service. We had to rehabilitate his whole image. He was a poison. Nobody wanted anything to do with him. Rickey based his measure on money, and he wanted to make sure he was getting whatever he'd heard somebody was, but I had to tell him those guys, Hank Aaron, Brooks Robinson—they were beloved. Those guys loved kids. Those guys are kissing babies. Brooks Robinson used to travel with a Sharpie in his pocket. You're not going to get any of that if you show up to a place and won't even shake hands with anybody."

Now that he was made, Rickey let the walls drop. Walt convinced him that people wanted to like him—he was Rickey, after all—and just a little of his sunlight could warm a meadow. And soon, the finicky baseball card world opened its doors. The big boys like Steiner Sports—the biggest memorabilia company in the business—wanted to do business with Rickey. A corporate meet-and-greet dinner with Rickey, sponsored by AT&T? Done. Rickey would wade into the crowd and laugh. Walt went on a social media offensive, posting photos of Rickey at public events, mugging for the camera with a politician's ease. Letting his admirers breathe a fraction of his air brought him closer to them. At one event a shy promoter asked Walt if his client could come over and say hello to Rickey. The client was the NFL legend Roger Staubach himself. "That was the real Rickey when he would let it happen. Even the people at his level were in awe of him," Walt recalled.

Now at shows everyone had a Rickey story to tell (in the third person of course), and those stories no longer symbolized the sport going to hell but rather all that was special and good and hilariously wistful about baseball—they missed Rickey. Too often baseball made the headlines only for labor feuds, drug use by players, or Black players disappearing from a game with which Black people once felt the closest kinship. And the game had become so goddamned boring! Who wouldn't kill to see a snatch-catch again? Just one. The game had lost its color. "The game has become so boring, if you steal a base, they give you a damn taco," Willie Wilson said. "How many tacos would they be giving out if Rickey was still playing? They'd be eating tacos for a year." Once, right in the middle of spring training, the Angels superstar Mike Trout, the best player in the sport, walked through a Nordstrom in Scottsdale, Arizona, as anonymously as an insurance salesman.

The new generation didn't come to the game by comparing Rickey to Mays or Kaline or Mantle and concluding that he was too gauche to be in that class. They came to the game comparing the newcomers who entered the clubhouse to Rickey. Stars had grown up with him and now walked with him, Rickey, in person. Bonds, the greatest player in the game, used the snatch-catch—just like Rickey did. Ken Griffey Jr., the other greatest player in the game, who used to run around the Yankee clubhouse when Rickey was there with his father, Ken Sr., wore number 24—Mays's number, but also Rickey's. In 1990, the *Chicago Sun-Times* veteran beat writer Joe Goddard profiled Sammy Sosa, a hot White Sox prospect whom scouts were calling "the next Rickey Henderson." That same year, when Tigers manager Sparky Anderson got a first look at Deion Sanders, who did he immediately see? He saw Rickey. When the old schooler Buck Showalter managed Sanders, the first guy he compared him to was Rickey—and it was to be taken as a compliment.

It wasn't just the fans and the writers who now saw him differently than the fans and writers of the past, but also his peers. What the older cranks saw as almost an insulting quirkiness was magic to the new kids.

It was June 27, 1994, and the California Angels were at the Coliseum. Rickey was having one of those Rickey games—he'd been on base all night. His first at-bat, Rickey singled, reached the bag, and looked at J. T. Snow, the Angels' first baseman, and said, "Hey, kid."

"So I've only been in the league a couple of years, and it's Rickey Henderson," Snow recalled. "The pitcher throws over once. Rickey dives back. Throws over again. Rickey dives back. Rickey gets up, dusts himself off, and says to me, 'You can tell him he don't gotta throw over here today. I'm not running today. Rickey tired.'"

The next two times up, Rickey doubled and homered. In the fifth, Rickey was on first again, and Mike Butcher, the Angels pitcher, threw repeatedly to first. "After he dusts himself off, like, after the third throw, he says to me, 'Man, you *better* go tell him he doesn't need to throw over here today. Rickey tired. Rickey ain't running today.'

"It's a true story," Snow recalled. "He would come down to first base and call me 'Kid.' It was kind of amazing, because here's the stolen-base king and he tells me he's not going. I mean, he's Rickey Henderson, so I kinda *wanted* him to go. In the dugout I told everyone, 'Rickey said he wasn't running.' I thought he was bluffing, but he was on base like five times that day and didn't even attempt a steal. 'Rickey tired.'"

Snow was 11 years old when Rickey made his big league debut, and he had seen Rickey run a million times—who hadn't? Yet it was different working the bag when Rickey was on first. Even 12 years after breaking Brock's single-season record, Rickey would still wear that big gold medallion with the number "130" etched in the center. "He was so quiet when he would run, you couldn't hear his feet at all," Snow remembered. "He had the chains and stuff on. That was the only thing you could hear, the chains rattling. It was my job to let out a yell when he took off, but you had to be looking at him to know, because his feet didn't make a sound when he took off."

Jimmy Rollins was playing shortstop for the Phillies the night Rickey broke Ruth's walk record. Rollins was born in Oakland, played Little League for the Oakland Dynamites, idolized Rickey, and was a star at Encinal High in Alameda, the same school that Hall of Famer Willie Stargell attended. When Rollins was in high school, Shooty Babitt, then scouting for Atlanta, lost out on him to Philadelphia. Jimmy's father, Jim Rollins Sr.—"Big Jim" to everyone around the way—was part of old Oakland. West Oakland. Mc-Clymonds Oakland. The family had migrated to Oakland along the familiar pathway from the South; like Stargell's family, the Rollinses had come west from Oklahoma. Big Jim and Rickey were good friends, linked by their mutual connection, Fred Atkins. Now the son—the next generation of the legend—had been on the field as Rickey broke a record that had been set a dozen years before Jackie Robinson's debut.

He was hoping he would also be on the field when Rickey broke Cobb's all-time runs scored mark, but the baseball fates did not cooperate. He did, however, remember the time he just wanted to get a glimpse of the man.

"I'd always heard that if you wanted to catch Rickey, it had to be early—Rickey worked out in the morning. It's an off day. I get to the ballpark, and Larry Bowa is like, 'What the fuck are you doing here?'" Rollins recalled. "I was too embarrassed to tell him I was there to see Rickey.

"So I'm hanging outside the weight room and I'm like, 'What *am* I doing here? What if he's not even here? I wasted an off day.' But I peek my head in the weight room—there he is! I duck my head back out, but he already sees me, so now I have to walk in, and there he is, doing curls. He's doing like, 35-pound weights. I usually start at 45 or so and progress downward, but I can't show him up by lifting more than him. That's disrespectful. So, I do 25 pounds. I try to act all cool, put some bass in my voice and say, 'Hey, Rickey.' He looks at me and says, 'What's up, Little James?'

"He acknowledged me directly—he knew who I *was*! And now all the bass is gone out of my voice and inside I wanted to explode. *Nobody* called me 'Little James' unless you were close, like family, and just by calling me that he was letting me know he had been following me. It was crazy. I felt that inside, like the elders were watching. Then he got up, said, 'All right now.' And then he left."

When Jimmy called Big Jim, his father didn't understand the fuss. Rickey was one of them, and Jimmy was part of that Oakland heritage. He could have met Rickey whenever he wanted. Over the years Big Jim would tell Jimmy he was going over to see Fred Atkins and Rickey was going to be there. Did he want to go? "I'd say no, because I was too shy, because it was Rickey." Now, decades later, not only had Jimmy Rollins become part of the legend of Oakland by making the big leagues, but he had also joined a special fraternity within the fraternity—those players, like Frank Robinson and Joe Morgan and Rickey, who started in Oakland Little Leagues and went all the way to Most Valuable Player in the major leagues, the best player in the game.

When Jimmy Rollins won the 2007 National League MVP, Big Jim threw a party at the house. Fred was there, Mike Norris showed up, and so did Rickey. The legend of Oakland was still alive, and it was Jimmy Rollins who had kept the line going.

With Rickey, the stories flowed, and talking about him made everyone forget for a moment the game's present lack of charisma. Rickey had become the ultimate baseball character, in the tradition of Dizzy Dean and Casey Stengel and Cool Papa Bell—but with the career numbers of Ruth and Cobb.

They told stories partly because Rickey wouldn't retire. He was still there, and that was a story in itself. *How* was he still there? His peers were now working in broadcast booths, managing or running teams, or missing the game in retirement, but there was Rickey, still in uniform. The stories about Rickey were not only tall tales of the past but also tales of the present. Rickey had begun his career *in the 1970s*. The surly, sullen, moody Rickey of the 1980s was now being massaged into the eccentric, quirky Rickey. The stories revealed a character like the wondrous Satchel Paige—the title of whose autobiography, *Maybe I'll Pitch Forever,* seemed to have given Rickey ideas as a position player—combined with Yogi Berra, for whom dialogue became a wonderful blend of legend and fact, impossible to detangle.

Pamela recalled that Rickey himself would invoke Satchel Paige, the ageless one. Paige pitched in parts of five decades. He belonged to time—he was of indeterminate age, or at least that's what he told people—and he reached the majors at the age of 42, in 1948. He even started for Charlie Finley as a 58-year-old with the 1965 Kansas City A's, pitching three scoreless innings against Boston on September 25. "Rickey had baseball in his blood," Pamela would say. "He was following Satchel Paige. He would say he was going to play as long as he could. He was going to keep taking jobs for any team that was willing to give him one, because once they stopped, it was all over."

As baseball characters went, Rickey had become a modern-day Yogi. In a nod to his former manager, some people even called the stories about him "Rickeyisms."

Did Rickey really frame a million-dollar check without cashing it?
Did Rickey really get frostbite in August?
Was the John Olerud story really true?

One explanation for Rickey's rehabilitation was that the old battlefields had disappeared—and so did many of its combatants. Professionally, Rickey had outlived so many of them, the old curmudgeons who had entered the sport before World War II, when the game was still segregated. Dick Young, who covered DiMaggio, and Red Smith, who covered Ruth, had both covered Rickey too. But they were long dead now, and even the generation they had influenced was aging out.

Many of the old fights were dead. Even if they still resented the athletes, the public had finally relented against the money—the players were super-rich now, and comparatively the money Rickey was fighting for seemed quaint. After so much warfare between owners and players during Rickey's time, only the crankiest old-timer could argue that the game wasn't a business and the players weren't entitled to their enormous share of a stratospheric bounty.

"Media-wise, the writers didn't help. It's easy to pick on the guy with a lot of money, and Rickey was more aggressive with that," recalled A's catcher Terry Steinbach. "Rickey didn't hide when he was unhappy about what he was making. He didn't hold back on that. That was easy fodder. It was very easy to get stuff, and some of it was not too appealing as far as Rickey's character went. Rickey gave you the stuff, and a lot of it was not untrue, but people are sick and tired about hearing about rich guys complaining when you're working 49 hours a week.

"I once asked Frank Blackman of the *Examiner,* I said, 'Blackie, why are you such a dick?'" Steinbach said. "He said, 'We're an afternoon paper. Everything good has already been written. We've got to find something else, another angle.' Because of his greatness, they were looking to bring the guy down."

The new generation no longer watched Rickey for what he wasn't, but saw him specifically for what he was—and that was Rickey. Far from being offended by Rickey Style, it was why they bought the tickets. For instance, on Christmas Day 1987, a nine-year-old named Kent Corser received a set of baseball cards as a gift. Kent was a Midwesterner, and the Royals were his team. Who did the kid gravitate toward? Rickey.

It was the start of a lifelong love of Rickey as Corser became the ultimate Rickey superfan. As an adult, he finished his basement to create a 1,000-square-foot "Man Cave of Steal," where he kept 4,500 unique pieces of Rickey memorabilia. He had even custom-made a green-and-gold tree ornament that read "RICKEY" and had in his collection a Christmas card from the Hendersons with a picture of Rickey, Pamela, and the girls on the front. Inside, it read:

Twas the night before Christmas in the Henderson home
Rickey was building a fire & Pam was on the phone
Angela was baking cookies & Lexi was peekin'

Little Miss Adrian was in bed sleepin'.
The stockings were hung on the chimney awaiting,
The arrival of St. Nick & the gifts he'd be bringin'.
From Our Family to Yours
Merry Christmas and Happy New Year

Corser had actually met Rickey twice, the second time when he drove himself and his seven-year-old son Dylan five hours to Iowa, where Rickey was playing in a 2013 celebrity softball game at the "Field of Dreams," the baseball diamond made famous by the Kevin Costner film of the same name. Ozzie Smith was there. Johnny Bench too. The place went wild when Rickey emerged from the cornfield—and then spiraled into a frenzy when Rickey hit the first pitch of the game into the corn for a home run. On a magical afternoon, Walt McCreary got Rickey to sign the ball for Kent, and Rickey took pictures with Dylan.

So many had grown up with posters of Rickey on their wall, waggling his fingers in his Kelly green Mizuno gloves. They had come to the game through baseball cards and television, and they played baseball because of Rickey, snatch-catching because Rickey gave them the snatch-catch. When he saw Rickey for the first time, standing on a street corner following a Dodgers-Cubs game in 2003—when Rickey's career was winding down—Corser took a shot. "I just said to him, 'I don't want an autograph. I just want to shake your hand. You're the reason I'm here. You're the reason I love the game of baseball.' He took my ticket stub and signed." Rickey was now an heirloom.

He was also mystical, showing up in the oddest places. Rickey could be anywhere. People would see Rickey at the ranch out in Coarsegold and no one would believe it—*Rickey? HERE?*—not realizing that Rickey had lived there for years. There was the time in 2017 when Rickey showed up at Game 3 of the NHL playoffs, first round, San Jose Sharks against Edmonton, wearing a custom HENDERSON 24 Sharks sweater, waving the team flag to hype up the San Jose crowd.

Then there was that time in 1998 when Walt McCreary got a call from his 11-year-old son's school—the principal wanted to arrange a meeting. This had to be trouble. "I get there and he says, 'We love your child, but he is telling all the kids that Rickey Henderson stays at his house, so we're asking if you can speak to him.' I said, 'He does,' and I still think they thought I was BS-ing too."

The new generation of baseball executives cared about the numbers, and not the old average-hits-runs standbys but the *advanced metrics*. That sophisticated mélange of statistical analysis didn't make Rickey look good to the Bill James crowd—they made him look *even better*. Rickey's numbers grew in importance over time because the new generation of baseball fans and writers and executives were evaluating the entire sport differently. As Rickey aged, his résumé left an even more impressive wake.

Another time some dude piped up with a post on Facebook, that online slaughterhouse, saying that Rickey was selfish, all about Rickey, overrated, *and* wouldn't be able to crack a team in the numbers era. That inflamed Chicago schoolteacher Jonathan Jordan, who taught Pythagoras's three averages—arithmetic, geometric, and harmonic. Jordan created a formula using harmonic average (as Bill James did in creating his power/speed formula) to determine where Rickey fit in the pantheon. Six months later, after creating a "Small Ball Harmony" formula—$(3*BB*1B*Sac + SB)/[(BB*1B)+(BB*Sac + SB) + (1B*Sac + SB)]$ for those scoring at home—Jordan concluded that Rickey was the greatest small-ball player ever, ahead of Cobb. When he added Rickey to what he called his "All Ball Harmony" formula for medium- and big-ball players—the slashers and power guys—the numbers put Rickey second all-time, behind Ty Cobb but ahead of Barry Bonds.

"The original slight was that Rickey couldn't play in a Sabermetrics world, so I created my own advanced analytics to prove he would not only make a team, but he was the greatest small-baller in the history of the game, decades after the heyday of small ball," Jordan recalled. "My argument was that he was not only one of the greatest when he played, but that he'd have been the greatest in Cobb's era . . . The numbers I created spoke for themselves."

Rickey was the statisticians' ideal player. He did everything they could have dreamed of, not just by getting on base but in the way he used his eye at the plate. Rickey ran up pitch counts, and they loved that—get that starter out of the game. Rickey saw so many pitches and walked so many times that any pitcher facing him once was throwing to the equivalent of three—maybe four—free-swingers up there hacking at the first pitch. Throw him a strike and he'd turn on it, upping both his on-base and slugging percentages. "If Rickey played today," Jimmy Rollins calculated, "he'd be making $500 million." Billy Beane, the front-office face of the analytics revolution, said, "If Rickey were playing today, you couldn't pay him enough."

Not everyone was enthralled by baseball's new statistical approaches—something big was missing. Dave Stewart was convinced that the analytics erred by discounting the value of wins to a starting pitcher and taking the position that wins weren't important to a pitcher's résumé. The new guard said that wins were a "team stat," and so were far more indicative of circumstance than the ability of the guy on the hill. Stewart was enraged by that claim and felt that it was missing the human heart, his specialty. A major part of a starting pitcher's job, he believed, was to provide stamina and competition—to stay out there and fight for his team—and that effort was never independent of the score. Stewart thought that this reevaluation of pitching was undermining the traditional definitions of pitching greatness. Now no one would know *who* helped the team win the most. The new numbers, however, absolutely benefited Rickey.

With their new interpretations of data, the new guys just laughed at the old guard (*What were they watching?*) when Willie Wilson finished fourth in the league in the 1980 MVP balloting. Sure, he had a great season, and the numbers bore that out. Sure, he had 230 hits, and sure, his Royals team won the pennant—but here was a guy who had 230 hits and *didn't even reach 300 total bases*. That's what happens when a player walks only 28 times in 745 plate appearances. Rickey, who walked 117 times that year, finished 10th in the MVP voting. The high-contact, low-walk guys, like Clemente, were still great players of course—nobody was going to knock the great Clemente out loud—and so was that Garciaparra kid up in Boston, who struck out with Mattingly-DiMaggio-like infrequency, but the praise sounded like a platitude. To the new baseball evaluators, see-ball, hit-ball baseball was dead, and they were determined to make sure it stayed that way.

The fearsome Red Sox slugger Mo Vaughn used to call Rickey "Gas" because, Mo said, "to walk him was like putting gasoline on a fire." Ball four, and Rickey would trot down to first. Mo would be there, a boulder of chaw ballooning one cheek.

"What up, Gas?"

"What up, baby."

Rickey would take a few steps toward second, and Vaughn's manager—didn't matter which one, Butch Hobson, Kevin Kennedy, Jimy Williams—would get nervous. So would the pitcher, even strikeout guys like Roger Clemens who could make base runners irrelevant merely by overpowering whoever was at bat. Vaughn recalled the familiar pattern: The manager would order a throw to first. Rickey would dive back, and Mo would slap a little leather on him.

Another throw, another retreat to first, another swipe of the mitt from Mo. Again. And again. Finally, Rickey would call for time, emerge from the dust cloud, wipe himself off, and look at Vaughn.

"He would say, 'Dawg, I gotta go. He's tiring me out throwing over here so much!'"

And then Rickey would steal second.

Another time Rickey was on first, Mo gave him a little glove tap on the hip, respect for the legend.

"What up, Gas? You going?"

"You know I am."

And then Rickey was gone.

For a quarter-century, Rickey played in every city in America, and all the clubbies aged along with him. Big Jim Kascinski was the visitors' clubhouse man in Milwaukee. Everybody loved Big Jim. He had been there since the old days, predating the Brewers, when Milwaukee was a National League city. Big Jim was a batboy in 1963 for the Aaron-Mathews-Spahn Braves, before the team packed up and left for Atlanta.

The A's started the 1994 season in Big Jim's town, and when the team arrived, Oakland strength coach Bob Alejo recalled, a representative from the Toronto Blue Jays met Rickey in the A's clubhouse and handed him a box and an envelope. In the box was Rickey's 1993 World Series ring. These were the days before baseball celebrated everything, turning both the biggest and most pedestrian moments into a Hallmark card—something to remind us that the grand old game could still pull at the heartstrings. In later years, teams would wait for a player who changed teams after winning a championship to return to his old team as a visitor and do a classy pregame, on-field tribute—give a guy his flowers.

In 1994 there was no pomp and no pageantry. After he was handed the box, Rickey put on his warm-ups and went out to batting practice. "You had to go down the stairs and around from the clubhouse to get to the field in Milwaukee. The place was a mess," Alejo recalled. "I warmed up some guys and threw some BP. The first inning goes down, and Jim is taking the practice uniforms to wash them. He's turning them inside out, emptying the pockets. Then he calls me over and says, 'I think you want to take a look at this.' He's got a pair of warm-up pants in his hand and says, 'These are Rickey Henderson's.' He empties the back pocket and there's a folded-up envelope: a check for a hundred thousand dollars. Rickey took the envelope, stuck it in his pocket, and went to go hit. It was his World Series share from the year before. He must have forgotten it in his pocket."

For the record, while Rickey was taking his hacks in the cage, the check sitting in his pocket was for $127,920.77—a full share for being part of the 1993 champs. "Big Jim looks at me and says, 'I guess he didn't need it,' which I thought was funny because you know what they used to say about Rickey: the only time Rickey let go of a dollar was to get a better grip."

There was a funny addendum to the story: Nearly 30 years later, Big Jim had no recollection of it. What he did remember was Jose Canseco doing something similar—forgetting an $80,000 check in the trainers' room.

"Jose went into the trainers' room and put the check down. It was 80-thou—take home. And it just sat in the drawer until a week later and I found it," Kascinski recalled. "I called the A's, got Jose, and I told him I found a check, and he said, 'I was *wondering* what happened to that.' I mean $80,000. He was just carefree about it. I don't know what I'd do. That would be my life if I lost an $80,000 check.

"Now Rickey, Rickey never bothered me," Kascinski said. "Rickey was a model as a visiting player. Didn't bitch about anything. You had guys who were complainers. Complained all the time. The uniforms weren't clean enough. They wanted this or that. They could find something wrong with everything. Not Rickey. He'd come in, say hi, and then three days later say goodbye. Unfortunately, I didn't get to know him very well.

"But let me tell you this: I had a nephew who got diagnosed with cancer when he was little and got his arm amputated immediately. Rickey took a liking to my nephew. They had a good relationship. You would not believe how many players went out of their way to be nice to him and when you asked him about players, Rickey was one of the guys whose name always came up. I was just so happy that I was in a position where I could help my sister out, having a son with one arm. When people to this day say bad things about athletes, they beat their wives and do their drugs and get in trouble, but there are so many who do good things and I'm an eyewitness to it. Rickey made a big impact on a little boy."

Rickey spent the final chapter of his career as an itinerant legend playing on so many teams that he even became something of an accidental innovator: teams rarely acquired future Hall of Famers at the trade deadline, but there was Rickey, from Mount Rushmore, still available as long as he had gas left in the tank. After Toronto, Rickey would play for Oakland, San Diego, Anaheim, Oakland, the Mets, Seattle, San Diego, Boston, and Los Angeles—nine stops in nine years. Where Bob Ryan saw Rickey being moved as proof of a team eventually souring on him, Rickey did not see himself as discarded. He saw himself as the missing piece for his new team. Other teams in contention saw the value in acquiring Rickey as a short-term rental. As Rickey crisscrossed the country, the money got bigger and it became customary for great players to wind up playing with many teams in succession. Once again Rickey was the leader in a category, albeit an unofficial one: the greatest player to play for the most teams.

"That's how it would go," Rickey would say. "You need a boost? Go get Rickey. You close to winning? Go get Rickey." He was the trade deadline spark plug for teams making a pennant drive. That was one way it was framed, and Rickey was more than happy to oblige, to make the legend fact. Steve Buckley, the *Boston Herald* columnist, wrote of Rickey when he signed with the Red Sox, "He has been a vagabond for most of the second half of his career, a hired gun of a ballplayer who has worked for so many teams the last ten years it's hard to keep track of the man's comings and goings."

In August 1997, when Rickey joined the hard-luck Angels—who had ditched the "California" by then and become the Anaheim Angels—they were a team in desperate shape. In a dogfight with Seattle for the AL West, the Angels needed a push—especially after Tony Phillips, their leadoff man and an old Rickey homeboy from the A's days, was caught stoned in a hotel room in Southern California. Some of the stories weren't so kind: the Angels found Phillips in a crack den, they said. After Phillips was nailed for cocaine possession, the Angels made a trade with the Padres and got 38-year-old Rickey.

For Tim Mead, the Angels' PR man at the time, his enduring memory was of Rickey playing cards in the clubhouse and talking throughout the game to get in everybody's head. "I just remember Rickey at the table, just a master," Mead recalled. "You could just hear Rickey and how delighted he was when he had a good hand—and he was always in the third person. 'Ahhhh. Rickey's got a good hand—a *goooood* hand. Rickey's not gonna tell you what to do, but . . . he would fold if he were you.'"

That was a typical Rickey play. Back in Toronto, he'd sit in the clubhouse and work the room at the card table. "He'd sit there, playing dumb when he was watching everything, paying attention to everything down to the last detail," the Blue Jays catcher Pat Borders recalled. "He'd be watching you. I'd be all self-satisfied with a full house and he wouldn't move, and just as you're about to reach across the table, he'd drop four of a kind and ask all shy, '*Did I win?*' And I'd say, 'You son of a bitch!' Let me tell you something about Rickey—I enjoyed the shit out of him."

Rickey didn't hit—just .183 with Anaheim—but the on-base was nearly double. Even at 38, he still stole bases at an 80 percent clip, 16 out of 20 bags. That made him valuable—even if he couldn't hit his weight, he could get on base and steal a bag. The Angels' bench coach at the time was Joe Maddon—the same Joe Maddon who tried to keep Rickey from snaring the stolen-base title for Modesto of the California League back in A ball 20 years earlier. During a game, Maddon was in the dugout with the stopwatch—timing the pitcher's speed to home plate. "If the pitcher's move is 1.4 seconds, I'm happy. If he's at 1.6, that's *waaay* too slow. Rickey would steal 250 bases.

"Now I've got Rickey in Anaheim. He's at first, and I'm doing the times, and the guy on the mound—I don't remember which pitcher—but his time was 1.21. That's fast. At 1.2, nobody goes. Too fast to the plate. And Rickey would get that step, you know, where he would get that step and move, get that step and keep time. And if he timed it, he didn't care what the guy was to the plate. He stole and he was safe. I couldn't believe it. I've never seen that, where a guy was that confident on a 1.2 move. It just doesn't happen. I doubt any of the great base stealers did that. Brock? No. Maybe ask Rock Raines, but no. That was a combination of technique and the Three Musketeers 'I'm better than you' confidence. That's just flat-out confidence. And he was almost 40 years old. That's what was incongruent to me.

"What Rickey did for the hitter and what he did to defenses, you just couldn't quantify the disruption. Who knows how many home runs were hit because of what he was doing to the pitcher? Who knows how many errors were caused because the defense was thinking about him and not on the situation? When you're standing on the top step of the dugout, you see that impact."

The old Oakland Raider fan in Rickey would take the Al Davis approach. He was going to impose his will—on the stats, on the manager, on the pitcher and the catcher. He didn't care what the numbers said. This was Rickey Henderson—are you really going to let a stopwatch decide if he was going to steal? "To me, what you're saying is you don't have confidence in me to beat this guy. It's like the Raiders. We don't take what the defense gives you. You *take* what you want!"

There were Rickey stories that were such pure Rickey that you had to laugh, because he could just do things that would get other guys killed. In a spring training game in Scottsdale, A's-Giants, Rickey went deep and styled *in a spring training game,* picking the jersey a couple of times and then high-fiving Dusty Baker, who was managing the Giants. He high-fived *the manager of the other team.* The stories that gave people chills, though, were the ones that contained the best, most sumptuous ingredients of the Rickey gumbo—Rickey Style with a dash of superhuman. Take, for example, the doubleheader against the Indians at the Coliseum on July 5, 1993, when Rickey homered to lead off both games. The legendary Oakland radio man Bill King was on the call:

> There's a swing and there's a long drive. That ball is belted far . . . deep . . . GONE! Another Rickey Henderson leadoff home run . . . fifth this year, 60th of his major-league career . . . The ongoing record . . . It is the 11th home run of 1993. The A's lead one to nothing. Holy Toledo . . . And THAT'S your A's replay!

And then to start the second game, Rickey was back for more. King was on the call:

> There's a drive to left field. It's hit deep . . . It is . . . GONE! Home run! HO-lee Toledo! Has anyone ever DONE that? Rickey Henderson has homered to lead off the A's first inning for the SECOND time in this doubleheader, and the A's lead one to nothing . . . Two-and-one as Rickey exploded for that line-drive shot just to left of the steps in left field.

King had to talk fast, *real* fast, on the second Rickey home run because it was blasted out of a cannon. The Cleveland pitcher, Mark Clark, didn't even look at the ball; it was one of the pull jobs the big cleanup guys hit. On contact, Rickey flipped the bat downward then took two backward steps to give his prodigious blast ample space to breathe. Rickey had backed up so far that he was on the grass nearing the on-deck circle before starting his home-run trot. That's how much of a no-doubter it was.

There was a story to that day.

"Tony had given Rickey the morning off. Periodically, he would tell the veterans they could skip stretch," Bob Alejo recalled. "I'm standing on the field, and it's like 10 minutes to game time. Tony says, 'Do you know where Rico is?' I said, 'No,' and Tony says, 'Because he's leading off. I run into the clubhouse. No Rickey. I look everywhere. No Rickey. Finally, I go into the bathroom, go into a crouch, and what do I see but Rickey's green Mizuno cleats in one of the stalls.

"I say, 'Rico?' He says, 'Yeah, B?' He used to call everyone 'B,' so with my name, I lucked out. I say, 'It's game time, you're up!' He says, 'Oh, shit!' You can hear his spikes against the bathroom floor and he's running down the tunnel. He tells me to grab his bats. He gets into the batter's box—and homers. You gotta remember: he's done nothing. No swings, no stretch, no warm-up. Sitting on the can was the most exercise he's had. From a physiological standpoint, it was the most amazing thing I'd ever seen because he literally hadn't done anything. Nothing."

There were no fluke elements to what Rickey could do. "There's 10 percent of guys in the game who are just better—Bonds, Griffey, Randy Johnson, Rickey. They're the 10 percent," recalled J. T. Snow. "There's the other 10 that just gets by on pure grit. The rest, the 80 percent, is in the middle."

Terry Steinbach recalled one of Rickey's moments when he separated himself as one of the 10 percenters:

"There's not a lot of players, I'm sure, who just have that extra ability. Gifted. Call it whatever you want to call it. They can turn on that next level. I can't remember when it was. I know I wasn't catching that day. We're on the road. I took infield and shagged in the outfield. I'm going into the clubhouse to grab a cup of coffee and get ready. I get up there. It's like five minutes to seven, and Rickey's stark naked. I say, 'Rico, it's game time.' He's talking to himself, *Rickey's gonna have a game. Rickey's gonna have a game.* I say to myself, *I gotta see this.* It's two minutes. I'm pretty sure the anthem is playing.

"He's still in the locker room, talking to himself, *Rickey's gonna have a good day.* It's 30 seconds before first pitch. He says, 'Rickey's ready to go!' He walks down the tunnel. Gets his bat. Hits a home run. Everybody else—and I emphasize *everybody else*—they'll do a few sprints. They'll look at the starting pitcher warming up, see what he's throwing. Checking him out, having their visualization. Some guys try to time his release. Rico doesn't even look at the guy and goes deep. I've never seen anything like it."

There was the time, in 1990 or 1991, late in the game, when the manager, either Stump Merrill or Bucky Dent, was giving out instructions. Buck Showalter was coaching the Yankees.

"Rickey was hitting against us, and he has us playing no-doubles defense," Showalter recalled. "Guarding the lines. Don't give up anything big. Don't let him get in scoring position. Then Mattingly turns around and yells into the dugout, *"What for? If he gets a single—IT'S A DOUBLE ANYWAY!"*

It's May 30, 1994, the A's made their first trip of the season to Toronto. The team bus left the Toronto Sheraton, rolled down Spadina Avenue, and as it rumbled into the SkyDome passed a billboard on Blue Jays Way containing just three elements: a photo of an elated Joe Carter, the date of his epic home run, and the time it landed in the seats to give Toronto the championship. No other words. The billboard sparked a question that bounced around the A's bus as it pulled into the ballpark: "Where were you when Joe Carter hit the home run?" From the front to the back, players, coaches, and staff recalled their whereabouts at Canada's most famous baseball moment. Dave Feldman, the statistician for KRON-TV, the A's television affiliate, said he was sitting on the couch, watching the game in his San Francisco apartment, totally stunned. More voices followed, with more recollections.

Then a lone voice boomed from the very back of the bus.

"I WAS ON SECOND BASE!"

It was Rickey.

16

ON JANUARY 22, 1998, a month after celebrating his 39th birthday, Rickey was back in Oakland. For the fourth time. He and the A's had agreed on a one-year, $1.1 million deal.

Money wasn't part of the game now. Those days were over—somewhat. Rickey was no longer in the top earning tier of the sport. Pushing 40, he was older than Billy Beane, the A's new general manager. It was a miracle of science that he was still out there playing. Not vying for the top dollar anymore, he wasn't pissed off for not having it—at least not *as* pissed off. The new guys, who had entered the game in the post-strike stratosphere, made Rickey's time look like they haggled over what was ashtray money compared to the zeroes on the paychecks today. Jerry Reinsdorf, the owner of the White Sox, complained like hell about salaries before the strike—then signed Albert Belle to a four-year deal at $11 million a year. Carlos Delgado of the Blue Jays got $17 million per. Derek Jeter got $189 million from the Yankees. And then, at the 2000 winter meetings in Dallas—on consecutive days, no less—Boston signed Manny Ramirez to an eight-year, $160 million deal and Alex Rodriguez would reel in the biggest fish of them all from the Texas Rangers—10 years, *$252 million.*

That wasn't to say money didn't matter to Rickey, but Rickey knew he wouldn't be asking any front offices for A-Rod money. The money that *did* continue to matter was the money that could be had by the wonderful fact of simply being Rickey—how much was a name worth?

Pamela would always say that Rickey was an old soul who listened to the wisdom of the elders around him, and it was true. The sweetest stories about Rickey usually revolved around him listening to his mother. Bobbie always knew best. The older guys also had Rickey's ear. When the A's had a problem, Jim Guinn could talk to Rickey because there was a better chance that Rickey would listen to him than anyone else. And when it came to the money in the game, another elder had Rickey's ear above all—the great Willie Mays.

Willie and Rickey were practically neighbors. Both lived in Hillsborough, across the San Francisco Bay on the Peninsula. Willie was baseball royalty; the word "legend" didn't really do him justice—nor, Willie always believed, did his salary. For all the bouquets tossed his way for being the best, most exciting player of his time, the standard of the modern, five-tool player of the integrated game, Willie never felt like he got his money. As the salaries rose high enough to be competing with the gross national product of small countries, Willie just burned. There wasn't a time when he was asked about the current game and money *didn't* come up. When news broke that some fourth outfielder was making $7 million, Willie reminded anyone listening that he topped out at $180,000. The words stood on his tongue for a half-century: "Can you *imagine* what *I'd* be making today?"

Of course, it was all relative. Willie was the standard—on the field and at the bank. He was making top dollar for his time until Henry Aaron passed him in 1972 at $200,000 per season. There was something else, though, that Willie never mentioned while he talked on and on about how much money he should have made—Willie did not support Curt Flood's fight to wrest the players from the grip of the teams and the reserve clause, the one fight that made the money possible.

In a sense, Rickey and Willie were similar in that both were at least partly responsible themselves for creating the obstacles that they felt undermined their maximum earning power. Willie didn't create the reserve clause, but he didn't do anything to fight it either. Rickey wanted his money, but Rickey wasn't willing to risk money to make it. Rickey's normal financial disposition was cautious—an odd trait for someone who loved the rush of gambling.

"We were naturally thrifty people," Pamela recalled. "He would say, 'What if I get hurt? If I get hurt, I couldn't play. How could I take care of my family?' We saw everyone spending. Everyone lived for the moment. Were they saving? There was nothing funny about Uncle Sam. That's not Rickey. Rickey didn't live for the moment. He lived for the future."

The image of Willie Mays racing across the outfield like a god had brought joy to a generation, and through him that time was glorious and so

were they—young, unlined, beautiful. Willie gave that to them. The reality
was that during those years when Willie Mays was giving the fans memories
that shaped their lives, he was also learning the cold lessons of the business
of baseball. That business taught him two things: nothing was free, and his
name was worth millions. To Willie's eye, everyone was making money off
of him. Sure, the guy writing the book on Willie had to do the work, but was
the guy getting paid to write a book or was he being paid because Willie was
the subject? Since Willie was the reason anyone was going to read it, Willie
deserved a piece of the profit. That meant no free interviews. Willie's voice,
his presence—that was money. You wanted Willie to appear at a banquet?
You had to pay Willie to honor Willie. He was Willie Mays. Who was doing
who the favor? (*And did you see how much money these guys are making
today?*)

It was these lessons that Willie passed down to Rickey, lessons forged
from decades of feeling exploited, like he was making everybody else rich. It
was an attitude common to the players of Willie's time, because, by custom,
they *were* exploited. Frank Robinson felt the same way. Everybody loved
Willie, and nobody loved Frank (Frank made sure of that), but they were
simpatico on one issue: no one got to make money off of his name. Players
took this attitude even when there was no money to be had. To them, *somebody* was making a dollar off of them. When Rickey superfan Kent Corser
attended a paid event, he discovered that Rickey did not sign bases. A signed
base from Rickey was a rarity. When Corser scored a signed base with the
inscription "1406 SB" for a cool $350—a steal, he thought!—he knew it was
a rare piece.

Willie reminded Rickey that his name was his currency, and that everyone was trying to earn something for nothing off of that name. Back as a
young player, Rickey had been told by Reggie not to sign his name too often.
Too many signatures flooded the market. It was better to wait until later—
scarcity drove up the price. "If you don't sign your name now," Reggie told
Rickey, "you can live off of it later." That was why Rickey never signed bases.
There might have been 12 bases, tops, on the face of the earth with Rickey's
signature.

While Rickey measured each deal by the dollar, Walt McCreary coun-
seled Rickey to employ a little more kindness and flexibility. It also could
pay bigger, untold dividends, like when Rickey was enraged that he had been
promised $25,000 at the 2013 Field of Dreams game, received a couple thou-

sand less, and planned to ditch the event. Walt talked him off the ledge, and as an unforeseen bonus, Rickey ran into a poker game and made himself another $20,000.

Being nice mattered. People remembered nice. Money was important, Walt told Rickey, but nice had to be part of the calculation, like when Rickey agreed to do a gig at a Toronto hospital at a heavily discounted rate—three days for $12,500. (There was another motive no ballplayer could resist—everyone knew Toronto women were gorgeous.) He had attached himself to an important fundraiser that helped better resource the burned victims unit. He had already won a World Series in that town, and now people loved him even more.

Mays's outlook may have seemed rather cynical coming from the celebrated Say Hey Kid, but it was born out of all those years of giving the world smiles while missing out on the *really* big paydays that came after he left the game. By the time Rickey returned to Oakland, the average big league salary was around $4 million—four mil for a basic, everyday ballplayer. That was why Mays couldn't help but remind everyone of what he'd have been making at those prices. Even when some good money came in the 1980s and 1990s, when the card show circuit exploded, the FBI and IRS showed up and decked the players faster than a Bob Gibson heater.

For this go-round in Oakland, Rickey got a personal assistant, Detra Paige, who was from the Bay and graduated from Kennedy High in Richmond. She arrived in 1998 to work in the A's community relations department, but Rickey and all the requests for Rickey became her personal responsibility. She coordinated Rickey's charity, Rickey's Heroes, a program in which three students from the Oakland Unified School District and their teachers were invited to a weekday day game when school let out as Rickey's guests. They were given access to the field and got to sit in the dugout as guests of one of the most famous alumni of the city.

Willie reminded Rickey that doing interviews, appearances, documentaries, all of it took money out of his own pocket. Being elected to the Hall of Fame? That made him even more valuable, sending the price up even higher. People paid premium dollars to talk to a Hall of Famer. That's where Detra came in on the team side: if a request for Rickey came to the team, it went to Detra before it went to Rickey. Willie made it clear to Rickey that he shouldn't do *anything* for free, often including requests from the team itself. MLB too. The honchos over on 245 Park Avenue had a marketing and

promotions budget, so if they wanted Rickey, they could pony up and give
him a slice of the pie.

The Byzantine memorabilia world was a way the players made some
of that money back—Rickey could clear $250,000 a year, easy, signing his
name at personal appearance shows, but the IRS was always lurking around
the fast-money, under-the-table-income card-show culture. They'd already
nailed Pete Rose for unreported income—he'd done time. They got Darryl
Strawberry for tax evasion from card-show money—six months home con-
finement in a plea deal. The feds got probation for the Hall of Famers Duke
Snider and Willie McCovey—and in 1996 the IRS was watching Rickey too.

Rickey rarely appeared on the pre- or postgame radio programs. He
might show up at FanFest right before spring training, but you couldn't
count on it. As the saying went, "Why buy the cow when you can get the
milk for free?" Walt made sure that Rickey's time was protected—a card
show lasting two to two and a half hours would fetch $20,000 to $25,000.
Rickey remembered what else Willie had told him: to not only *not* give
away the milk for free, but to make sure to always get it in cash. You never
knew when an unscrupulous promoter would promise you the moon—and
bounce the appearance check.

That bit of wisdom explained what happened when Rickey was doing a
signing in Oakland along with Cecil Fielder and a storm knocked out the
power. Rickey immediately yelled at Walt, "The *box! GRAB THE CEREAL
BOX!*" That was where the payments were stashed—25 grand, in cash, just
sitting in a box of Cap'n Crunch.

Rickey's fourth time in Oakland very much resembled his first tour in the
late 1970s, with one major exception: this team was full of kids, and he wasn't
one of them.

After bottoming out from the last dynasty, the A's hadn't yet recovered—
they lost 97 games in 1997 and the losing-season streak was now at four
years—but at least on paper the future looked promising. The 1998 team did
not advertise itself as a good team—and sometimes didn't advertise itself
at all as its never-ending quest to escape Oakland continued. (The potential destinations now included Las Vegas, Portland, San Jose, Fremont, and
maybe Sacramento.) There were reasons for optimism in a year when they
weren't expected to contend but the kids could gain experience and the team
could reap the secondary benefit of offering the fans one last chance to see

Rickey. Many baseball people thought he was more than likely going to retire at the end of the year.

The kids loved Rickey—and there were so many of them. The baby-
faced right fielder Ben Grieve couldn't walk 10 feet without a salivating Billy
Beane comparing his golden baseball swing to Tiger Woods's golf swing.
A. J. Hinch played on Team USA, and everyone around camp said he was
wiser than his years, a Stanford whiz kid who was penciled in as the starting
catcher—as a rookie. The shortstop was Kurt Abbott, but he was just a placeholder. The shortstop of the future was Miguel Tejada, a Dominican kid who
stopped going to school at 12 in favor of the education of fielding ground
balls and hitting curveballs—preparation for the big leagues. Two more, the
third baseman Eric Chavez and pitcher Mark Mulder, didn't start the season
with the team, nor did a third, Barry Zito, a quirky left-hander the team
was high on for 1999, but all of them were expected to arrive at some point.
Maybe they would be September call-ups. Another one, an unheralded
pitcher named Tim Hudson, was in the minors. Hudson didn't come with
all the trimmings, but he was grimly serious, all business, on the mound.

Tony La Russa was gone. He left in 1996 to manage the Cardinals, eventually taking Dennis Eckersley and Mark McGwire with him. When Sandy
Alderson announced in the off-season that Billy Beane would succeed him
as GM in 1998, the A's had rookies not only all over the diamond but now in
the front office too.

Billy was four years younger than Rickey. The two had not only been
teammates on the 1989 title team but shared adjacent lockers. Billy would
never forget June 12 of that year, the day he was sent down to Triple-A Tacoma.
When Billy got the return call on August 18, Rickey looked at him quizzically
when he showed up in the clubhouse and said, "Where you been?"

"Rickey," Beane said incredulously, "I got sent down. I've been gone two
months."

"Really?" Rickey said. "I was *wondering* why I hadn't seen you around
here."

The two young center fielders, Jason McDonald and Ryan Christen-
son, were warned not to play cards with wily old Rickey (they didn't listen), and Miguel Tejada followed Rickey around like a golden retriever pup.
Even though Tejada was earning the big league minimum salary of more
than $300,000, Rickey still gave him $10,000 to get himself a car. When
Tejada eventually became a big star, winning the AL MVP and signing an

$80 million free-agent deal with the Orioles, Rickey wanted (and got) his 10 large back (*It's always a loan*).

The emerging leader of the young band, slugger Jason Giambi, was a Mc-Gwire protégé who was a rookie with the A's when Rickey was on the 1995 team. Giambi loved the accomplishment and exclusivity that came with being in a big league clubhouse, and now it was his turn to be the big man on campus. Giambi used to marvel at Rickey's physique, even at 39. "Rickey's so cut," Giambi would say, "he might bleed to death if he got a paper cut." With his breathless surfer cool, Giambi once described the aura of Rickey's clubhouse regality: "Who? Rico? Two percent body fat, first-ballot Hall of Famer, President, All-Tripod Club [because Rickey was so well hung]. What more could anyone ask?"

These 1998 A's were entirely focused in the present on preparing for the future, on putting the pieces in place to take off—but not Rickey. He was 39 years old. His present *was* his future, and there was a poignancy, a sadness, and an irony to the way he carried himself that year.

Ever since he made his big league debut, the enormous size of Rickey's ego was something all parties in the sport thought they could agree on, proving that Rickey was right: he would never live down the "Today, I'm the greatest of all time" speech when he passed Lou Brock. Yet it was Rickey's lack of ego that would now define him. He was nearly 40, and at the plate it showed. He still had the eye of a hawk, but pitchers could beat him with sheer power because he had the reflexes of a 39-year-old. As much as the writers and the fans might love the ceremony of torch-passing, the game itself is ruthless, and no sentimentality was shown toward Rickey.

But he was still on the receiving end of something better than sentimentality: awe. The A's played an exhibition game against the University of California in the spring, and A's public relations man Jim Bloom remembered the Cal starting pitcher being frozen by the prospect of facing the great Rickey Henderson. "His knees were knocking. You could just see how nervous he was. He ends up hitting Rickey with the pitch. The umpire tells Rickey to take his base. Rickey picked up the ball, tossed it back to the pitcher, and said, 'Nope,' and he stepped back into the box and the pitcher finished pitching to him."

The A's started the season against the Big Boys. On opening night at the Coliseum against Boston, the great Pedro Martinez made his American League debut by breezing through the A's lineup, striking out 11 in seven innings and overmatching Rickey in three easy at-bats—though Rickey did manage a walk. Three weeks into the season, whether against Hall of Fame–caliber or scrub pitching, Rickey was hitting just .189. Even his jets were sputtering. He had stolen four bases—but was caught three times.

Art Howe, the A's manager, just watched. Howe was one of baseball's greatest gentlemen, a good and decent man. Once a season, Howe would take the traveling beat writers out to dinner—to Ruth's Chris in Toronto, the Cheesecake Factory in Chicago. Unconcerned about Rickey's oddities, Howe let him play—the guy was gonna be a Hall of Famer, for God's sake. He was too much of a gentleman to voice his deep suspicion that Rickey probably didn't even know his name, but he didn't need to: the team medical staff noticed how many times Rickey would call to Art with "manager," and deduced the truth—he didn't.

But Art Howe had been around the game for decades. He'd had his moments too, and he assessed baseball with the unsparing judgment and pessimism of the most weather-beaten scout. Night in and night out, it was painfully clear that pitchers were easily pumping fastballs by Rickey. They were throwing nothing cute at him—no setup breaking ball to disguise the fastball—but just throwing the gas. Right by him. All you had to do was challenge him.

Watching his underpowered club, Howe maintained the requisite low expectations for the present. The team might have been built for the future, but managers have to win today. *He can't get around,* Howe would say to himself as he watched Rickey from the dugout, remembering the end of his own career. "I was never a superstar like Rickey, but I played till I was 39. The reflexes start to go, and you yourself, you're the only one who really knows how much you're slipping. I'd foul a ball off and say, *Man, you shoulda killed that. What's* wrong *with you?* It was frustration more than anything else. In a way, it makes it easier to say goodbye. You know you're not yourself."

For the guys who resided at the top, Mount Everest guys like Rickey, getting dusted by dudes whose asses he used to wear out would surely have led to nightly eruptions of frustration. The biggest guys? They just let it go and walked away from the game without letting the chumps they used to own get comfortable embarrassing them. They wouldn't let them have the satisfaction of catching them on the way down, of returning the favor for being dominated all those years.

When he gave up a pinch-hit grand slam to the Cubs' Pete LaCock on

September 3, 1975, Bob Gibson left the mound and never pitched again, later saying, "When you give up grand slams to Pete LaCock, you know it's time to walk away." They all knew the rules. When it came to retirement, there were only three realistic outcomes for professional athletes: (1) the game retires you because you just can't play anymore; (2) your body sends you home through injury; or (3) you leave while still on top, on your own terms, the way Ted Williams did (.316, 29 home runs in his final season, as a 41-year-old!). Everyone knew it was already too late for Rickey to take that last option, and the fact is that few athletes ever decide to leave while they're on top. True kings rarely surrender the throne willingly.

Yet while everyone else was lamenting that the great man was just a withered facsimile of his old self, wincing at the outs because they remembered when he was once the most explosive force in the sport, Rickey himself was uncommonly secure. He still laughed in the clubhouse and still talked to himself at the plate, still never caring who heard him (*Now, you know better than to swing at that, Rickey!*). His willingness to keep competing, given his limitations, revealed a surprising lack of ego to the people in the game who thought they knew him but clearly did not. He even found a way to laugh at himself during the April 25 game in Baltimore when Rafael Palmeiro doubled him off first—the greatest base stealer in history fell for the hidden ball trick.

Of course, there was another possibility for why he accepted these humiliations—maybe Rickey did not know how to walk away. For 30 years, he had been marked by a singularity—by the indomitable will of the world-class athlete (*You must not know who I am!*). Ahead of everything else, Rickey was always what mattered to Rickey. It had always been this way. When Rickey needed to turn it on, he had often seemed capable of just bending life to his will.

Nobody understood this better than Pamela. He was still Rickey, but time and age would remain undefeated. It was during this stage that she hoped the great athlete would understand that, as his skills dissipated, he could become a great man by returning the sacrifices she had made to support him. Maybe it was time to give his energy to her. Nobody else had seen or felt or lived Rickey's journey more personally than Pamela—and nobody had been more devoted to his greatness over of the course of almost his entire life.

In his autobiography published six years earlier, Rickey had written, "High school is where I met the woman I've been with for 17 years, Pamela

Palmer. One thing Pamela and I don't have—and it's not a big deal for us—is a marriage certificate. We've been together for so long, a marriage certificate wouldn't make a lot of difference. We will get married some day. I always say we'll get married in February or November, just before the season or just after the season. I've been saying that for seventeen years."

The reality was that Pamela was hurting in 1998. While her love for Rickey was real, she was deeply questioning the price it often demanded she pay—the sacrifice of her own goals and her self-esteem. For 23 years, her life had been Rickey. The A's would call Pamela his wife, but Rickey and Pamela were not officially married. It may not have been a big deal to Rickey, but by 1998, after nearly a quarter-century spent with Rickey as he climbed from high school to the top of the game, as the empty nest neared, and as his time in the game was coming to an end, not being married to Rickey was certainly a major issue for Pamela. One consequence of Rickey's singularity, of being a one-namer, was that many people in baseball didn't even know he *had* a wife.

"Because of the fact that he was such a well-rounded athlete, I never made a fuss about it or got to the point where I got upset," Pamela recalled. "I thought he would see things a little differently, and that he would want to settle down. But that was scary to him, shutting down, getting old, letting his body get weaker."

That summer Pamela had a message for Rickey: without greater commitment from him, she was leaving. Because she was so young when they met, just 14 years old, her life had been all about Rickey before it was ever her own life to live. She had come increasingly to realize that her life had *never* been her own. She had been the silent anchor of the entire operation, and she had done it without even the respect of a legal commitment. His greatness was hers—except that she had become ever more aware that, after a quarter-century together, this wasn't exactly true. His greatness had come at the expense of her development as an adult woman. But now, she felt, his greatness and her development did not need to stand in opposition to each other. Pamela had accepted the most difficult elements of the baseball life for which the millions of dollars were no salve: the time away, the uncertainties, the constant competition for a part of Rickey, and naturally, the volume of women who came with the baseball life. What she required now was reciprocity.

"It broke me because I never did receive that full attention," Pamela recalled. "It was always because of something else, someone else. It was never about me. That was very hard for me. It was such a trying time. No one was there for me to express what was going on with me."

It was then, in the summer of 1998, that Rickey and Pamela eloped, with plans to have a proper honeymoon at the end of the season in Hawaii. Pamela came home to create more stability. By then she had been settled with the girls full-time in the Ahwatukee section of Phoenix, ending the dual-city living between the Bay Area and Arizona. Even as Rickey navigated the mortality of his playing career, Pamela was ensuring that her life would contain a certain level of permanence.

"It was one of the reasons we cherished the holidays so much, because it was the one time we had him," Pamela recalled. "We didn't have to share. We didn't have to be in public. It was just us. I had wished there was more times when he was devoted directly to his family, but when we had the holidays, we did not have to share him, and that was our cherished gift."

In lieu of retirement from the game, Rickey would subject himself to the humiliation he knew—competing on the baseball diamond, even if it meant getting beat more than he'd ever been accustomed to. Striking out was easier than succumbing to the unknown cruelties of age—at least he was still playing, still in the arena. Like most players, Rickey was so convinced of his abilities that he never believed his struggles couldn't be corrected. Surely a hot streak was right around the corner and he'd soon rediscover what set him above the rest—but that was no longer happening. His new reality was that the great Rickey was now a mediocre hitter—like most guys pushing 40.

Nevertheless, after all the contract squabbles and sniping, the money demands, the moods and volatile relationship with the business, watching the legend expose himself to the cruelties of age and the limitations commonplace among players who didn't have his talent made the writers and fans see a side of him they had never truly considered during the last 20 years— maybe he really *did* love the game.

Rickey neither carried himself bitterly as he struggled, unable to accept what his body could no longer do, nor become a bore. He didn't blather on about the old days when he was king, refusing to accept yet another strikeout and proclaiming to everyone that these whippersnappers were only outclassing him because they had youth on their side. As a result of his equanimity, a compassion developed for him, and people began to enjoy him in ways that hadn't happened for much of the two decades he had dominated the sport. In a considerable departure from the retired legends who never stopped being pissed off that they couldn't beat time, Rickey's willingness to fail now made him just like everyone else. He played with the skills he currently possessed, in the moment, without looking for pity, ever willing to accept the challenge of succeeding at the world's highest level of competition even as his legendary body inevitably wore down.

"Rickey was very comfortable with who he was," Steve Sayles recalled. Sayles was the A's assistant trainer who went back with Rickey to the Padres days and for years was the only Black head trainer in baseball. "They were throwing fastballs right by his ass, but Rickey figured at some point you were gonna slip, and when he caught you slipping, he was gonna get you. And he knew once he got on, he could swipe a bag, he could affect the game. He always knew that even if he wasn't the player he once was, he could always do something to hurt you."

When the new generation tried to put Rickey's career in the grave, like they did that night of April 29, 1998, in Cleveland, the ego came back, furiously protecting him, fueling him.

The Indians were in love with this new kid Jaret Wright. Big kid, six-two, 220 pounds, nasty fastball, nasty attitude, unafraid—Wright had all the tools. Even Rapid Robert—the crotchety old Hall of Famer Bob Feller himself—paid attention to this kid. During homestands, Feller could be spotted in one of the back rows of the Jacobs Field press box, spending most of his time on the phone, being a bastard, berating people, well-wishers and sycophants alike. ("Hello? This is Bob Feller. I received your message. *Don't ever fucking call me again.*") But when Wright was pitching, even Feller stopped yelling at people just long enough to watch the game.

The kid Grieve went 5-for-5 with two doubles, his Tiger Woods swing so beautiful that night that in the fourth inning Wright drilled him. (After the game Grieve took off his uniform and revealed the baseball's stitching imprinted into the roasting pink flesh of his back.) Rickey struck out three times, couldn't even get the bat off his shoulder to catch a fastball. Eric Plunk, still in the league, blew Rickey away after Wright had whiffed him twice, but in between the strikeouts he went 2-for-5 with two runs scored. One of those hits was a single that should have stayed a single except that Rickey hauled ass out of the box and slashed into second with an RBI double. He even threw a message pitch of his own—a straight steal of third when the A's had a three-run lead.

Wright being the phenom in the Indians system wasn't a big deal. There was a Next Big Thing on the mound every day in baseball. It wasn't Wright who set Rickey off. That honor went to Kenny Lofton, the Cleveland center fielder who blazed his way to the American League lead in steals in five straight years. Four months after Rickey beat Brock's all-time record, Lofton made his big league debut, on September 14, 1991, with Houston (playing for and irritating the shit out of Art Howe). Wright was the headliner, but it was Lofton that night who decided that Rickey belonged in the nursing home.

"One time we were in Cleveland, and Kenny Lofton was leading the league in stolen bases," recalled Ron Washington, the A's third-base coach at the time. "And here's Lofton across the diamond chirping at Rickey: 'See that old man on the other side of the field? There's a new sheriff in town. That dude is *done.*' And don't you know, Rickey just went on a tear. Second . . . gone . . . third—*gone.* He'd come back into the dugout and say, 'If Rickey sleep, let Rickey sleep.' He just took whatever he wanted. When you talked shit to him the way Kenny Lofton did, he reminded you that he was still Rickey Henderson. That bitch was special."

The new "sheriff in town" took the collar that night, going a meek 0-for-4.

These were the beautiful moments, the snatches of sand before they flowed to the bottom of the hourglass. Rickey was the third-oldest position player in the game. Pitchers lasted forever, but only Wade Boggs and Paul Molitor were older than Rickey, and for them, reaching first was like pulling in to a rest stop. Rickey could still be the best player on the field, as he did in a weeklong stretch May 3–10 when he raised his average 50 points to a season-high .275 and had three straight multiple-hit games. Or in that May 17 game in Oakland when Howe put him in center field against the White Sox and he went double, single, triple—a bomb away from the cycle.

The triple, which came in the ninth to cap a furious comeback, would be his only triple of the year. It was one of those special three-baggers, ripped down the left-field line so he had the play in front of him the whole time. Usually in that situation a runner could see that he better *not* take the extra base, but Rickey never slowed down. Picking up Ron Washington's sign at third early, he rounded second and flew into third, legs pumping hard and cutting into the wind as aerodynamically as a sprinter. He was using the jets one more time. "Let me *tell* you something," Washington said beaming after the game. "*Tonight,* Rickey was *low*-flying around those bases!"

By June 24, the 20th anniversary of his major league debut, Rickey had fallen back and was down to hitting .235. That same day his voice boomed through the A's clubhouse: "*Little Bip!*" Across the room by his new locker was Bip Roberts, acquired by the A's in a deal with the Tigers—in part so as to spell Rickey once in a while. Bip could play both infield and outfield. Being able to play five positions always made it easier to get into the lineup.

Another circle in the legend of Oakland had been closed. Bip and Rickey in Oakland. Oakland Tech and Skyline, Bushrod and McConnell, North Oakland and East Oakland, batting 1-2 in the A's lineup. It was Bip's last stop in the big leagues after 12 years, and for the second half of the season the two would share the clubhouse. At 34, Roberts would be finished as a major leaguer after the season. Even though he would hit .280 for the A's in 61 games and could have played a few more seasons, the life of a big leaguer had run its course for him. Being present for his family was more compelling than the itinerant and nomadic life of a baseball player.

"Rickey was like a big brother to me," Roberts recalled. "He was always looking out, in his way. I remember there was one time on the road we were playing cards in my room and he was about to go to the ballpark, because Rickey always liked to get to the clubhouse early. He left my room, and a little while later there was a knock on the door, and it was Rickey with a bag of cheeseburgers to make sure I had some food in me. 'Idolize' isn't the right word for how I felt about him, but absolutely I admired him. Absolutely."

Even though he was five years older than Bip, Rickey had no intention of quitting. When he needed to go to his reserve, he could tap into it with a big game now and then, but his baseline game at the plate was subpar. Washington was amazed by Rickey's professionalism—a word not often associated with him over his career—as he managed the unforgiving season while still trying to play like Rickey. He wasn't a full-time DH, as Molitor was, and he wasn't a guy like Boggs, whose work was done after he hit the ball. "He'd have that burst, and then for the next two to three games he'd go through the motions," Washington remembered. "There's a difference between pacing yourself and jaking it. Jaking it means you're trying to fool somebody. Rickey wasn't trying to fool someone. He knew what his body could do. He knew with his style of play and the things he put his body through that he wouldn't last very long in the game. When he was right and feeling good, you couldn't stop him. He'd come into the clubhouse and say, 'Rickey Time . . . Coming to get 'em tonight.' And he'd go hit a leadoff bomb."

Rickey was still dangerous when he got on base, and because of his eye, he got on base a lot. This was why Billy Beane knew Rickey was still valuable. When the fans and writers would suggest that Rickey was done because he couldn't get his batting average above .240, Billy would coolly reply, "He's got a .400 on-base." After that first month of the season when he couldn't steal two bases without getting caught once, the night in Cleveland with Kenny Lofton had woken him up ("If Rickey sleep, let Rickey sleep") and now Rickey was a force. At one point in the season, he stole 29 straight bases. After May 7, when Detroit's Joe Oliver got Rickey in the fifth inning trying to swipe second, he wouldn't be caught again until June 13, when Randy Johnson picked him off first. The next time a catcher caught him was on July 4 in Anaheim, when Matt Walbeck caught him at second.

By the record books Rickey had stolen 29 of 30 bases over that stretch. By his math, he had stolen 29 straight bases. "If the stats show I steal off the catcher, then why do I get a caught stealing when the pitcher picks me off?" Rickey would ask, still sore about that rule. Either way, Rickey remained, at 39, the premier base stealer in baseball.

Rickey was at the stage where he could fall out of bed and break one all-time record or another. Jim Bloom had been tracking the numbers and a Big One was fast approaching: 2,000 runs. It wasn't just a Big One—scoring 2,000 runs was the *biggest* record Rickey craved. For all the years Rickey was defined as a base stealer, he always defined himself as a run scorer.

Bloom loved Rickey and immediately went to management to prepare a celebration of the historic milestone. But he didn't find a particularly receptive audience in Sandy Alderson. "He asked me, 'How significant a statistic is it? Who else has done it?'" Bloom recalled. "I told him, 'Mays, Aaron, Ruth, Cobb.' He said, 'Okay, we should definitely do something.'"

For nearly four hours on the night of August 28, the A's and Indians threw haymakers at each other. In extras, the A's scored eight runs in the top of the 10th, the final three on a Jason Giambi three-run homer that scored Rickey, who had already driven in a run in the rally. The run was Rickey's 1999th of his career. Three nights later, with Rickey on third, Giambi lifted a sacrifice fly to center, caught by (who else?) Kenny Lofton. Rickey trotted home, but not before slowing down to softly step on home plate with both feet. The on-deck hitter, Matt Stairs, gave Rickey a fist bump. Rickey pointed at home plate—he wanted the base, a ceremony, and for Dale Ford to stop the game. The home-plate umpire didn't budge, and while Giambi was hugging him in the dugout, Rickey had to settle for the ball. The next day Bloom called the Indians and asked John Hart, the Cleveland general manager, for home plate. Hart agreed that Rickey could have it—but after the season.

Saturday, September 26, 1998: the A's called it Rickey Henderson Day. In anticipation of the A's 100th anniversary, the team voted Rickey the A's player of the century. "He knew the fans liked him," Bloom recalled, "but didn't know they held him in such esteem. That really touched him."

Rickey was always cagey about retiring, but in everyone else's mind his retirement was a given. After the season, Bip Roberts quit. Across the country in Boston, so did Dennis Eckersley. It wouldn't have been surprising if Rickey did too, but even if he didn't, Rickey and the 1998 season had served their purpose for the A's. The kids got to play, and now, moving forward, the A's were going to play their young players. Nothing was official, and the A's never officially closed the door on Rickey, but all the signs were clear that the chance of Rickey returning to the A's in 1999 was even money—at best.

Rickey played 152 games in 1998, the first time he'd topped 150 in a decade. He led the league in walks and finished 12 steals ahead of his nemesis, Kenny Lofton, the first time he'd led the league in stolen bases since 1991, and the 12th time overall. He was now the oldest stolen base champ in history. He scored 100 runs for the 13th time. The bat was slower—that was no illusion—and he struck out 114 times, the most ever in his career and the first and only time he'd ever struck more than 100 times. But even with a career high in strikeouts, Rickey had more walks than whiffs with 118.

So, with retirement on everybody's mind but his, Rickey stepped on the field against the Angels. On the mound was the knuckleballer Steve Sparks (who was nicknamed "Phone Book" because he once dislocated his left shoulder trying to tear a phone book in half). There were 22,661 in the stands, all waiting for Rickey to give Oakland one more thrill, and he delivered: nearly perfect that game, he went 3-for-3 with two walks and two stolen bases.

In the bottom of the ninth, with two on and two out in a 3–3 game against the Angels' flamethrower Troy Percival, it was Rickey, who couldn't hit a good fastball all year, who ripped a game-winning single to center. Frank Blackman, who did not always think of Rickey as a great player or a great teammate, wrote the game story for the *San Francisco Examiner*. He wondered aloud what Oakland baseball fans were thinking:

RICKEY SHOWS HIS WORTH—FOR LAST TIME?

The A's honored Rickey Henderson before Saturday's 4–3 victory over Anaheim at the Coliseum, celebrating the future Hall of Famer's accomplishments in the game.

Was it also a going-away party?

"I will probably talk to them next week sometime," Henderson said. "I want to see where I stand with them. And if everything works out, we'll have something going. But I intend to play next year somewhere. Hopefully, it will be here."

Saturday's was his 151st game, a demonstration that even at 39 (he'll be 40 in December) he is durable. He is tops in the majors with 66 stolen bases and will become the oldest player ever to lead his league in thefts. He's walked 118 times, also best in the league. He's played a solid left field. And he's been a leader in the clubhouse, an influence on the younger players with his constant good humor and outstanding work ethic.

"The thing I remember most about Rickey that season was Rickey Henderson Day," Art Howe said. "He had a perfect day at the plate. He was still able to turn on the switch. Because of his age, he couldn't do it every day anymore, but that was a big day for him. He knew the lights were on. It was because of him that people came to the ballpark that day, and he delivered."

That day and going into the first days of the off-season, a wistfulness and melancholy enveloped Rickey. The A's had treated the ceremony as the goodbye to the game they believed it to be—but as Christmas rolled around and Rickey celebrated his 40th birthday, he made it clear that he had no intention of retiring. No pomp. No circumstance. No retrospectives. Pamela was secretly hoping that Rickey would call it a career, but he wasn't going anywhere—except to announce to the league that his services were still available.

Something as seemingly inconsequential as a 40-year-old trying to catch on with a team continued to have a story attached to it—because it was Rickey. A story went around that Rickey was personally cold-calling teams—no agent, no representative—in search of a tryout. One of those stories was true: Rickey did call Billy Beane, but the A's were uninterested in Rickey's act 5—especially when Rickey said that he didn't just want a raise for 1999 but was thinking *double*. "I think," Rickey said as the calendar came to a close, "I can still help a team."

Meanwhile, after Sandy Alderson gave the keys of the A's front office to Billy Beane, he went to the Padres, and then to the Commissioner's Office, where there had once been loud talk of him one day becoming the next commissioner of baseball. (Bud Selig, of course, had about as much intention of walking away from the game as Rickey did.) One year Sandy filled out a questionnaire for a college reunion. Under the heading "Hobbies," Alderson wrote, "Trading Rickey Henderson."

THERE WAS NEVER a limit to Rickey Style, and the closer he came to the end—whatever that really meant—the more people in the game remembered and celebrated each lustrous facet of his showmanship, recalibrating it whether from disrespect or nostalgia, even when they couldn't have been more disapproving at the time. The new technology contributed to the nostalgia—old clips of Rickey posted to social media served as a periodic but constant reminder of just how different a ballplayer he was and gave the youngsters a taste of what they had missed. The past that was built on legend endured, and the stories about Rickey just kept growing in the retellings.

The legend of Rickey was also aided by the growing sentiment in the contemporary world that baseball had gotten so bland, both in how it was played and who was playing it, that it was as if the sport had lost its collective taste buds. Fans yearning for a little flavor created YouTube compilations of Rickey, video clips of his greatest hits—the Pick after the home runs; the Cadillac, Rickey's signature glacier-slow trot around the bases; his titanic demolition of the Blue Jays in '89—first wearing number 35 and then number 24, early on in green and gold and then in pinstripes; and finally as the legend, the journeyman player, the temporary spark for any team that called. Rickey had excited the palate with a menu of delights, and the new generation who had missed the snatch-catch days now got to see the blinding glitter of Rickey Style go viral.

Showcased in those old clips was the most famous and notorious Rickey move—that exaggerated wide turn as he left the batter's box before beginning the home-run trot. Rickey's turn was so wide that he looked like he

was looping down a cloverleaf off-ramp before approaching the highway of
the bases. You could argue that the wide turn was just one of Rickey's many
touches, one that upped the volume of his showmanship quotient, or that it
was an addendum to the Cadillac, like putting fins on the latest model—but
neither was true. The wide turn certainly made the Cadillac all the more
memorable, but it had a history of its own.

The wide turn trot was special. Very special. Rickey would always say
that none of his moves were planned. They were spontaneous—he just had
style—but the wide turn wasn't about style. It was about revenge. In later
years he would see baseball's attempts to manufacture cool as desperate. The
bat flips, the home-plate celebrations for a nondescript win in April for the
sake of attracting a highlight show—all this just made the game look worse.
Contriving a style was just as bad as trying to douse Rickey's organic flair.
"You can't turn a Jaguar into a Volkswagen," he would say. The wide turn,
however, was different. It was a direct response, Rickey said, to years of being called a show-off by the game's self-appointed gatekeepers. The particular gatekeeper in question was Rickey's old coach with the Yankees and his
Double-A opponent from way back in the day, Buck Showalter, who at the
time was not only managing the Yankees but doing so at a time when Rickey
was exacting his revenge on them for the New York years.

Buck was rebuilding the Yankees into a team on the rise. The new kid
leading off, 24-year-old Bernie Williams, was showing promise in his first
full season. A future Hall of Famer, Wade Boggs, had come over from the
Red Sox. Paul O'Neill, whose Reds had stunned the A's in the World Series three years earlier, was the hot-tempered, water-cooler-smashing right
fielder. And Mattingly, Rickey's favorite teammate, was still there. The building blocks of a good team were being assembled.

It was April 20, 1993, at the Coliseum, A's against the Yankees. A wild
game. A Rickey game. Rickey was on base three times, two stolen bases, a
run scored—all without a hit. The A's were in a laugher until Showalter's boys
stormed back with four runs in the ninth in a rally off Eckersley, capped by
a Bernie Williams double that gave the Yankees a 7–6 lead. The A's tied it in
the bottom of the inning, and in the tenth, with a runner on, Rickey blasted
a two-run homer to end the game. The ball cleared the fence. What was left
of the 20,456 fans who had shown up were out of their seats. The beaten Yankees were skulking off the field . . . but Rickey hadn't moved a muscle. As the
ball was clearing the fence, he was still standing at home plate—like a statue,

like a glorious statue of . . . of . . . Rickey. Finally, he began his victorious trip around the bases. In *Newsday,* Jon Heyman described the scene:

RICKEY PLAYS SPOILER

Rickey Henderson simply stood at the plate, watching the two-run homer that ended the battle of the bumbling bullpens. Henderson's two-run drive with nobody out in the tenth inning off John Habyan barely cleared the leftfield fence. But it was convincing enough for Henderson to admire the clout that won it for the Athletics, 9–7.

As he began rounding the bases, Heyman noted, Rickey "did some major hot-dogging, giving the home-run signal as he jogged to first base." That was on top of the rest of Rickey Style—the Pick, the Cadillac, the works.

In the fourth inning the next day, Rickey took a ball from Jimmy Key and blasted it—and admire it he certainly did—but the ball never left the park. It meekly curved foul. Rickey recalled Showalter yelling at him for show-boating, for *disrespecting the game,* and in response, Rickey deposited a Key breaking ball three pitches later into the left-field seats. Three decades later, Rickey said he never forgot that exchange.

"I hit a ball at home. I hit it, but it didn't really go, and he was over there cursing me out," Rickey recalled. "Next pitch was up. Next pitch, they throw behind me—and now I'm pissed off. Now, next pitch, he threw that cock shot and . . . *Whammm!* I *know* this ball's gone! I curled so far out the base-line I almost went into their dugout to give them all high-fives. They're yell-ing at me, 'You crazy!' And I'm like, 'See, you had it coming!' You trying to get me for something cuz you think I'm trying to show you up? I wasn't. But okay, *now* I'mma show you up. Now when I hit one, I'm coming to high-five you before going to first base. They were saying, 'Get out of here! Get in the baseline, you son of a bitch!' And I was like, 'I'll get back in the baseline— but I gotta come say hello to you first.' And that's when I had that wide trot. That's where it came from.'"

As origin stories went, it was completely plausible, full of the requisite ele-ments of insult, machismo, revenge, and Rickey, and it's true that the general recall of baseball players is nothing short of remarkable. Rickey had a big se-ries against a team with whom he'd had history. Showalter had a rep as a no-nonsense manager who wanted the game played the right way—you might beat them, but you don't make a Buck Showalter team look bad. Everyone knew Buck could be a hard-ass—he was a real spit-and-polish man, having come up in the Yankees system—so it tracked that he might take umbrage at Rickey making the world his stage at Buck's expense, especially after Rickey walked him off the night before.

Additionally, Rickey had been wearing out Jimmy Key for a decade. Over a 25-year career, Rickey faced only Frank Tanana and Jack Morris more than Key—and there was no pitcher he'd faced as many times with as much success. "I wore his ass out," Rickey would say, and the numbers backed him up: .409 average, nine homers in 102 plate appearances. If Key had finally decided to throw one behind Rickey in frustration after years of being cuffed around by him, well, that made sense too—the universe needed to be kept in balance. A guy had to stand up for himself.

Besides, it wasn't as though there hadn't already been an ongoing price for Rickey Style. "He was such a dynamic ballplayer, and the opposing team didn't really like Rickey Henderson," the umpire Richie Garcia recalled. "What Rickey did didn't even come close to what they do today, but in our day he had a little bit—a lot more—flair, and it wasn't accepted. He was down on his butt a lot. He was made to jump around that batter's box."

There was that crusty old bastard Danny Darwin. Eckersley just referred to him as "a prick." Mean streak Danny Darwin. It was August 25, 1992, at Fenway against the Red Sox, and Rickey was just wearing Darwin out: walked his first time up, singled the next time and drove in a run, and then stole second in his third time around. Next time up, with two out and nobody on base, Rickey worked a 3-0 count. Instead of walking him, Darwin just reared back and smoked Rickey—fastball right to the ribs. "Fucking prick," Eckersley recalled. "He knew he was gonna walk him, so he just fucking threw it right at him." Rickey was writhing in the dirt, but this was a night when his nose was in it. Rickey climbed up off the dirt, headed to first, then immediately stole second and scored a two-out run.

So all of the pieces had fallen into place to create a familiar-sounding Rickey story. The only issue with this particular Rickey–Buck Showalter story, however, was that it wasn't true. At least, the Buck Showalter part of it wasn't. Rickey happened to be one of Buck's all-time favorites.

"I think he's embellishing that one. I loved watching Rickey," Showalter recalled. "Absolutely loved it. People would get all upset at what Rickey was doing. Not me. To me, I loved that Rickey had that Muhammad Ali style—it wasn't bragging if you could back it up. Was it the dugout? I'm sure. I would never yell at Rickey, but I guarantee you somebody in that dugout probably did. Clete Boyer or Frank Howard. That'd be my guess."

There were few people in the game who absorbed baseball the way Buck Showalter did. If basketball guys who hunger for the game nonstop are gym rats, Buck Showalter was a baseball sponge. He came up in the coaching ranks with Billy Martin and had been in the Yankees system as a player. He was a perfect Steinbrenner manager because George's policy of prohibiting facial hair below the lip suited Buck just fine—ballplayers were supposed to look professional. But all the objections to Rickey's game? Count Buck Showalter out on that one. He marveled at Rickey. Buck Showalter respected talent and knew the rules were different for the one who had bags full of it. Buck was, after all, the guy who once intentionally walked the great Barry Bonds—with the bases loaded.

Buck talked about Rickey with a surgeon's precision, or an engineer's attention to detail. He was one of the few white men in the game who tried to take Rickey's view of the elements of the game where he took the most criticism. "Everyone always fixated on Rickey because he wasn't good with words, because he sounded inarticulate, so they assumed he wasn't bright. If you were worried about being made fun of every time you spoke, would *you* want to give interviews?

"He spoke in Rickeyisms, but sit down and listen to him talk baseball. Listen to the way Rickey could break down situations, the way he talked about pitchers, the way he read pitchers, the way he used his legs for leverage to take off. Let me tell you, Rickey was a sharp baseball thinker. When I was coaching him, you couldn't bullshit Rickey. He wanted to know why we were doing this, or why we were doing this type of drill. He wanted to know that *you* knew why we were doing it. Sometimes we'd do some drills just to look busy, and Rickey would say, 'Why are we doing this?' And I would say, 'To keep Steinbrenner off my ass.' And he would say, 'Yep. That's a good reason!'"

While everyone told stories about Rickey, padding the legend of an aloof, timeless savant of a character who couldn't be real, Showalter saw beyond all that. The "Planet Rickey" stuff undermined a word that was rarely if ever associated with him: professionalism. "I remember when we were in spring training in Fort Lauderdale with the Yankees. It had to be 1985 or 1986. I'm driving and I see Rickey at a little fruit stand. I pull over and I say, 'What are you doing here?' Rickey's got a bag of fruits and vegetables and says,

'Gotta keep this Cadillac running. Gotta put the right fuel into it.' I know it runs counter to all the other stuff, but Rickey wasn't into the long nights and the hard living . . . There are so many stories. Harold Reynolds by himself could tell you stories about Rickey that would make you piss your pants, but Rickey was serious about being a great player. He was dedicated to his craft."

Now Rickey was competing against time, against history and its ghosts. When it wasn't exactly clear why he was still playing, his competition with history was the easy answer. As glorious as it was to still have Rickey on the field, there was the counterargument about players who hung on too long, diminishing their own hard-won reputation. Hanging on too long left people with bad last impressions. Also, Rickey's career totals may have been rising because of his longevity, but his career averages were dipping. He would finish with a career batting average of .279 in 2003, five points lower than just a couple of years previous.

So why did he do it? The reason, of course, was the competitiveness, the drive to outlast the rest. He was too close to too many of those good, round milestones that separated the immortals from all the rest. What sounded better—having a career .284 batting average and 2,816 hits, or a .279 average and 3,055 hits? Rickey wasn't just doing his best Peter Pan impersonation, refusing to grow up. He knew the inherent value of the raw numbers. He knew exactly what 3,000 hits meant, the significance of breaking records held by Cobb and Ruth. No way would Rickey walk away to protect a couple of points on the average when Cobb and Williams and Mays were close enough to touch.

There was also a victory in just being in the lineup at his age, playing the game the way he did, beating some 20-something out of a roster spot. Ruth played until he was 40. Cobb was 41. Henry Aaron played until he was 42. So did Willie. So, then, would Rickey. He would play even longer. He wouldn't just happen to outlive the legends as an active player. It would be his goal.

As Rickey's lights flickered, they were all worrying about his legacy, about what the final totals were going to look like when they presented his case to St. Peter—in this case, entry through the pearly gates of the Hall of Fame. The great Tim Raines, one of the high standards himself for stolen bases, was 38 years old with 803 stolen bases to his name when he said he wanted to reach Cobb's mark of 892 stolen bases. Raines had won two World Series with the Yankees, but stolen only 26 bases in the previous three seasons.

By this point, with Rickey the undisputed stolen-base champion and recognizing the game wasn't paying the big money to steal bags, Raines had recalibrated his memories of the 1980s, downplaying the emphasis on stolen bases—even though it was the category in which both he and Rickey had made their mark. "I really stopped focusing on stolen bases and wanted to think more about being a complete hitter," Raines would say. In a twist of fate, he would begin his final kick by signing with none other than Oakland—to replace Rickey. So too did Tony Phillips, who rejoined Oakland in 1999 for the third time. The A's signed two of his 40-plus contemporaries to replace one Rickey.

Meanwhile, Rickey was on the market again, looking for work. In previous years, in a different time, he most likely would have been done, having fallen short of the milestones, unable to catch Ruth and Cobb on the walks and runs list, but these times were different. The eye test said Rickey couldn't get around anymore. Art Howe knew it, but the analytics said that he didn't have to: his eye still made him valuable. To what would be called the Moneyball generation, those 118 walks gave Rickey immense value—at a decidedly low price.

Rickey and New York just couldn't quite quit each other. After the 1998 season ended, Steve Phillips, the New York Mets' general manager and a great friend of Billy Beane, called about Rickey. The Mets were a good team, but awful at leadoff. Was it true that Rickey had been the first player since 1937 to score 100 runs while hitting .236 or less? Yes, yes it was. It was also true that during those six decades in between few players would have much of an opportunity to do so because hitting that low led to not being on the roster. But that wasn't the case for Rickey, who ended up not only on a roster but getting the money he wanted.

The Braves were the class of the NL East, but the Mets were close, and they needed a spark plug. They needed star power. They needed to believe the way champions believed—and Rickey was a champion. Phillips had done his due diligence and found out as much as he could about Rickey's time with the Yankees. Now he asked Beane, what did he think about 40-year-old Rickey? Beane told him straight—100 walks a year and a nearly .400 on-base was worth way more than Rickey's asking price. Billy Beane also told Phillips that Rickey needed to be rested more often and was, well, *unique*. Nevertheless, Billy vouched for Rickey, so Phillips signed him to a $2 million deal for

two years. A decade after being traded from the Yankees, Rickey w
in New York—almost.

Phillips had been forewarned that Rickey was cut from a different cloth,
which he discovered when it was time to finalize the deal. "We were done
negotiating with his representatives, but then they say, 'You have to talk to
Rickey. He gets involved with every negotiation.' So I call him. He never
called me Steve. He used to call me 'GM.' He'd say, 'Hey, GM,' because he
doesn't ever remember names.

"We start talking and Rickey says, 'What are you going to give me when
I break the records?'

"'The records?'

"'All-time walks and all-time runs scored.'

"'We'll do it up right. A special ceremony on the field. We have something
made, in crystal, to commemorate the record.'

"'Whose crystal?'

"'A crystal. It will be from Tiffany's.'

"He says, 'Who's Tiffany?' I say, 'It's glass, with your name etched . . .'

"'What the hell I want with glass?'

"Finally, I said, 'Rickey, what do *you* want? What do *you* have in mind?'
He says, 'I want one of those things Madden drives around in.' He wanted a
bus, a Madden Cruiser. I said, 'Rickey, this is your first year with us. Most of
the numbers you accumulated came when you were with other teams. We
will do a great, respectful ceremony. I understand breaking Babe Ruth and
Ty Cobb records are incredible accomplishments, but I cannot convince our
ownership to invest in a Winnebago."

The negotiation was moot, because Rickey wouldn't break either record
for another two years, when he was with the Padres, but at the time Rickey
had been making his contingency plan to cash in on every record he broke.

"Everything I'd heard about was true before he took the field for us," Phillips said. "When spring training arrived, I called Rickey in to sign his contract. He read the contract, and said, 'If I'm the MVP, all I get is $100,000?'
And he wanted to know if the vesting option rolled over into the second year.
I was impressed because he had clearly read the contract himself and wanted
information on the vesting mechanism. I told him this was the agreement
his agents approved.

"He says, 'Well, you've got a problem because now Rickey's got a black
circle around his heart, and the last time Rickey had a black circle around

his heart was with the Yankees—and you saw how that worked out.' I said, 'Rickey, your agents *agreed* to this.' Rickey said, 'Rickey's got a black circle around his heart. What are you going to do about it?'

"I told him I couldn't change the language. The paperwork had already gone to MLB. I said to him, 'Okay, Rickey, if you win the MVP, I promise you right now I will renegotiate the deal and make you a free agent. You have my word. Handshake deal.' He said, 'All right. The black circle's gone.'"

For a few stretches during the season, Phillips wasn't sure if 40-year-old Rickey *wasn't* going to win the MVP. He hit .130 in the spring—but that was spring. The lights hadn't yet come on. When they did, Rickey was there. April 7 at Florida—two home runs. It was only the first week of the season, but Rickey was hitting .545, and that was the funny thing. Rickey hadn't hit .300 in five years, but 1999 was nothing like 1998, when tracking a ball as it strayed out of the strike zone had been Rickey's best chance to get on base. Rickey wasn't tricking them with a low batting average but a high on-base with the Mets. As a 40-year-old, he hit a robust .315 and would be named the National League Comeback Player of the Year. The fans loved the old man as underdog, and the Mets captured the city again. Rickey was the rehabilitated Rickey. Even Mike Lupica, never shy about letting Rickey have it, said he was a joy.

Rickey, famously aloof, was even a mentor. The kid Roger Cedeno was having his best year as a pro and was already a blazer on the bases. Rickey helped him work on his technique and also got on him for his eye at the plate. "That first year for us, Rickey was such a big personality," Phillips recalled. "When Rickey walked up to the plate, he set a tone. He had a swagger that the Mets had arrived."

Even when Rickey was ornery, the fans still forgave him and loved him in a way they might not have a decade earlier. The fans would descend on Port St. Lucie, where the Mets held spring training, desperate to get a glimpse of Rickey—and an autograph. Dutifully lined up, the fans would see him coming and then be left crestfallen when he greeted them with these five words:

"Rickey don't sign on Mondays."

The next day, fans would line up for Rickey, then form a cluster as he approached.

"Rickey don't sign on Tuesdays either."

Periodically, Rickey might sign autographs, but his reluctance stemmed from apprehension about the runaway and exploitative memorabilia racket.

Unable to separate the vultures from the die-hards, Rickey remained adamant about not signing autographs, but he'd sit and take pictures with fans
for an hour. That split the difference. He gave something to the fans while
reducing the volume of Rickey signatures that could be sold on the open
market.

The Mets lost the division to the Braves by six and a half games, but their 97
wins was enough to get them into the playoffs for the first time in a decade—
baseball had the wild card now. When they beat 100-win Arizona in four
games to head to the National League Championship Series and play the
dreaded Braves, there was even talk of a long-awaited Subway Series against
the Yankees. New York hadn't had one of those since the Yankees beat the
Dodgers in 1956.

Rickey hit .400 against the Diamondbacks in the Division Series and kept
Randy Johnson flustered in the opener in his unique way (two walks, two
stolen bases, of course). Then the milk went bad.

The discord had started brewing during the regular season because two
players, Rickey and Bobby Bonilla, couldn't stand the manager, Bobby Valentine. None of that was supposed to matter, though, because the Mets were
now in the NLCS against the dynastic Braves, the Maddux-Smoltz-Glavine
Braves, the Braves who would win 14 straight division titles. Bonilla, the
Bronx kid who was fresh off a 1997 championship with the Marlins, was back
with the Mets as he neared the end of his career, getting a second chance
after his first disastrous stint with the team.

With the World Series at stake, the Mets lost the first three games before
making a furious comeback. In the fourth game, Valentine removed Rickey
from the game, but because he was late in making the substitution, he had
to call Rickey off the field back to the dugout—an embarrassing move for a
big leaguer, especially one at Rickey's level. Valentine would say that pulling
Rickey off the field was an oversight, but Bobby V was a stickler for details
who didn't miss a thing. Rickey was sure his manager had shown him up.

The Mets won the game, 3–2, to stave off elimination and then did it
again in Game 5, highlighted by Ventura's famous "Grand Single," a game-
winning grand slam that counted only as a single—the longest single in Mets
history—because Ventura never completed his trip around the bases as the
Mets mobbed him between first and second base in celebration. Despite the
win, Rickey was mad about Bobby V.

Rickey played well in Game 6, going 2-for-5 with a double and a stolen base. Valentine replaced him on a double switch with the Mets six outs away from forcing a deciding seventh game. Bonilla didn't start, but he contributed a clutch pinch-hit single. The closer, John Franco, couldn't hold the lead.

The game went into extras, and in the bottom of the 11th, with the bases loaded in a 9–9 game, Kenny Rogers—Rickey's teammate in Oakland the year before—walked in the winning run. The comeback was over. The season was over. On the top step of the dugout, the Mets were stunned. Some players were crying, bawling like they'd lost the township Little League title. In that moment, it was a game, not a business. At that moment, it was the most important game of their lives and they had lost.

Where was Rickey? He wasn't in the dugout watching the game. Where was Bonilla? He was gone too. When the broken Mets filed into the clubhouse, the mystery was solved: there was Rickey in the Mets clubhouse with Bonilla, laughing, playing cards.

Nobody knew who leaked the story to the papers the next day, but Bob Klapisch of *The Record*—the same Klapisch whom Bonilla threatened in the clubhouse six years earlier during his first Met tenure with the immortal line, "I'll hurt you, I'll show you the Bronx right now"—dropped a bombshell on the heartbroken Mets fans: as the season ended in the most gut-wrenching way possible, Rickey was playing cards like it was spring training. A week later, the Yankees had finished off the Braves in four straight for their second consecutive World Series, but the talk in Queens was all about how two guys could care so little. Lisa Olson of the *Daily News* zeroed right in on Rickey. It was not a lapse in judgment, she wrote. This was who Rickey always was.

THROW THE BUMS OUT!
RICKEY, BONILLA HAVE TO GO

Henderson's role in this escapade was no surprise. After all, George Steinbrenner once invented a whole new word to describe Henderson's tendency to lollygag when he didn't feel up to doing something that wouldn't benefit him. The term "jaking it" isn't found in any Webster's, but Steinbrenner left nothing to the imagination when he accused Henderson of doing just that.

Two years before Henderson had broken the ceiling with his fat contract, but then the A's signed Canseco to a deal that made Hen-

derson's look like the change behind his couch, and he was livid. He
spent the rest of the season jaking it, which appears to come as naturally as stealing bases.

When spring camps opened and Rickey arrived after the first day of voluntary workout, he had no idea about the buzz saw that awaited him. The
season had ended the night of the infamous card game, and so he didn't
know it was the story of the off-season. As was his custom—and his right
under the collective bargaining agreement—Rickey arrived after the voluntary reporting date but before the mandatory date. The papers said that
Rickey was late, that he was in Vegas.

Still, Rickey owned his rebellion—at least his issues with Valentine—and
didn't care much about the optics, the way you're supposed to look after
victories and defeats. That stuff was for the writers and for the fans, the people whose only investment in the game was their emotions. Rickey was not
going to apologize for failing to be funereal in a loss, even though the baseball culture said there was a way to grieve tough losses, to show you cared.
"Rickey doesn't have a mean bone in his body. He's much less nefarious,"
recalled Bob Alejo. "He's the person laughing his way out of stuff if things
ever get heated."

This time, though, there was no massaging what happened as Rickey being Rickey. The city was dying after losing to the Braves, the players in the
room were devastated—and Rickey wasn't there because he was mad at his
manager? The rage from the newspapers was echoed throughout Queens.
Olson's rage either blinded her to the facts or kept her from looking them up
(Rickey didn't jake it when Canseco got his megadeal—he won the American League MVP that year), but her column echoed the sentiments of the
hard hats listening to drive-time sports radio. In the spring, Rickey was back
with the Mets, but his days were numbered. Bonilla—who'd hit only .160 in
60 games in 1999—was already gone.

"Bonilla wasn't a real Met. He was on his second tour, and he was just
passing through. And Rickey? I never got the impression that Rickey cared
about anything but himself," Klapisch recalled. "These guys were just gutted.
They had the worst loss of the year, ended their seasons, and these two fucking guys were laughing and playing cards. There were guys who wanted to
bash their heads in with baseball bats. And it was a big 'fuck you' to the manager. Everyone knew they didn't get along. There were guys in that room

thinking, *How could you?* and the worst thing about it was they didn't even try to hide it. They didn't get caught in some back room. They were in the middle of the clubhouse playing cards. It was bad. It was a very bad scene. Everything bad about it then is just as bad as it sounds now."

On its face it always seemed that Rickey belonged in New York—there was no more appropriate bright-lights player in his time. But perhaps nobody was a worse fit for New York because of the enormous gap between how Rickey was viewed by most of his teammates in the clubhouse and how the papers sold him to New York.

New York was all about reverence and tradition and deference, and Rickey was all about what Rickey could do. Fifteen years earlier, Rickey and New York immediately clashed when Rickey stiffed the writers before his Yankees debut (*I don't need no press now, man*). This time, crosstown, long before he played his first game with the Mets, it was Rickey saying he wanted to wear number 24. *But that was Willie Mays's number!* So of course the call went out to the San Francisco Bay peninsula and the 68-year-old Mays said he didn't want *anyone* wearing his number, and of course when the season started there was Rickey wearing number 24, which frosted Mays. Mays said he wasn't mad at Rickey, even though it was Rickey who made the request. Mays said he was mad at whoever approved it.

Outside of a couple of tough guys like Turk Wendell, the Mets reliever Rickey clashed with and the player the writers held up as the conscience of the clubhouse, the 1999 season was a memory. In general the card game was like most things in a clubhouse—an issue to some, a deal-breaker to others, a non-issue to still others. "It really wasn't that big a deal," recalled Robin Ventura. Of course, Ventura was the most chill guy in any clubhouse.

"Rickey was a great teammate. He totally ingratiated himself within the clubhouse. He was fun to be around—and he loved playing. He wanted to play every day," he said. "My whole career existed within his. Rickey played before me, and he played after me. A's, Toronto. No matter what team he went to, he made them better.

"The card game? Nah, that wasn't that big of a deal. It was all because we lost the game. If you win the game, it would have been totally different. Look at the 1986 Mets. A few of those guys missed Mookie's ground ball, but they won the game and now they're revered."

Bobby V, though, absolutely thought the card game was a big deal. Rickey's brazenness had undermined his authority in the room with the other 24 guys. All the good things Rickey had done in 1999—mentoring the young guys, keeping the room loose, ruining pitch counts—had been undone by what he did after that one game. You also couldn't have the fans thinking the players cared less than they did—especially in New York, where the scrubs who hustled got dispensation over stars because they wore their lack of talent on their sweaty faces as proof they were trying.

Valentine told Phillips that Rickey had to go. When Rickey started off hitting .219 with nearly as many strikeouts as walks, Phillips released Rickey—but the specter of New York wasn't quite finished with him. Seattle—whose GM, Pat Gillick, had traded for Rickey in Toronto in 1993 and whose manager was Lou Piniella, the very man who affixed the lifelong tag of "jaking it" to Rickey—signed him a week later.

The 2000 Mariners were in the same position as the Mets a year before. They were knocking on the postseason door and needed a leadoff hitter, someone to show them how to strut like winners. Thirteen years removed from 1987 and Rickey's hamstrings, Piniella said that he loved Rickey. That New York stuff? Water under the bridge. A long time ago.

He was still Rickey, so first at-bat as a Mariner? Rickey homered. There was always a tale at the ready. "I was a batboy for the Mariners in 2000, when they picked him up on waivers, I think," recalled Jason Beatty. "Rickey was staying at a hotel in downtown Seattle, and I was asked to pick him up and bring him to the ballpark for the first couple of weeks until his car got into town. I played Little League in the '80s and loved his flash with the Athletics. For two or three weeks I got 10 minutes one on one with one of the greatest ballplayers ever. We'd walk into the park together from the players' lot. He let me park my '92 Honda Accord in his spot.

"Dave Henderson was in the clubhouse often and loved to interact with Rickey and talk about their times playing together on the A's," Beatty recalled. "I started telling them how I was a fat white kid playing catcher for a Little League team, on the Pirates wearing black and gold, but I rocked the padded Mizuno lime green batting gloves Rickey wore. That sent Dave Henderson into a tailspin story [about] how those were actually his batting gloves but Rickey walked by his locker, picked up a pair and put them on, and decided that pair would then become his—and he rocked them the rest of his time in Oakland. Rickey sheepishly acknowledged that that was the true story."

On July 24, 2000, Rickey wasn't hitting. He hadn't homered in two months

and was 2 for his last 15. Oakland had come to town, and Dave Henderson
was there too, doing a slate of games for the Mariners' television broadcast.
With the possible exception of Dave Parker, nobody's humor in the A's clubhouse had been more ruthless, more cutting, than Hendu's, and when he
saw Rickey at the cage before the game, the two shared moments of laughter. Right as Rickey was about to walk into the cage, Hendu stopped him,
whipped out a black Sharpie, drew a pair of glasses on the barrel of Rickey's
bat, laughed, and walked away. Rickey played two games in the series and
went 4-for-8.

For Rickey, Seattle was just another stop on the railroad, one that lasted
half a season, with the Mariners winning a round in the playoffs. Seattle
brought the total to five different teams that went to the postseason with
Rickey on the roster. Rickey hit .400 in the ALDS and the Mariners swept
the White Sox, but the Yankees were too much, knocking them out of the
Championship Series. New York, a year late, got its Subway Series.

Seattle was notable in Rickey's nomadic journey for two reasons. The
first was that with the Mariners 41-year-old Rickey returned to wearing
number 35, for the first time since 1984. The second? Seattle was the site of
the downfall of the most famous Rickey story of them all—though it still
couldn't be killed.

When Rickey arrived, John Olerud had never heard the helmet story,
though, to be fair, the story was still in its infancy—just a few weeks old. He
and Rickey had been teammates in 1993 with the Blue Jays. It was Olerud's
greatest year: he was a World Series champion for the second time, hit .363,
won the batting title, made his first All-Star team, and finished in the top
three for the MVP for the first (and only) time. When Rickey joined the
Mets in 1999, Olerud was the first baseman, but he had signed in the off-
season with the Mariners, his hometown team. When Seattle picked up
Rickey after the Mets let him go, Olerud and Rickey were now teammates
for the third time.

Olerud had been distinctive in the game for many reasons—the sweet
swing, the subtle consistency of his offense, the nicest-guy-in-the-world
demeanor of an easygoing Pacific Northwesterner. Most of all, Olerud was
known as the guy who wore a batting helmet in the field. As a phenom at
Washington State, Olerud suffered an aneurysm and underwent six hours
of brain surgery. When he resumed playing baseball, he took to wearing a
batting helmet in the field as a precaution.

When Rickey arrived in Seattle, he saw Olerud—a man who had been his teammate just months earlier—and asked him about the helmet. Olerud explained why he wore the batting helmet, about the operation, and Rickey said, "Man, I used to play with a guy who did the same thing in New York," to which Olerud replied, "Yes, Rickey. That was me."

"Here's how I heard about it," Olerud recalled. "I was taking BP, and Dave Niehaus, he comes walking up to me chuckling, and he tells me the story, and says, 'Olie, tell me if this is true: they say Rickey came up to you and asked you about the helmet. And you said, "Yeah, I wore the helmet because I had surgery when I was in college." He goes, "That's so funny. I just played with a guy last year, same thing." "Yeah, Rickey, that was me."'

"He says, 'Is there any truth to that?' I said . . . 'That's *really* good.' I said, 'But no, there's no truth to that.' And so I thought that was it, and it just kind of had a life of its own. It just kept being talked about, and I kept telling people, 'No, it's not true.' It's a great story. I love it, but it's not true. And to this day it continues.

"Smart baseball fans would come up to me and say, 'Can I ask you a question? And that was always code for 'I'm going to ask you this Rickey question.' Or it was usually, 'I have a neighbor who's a big baseball fan, and he wanted me to ask you this.'

"What happened was the New York Mets assistant trainer was Scott Lawrenson—great sense of humor, very dry sense of humor. And what he would like to do is, he'd see a picture in a magazine or in the newspaper that looked like one of the guys on the team, and he would cut it out and make up a little story underneath. The one that strikes me that I remember: he had this Latin guy shaking up margaritas, and it looked like Rey Ordonez. And he cuts that out, and it would say, 'Rey Ordonez was seen on Cinco de Mayo . . .'

"So it was always fun to go into the clubhouse and see if there was anything new on the bulletin board, if anyone made the bulletin board. There were some really good ones. He'd come up with a list of what guys would do if they weren't playing professional baseball, and he had me as a Wal-Mart greeter because I was so quiet, and he thought, wouldn't that be funny to see Olie trying to say hi to everybody.

"My understanding is, he told the clubhouse guys when he found out that Rickey got signed with Seattle, and knowing Rickey wasn't always the best at remembering names, he told the story to the clubhouse guys. The clubhouse guys laughed. They go into the clubhouse to tell the players, and somebody must have overheard them. They wrote it down. It gets in the newspapers. Then the TV guys read it, 'Did you hear the story about what Rickey said to Olie'—just took on a life of its own—until they did the story on *ESPN SportsCenter,* and all the Mets guys were watching in the clubhouse and they were just laughing. They couldn't believe it kept going. It even got to the point where Scott Lawrenson called me at the All-Star break and said, 'Hey, Olie, I'm sorry. I was just goofing around. I had no idea it would turn out this way.'

"When I would go to a new team, I'd be sitting across from a guy after a game, and someone would say, 'Can I ask you a question . . . ?' I think in Boston Jason Varitek would say, 'Rickey was here last year, and he says it's true.' I remember playing against him and I saw him in the outfield, I went running out to him to say, 'Hey, Rickey, would you tell these guys . . .,' and he would just go, 'Aww, man . . .' So I don't know if Rickey kind of liked the story, enjoyed the humor of it, and just wanted to keep it going."

Olerud's recollection of the story's origin was accurate, but there was another detail to the story: the original fire-starter was Robin Ventura, who lit the fuse talking to Todd Zeile and Al Leiter. "We were in the trainers' room," Ventura remembered, "and Scotty was taping my ankles when he heard that Rickey had gone to Seattle, and he just said it as a joke. 'Imagine if Rickey said that to Olie.' And I said, 'I wonder how long it would take for that to become a story?' So I went into the clubhouse and I was talking I think to Al or Zeile, and I said it just loud enough where I thought people could hear me. Somebody heard it, and it just took off ever since. It will not die. It didn't happen, and they don't even care. Even when I managed, guys would say, 'Did you hear this Rickey story?' and I say, 'Uhhh, it never happened.' As long as they want to believe it, it will always have legs because it was Rickey, it was very believable."

Some of the stories were not true of course, like the infamous Olerud tale and also another doozy of a fish story that supposedly took place in Philadelphia, when Rickey went there in 1996 with the Padres. It was his first go in the National League, with new cities and new routines. One night after playing the Phillies, Rickey called for a car service to take him back to the hotel. Apparently, the car was parked at the wrong gate and he was left out there roaming the Veterans Stadium parking lot, looking for his ride. When a security guard noticed the great Rickey Henderson wandering around the grounds, he went to ask him if he was okay, and, according to the tale, Rickey replied, "No, I'm not okay. Rickey don't like it when Rickey can't find Rickey's limousine."

These were the Rickey stories that the Black players in the league would hear and react to with an eye roll—and a groan. Most times they would wince. Rickey was a character. Rickey was unique. Rickey was bizarre and funny and aloof, but there was a difference between Rickey being on his own program and the fictionalized minstrel stories that diminished him and used him to reinforce the Black stereotypes so many had spent their careers trying to shed. Those stereotypes might have been funny. They might even have been hilarious examples of Rickey being Rickey, and a lot of them just happened to be true—but the stereotypes weren't harmless.

Finding work in baseball after their playing careers had ended was hard enough for Black players, but it was even harder in a game saturated with Rickey stories. Doubts about being respected as baseball thinkers and leaders, as men who the white billionaire suits could trust not just to run spring training and draw up lineups but to speak to civic organizations and represent the club, followed every Black player who wanted a future in the game after their playing days were over. Laughing at Rickey may have made for hilarity at the bar or in the press box, but every Black player hoping to one day be a manager or a general manager knew the stories were just making it that much more difficult to be taken seriously. What belonged to one stuck to the rest. They knew that laughter directed at Rickey was also directed, however subtly, at all of them. Anyone who doubted that could simply look at the percentage of managerial jobs that went to Black candidates. The numbers didn't lie, and no amount of apologias in *The Sporting News* could change what they said.

When the players winced, they were also wincing for Rickey, because underneath the laughter was the cruelty of inequity. There was no question that Rickey suffered from an early reading disability that had not been addressed, that his education had not received adequate attention, and no question that his athletic ability had reduced the academic rigor required of him in the classroom, allowing him to play sports and not learn.

The Black players could often spot those three-dollar-bill Rickey stories, because they knew Rickey didn't always speak in the third person. It was one of the first things Dave Parker noticed when Rickey joined the A's in 1989.

"He was every bit as good as advertised, and a lot of people resented him for it, but the amount he spoke in the third person was an exaggeration."

The Black players always knew when to call bullshit on Rickey stories. They knew, and would say to each other, that the third-person stuff was for white people. They also knew that lots of Black players told Rickey stories, but very few routinely told third-person Rickey stories. It wasn't that he didn't speak in the third person, because he did. It was the embellishment and overemphasis on it that made some Black players uncomfortable with the racial overtones embedded in the retellings of such obvious fabrications.

When John Shea was collaborating with Rickey on Rickey's memoir *Off Base*, Rickey's speech was one of the first things he noticed. Shea had heard all the legendary third-person Rickey stories, but he didn't hear Rickey speaking in the third person himself. Rickey stories were told like a game of telephone—each version further embellished with each retelling. Shea, too, was uncomfortable with the stories highlighting Rickey-speak because of the racial connotations, but also because of the class insults in those stories. He had already heard a story that the Oakland beat writers made a T-shirt mocking Rickey based on something he'd said, complete with his grammatical and phonetic errors. That was another example of the white press ridiculing a Black athlete for his upbringing—and more proof that Rickey had good reason to be naturally skeptical of the media.

Third-person Rickey would emerge when Rickey was animated about something—like when he would walk into the clubhouse, feeling a good game in his bones, and announce *"Rickey time! IT'S RICKEY TIME!"* That meant something spectacular was due to happen—a couple of hits, a couple of steals, maybe a leadoff jack. This was something Rickey absolutely, undeniably did, just as it was also true that Rickey was terrible with names—he would just call everyone "Baby." One time in 2001, on the Padres team bus, third baseman Phil Nevin told Rickey he'd give him $100 for each person on the bus he could name. Rickey was quiet. Nevin's face began to curl into a satisfied smile. He was right. Rickey *didn't* know the names of his own teammates—not even one. After several moments of silence, Rickey then looked at Nevin and said, "Fuck you . . . *PHIL!*"

Usually when Rickey went into the third person he did so to motivate himself. ("Come *on*, Rickey. You *know* that ball is gonna be outside.") When

David Cone was a young pitcher for the Royals and first faced Rickey, he thought Rickey was trash-talking *him*. "After every pitch he's got something to say, and I'm listening to him. He'd be like, 'Nooooo, no, no. Rickey. Stay *off* that slider,' and I'd be looking back at him, and he wasn't even looking at me. You know who he was talking to? He was talking to his bat."

It was 2002, and Rickey was 43. He'd already broken all of the records he'd coveted, and he'd gotten his 3,000th hit on the last day of the season—just as Roberto Clemente did way back in 1972. December and January passed without anyone expressing serious interest in him, and as spring camps opened Rickey was still without a team.

Then in 2002, Rickey's eighth team, the Boston Red Sox, came calling. The Red Sox were now owned by the trio of John Henry, Tom Werner, and Larry Lucchino, who'd bought the team weeks earlier for $700 million. The Red Sox had always been adversaries, but the front office now included, in Lucchino and Charles Steinberg, two of Rickey's pals from San Diego.

The Red Sox needed depth in the outfield, and Rickey was available. It was just a minor league deal they offered, $330,000, which was the big league minimum. Even if he made the team, which was no given, he wasn't going to be a starter. A year earlier the Red Sox had signed Manny Ramirez to an eight-year, $160 million deal to play left, and a month before Rickey signed, Johnny Damon had signed a four-year, $32 million deal to play center—and bat leadoff.

The Red Sox also had Michael Coleman. Once one of their hottest prospects, Coleman was trying now to make a comeback. Before he'd swung a bat in the big leagues, Coleman had seen himself as a marquee player. Coleman talked a huge game, but never backed it up. He had nicknamed himself "Prime Time" before being humbled as a big leaguer: after three seasons, he had a .194 career average, one walk, 26 strikeouts. After stints with Boston, Cincinnati, and the Yankees, Coleman now had a chance, at just 26 years old, to win the fourth outfielder spot and rebuild his career. But the Red Sox hitting coach, none other than Jim Rice—one of the greatest Red Sox of them all, a former AL MVP in 1978, and on the cusp of the Hall of Fame—told Coleman not to take the competition lightly. Even though Rickey was 43 years old, if there was one thing he knew how to do it was how to make a ball club.

So there was Rickey running sprints with players young enough to be
his kids. There was Rickey arriving early. There was Rickey giving Johnny
Damon tips on how to steal bases. There was Rickey *outworking* players half
his age. When spring games started, there was Rickey hitting .340, including
that wild game against the Yankees with new ownership in the box.

Leading off, Rickey stood in against that Cuban magician Orlando
"El Duque" Hernandez—one bright-lights guy against another. Duque
threw Rickey three pitches. On the fourth, Rickey skyed it to left, deep and
over the fence. Duque turned and watched it leave the ballpark and then
turned back to the plate—to see that Rickey hadn't yet left the batter's box.
It was spring training, the game didn't count, and Rickey was admiring the
beauty of his home run as if it belonged in the Louvre. "I'm not a big home
run hitter, but when I hit 'em, I enjoy 'em," Rickey would say after the game.
Rickey started the Cadillac, took a month or two to get around the bases,
and then, just before reaching home, stopped jogging and started walking
toward home. Finally, he stepped on home plate.

Duque wanted to kill Rickey. Next at-bat, Duque got Rickey on a pop-up
to end the inning—and returned the favor by jogging to the dugout *before*
the ball was even caught. He passed Rickey across the first-base line and
immediately fired off a torrent of curses. They approached each other. The
Red Sox first-base coach, Ino Guerrero, restrained Rickey, while Yankees
manager Joe Torre grabbed El Duque. It was spring training.

After the game, Duque had nothing to say, but Rickey had plenty to say.
"Maybe he needs to grow up a little bit. I'm not a kid. I've been playing in
this game a long time. Ever since he's been crawling on his knees I've been
playing baseball—unless he's as old as I am, and he probably is."

When camp broke, two things happened. First, Rice turned out to be
right: Rickey beat Coleman out for the final outfield slot. And second,
when the Red Sox purchased his minor league contract and put him on
the big club roster, Rickey wasn't happy with his contract. He said he deserved more. Internally, the Red Sox were confounded, unsure if Rickey
was serious—or delusional. *Was he serious?* Rickey was a fourth outfielder,
not a starter. He was 43 years old, not 23. He'd hit .227 the year before, and
.233 the year before that. He had already agreed to a minor league deal.
The terms were set, and it wasn't as though 29 other teams were knocking
down his door. But he was still Rickey, and he negotiated as if he were a
first-round draft pick.

RICKEY DOESN'T LIKE THESE NUMBERS
WANTS MORE INCENTIVES IN CONTRACT

"They have to figure out if I'm going to be with them," Henderson said. "That's the next question. It seems like it shouldn't be a question, but it's a question right now. It's a real big question.

"I made the club. Other than that, we just got to work out the details. It's a little bit more complicated with my contract. If the contract don't work, I'll go home. Say it like that. I might be going home in Houston. I don't think I can play until they work it out."

Inside the visitors' clubhouse in Houston, Rickey was adamant that the details of his deal had not been resolved. Jeff Horrigan of the *Boston Herald* and Bob Hohler of the *Boston Globe* were in the media scrum listening to Rickey. In his previous life, Hohler had covered Congress and the Clinton White House for the paper. Relying on his old Beltway language, Hohler asked Rickey if he felt the Red Sox had reneged on previously agreed-to stipulations. Hohler recalled Rickey as responding, "That's right. I want my stiffulations." Horrigan recalled emerging from the interview utterly confused. "It was hilarious," he said. "We had no idea what he was talking about."

Rickey ultimately signed his deal, and on April 27, at Fenway Park against Tampa Bay, he led off the game with a home run—for the 80th time of his career. It was also the game-winning RBI. The Red Sox won 10–0, when Derek Lowe, the starting pitcher, tossed a no-hitter.

Being around Rickey completed an arc for Glenn Wilburn, a member of the Red Sox public relations staff. He was a Bronx kid, grew up in Fordham, and the Rickey-Mattingly-Winfield Yankees were his sweet spot as a fan. Working with the Red Sox, he was now working with Rickey too.

"It was just so bizarre. Rickey got traded to the Yankees, and I was at the game when he played his first game as a Yankee," Wilburn recalled. "And I was a vendor at the Stadium—soda, popcorn, frozen fruit bars. Day game weekdays they let me sell hot dogs, but they put me in the upper deck. I was 150 pounds soaking wet. No harness, no kind of back support, nothing. We just had the crate that held like, 25 sodas.

"Rickey was a character. He and I got along great. There were a couple of things that stood out. The one time we went back and played the Padres. It was a family trip—Atlanta, San Diego, and the Dodgers," Wilburn recalled. "And the Padres honored Rickey for breaking the all-time runs [record].

And I remember that, when he slid into home plate. It was huge, I remember. You know how far the dugout is from the clubhouse? It's a football stadium, a long, winding way away. The Padres made an award for Rickey, a framed home plate, and gave it to him. He gives his speech and starts walking in my direction, and he just fucking hands me the award. Doesn't say a word to me, and I'm like, 'Ohhhh . . . I guess *I'm* supposed to bring this back to the clubhouse.'"

Rickey went dark in Boston. During the first week of May, the Red Sox owned the best record in baseball, but Rickey was on the bench. "He wanted a bigger contract, and he was being bitter about it. It didn't play," Wilburn recalled. "After the game he says, 'I want to call a press conference about my contract.' I told him, 'Rickey, I'm not a GM. I'm just a PR guy, but this is gonna look bad for you. You cannot renegotiate your contract during the season.' He was old, in his early forties, and we were in Oakland, his hometown. But he kept saying, 'Man, these guys aren't paying me.' I told him, 'Rickey, it's gonna open a whole can of worms.' He said, 'All right, I'll think about it.' So I talked him out of a silly press conference."

He was still Rickey. That meant he was different. That *made* him different. The big ones, the stars, they were always different. There was always some situation big or small that reminded you of what made them stars. "Getaway day, Kansas City. For some reason, we couldn't go from the bus straight to the tarmac, so we had to walk through the terminal," Wilburn recalled. "So all these people start seeing the Red Sox. They notice Rickey and start yelling, 'Rickey! Rickey!' Rickey's got this sullen face, and you can just tell he doesn't want to be bothered at all. These two guys start yelling, 'Rickey! Rickey! Can we have your autograph?'

"And suddenly, just like that, he's got the biggest smile on his face. He's engaging them, and I'm thinking, *How does he turn it on like this?* I was there and I'm like thinking, *He's about to tell these guys to fuck off.* And now he's got his arm around these guys. Taking pictures, signing autographs. It was incredible."

The 2002 Red Sox won 93 games but fell out of the race in September. Rickey had played 24 seasons, 23 of them away from Boston, but even though he had only played 72 of his 3,051 big league games with the Red Sox, the new ownership of John Henry, Tom Werner, and Larry Lucchino announced that they would cap a legendary career with a day for Rickey, on the field, with all the trimmings. These Red Sox wanted to do things with class. The front office decided to give Rickey a car in a pregame ceremony. Walking along the Red Sox concourse with Charles Steinberg and Larry Lucchino, Rickey eyed a tasty, sleek Mercedes roadster. "You want a car like that one?" Steinberg asked.

"Not one *like* that. *That* one," Rickey said to Steinberg.

"But . . . that's John Henry's car."

On September 30, the Red Sox presented Rickey not with a Mercedes but with a red Ford Thunderbird in a pregame ceremony. "They were showing me respect," Rickey told the *Boston Globe,* adding, "I was really proud of that."

Laughing and shaking their heads, Red Sox employees for years would tell *another* version of that day—and the story spread across baseball like a prairie fire. When Rickey arrived at Fenway that morning, he passed the rows of cars that lined the players' lot along Van Ness Street—and there sat the Thunderbird. Rickey looked at the lot attendant and said to the kid, "Whose piece of shit is that?"

The attendant stammered, "It's . . . umm . . . it's *yours,* Rickey. They're giving it to you on the field today."

"Oh, okay. I think I'll give it to one of my daughters."

And there was *yet another* version of that day. This one came from Mike Port, the Red Sox general manager at the time. The day for Rickey was not the by-product of the Red Sox magnanimity, but of Rickey shaking the Sox down during the contract stalemate that occurred way back at the end of spring training when Rickey made the team and Bob Hohler and Jeff Horrigan were perplexed by his "stiffulations." As it turned out, his *stipulations* were a guarantee that he would be honored by the Red Sox at the end of the season and feted for his greatness.

"We signed Rickey to a minor league contract, and within custom, it called for a salary of X if we purchased his contract," Port recalled. "We were in Houston. Rickey makes the club. I went to him and congratulated him. I say, 'Here's a major league contract. Let's go!' Rickey says, 'No, no, no. I need more money.' I say, 'Rickey, this is how it works: you signed a contract that pays you this amount.' He says, 'I'm *canceling* the contract.' I'd only been in the game 30 years and I have no answer. What do I know? Canceling the contract? But he's firm. 'I changed my mind. I'm canceling that.'"

Now Port had to go upstairs. He called Lucchino, who told Rickey, essen-

tially, that there was no turning back. They could not renegotiate his contract. His paperwork had already been filed with MLB. Opening day was in
24 hours.

"So," Port recalled, "Larry says, 'Maybe we can have a night for him later
in the season,' and Rickey says, 'What would be the gifts?' Do *you* ever ask
what someone is going to buy you as a present? Rickey said, 'I just like to be
farsighted on occasion.' I said, 'Well, since you brought it up, what would you
like?' First, he asked for a mobile home. John Henry had the latest roadster
convertible, and Rickey said he wanted it. John Henry's car. Not a model like
it. *John Henry's car.*"

Port misremembered the red Thunderbird as a burnt orange Mustang,
but the punch line was pretty much the same. When Rickey saw the car, Port
recalled Rickey as saying, "'Whose ugly-ass car is that?'"

There was a nice crowd that day, and Rickey soaked it up, but like the
last Rickey Henderson Day in Oakland back in 1998, Rickey used his afternoon of memories and farewell gifts and memories to make an announce-
ment—he wasn't going anywhere.

"I think, "Rickey said, "that I want to play one more year. I can still help
a team."

Rickey was now trying to make good on his desire to play forever, but
after Boston, no teams called. Pamela was convinced that this was finally it
and Rickey could now give the family what he had given to millions of fans
across a quarter-century—his primary attention. Rickey wasn't quitting,
though. He said he had more baseball in his system and could not quit while
he still had the desire to play—so he canvassed and auditioned.

Was it true that Rickey called Padres GM Kevin Towers and left him the
voice mail: "This is Rickey, calling on behalf of Rickey"? No, that was one of
those three-dollar-bill Rickey stories, a third-person confection that white
people loved and that made the brothers cringe. It scarcely mattered at this
point because that persona was how the public would choose to remember
him, and at least it was far more palatable than the persona of the 1980s: the
prototypical money-driven mercenary. What was true was that Rickey still
wanted to play, and if there was a place that would have him, he would go
there. In the spring of 2003—and again in 2004, when he believed that he
could make a big league roster at 45 years old—that place was Newark. The
independent Atlantic League Newark Bears.

Rickey Henderson was now playing in the minor leagues. In the minors,

everybody was scrambling for customers. Promotions were a big deal—
Bring Your Dog to the Ballpark Day, fireworks extravaganzas, anything to
get people to come to the yard. Atlantic League teams now had another
attraction—Rickey. When the Somerset Patriots advertised their games
in the paper, the home games against Newark were billed as "Somerset vs.
Newark—With Rickey Henderson."

There were a few big leaguers on the 2003 Bears. The manager was Bill
Madlock, who'd won four National League batting titles and the 1979 World
Series with the Pirates. There was Ryan Minor, who played four years in the
majors, and 12-year veteran pitcher Jaime Navarro, who had faced Rickey
40 times in the big leagues, but Rickey didn't wear his ass out—Navarro
held him to a .226 average. Michael Coleman, the guy trying to restart his
career but who lost out on the final Red Sox outfield spot to Rickey a year
earlier, was also on that team. Coleman hit .320. Rickey hit .339, which led
the team, even though he was 44 years old and the average age on the team
was 27.

"The guy was in his midforties, and he was our best player," recalled Michael Collazo, who was with the Bears' sales department. "You didn't get
any whiff of him saying he was the greatest of all time. Didn't get a lot of
words out of him. The little I dealt with him, he was a quiet, to-himself dude
compared to his media image. I grew up in Philly, so I knew certain athletes
got a bad rep. It was very clear what his media perception was compared
to real life. He wasn't hanging out at the bar or anything, but people loved
Rickey. There was no beef. Bill Madlock was the manager. He was the pain
in the ass."

Rickey was even selected to the All-Star team, and the league thought
it was a great thing to promote—until Rickey didn't show up. Initially, he
thought the game was being played in Nashville, Tennessee, and that was
great. Good town, good food. He'd be there. Then he realized Nashville
didn't even have a team in the league. The game was being held in *Nashua*.

Nashua, New Hampshire.

"There was a team called the Nashua Pride. Small bullshit town. Crappy
ballpark. Nothing to do up there," Collazo recalled. "Rickey was named to
the All-Star team and never showed. 'Come see Rickey Henderson!' He
thought they said *Nashville*. They tried to use his appearance as a carrot to
sell tickets—and he never showed.

"He didn't say three things to anybody, but the players loved playing with him," Collazo said. "He didn't do any of the generic minor league things, but he was pretty chill. He wasn't like, 'I don't wanna be here. This is fucked up.'"

In 2003 the Dodgers had called. In 2004, when Rickey played 91 games in a return to Newark, no one called, and no major league team would ever call again. But Rickey wasn't done. He went back to San Diego and played 73 games with the San Diego Surf Dawgs of the Gold Coast League. The manager was the old Giants catcher Terry Kennedy, the same Terry Kennedy destroyed by Rickey in the 1989 World Series. Rickey hit .270 with 16 stolen bases. In his final two years of professional baseball, at ages 45 and 46, Rickey stole a combined 53 bases—and was caught four times.

One day during Rickey's first season in Newark, a giant of a man from his faraway past approached him at the batting cage. Nearly a foot taller and two years younger, it was six-foot-eight Jim Hague, the old jack-of-everything for the Jersey City Indians when Rickey was 19 years old back in 1978—the days of rooming with Mike Norris, hating John Kennedy, calling Charlie Finley, and being carted around in Hague's red-and-white 1976 AMC Pacer.

JIM: Rickey, do you remember me?
RICKEY: No.
JIM: I used to drive you home after Jersey City. You don't remember?
RICKEY: No.
JIM: Used to bring you food. Clothes. Every day.
RICKEY: No.
JIM: You don't remember? I picked you up, and drove you home.
    Every. Single. Day. Back and forth from the ballpark.

Then it clicked.

RICKEY: In the bubble car?

"So," Hague said, recalling the story, "he remembered the bubble car, but he didn't remember me. That was okay, because there were several people whose names he didn't remember. I'll say this: he was fascinating. He could be the best teammate and do anything for you, and then the next minute he'd be sullen and dark and not want to talk to anyone. Rickey Henderson was clearly the most fascinating and bizarre person I've ever been around in sports."

FOLLOWING THE MANDATORY five-year waiting period, Rickey's induction into the Baseball Hall of Fame was a no-doubter, especially for most of the newer generation of voters, who were more persuaded by his raw numbers than put off by the jagged edges of his personality. The only suspense would be the percentage; after the results were in, 28 voters left Rickey off the ballot in his first year of eligibility. An odd reversal of logic was applied to Rickey. His demolition of analytic models made the voters who had *not* seen him play view him even more favorably than did many of the ones who had.

Frank Blackman had covered the A's for the *San Francisco Examiner* during three of Rickey's four stints with the A's. He had seen Rickey during his powerhouse years, and he was an eyewitness to the Rickey-Canseco soap opera as the two players jockeyed for days off, jockeyed for salary, jockeyed for respect. Blackman also covered Rickey in 1998, his last year in Oakland. Blackman's opinion of Rickey was similar to La Russa's: he felt that, while unquestionably great, Rickey was often held back by his own unprofessionalism and simply did not always meet the threshold of consistent, team-oriented greatness set by Aaron, Mays, and DiMaggio. There was more to greatness than numbers.

During a road trip to Anaheim during the 1998 season, the writers in the press box tossed around a question: Which active players were first-ballot Hall of Famers? The list was impressive: Greg Maddux, Wade Boggs, Cal Ripken Jr., Barry Bonds, Roger Clemens, Tony Gwynn, among others—but Blackman's list did not include Rickey. "The reason why Rickey Henderson is not a first-ballot Hall of Famer," Blackman said, "is because he took too many days off. There was always a reason. Rickey played whenever he felt like playing—there were just too many days when Rickey didn't want to play." Whether or not Blackman eventually voted for Rickey was, in the end, immaterial, because 511 other voters did, delivering 94.8 percent of a vote that required 75 percent for induction. There was no suspense after all: Rickey sailed overwhelmingly into immortality.

Up until then, only 13 players in history had amassed a higher vote total than Rickey did. His percentage of the vote was even higher than the percentages for Willie Mays, Ted Williams, and Frank Robinson. Rickey's numbers were as high as they were because of the times. It was a celebratory age, with no tolerance for nonsense like Jackie Robinson receiving 77.5 percent of the vote on his first try or DiMaggio getting in on the fourth ballot. Jackie's original 1962 Hall of Fame plaque did not even mention his being the first Black player of the modern age. In Jackie's day and DiMaggio's, the writers saw themselves as gatekeepers of the grand game, and the first job of any gatekeeper was to deny admission, to reinforce the exclusivity of what lay beyond the gate. The default impulse among modern Hall of Fame voters, however, was the opposite—to say yes rather than no to the induction of the great players.

After the vote, all that was left was for Rickey to appear onstage at Cooperstown. That was what everyone was waiting for—Rickey's induction speech. From the beginning of January, when his election was announced along with the overdue election of Boston legend Jim Rice, Rickey at Cooperstown in July was the anticipated popcorn moment of the year. Nobody could wait for The Speech. If Rickey had said he was the greatest of all time with Lou Brock sitting a foot away from him, what on earth was he going to do at the Hall, when he'd reached the ultimate goal and had the ultimate baseball audience all to himself? How many Rickeyisms would he spout? How many times would he refer to himself in the third person? How many times would he tell an audience full of greats just how great *he* was? Baseball was tantalized by the prospect of Rickey on Rickey, which was certain to be unforgettable.

What Rickey saw in the anticipation, however, was not a respectful enthusiasm for his arrival at Mount Olympus, but a trap. He had never lived down the widespread belief that his megalomania had humiliated poor Lou Brock. Even the people who laughed it off as a harmless Rickey quirk felt sorry that day for Brock, the game's humble gentleman—just as Jeff Idelson had felt for Pamela. Rickey believed that what really awaited him was not a celebration but the ultimate opportunity for the entire baseball world to watch Rickey embarrass himself, to be on display as a self-absorbed superstar butchering the English language.

The potential for laughs wasn't the only reason everyone was anticipating Rickey's speech. Jeff Idelson, the president of the Hall of Fame, feared for the players, for the Hall of Fame itself—and for Rickey. Nobody wanted to see great players embarrass themselves during their finest hour. Induction was the culmination of a life's work, and it was Idelson's job to position the inductees for success.

When Rickey submitted his first speech to the Hall, Idelson kindly recalled that it was "not great." So what did Rickey do? He went back to school. Telling hardly a soul, he had Fred Atkins connect him with the communications department at the local junior college, Laney College in Oakland. Rickey would work on his speech in a college setting.

Guiding this process was not just any old professor but Dr. Earl Robinson, who was part of the great Berkeley High tradition of baseball players. Robinson even made the big leagues, with the Dodgers in 1958—the year Rickey was born. Robinson also played for the Orioles. He wasn't in the majors long—just 170 games over four years—but he was one of the few people on earth who could say that he had played in the major leagues.

Fred had taken a broadcast course at Laney years earlier, and Dr. Robinson was his instructor. When news broke of Rickey's induction, Dr. Robinson, with Fred's help, got Rickey into his class. Dr. Robinson told the class that Rickey could use some help with his Hall of Fame speech because he didn't love public speaking and always felt ill at ease in academic settings. Then Rickey showed up every day and Dr. Robinson's class critiqued his Hall of Fame speech for content, cadence, and physical delivery.

The Hall had provided inductees with a neat three-ring binder to hold their speech, each page fitted into a plastic sleeve in order to avoid the possibility of disaster, such as the pages falling out of order, or getting blown away or wet from rain. Rickey was ready. To slow down his pace and calm his anxiety about public speaking, Rickey had put the pages of his speech in reverse order. That way he wouldn't rush.

Dressed in a loose, cream-colored suit, Rickey took the podium:

Hey, hey. I hope everyone is having a great time. First, I would like to thank God, the Baseball Writers' Association of America, and the Commissioner of Baseball for this true honor. I also want to thank the members of the Hall of Fame for being here today. Thank you.

I love the game of baseball. That's why it was so hard for me to walk away from the game. I thought if Satchel Paige can still play in major league baseball at the age of 45, then with my dedication, hard work, and desire, I can play the game until my body said it was time to hang it up.

I wouldn't be standing here today if it wasn't for my wife, Pamela, who took care of the home while I was away, and brought up our wonderful daughters and supported me in my career. Thank you, and I love you.

To all my beautiful and intelligent daughters, I wouldn't be a complete man without your love and support. I love you, girls.

A special thanks to my mother, Bobbie. Back in high school, I played football, a little hoops and baseball. My dream was to play football for the Oakland Raiders. But my mom thought I would get hurt playing football, so she chose baseball for me. I guess moms do know best. Thanks, Mom.

I would like to say thanks to my father, my brothers, and my sister for their support. To my father and mother-in-law for always being there when I need them. I would like to say thank you.

Several of my high school friends are here today to help me celebrate this wonderful and important event. I want to say thank you.

Now let me tell you a story about how I got into playing baseball. When I was a kid in Oakland, Mr. Hank Thomas [*sic*] tricked me into playing Babe Ruth baseball by coming to pick me up with a glazed doughnut and a cup of hot chocolate. (*laughter*) That was the way he would get me up and out of bed and on to the ballpark.

My first year in high school, my favorite sport was football. I did not like baseball. My counselor, Mrs. Wilkinson, bribed me into playing baseball (*laughter*). She would pay me a quarter every time I would get a hit, a run scored, or stole a base.

After my first 10 games, I had 30 hits, 25 runs scored, and 33 steals. Not bad money for a kid in high school. (*laughter*)

As a kid growing up in Oakland, my heroes were Jackie Robinson, Willie Mays, Hank Aaron, Reggie Jackson. What about that Reggie Jackson? (*laughter*) I stand out on the ballpark in the parking lot waiting for Reggie Jackson to give me an autograph. Reggie used to come out all the time and I'd say, "Reggie, can I have an autograph?" He would pass me a pen with his name on it. (*laughter*) He never gave me an autograph. (*laughter*)

To all my coaches out there that taught me along the way, I want to say thank you for believing in me.

I would like to give a very, very special thanks to James Guinn, the scout that signed me out of high school. He believed in my talent as a baseball player when teams was afraid to draft players that throw left-handed and bat right-handed.

In 1976, my first year in the minor league, my coach, Tom Treblehorn, helped me develop my skill in baserunning and taught me to play the game hard. I had not perfected how to take a lead or how to slide. Tom asked me to come to practice early every day and work on my sliding and base-running skill. I guess, Tom, that hard work paid off for me, and I am very grateful.

In June of 1979, I received a call from Charlie O. Finley. He wanted me to play in the big league for the Oakland A's. That was the most thrilling time of my life, playing the game that I loved in my hometown in front of my family and friends was a dream come true. Charlie, wherever you at, and that donkey (*laughter*), I want to say thank you for the opportunity.

In 1980, the A's hired a new manager that I would look up to for the rest of my life, one of the best teachers and managers anyone could ever play for, Mr. Billy Martin. Billy always got the most out of me. He taught me to compete at the highest level and respect the game of baseball. Billy, I miss you very much, and I wish you were here with me today.

To the Haas family, Mr. Wolff of the Oakland A's, the City of

Oakland, John Moores of the San Diego Padres, George Steinbrenner of the New York Yankees, and the other general managers and owners of Major League Baseball teams, I would not
be here or the player that I became. Thank you for giving me the
chance to play the game that I love so much.

I played with some of the greatest players in the game, Jim
Rice, Don Mattingly, Dave Winfield, Tony Gwynn, I called him
"Dennis the Eck," Cal Ripken Jr., Dave Henderson, and my best
friend and loyal friend Dave Stewart, and so many other players
that I will never forget.

It's an honor to be inducted into the Baseball Hall of Fame
and have my name next to players like Jackie Robinson, Babe
Ruth, Willie Mays, Hank Aaron, Lou Gehrig, Roberto Clemente,
and the list goes on and on.

I would like to congratulate Jim Rice and Joe Gordon. It
is a pleasure to be inducted into the Hall of Fame with you
gentlemen.

In my career, I had the good fortune to play for nine teams.
It was wonderful because this allowed me to meet fans all over
the country. It's the fans that makes the game fun. To all the fans,
thank you. Thank you. Thank you for your wonderful support
over all these years.

I would like to thank everyone here and all over the country
for sharing this special moment with me and my family. To all
the kids out there: Follow your dream. Believe in your dream.
Because dreams do come true.

When you think of me, I would like you to remember that kid
from the inner city that played the game with all of his heart and
never took the game for granted. (*applause*) Thanks to everyone
here for making my dream come true today.

In closing, I would like to say my favorite hero was Muhammad Ali. He said at one time, "I am the greatest." (*laughter*) That
is something I always wanted to be. And now that the association has voted me into the Baseball Hall of Fame, my journey
as a player is complete. I am now in the class of the greatest
players of all time. And at this moment, I am very, very *humble*.
Thank you.

Rickey walked away from the podium to a standing ovation. Jim Rice, Tom Seaver, Rod Carew, Robin Yount, Henry Aaron, and Sandy Koufax all congratulated him. On the dais, when Rickey mentioned Ali, the crowd murmured with anticipatory laughter. *Here it comes. It's Rickey Time.* When he repeated Ali's famous refrain, the murmur grew. *Rickey was going to say it again.* He was going to do it. He was going to say he was the greatest of all time. When he didn't, when he pivoted toward humility instead, Rickey and baseball had achieved a rapprochement that had eluded both for 40 years. Rickey had lowered his defenses; it was safe to be vulnerable now. All of the fights—for money, for respect, for status, for being seen as a great competitor—they were all over now.

The game could in return go beyond acknowledging Rickey's greatness and finally accept him not just as a legend—as a player he had already secured that status long ago—but as a full member of the institution. Rickey could now be counted on to give the game the requisite gratitude that softened the edges of even the most ferocious competitors once the competition ended. When he professed his love for the sport, the game could accept it now without the conditions that had always kept Rickey at a certain distance from the inner circle of greatness. He had finally overcome the accusation of jaking it, and he was also now forgiven for the record-breaking speech of 1991. The Hall of Fame speech permanently rehabilitated Rickey in the public's mind. "Basically, I'm reflecting back to when he broke Brock's record and what he was saying then," Jeff Idelson said, "and all I could think was, 'This guy has come full circle.' He crushed [the speech]. He crushed it in terms of content, and in terms of delivery."

The ones who loved him most had feared that Rickey would embarrass himself in front of one of America's august institutions, before a predominantly white audience. That Rickey would just give them more fuel to tilt their opinion of him toward the third-person clown and away from dignified Hall of Famer. Mike Norris, who was with Rickey in Jersey City back in '78, helping him improve his reading, called Rickey months before the induction and offered him assistance with his speech. Rickey didn't tell him he was taking speech classes at Laney.

"I told him I'd help him with the speech if he needed it. He said, 'I got this,'" Norris recalled. "I said to myself, 'You sure about that?' I was so proud of him because you could see how important that moment was to him. People treated him like he was some kind of joker, but Rickey took what he could do *seriously*. When he finished, I said, 'I'll be damned. That nigga knocked it outta the park.'"

Rickey accepted the congratulations he received after the speech, but he wasn't fooled. He knew he was being lauded because he expressed a humility before an audience of people who had not believed he possessed humility and were convinced of his self-centeredness. Rickey knew it was no compliment to exceed low expectations. He also knew he had surprised the many who thought he was dumb.

"I was analyzed by the students. They were saying, 'Whatever you're trying to get to, we're going to analyze you and say if it's good, bad, this and that, analyze how you approached it," Rickey recalled of his prep at Laney. "I didn't want to mess up that speech. And everybody was saying, 'The third person, and what's he gonna say?' and I said, this time, I'm going to take the time and go and learn, take the time we never got growing up. It's gonna make a big difference.

"I didn't make a fool of myself, and I'm going to tell you the honest to God's truth: that's what they were waiting on. And when I didn't, they were *shocked*. When it was over, people said, 'Oh, great speech! That was great!' Nah. You were shocked I didn't make a goddamned fool out of myself."

When the A's traded Rickey to the Yankees in 1984, his number 35 became available. Although the old-school A's fans still associated 35 with Rickey, during the big years the number belonged to Bob Welch. When the A's said that Rickey was no longer in their plans and he went to the Mets after the 1998 season, his Hall of Fame credentials cemented, the A's didn't save number 24 for Rickey's eventual retirement. They were quietly upset that he had left—again. They didn't even wait a season to give away his number, and they didn't even give it to some five-tool outfielder. They assigned the famed number 24 to a *pitcher*—that old, cantankerous St. Bernard of a reliever, Doug Jones.

Now, though, 24 would be immortalized. Days after Cooperstown, the A's retired number 24 during a pregame ceremony on August 1. Rickey joined Catfish Hunter, Rollie Fingers, Dennis Eckersley, and Reggie as one of five Oakland players whose number had been retired since the franchise arrived in 1968. The catcher Ray Fosse handled the proceedings. Rickey held a bouquet of roses before stepping to the podium, where he gave the crowd some third-person fan service.

"I'd like to share a little Rickeyism with you: Rickey has tears in his eyes . . . Rickey has love in his heart for you . . . Rickey is so very, very, very humble." The place went wild.

The public edges may have softened, but he was still Rickey. Behind closed doors Rickey was still all business. He never forgot what Willie Mays had told him: nobody gets anything for free.

When his election to the Hall was announced, MLB Network, the house organ of Major League Baseball, wanted to do a sit-down with baseball's newest Hall of Famer. Rickey's people spoke to MLB, and when it was over, Rickey had agreed to do the interview—for $5,000.

In 2017, as part of the A's positioning Rickey as the centerpiece of its commitment to Oakland, the team decided to honor Rickey. They weren't going to name the stadium after Rickey—naming rights were far too lucrative to allow that—but the team president, Dave Kaval, had another idea: naming the field after Rickey. That would solidify the A's new marketing slogan, "Rooted in Oakland," and keep people from thinking the A's were constantly trying to engineer their way out of town. With the A's playing on Rickey Henderson Field, there were now three baseball fields in Oakland named after him. Arroyo Park in East Oakland and the new baseball diamond at Oakland Tech also bore his name.

For honoring him by naming the field after him, Rickey, again, wanted gifts. His wish list included a boat as well as that most elusive of prizes he had not received from the Mets: he told the A's he was open to the gift of a Winnebago—the return of the Madden Cruiser. The A's gave him a brand-new Cadillac Escalade.

Pamela wrote the speech, as she had always done on so many of the big occasions in the past 40 years. Their routine for handling Rickey's public appearances had been solid. Forever devoted to his greatness, Pamela did the writing; she knew how to make sure he always looked good and how to remind everyone of all of the hard work, sacrifice, and single-mindedness that went into the making of the legend. His talent was natural, but it was also cultivated and nurtured. This speech for the naming ceremony wouldn't be very different from all the others and would hold no surprises—until the big surprise came.

Rickey stepped onto the field, serenaded the crowd, soaked up the honor of the green-white-and-gold-painted patch of field behind home plate where his name and number now adorned the A's home field—and then went completely off script. He did not mention Pamela, and he barely mentioned the family. In that moment Rickey reverted back to a level of conceit that the afterglow of the Hall of Fame induction had done so much to eliminate.

When Rickey didn't mention her by name in the ceremony for breaking the record in 1991, Pamela had let that one slide. This time she was furious. But the public ate it up, not knowing the difference between this Rickey and any other Rickey. He was still their guy, but Pamela saw a change in him. Periodically, Pamela would grow upset with Walt McCreary's charm offensive on social media—posting photos of Rickey kissing babies and glad-handing with the public while he was becoming less connected to family, more unto himself. Walt was rebuilding Rickey's public brand, but in his speech for this latest moment of glory, when he had deliberately ignored her, throwing her off the team when they had always been together, was painfully defining.

"It took a *lot* of effort not to make a scene, I was so upset," Pamela recalled. "During that period, when they named that field after him, it was like he was turning into a monster. It was like the persona of Rickey began to take over, and he was becoming more persona than he was the actual person.

"But that's Rickey. I understand it too, that single focus, to shut everything out. To be the center is what it takes to achieve all the things he has achieved. You have to put yourself first. Always. Above everything. That is one of the things that I always admired about him—when he sets his mind to doing something, nothing gets in the way. But there's also a price, and the people close to you pay that price. There have been opportunities where he has had a chance to be both, to be as great a man as he was an athlete. Those opportunities have been there, but sometimes . . . it was why we always knew the time we were able to spend as a family was so important. I always said Rickey lived his life with the same philosophy he used to steal bases: If I don't get caught, I'm safe." He had been put on that pedestal for so long, he lost some of himself."

Rickey was not only a Hall of Famer, but a vindicated one. The century-old culture had said that the prerequisite for any outfielder worth his salt was playing 150 games. Beginning in 1954, and after losing his second and third seasons to military service, Willie Mays played 150 games in 13 *consecutive seasons,* in the first eight of which baseball was playing a 154-game schedule. In those eight years, 1954 to 1961, Mays missed a grand total of 15 games. During the 13 straight years of playing 150 or more games, he missed 40. Henry Aaron played 150 games in nine straight years and in 13 of 14 seasons.

In those days, games played was a bedrock statistic of durability, dedication, toughness—but those were also the days when players had virtually no power to say they needed a break. While Bob Ryan argued that Rickey could have been even better had he played *more,* how much better could Mays or Aaron have been if they played *less?* During that 13-year stretch, Mays played 2,002 games and hit .318 with 518 home runs, but would those numbers have been even higher if he'd played at a time when the game believed that his body was worth protecting and he'd had a say in how to protect it, as Rickey did? The practices of Mays's time and earlier had filled a virtual graveyard of dead, shortened, or never-was careers; victims of overuse, players had been afraid of being discarded if they disclosed an injury. This was what had happened to Rickey's best friend, Fred Atkins, years earlier when he joined the Yankees system as a high school kid with a bum arm and no leverage to tell anyone who might have been able to help.

The players knew they were disposable, even when they were making the big dollars, even when they were on top, the best in the world, because the owners knew that eventually *all* the players could be replaced and that one day, through advancing age or declining performance, they would be. Nobody played forever, and at some point on the way down the owners and their minions would be waiting.

The players who didn't know this, well, all they needed to do was open a history book and read about how the game treated the Babe when he was done: the game tossed aside the great Babe Ruth like a used dishrag, after all he'd done to transform baseball into the national game. Everybody aged, and only the truly naive or the astonishingly arrogant had any illusions about the power dynamics at play. All anyone had to do was look at the litany of players' bodies that had been broken trying to please the fans and the owners, trying to color inside the lines of the culture. What was baseball culture anyway, other than a set of customs the players inherited but did not create when they first put on a uniform? Maybe the culture was wrong.

What, in the end, did being a good soldier get players anyway? Tim Raines was a good soldier—the writers never said *he* jaked it. But after Raines played 150 games in five straight seasons, he would never be the same player again. He'd play 14 more seasons and only hit 150 games once. Previously, he'd stolen 70 bases in six straight years. After 150-plus games in each of those five pounding straight years, Raines would reach 50 steals just twice. When it was over, it was Raines who paid the price: he was ultimately elected to the Hall of Fame, but only after being omitted from consideration—the voters' penalty for having a worn-out body too early, for being a part-time player much of the time in his last 11 years in the big leagues, for not being good enough long enough.

Mattingly poured his everything into the sport. Steinbrenner still penny-pinched him every off-season, even as Donnie Baseball kept up a Hall of Fame pace, playing 153, 159, and 162 games from 1984 to 1986. Then the body gave out, but Donnie grimly soldiered on at first base with a bad back. Despite his relentless power and his devastating ability to produce runs, his Hall of Fame trajectory faded as his story became one of baseball's what-ifs. Vince Coleman dutifully played his 150 games in each of his first four seasons—he had even more stolen bases over that period than Rickey—but after his sixth year Coleman would never again surpass the 145-game plateau and he stole more than 45 bases just once more.

Rickey, meanwhile, played 150 games just four times over a quarter-century, but still reached several Aaron-Mays-Ruth-Cobb benchmarks. "If Rickey had done what everyone told him to do, played when he knew better, played when every manager told him to, he would have never, ever produced the kind of all-time numbers that he did," Dave Stewart said. "He would have never made it. Nobody put their body through as much as Rickey did. I say this all the time: nobody played the game harder than Rickey. His game was far too physical. He would have never been able to withstand what the season would have done to his body."

"They tried to control him," Shooty Babitt said. "That's the one thing baseball wants you to do, and that's conform. Rickey wouldn't conform. He couldn't be controlled. And now look. After all those years, baseball has come around to his position. Now they're resting guys to preserve their legs after all those years of criticizing Rickey for protecting his body."

Even Tony La Russa, Rickey's toughest manager, admitted years after the fact that he had been wrong. "Rickey knew his body better than anyone else," La Russa recalled. "I have to admit I was wrong about him. He knew his body, how it felt, what it could do. As manager, I would ask him how he felt, and he would tell me '70 percent.' Seventy percent wasn't good enough for him to play, but I'd tell him that 70 percent of Rickey Henderson was better than 100 percent of anybody else I had on the bench. There were times he did not play even when that 70 percent, I thought, could have benefited the team. But when you look at the end results of what he did, the totality of his career achievements cannot be argued."

Now the sport was catching up to him. Teams routinely used terms like "load management," sports corporate shorthand for resting players, a practice Rickey employed for himself when the game wouldn't. It had evolved as managers, GMs, and front offices witnessed attrition masquerading as machismo or worse, as "professionalism." People were already saying that the big guy in Anaheim, Mike Trout, just might be the greatest player of all time. Three-time MVP, with nine straight top-five finishes, $430 million Trout played at least 157 games in four straight years and hadn't reached 140 games since. He was plagued by injuries—just as had happened with so many of the greats who needed their legs as much as their bat.

The evolution of the game gave Rickey a measure of satisfaction. Ultimately he had been right, but he could never forget his bitter memories of 1987, the fights he did not believe had needed to be fought. Only three players in the history of the sport, Pete Rose, Carl Yastrzemski, and Henry Aaron, played more games than Rickey, and yet the one person who bled to play baseball was accused for most of his career of not wanting to; no volume of redemptive Rickey stories and myths could change that. As an undisputed legend, Rickey would now be celebrated for his longevity, and with those commendations came tacit acknowledgment that, in the end, he had understood the game better than the people who gave the orders. He was vindicated.

"Tell me something," Rickey said. "How in the hell you gonna steal fourteen hundred bases jaking it? How could you do what I did, for as long as I did it, and say I didn't want to be out there?"

Epilogue

I N FEBRUARY 2020, weeks before the coronavirus pandemic shut down baseball, Rickey was walking along the back fields being quizzed about his successes, about the catchers whose lives he made miserable. He said that he went by feel and memory, never looking at numbers. No stats.

Rick Dempsey?

"Wore his ass out."

Jim Sundberg?

"Wore *his* ass out."

Ernie Whitt?

"What you think?"

The records show that Rickey stole 37 bases in 44 attempts against Dempsey, 54 of 67 against Sundberg, and 48 of 58 against Whitt. Reflecting on past battles, he summoned his gut and guessed that his worst percentages were against Bob Boone and Lance Parrish, stalwart receivers with the Angels and Tigers—and he was right. The records show that Rickey stole bases at an 80 percent success rate in his career, but that Bob Boone threw Rickey out 56 percent of the time and Parrish threw Rickey out the most—17 times on 53 attempts.

"Hmmm," Rickey said. "Boonie, I could never read him. He had my number, but Parrish? That wasn't Lance. That was Sparky Anderson in the dugout. Sparky had that magic."

He cannot believe that over his career he hit just .163 against Eckersley—8-for-49, one double, no homers, 11 punchouts.

"Damn. That bad? Can't be," Rickey says. "I musta got him when it counted."

In the Hohokam Park clubhouse, the A's Mesa, Arizona, spring training home, Rickey sat at a table with the players. They really were kids to him now—a couple of A's prospects were young enough to be his grandchildren. Some of these players were born in the 2000s. Rickey was where he had always been at this time of year—playing cards before the morning stretch.

So much of the A's clubhouse was unchanged. The A's trained in Scottsdale and later Phoenix when Rickey played, but in Mesa the clubhouse man, Steve Vucinich, was exactly where he had been since day one when the team first arrived from Kansas City in 1968. Mickey Morabito, the traveling secretary, was there too, just as he had been since 1980, when Billy brought him to Oakland from the Yankees. The continuity of the A's clubhouse was special in baseball, Oakland being the last mom-and-pop shop in the game. GM Billy Beane, the celebrity architect of Moneyball, had been with the organization for 35 years—and counting. Sandy Alderson, who started with the A's 40 years earlier—and launched Beane's executive career—had returned as a special assistant.

The great championship run of 1988–1990, fueled by Rickey and Stew in 1989, had grown distant. Bob Welch, Dave Henderson, Tony Phillips, and Don Baylor, as well as broadcasters Bill King, Lon Simmons, and Ray Fosse, the legendary voices of Oakland, had all passed. In June 2020, Claudell Washington died of prostate cancer at age 65, his murky estrangement with Rickey over money and other issues never quite resolved. Although slowed by the effects of Parkinson's disease, the great Dave Parker carried on; he wrote a memoir in 2020 because, he said, "I didn't know how much more time I would have if I didn't do it now." Time is calling.

At the end of the 2021 season, even Vucinich would call it a 54-year career, and as if on cue, the A's renewed their threats to leave town. The target was once again Vegas, but this time things were different: Las Vegas was now a legitimate destination for professional sports teams. The tacit prohibition against the city had been lifted when the NHL awarded Vegas the expansion Golden Knights, and then again in 2020 when the Raiders left Oakland again, for the second time. The NBA's Warriors left Oakland too, moving back to San Francisco in 2019.

With Oakland's other two professional sports teams already gone, the door had never been more open for the A's to leave too, closing the longest tenure of the Athletics franchise in any of its three cities. Dave Stewart, one of the true sons of Oakland, put his hands in the soil and made a bid to buy a portion of the Coliseum footprint in an attempt to keep the A's and revitalize East Oakland, but the A's had long decided that the Coliseum site, just blocks from his childhood home, had run its course.

The legend of Oakland continued, but the baseball players it nurtured began inevitably succumbing to age. The first generation, once the gold standard of talent for any city, yielded its grip. In 2019, the indomitable Frank Robinson passed at 83. Joe Morgan, the premier second baseman of his time, died the next year, at 77. Vada Pinson and Curt Flood were already gone.

After the second generation—led by Rickey and including Lloyd Moseby, Gary Pettis, Bip Roberts, and Dave Stewart—retired, Oakland would turn away from baseball just as much of the rest of Black America did and become better known for A-list superstars who dazzled in other sports. Marshawn Lynch from Oakland Tech was a champion running back in the NFL. Damian Lillard was unheralded at Oakland High (a two-star recruit!) but became one of the great players in the NBA. Jason Kidd, once a star basketball *and* baseball player at St. Joseph's in Alameda, landed in the NBA Hall of Fame.

As baseball diminished nationally, so too did its influence on the Oakland streets. The last A-list, Oakland-born heir to baseball glory was Jimmy Rollins—who retired from the game in 2016. And the kids who now played on the diamonds that bore Rickey's name? Well, so many of them who were just like he once was—same swagger, same Oakland style (*You must not know who I am!*), hitting line drives and breaking tackles—were now making a different choice from the one Rickey made when he was 17. These kids were choosing football over baseball. Baseball had once held their parents and grandparents tightly in its grip, but then it lost them all. At the big league level, the game was now only 7.7 percent Black. Rickey's name was painted into the grass at the Coliseum, his high school baseball field carried his name, and there was talk about erecting what he *really* wanted—a statue—in front of the Coliseum, but all this was happening at a time when fewer Black kids were choosing baseball. His style of play grew more singular than universal, and his team was trying to engineer itself out of town, a move that threatened to produce the opposite of a legacy.

Yet Rickey remained. Each year he would arrive at Hohokam Park as an instructor. Nobody, not even the manager, Bob Melvin, knew exactly *when* Rickey would show (he was always on Rickey Time), but they knew he was coming. Melvin kept a schedule of instructors, entering the dates they'd be instructing next to each name—Dallas Braden or Dave Stewart, for example. Next to Rickey's name? A string of question marks.

When he did arrive, Rickey could be found in his most familiar place— the clubhouse. Eating breakfast on a paper plate, in uniform, getting ready for work with the outfielders, but not before playing cards, looking for a mark. Making a little extra money off the greenhorns never hurt.

In the present, Rickey was there in the flesh, admired and revered, but even he of the low body fat and never-ending youth often seemed like a ghost of another era. Out in the field, he gave players clinics on baserunning—and especially that lost art to the game that he once dominated, base stealing. Invariably, he heard the same words at least a couple of times a day: *Rickey, you look like you could still play.* At Fitch Park, the A's minor league complex, Rickey stood in the outfield, balancing himself on a fungo, a ring of kid prospects and big leaguers forming a circle around him as he broke down his techniques—the stone tablets from the mountaintop.

The sport would always marvel at what Rickey could do on a ball field, but what Rickey did essentially no longer exists. During the 2019 season, 13 *teams* stole fewer bases than the 66 Rickey swiped in 1998—*when he was 39.*

When Billy Beane assessed Rickey's game and projected how he would be utilized in today's modern game, the player he returned with was not quite Rickey Henderson. "I think he would be closer to [Mike] Trout," Beane said. "Even with the risk associated with stolen bases, Rickey would still be a great player, but I think today his power would be emphasized over his speed—fewer stolen bases in exchange for more pop from his bat. Rickey doesn't have Trout's power, but he has more than enough power to be a consistent 30-homer guy today. No one is ever going to steal 130 bases again, but because of Rickey's eye at the plate, the power from the leadoff position, he'd still be a very valuable commodity. He'd still be a dominant, dominant, player."

The big numbers would still be there, Beane argued, just in different columns. That sounded good, but a Rickey Henderson who is not a threat to steal, whose work is done mostly in the batter's box and not just as importantly across the basepaths, is a more homogenized, less dangerous Rickey. The Rickey of 1982 would not be allowed to be Rickey today, for the numbers say his old game would be bad for business. There's too much risk in it, and with today's instant replay challenges to stolen bases, when players are being called *out* for being one one-millionth of a millimeter off the base, the risk has increased.

Rickey looked across the expanse of the outfields and saw an increasingly unrecognizable game. "A lot of today's players don't have that instinct," he said in the dugout. "They're vulnerable. They don't think, *I know good and doggone well I'm fast as hell. I know my chances are 85 percent I'm going to be safe. So why aren't you letting me go?* I said that to Billy Martin, 'Why would you give me the "stop" sign?'

"The only way I'd agree with that is if I'm getting thrown out 50 percent of the time. Then I'd say, 'Okay, you can control that part of the game.' But if I have a guy who can run, why would I keep him from running? Risk. *Risk?* But what is the risk you're taking thinking this fool in the batter's box can get me over? So now we might not score. We have a harder chance to score, and we gotta get more hits."

Rickey told the players to be fearless, to make the pitchers know their names. He reminded them that being on the basepaths wasn't a rest stop, but a place where they earned their money. He encouraged them to dig into themselves and find their inner Rickey Style. The players listened and nodded and smiled at the Hall of Famer, and that was the thing with Rickey: he could make swiping a bag *sound* as easy as he made it look. One year during a master class on larceny the A's third baseman and future AL MVP Josh Donaldson would say, "Rickey, that's easy for *you* to say. You're Rickey Henderson. *You* can do that. *We* can't."

The players headed out to the field, spikes clacking against the stairs and down into the tunnel leading to the dugout. Rickey followed along, in uniform, lines deepening across his face, a dusting of gray along his jawline, but still trim, still effortlessly fit, even though he hadn't swung a bat in the major leagues in 17 years.

Back in 2009, after his induction was announced, Rickey appeared at a press conference in New York, joined by fellow inductee Jim Rice. A reporter asked Rice about Boston second baseman Dustin Pedroia's availability for baseball's newest showcase, the World Baseball Classic. While Rice answered questions about the WBC, Rickey leaned over and whispered to Jeff Idelson, the president of the Hall of Fame.

"The WBC? What is it? Some kind of wrestling thing?"

"No. It's baseball. The World Baseball Classic."

Rickey asked Idelson, "Can I play?"

He was 50 years old, and indeed he intended to play forever—but not at the cost of immortality. He then whispered to Idelson: Would playing in the WBC affect his Hall of Fame chances?

"Chances?" a confounded Idelson said. "What chances? You're already in."

As of July 2021, 22,467 players had appeared in a Major League Baseball game, and no position player who began his career in the 20th century had played more seasons than the legendary Rickey Henderson.

Mark Kotsay, an A's instructor and Rickey's former teammate in San Diego, had heard a lot about the Rickey legend. As a young center fielder, Kotsay once played between Rickey in left and Tony Gwynn in right—that's 6,196 combined hits if you're scoring at home. Kotsay had heard all the stories, like the time Rickey was sitting in the seat on the team bus reserved for Gwynn, the greatest of the Padres. When Gwynn boarded and saw Rickey in his seat, the other players started to tell Rickey the rules—that was Tony Gwynn's seat. Gwynn was unaffected. "It's okay," Gwynn said. "Rickey's got tenure."

"*Ten*ure?" Rickey said. "Rickey's got *sixteen* years."

It was another of those stories repeated so many times that it was passed off as fact, and it might have been, but it also very easily could have been another apocryphal Rickey story. Kotsay reminded Rickey of one fact that was indeed true: Rickey never actually retired from baseball. Having never filed the retirement papers required by the league, Rickey never appeared on baseball's voluntarily retired list—and technically that made Rickey Nelson Henley Henderson, age 61, an eligible free agent.

Nodding his head in proud affirmation, older than all but four *managers* in the game at the time, Rickey confirmed it: he *hadn't* officially quit, even though he hadn't appeared in a big league game in nearly two decades. Pamela knew it was true, because at home Rickey would still express surprise that the phone no longer rang. "He couldn't understand it. He could still run. He still has his reflexes. He still has his eye at the plate, and he thinks he can do better than some of these guys making $50 million."

It was in that spirit that Rickey headed toward the dugout and, without a hint of sarcasm, reaffirmed his position. "I think," he said, "I could still help a team."

Acknowledgments

The genesis of this project began in February 2014 at the National Portrait Gallery in Washington, DC, during a celebration of Henry Aaron's 80th birthday. In between events with Henry, I met Pamela Henderson, who mentioned that, with his staggering career achievements, Rickey was deserving of a full-length biography. The book would not have been possible without Pamela's guidance, recollections, and candor. It was her insistence that Rickey not be diminished as the decades move forward—or worse, be forgotten, as eventually even the greatest of players will be without surviving stories. May we all be so fortunate as to have someone as devoted to our lives and committed to our successes as Pamela has been to Rickey's over nearly a half-century—and may we be wise enough to recognize our good luck should it ever occur.

For his part, Rickey was not particularly enthusiastic about being written about, especially in an unauthorized format—meaning, without his control. Nevertheless, between 2018 and 2020 he and I sat down for four interview sessions, and I am grateful for his time. No secondhand story or video can match the power of witnessing Rickey Henderson in person or listening to him tell his tale. You had to be there.

The original subtitle of this book was "Rickey Henderson and the Legend of Oakland." There may be no more unique place in America that combines the story of Black America, the promise of the Great Migration, and the influence of sports on American culture than Oakland. Special thanks go to one of the great legends of Oakland, Dave Stewart, for his unflinching recollections, guidance, and patience. Thank you to the other legends of Oakland for their time: Monte Poole, Gary Pettis, Lloyd Moseby, Mike Hammock, Fred Atkins, Bip Roberts, Jimmy Rollins, and two of their Berkeley counterparts, J. J. Guinn and Shooty Babitt, who were instrumental during a pandemic in putting me in contact with so many hard-to-find sources. Mr. Guinn, who signed Rickey as a 17-year-old and has been a godfather of Oakland baseball for more than a half-century, was unfailingly gracious with his time. Shooty is a living encyclopedia of East Bay baseball and a living part of that heritage, and was willing to vouch for me with potentially difficult interview subjects. The same was true with Bip Roberts, whom along with Rickey I was fortunate to cover during the 1998 season when I was the Oakland A's beat writer for the *San Jose Mercury News*. Lonnie Murray was invaluable to the completion of this book in far too many ways to count.

Special thanks also to one of the Black Aces, Mike Norris, whose generous recollections of his baseball life over dozens of text messages and conversations did so much to shape this project.

I always call the Oakland A's the last mom-and-pop store in baseball, and none of these stories would have been possible without the deep institutional memory of its alumni: Steve Vucinich, Art Howe, Billy Beane, Ron Washington, Larry Davis, Dennis Eckersley, Mickey Morabito, Pamela Pitts, Mike Selleck, Bobby Alejo, Sandy Alderson, Detra Paige, Steve Sayles, Debbie Gallas, Chad Huss, Mike Thalblum, Andy Dolich, and Roy Eisenhardt. Thank you to the photographers whose images of Rickey appear in this book: Matthew J. Lee, Brita Meng Outzen, and Ronnie Riesterer. A special thank-you goes out to both the legendary Z Man, photographer Michael Zagaris, who was there for it all and has the pictures to prove it, and Brad Mangin, another legendary Oakland-made photographer, who selflessly and on extremely short notice helped research, choose, and arrange the photos in this book.

Baseball is full of great professionals. On the public relations side of things, my thanks go to Pam Ganley Kenn at the Boston Red Sox, Richard Griffin with the Toronto Blue Jays, the Texas Rangers' John Blake, the A's Fernando Alcala, the Angels' Tim Mead, Chris Dahl from the Players Association, and John Thorn at MLB, all of whom were extremely helpful.

The publishing industry underwent a metaphorical hurricane during this book's writing as Houghton Mifflin Harcourt's trade division was acquired by HarperCollins, but thank you to Susan Canavan, the original HMH editor who believed in this book. Having written two previous books with her, I am grateful that Rakia Clark, who is not a hard-core baseball person, undertook the difficult task of shepherding a book already in progress. Rakia admirably pinch-hit to see this project to the finish line.

Special thanks as always to my agent, Deirdre Mullane. The inner circle invariably begins with Lisa Davis for all things research, journalism, and friendship. Christopher Sauceda and Toni Smith-Thompson read each chapter of the manuscript and offered much-needed guidance. Thank you to Joanna Cornish for assistance with research and interviews under difficult circumstances, and to Dart Adams for research, encouragement, and support. Professor Lou Moore could always be counted on at a moment's notice for wisdom, with voluminous archival support at the ready.

Cassidy Lent and the research staff at the Baseball Hall of Fame were always courteous and professional and an invaluable resource, especially Bill Francis, who over several books of mine over two decades now has always been so selfless with his time. Thank you to El Presidente, former Hall president Jeff Idelson, for his Rickey thoughts. Journalism is a competitive business, but thank you to Brian Murphy, Susan Slusser, Gary Washburn, Bob Nightengale, Jeff Passan, Jeff Pearlman, Claire Smith, Steve Kettmann, Dave Sheinin, Sweeny Murti, George King, Ray Ratto, Jack Curry, Drew Olson, Jeff Horrigan, Bob Klapisch, Marcus Thompson, and Ken Rosenthal for their willingness to make a connection, provide a phone number, and share recollections.

A special thank-you also goes out to Rickey superfan Kent Corser for his insights on the collectibles market and for introducing me to Walt McCreary, who was uncommonly generous with his recollections and whose more than 45-year friendship with Rickey should one day be its own movie.

Retrosheet.org, www.baseballreference.com, Newspapers.com, and the Society for American Baseball Research are invaluable baseball resources for any baseball project, and even as it destroys democracy as we know it, Facebook nevertheless offered extremely helpful resources locating sources in the numerous Oakland A's and Oakland History fan pages.

Lastly, but never forgotten, thank you to my late friend Pedro Gomez, who took an interest in the work and in the people that came with it like no other. Pedro had a watchful eye on me from the first day I set foot in a big league clubhouse back in 1993, and throughout the researching and writing of this book, he could always be counted on to send a text or to call, asking, "Have you spoken to . . . ?" or "I have a number if you need it," or "Did I ever tell you about that night in '92 when Rickey . . . ?" Pedro made sure I understood the context of a given year, event, or issue, and he turned the isolation of book writing into community, its own home movie. The only thing bigger than Pedro's rolodex was his heart.

Interviews

Sandy Alderson, Bob Alejo, Fred Atkins, Shooty Babitt, Dusty Baker, Billy Beane, Jason Beatty, Paul Beeston, Jerry Blevins, Jim Bloom, Vida Blue, Bruce Bochy, Bob Boone, Pat Borders, Ian Browne, Ellis Burks, Greg Cadaret, Bert Campaneris, Joe Carter, Peter Chase, Dawn Chmielewski, Tony Clark, Michael Collazo, David Cone, Jim Darby, Brian Davis, Mike Davis, Rick Dempsey, Dennis Dixon Sr., Andy Dolich, Dennis Eckersley, Roy Eisenhardt, Steve Fehr, Dave Feldman, John Flaherty, Cliff Floyd, Dave Forst, Terry Francona, Richie Garcia, Cito Gaston, Rich Gedman, Jason Giambi, Pedro Gomez, J. J. Guinn, Jim Hague, Mike Hammock, Jeff Hammonds, Rickey Henderson, Pamela Henderson, Pat Hentgen, Bob Hohler, Daniel Horowitz, Jeff Horrigan, Willie Horton, Johnnette Howard, Art Howe, Chad Huss, Jeff Idelson, Reggie Jackson, Kathy Jacobsen, Steve Karsay, Jim Kascinski, Pamela Kenn, Steve Kettmann, Bob Klapisch, Ken Korach, Kent Korser, Mark Kotsay, Carney Lansford, Tony La Russa, Joe Maddon, Buck Martinez, Don Mattingly, Lee Mazzilli, Walt McCreary, Tim Mead, Bob Melvin, Gene Monahan, Jackie Moore, Mickey Morabito, Lloyd Moseby, Lonnie Murray, Phil Nevin, Mike Norris, John Olerud, Detra Paige, Dave Parker, Gary Pettis, Renee Pinson, Pamela Pitts, Monte Poole, Mike Port, Tim Raines, Willie Randolph, Harold Reynolds, Bip Roberts, Dave Roberts, Andrew Robinson, Jimmy Rollins, CC Sabathia, Billy Sample, Mike Scioscia, John Shea, Buck Showalter, Mark Simon, Ken Singleton, Susan Slusser, Claire Smith, J. T. Snow, Terry Steinbach, Charles Steinberg, Dave Stewart, Todd Stottlemyre, Mike Thalblum, Mo Vaughn, Randy Velarde, Steve Vucinich, Suzyn Waldman, Ron Washington, Devon White, Ernie Whitt, Glenn Wilburn, Ralph Wiley (1995), Willie Wilson, Dave Winfield, Peter Woodfork, and Michael Zagaris.

Notes

Prologue

Chapter 1

18 *"Rickey ran directly"*: Interview with Fred Atkins.
    "Rickey was all-world": Interview with Dennis Dixon.

19 *"Gotta concentrate on football"*: Interview with Lloyd Moseby.
    "Now, Rickey will tell you": Interview with Lloyd Moseby.
    "There was this counselor": Interview with Rickey Henderson.

20 *"I just wanted him"*: "The Home Boys: Rickey's Caring Godmother," *San Francisco Chronicle*, October 13, 1989.
    "One year he was behind me": Interview with Fred Atkins.

21 *"Rickey was a Babe Ruth legend"*: Interview with Fred Atkins.

Chapter 2

23 *Mike Norris, a native*: Interview with Mike Norris.
    "My aunt was brown-skinned": Interview with Pamela Henderson.
    "I'd watch the games": Interview with Pamela Henderson.

24 *"They pushed me through"*: Interview with Rickey Henderson.
    Once he was at Tech: Interview with Fred Atkins.
    "He said, 'Y'all need some batting gloves?'": Interview with Fred Atkins.

25 *"He could just do things"*: Interview with Pamela Henderson.

27 *"When I finally"*: Interview with Lloyd Moseby.
    "In all the years": Interview with Dennis Dixon Sr..

29 *"They were our heroes"*: Interview with Lloyd Moseby.
    "I lived a block or two away": Interview with Gary Pettis.

30 *"A lot of Negro groups"*: Robinson and Silverman, *My Life Is Baseball*, p. 16.
    "You'd look into the stands": Interview with Fred Atkins.

31 *"Send me my records"*: Interview with Mike Norris.

32 *"My daddy used to"*: Interview with Jim Guinn.
    "I was the only Black player": Interview with Jim Guinn.

35 *"something like 45 to 7"*: Interview with Andrew Robinson.
    "I've seen enough": Interview with Jim Guinn.
    "I got him the first two times": Interview with Andrew Robinson.
    "He said, 'Rickey?'": Interview with Jim Guinn.

37 *"You're not watching"*: Interview with Jim Guinn.

39 *"We were looking"*: Interview with Jim Guinn.

41 *"The biggest difference"*: Interview with Jim Guinn.

Chapter 3

42 *"We figured he needed"*: Interview with Rickey Henderson.

44 *"When Charlie Finley heard"*: "A's Have Farmhand Who's Quite a Steal," *Sacramento Bee* (Associated Press), June 15, 1977.
    "I was ready to take off": Interview with Fred Atkins.

45 *"When I got to LA"*: Interview with Fred Atkins.

46 *"I was running, running"*: Interview with Rickey Henderson.

47 *"He took me to the field"*: Interview with Rickey Henderson.

49 *"The guy is impossible"*: "Strokin' and Stealin,'" *Modesto Bee*, June 8, 1977.

50 *"That was the shithole of America"*: Interview with Buck Showalter.

51 *"Charlie sent me down there"*: Interview with Mike Norris.
    "Unlike the other 21 guys": Interview with Jim Hague.
    "The first was that he was cheap": Interview with Jim Hague.

53 *"I encouraged my players"*: Paul Hirsch, SABR Bio Project.
    "Kennedy was a redneck": Interview with Rickey Henderson.

54 *"Redneck-ass John Kennedy"*: Interview with Mike Norris.

55   *"Mike almost killed him"*: Interview with Rickey Henderson.
     "I called Charlie O. Finley": Interview with Rickey Henderson.
56   *"He was looking at me"*: Interview with Jim Hague.
58   *"He said, 'Mike'"*: Interview with Mike Norris.
59   *"I enrolled in Tech"*: Interview with Lloyd Moseby.
     "Because of the athlete": Interview with Rickey Henderson.
     "Rickey was so far from home": Interview with Mike Norris.
60   *"According to the* San Francisco Chronicle*"*: *San Francisco Chronicle*, November 7, 1962.
     Mike Norris would grow up: Interview with Mike Norris.
62   *"'I'm not messing this up'"*: Interview with Jim Hague.
     "One day, Rickey told me": Interview with Mike Norris.
63   *"There's nobody out there"*: Interview with Jim Hague.

Chapter 4

65   *"Those guys fucking let you* know*"*: Interview with Dennis Eckersley.
67   *"It is evident"*: "A's: Baseball's Only Contraction Team," *Los Angeles Times*, March 29, 1979.
68   *"I shouldn't have been"*: Interview with Rickey Henderson.
     "Rickey Henderson could be": "A's Send down Rabbit Henderson," *Modesto Bee*, March 31, 1979.
     "Billy Martin always knew": Ralph Wiley, "Rickey Was a Run Walking," ESPN, January 10, 2005.
70   *"I tell you, every day"*: "Hot Dilone Given A's 'Passport' to Ogden," *The Sporting News*, July 14, 1979.
71   *"We used to kick their ass"*: Interview with Steve Vucinich.
72   *"Rickey Henderson has been showing"*: Tom Weir, "A's Wonder over Finley's Lack of Interest," *The Sporting News*, October 6, 1979.
     "Rickey loved music": Interview with Walt McCreary.
     "Rickey Henderson's life": "Henderson Seeks A's Green Light," *The Sporting News*, December 8, 1979.
73   *"'If they took the brakes off'"*: Interview with Mike Norris.

Chapter 5

75   *"I just threw my fists"*: "Keough's Boost May Carry Some Weight," *The Sporting News*, April 19, 1980.
     "Billy had short man's complex": Interview with Rickey Henderson.
     "Part of Billy's strategy": Interview with Mike Davis.
77   *"If there was one thing Rickey knew"*: Interview with Mike Norris.
78   *"The style, the styling"*: Interview with Dave Stewart.
80   *"Rickey Henderson is"*: "One-Man Show," *Minneapolis Star*, August 14, 1980.
81   *"You ever been in an airplane"*: Interview with Jeff Idelson.
83   *how they wet the ball*: Interview with Jim Hague.

Chapter 6

87   *"He can be the most"*: Interview with Jim Darby.
     "I think Rickey trusted me": Interview with Jim Guinn.
88   *"Yeah, it's me"*: Interview with Johnette Howard.
89   *"I've never faced him"*: Gammons, *Beyond the Sixth Game*, p. 99.
     "an old bush nigger": Marie Brenner, "The Confession of a Rookie in Pearls," *Esquire*, July 1, 1980.
     "Rickey was a true competitor": Interview with Mike Davis.
     "Billy used to love him": Interview with Rickey Henderson.
90   *"Now, me and Billy"*: Interview with Rickey Henderson.

91 *"I thought I was the closest"*: Interview with Mike Norris.
92 *"I knew his father"*: Interview with Jim Guinn.
 "Shooty was one of my best friends": Interview with Mike Davis.
93 *"Billy was the one"*: Interview with Jim Guinn.
 "Billy was an arrogant": Interview with Shooty Babitt.
 "Billy wanted to win": Interview with Jackie Moore.
 "Of course he loved": Interview with Shooty Babitt.
94 *"Anybody who would have to ask"*: Interview with Reggie Jackson.
 "When Billy took over": Interview with Jim Guinn.
 "Tom Underwood and Bo McLaughlin": Interview with Shooty Babitt.
 "They wanted to call it": Interview with Jim Guinn.
95 *"Better me than him"*: Interview with Lloyd Moseby.
 "I was in the doghouse with him": Interview with Shooty Babitt.
97 *"In less than two full"*: Peter Gammons, "The New Mays," *Boston Globe,* August 27, 1981.
100 *"Fingers was a relief pitcher"*: Henderson and Shea, *Off Base,* p. 70.

Chapter 7

104 *"Rickey Henderson can think"*: "Martin May Stand in Way of Speedy Henderson's Goal," *Johnson City Press-Chronicle,* March 13, 1982.
 "When I went out there": Interview with Rickey Henderson.
105 *"Usually"*: Interview with Roy Eisenhardt.
106 *"We're going to break the record"*: Interview with Rickey Henderson.
107 *"He would literally tell me"*: Interview with Mike Norris.
 "Rickey is probably the most feared": "Henderson Rated a Triple Threat," *The Sporting News,* August 9, 1982.
108 *"As Rickey Henderson dashes"*: "Twins' Calvin Faces a Selling Job," *The Sporting News,* May 24, 1982.
 "The thing that drives pitchers": "New DH Strategy: Second Leadoff Hitter," *The Sporting News,* June 14, 1982.
109 *Ott told Rickey:* "A's Fists Ready, Martin Warns," *The Sporting News,* March 13, 1982.
110 *"Sangy would just sit on you"*: Interview with Lee Mazzilli.
 "Rickey was about Rickey": Interview with Willie Wilson.
 "I had good help": Interview with Bob Boone.
111 *"That was the only thing"*: Interview with Rick Dempsey.
112 *"Obviously, he was a very"*: Interview with Richie Garcia.
 "He was perfectly willing": Interview with Buck Martinez.
113 *"He didn't know anybody's name"*: Interview with Richie Garcia.
114 *"Rickey had a habit"*: Interview with Jackie Moore.
 "What makes Rickey run?": Jim Murray, "What Makes Rickey Run?," *Lancaster Sunday News,* August 29, 1982.
115 *"He breaks the record"*: Interview with Jim Darby.
116 *"From then on"*: Interview with Monte Poole.
117 *"Billy would get drunk"*: Interview with Mike Norris.
 "I was still adjusting": Interview with Sandy Alderson.
118 *"What kind of manager"*: Interview with Shooty Babitt.
 "When Billy sent him": Interview with Jim Guinn.
119 *"That happened by chance"*: Interview with Sandy Alderson.
 "What people don't really seem to get": Interview with Shooty Babitt.
120 *"Signing a deal with Rickey"*: Interview with Jim Darby.
 "Rickey has been styling": Interview with Dave Stewart.
 "What I loved about him": Interview with Reggie Jackson.

121 *"Once he got out there"*: Cramer, *The Hero's Life*, p. 123.
122 *"It started off in Oakland"*: Interview with Rickey Henderson.
123 *"That's where it started"*: Interview with Rickey Henderson.

Chapter 8
127 *"The fans were fascinated"*: Interview with Roy Eisenhardt.
128 *"Salaries are as much a part"*: Interview with Roy Eisenhardt.
    reported that Rickey in 1983: Murray Chass, "Big Interest in Henderson," *New York Times*, December 3, 1984.
129 *"I hated it"* Interview with Roy Eisenhardt.
130 *"Rickey beat me"*: Interview with Sandy Alderson.
131 *"Power guys like"*: Henderson and Shea, *Off Base*, p. 84.
    "Arbitration never bothered me": Interview with Mike Norris.
    "We thought we could": Interview with Roy Eisenhardt.
132 *"And one to grow on"*: "Owners Won't Be Losing by Paying Big Salaries," *The Sporting News*, March 12, 1984.
    "Left fielder Rickey Henderson": *The Sporting News*, March 12, 1984.
135 *Boros told Gammons*: Peter Gammons, "Henderson May Be Truly Devastating," *The Sporting News*, April 23, 1984.
136 *"I'm just swinging the bat"*: Peter Gammons, "Henderson May Be Truly Devastating," *The Sporting News*, April 23, 1984.
138 *"was like putting red meat"*: Interview with Mike Norris.
    "I don't know why": Interview with Rickey Henderson.
139 *"Wore his ass out"*: Interview with Rickey Henderson.
    "If the pitchers": Interview with Rick Dempsey.
140 *"Rick, I'll make a deal"*: Interview with Rickey Henderson.
    "When you had a Rickey": Interview with Rick Dempsey.
141 *"After Roy told me"*: "Boros Wants Second Chance," *The Sporting News*, June 11, 1984.
    "Boros said there were": "Boros Wants Second Chance," *The Sporting News*, June 11, 1984.
    Gammons piled on: The Sporting News, June 4, 1984.
    "With Rickey's talent": Interview with Jackie Moore.
    "I'm fast. Let me be": "Henderson Dazzles Yankees," *The Sporting News*, June 11, 1984.
142 *"The bottom line"*: Interview with Roy Eisenhardt.
143 *"Lasorda was there"*: Interview with Sandy Alderson.
144 *"Jose Rijo, rhp"*: Baseball America.
    "The most interesting part": Interview with Sandy Alderson.

Chapter 9
147 *"I'm not going to give up"*: Martin and Pepe, *Billyball*, pp. 253–54.
149 *"I asked him"*: Interview with Fred Atkins.
    "Rickey hadn't cashed": Interview with Mike Norris.
151 *"People who don't know Rickey"*: Interview with Jim Darby.
    "This is Rickey Henderson": Murray Chass, "This Is Rickey Henderson: Speed That Terrorizes," *New York Times*, December 16, 1984.
152 *"If Rickey wants"*: Dave Anderson, "Henderson, at Last, Gets Center Stage," *Southern Illinoisan*, April 24, 1985.
153 *"Henderson developed a reputation"*: "Glide of the Yankee," *South Florida Sun-Sentinel*, March 12, 1985.
    "He was a team player": Interview with Jim Darby.
    "I think I'm a great ballplayer": "Glide of the Yankees," *South Florida Sun-Sentinel*, March 12, 1985.

"Then, I was trying to prove": "Slow-Starting Henderson Remains Patient," *Newsday*, April 26, 1985.

154   *"I told him"*: "Henderson, at Last, Gets Center Stage," *Southern Illinoisan*, April 24, 1985.

155   *"When the trade was chronicled"*: *Sports Illustrated*, April 15, 1985.
         "I didn't take 24": "Henderson, at Last, Gets Center Stage," *Southern Illinoisan*, April 24, 1985.

157   *"Totally closed"*: Interview with Bob Klapisch.

158   *"No hard feelings"*: Interview with Billy Sample.

159   *"Rickey Henderson, Willie Randolph"*: *The Sporting News*, February 18, 1985.
         "Our deficiency": Interview with Pat Gillick.

160   *"It did not take long"*: Baylor and Smith, *Nothing but the Truth*, p.

161   *"I don't need no press"*: Mike Lupica, "Rickey Day Hits Height of Yank Wit," *New York Daily News*, April 23, 1985.
         "There was some question afterward": Mike Lupica, "Rickey Day Hits Height of Yank Wit," *New York Daily News*, April 23, 1985.

162   *"I don't care about them"*: "Henderson Speaks for Himself," *Hartford Courant*, April 24, 1985.
         "Steinbrenner couldn't have been": "Henderson's Attitude Has Yankees Perturbed," *Miami Herald*, August 13, 1985.
         "Yankees manager Yogi Berra": "Berra Could Be History before the Weekend," *Star-Democrat*, April 26, 1985.

164   *"an on-base machine"*: Interview with Rich Gedman.
         "After the trade": Steve Fainaru, "Coming Home," *Arizona Republic*, May 25, 1985.

165   *"Murph cannot carry a team"*: Steve Fainaru, "Coming Home," *Arizona Republic*, May 25, 1985.
         "A's centerfielder homers": "Murphy Hits a Giant Silencer," *San Francisco Examiner*, May 28, 1985.

166   *"Let me tell you"*: Interview with Rickey Henderson.

167   *"Billy was fascinating"*: Interview with Claire Smith.
         "A lot of it": Interview with Billy Sample.
         "'Now, we were always taught'": Interview with Rickey Henderson.

169   *"Do we have a game tonight?"*: "Henderson's Attitude Has Yankees Perturbed," *Miami Herald*, August 13, 1985.

170   *"The young man has things"*: "Boss: He's Mixed Up," *New York Daily News*, August 13, 1985.
         "Do you think I'm going": "Boss: He's Mixed Up," *New York Daily News*, August 13, 1985.

171   *"It started with a wedding"*: Interview with Walt McCreary.
         "I had a really good relationship": Interview with Claire Smith.

172   *"I-me-mine time"*: "Henderson's Attitude Has Yankees Perturbed," *Miami Herald*, August 13, 1985.

Chapter 10

175   *"He's the best leadoff hitter"*: "Your Basic Baseball Terrorist," *The Sporting News*, September 1, 1986.

176   *"Henderson is a phenomenon"*: "Your Basic Baseball Terrorist," *The Sporting News*, September 1, 1986.
         "Rickey Henderson is baseball's": "Henderson: A Frustrating, Complex Star," Associated Press, September 2, 1986.

177   *"I was like, 2-for-43"*: Interview with Rickey Henderson.

178   *"Whenever a Red Sox pitcher"*: Interview with Rich Gedman.
         "Every time a strike is called": *The Sporting News*, May 26, 1986.
         "The basic problem": "Henderson Will Testify Baltimore Is a Wonderful Place," *Baltimore Sun*, June 16, 1986.

179   *"ticks everybody off"*: "Steinbrenner, Umps, at Odds," *Hartford Courant*, June 5, 1986.

"Rickey loved the fans": Interview with Claire Smith.

"Isn't it about time": "Rasmussen May Be Only Yankee to Reach Double Digits in Victories," *Jersey Central News,* August 31, 1986.

182 *"I'm in that dirt"*: Interview with Rickey Henderson.

"We were in the apartment": Interview with Walt McCreary.

183 *"Was he or wasn't he?"*: *The Sporting News,* August 10, 1987.

184 *"Don't come past this line"*: Interview with Rickey Henderson.

"The Yankees' need for pitching": Moss Klein, *The Sporting News,* February 2, 1987.

185 *"Rickey is a once-in-a-lifetime player"*: Martin and Pepe, *Billyball,* p. 255.

186 *"We were great"*: Interview with Rickey Henderson.

"Unless Billy Martin returns": Moss Klein, "Lack of Quality behind Repeater Jinx," *The Sporting News,* October 12, 1987.

187 *"Too busy. Too noisy"*: Interview with Pamela Henderson.

188 *"They were missing in action"*: Howard Bryant, *The Heritage: Black Athletes, a Divided America, and the Politics of Patriotism* (Boston: Beacon Press, 2018), p. 92.

191 *"They have fat contracts"*: *Journal News,* April 30, 1985.

"an equal-opportunity abuser": Interview with Claire Smith.

"If Tom Yawkey was flawed": Riley, *The Red Sox Reader,* p. 257.

192 *"A lot of people are afraid"*: Baylor and Smith, *Nothing but the Truth,* p. 216.

"The fact is": Winfield and Parker, *Winfield,* p. 314.

193 *"Rick's like me"*: Bryan Burwell, "Rickey's a Reggie on the Field, Not Off," *New York Daily News,* June 8, 1987.

"Reggie was always the kind of guy": Bryan Burwell, "Rickey's a Reggie on the Field, Not Off," *New York Daily News,* June 8, 1987.

194 *"Rickey Henderson came out"*: *North Jersey Journal News,* August 2, 1987.

197 *"We have trouble"*: *Michigan Chronicle,* August 15, 1964.

"Dark would sit": Interview with Jim Guinn.

198 *"They used to talk"*: Interview with Rickey Henderson.

Chapter 11

200 *"They give you money"*: "A Rare Outburst by Mattingly," *The Sporting News,* August 29, 1988.

201 *"busted his ass for this town"*: Interview with Jack O'Connell.

202 *"Man, Rickey got 60"*: Interview with Harold Reynolds.

"If you stopped him": Interview with Bob Boone.

"Throw something in the wrong spot": Interview with Rickey Henderson.

"and when you did": Interview with Dennis Eckersley.

203 *"Most people, even Red Sox fans"*: Moss Klein, "Overlooked Evans Building Hall of Fame Case," *The Sporting News,* July 11, 1988.

"Another criticism leveled": Moss Klein, "History Should Tell Red Sox to Keep Boggs," *The Sporting News,* November 28, 1988.

204 *"If the Yankees fade out"*: Moss Klein, "Sparky's Dial-a-Hero Misfits Still in the Hunt," *The Sporting News,* July 11, 1988.

206 *"Things started off"*: Interview with Claire Smith.

207 *"Rickey, he was a character"*: Interview with Dave Winfield.

208 *"How many grandmothers"*: Interview with Claire Smith.

"Rickey Henderson is not": "Green Rips No-Show Henderson," *Indiana Gazette,* February 24, 1989.

"Maybe Rickey can't read": "Dallas, Rickey, Deion Star in Yankees' Sitcom," *The Sporting News,* March 13, 1989.

209 *"He wasn't late"*: "Henderson's Remarks Raise Rhoden's Ire," *New York Times,* March 3, 1989.

210 *"I think we all expected"*: "Henderson's Absence Upsets Dallas Green," *Star-Gazette* (Elmira, NY), February 23, 1989.

"I don't know": "Henderson Misses 2nd Day," *Jackson Sun* (Associated Press), February 24, 1989.

"At least we found out": "Rickey's Absence 'Ticks Off' Green," *Hartford Courant*, February 24, 1989.

211 *"When Rickey Henderson arrived"*: "Henderson: Boozing Cost Yankees the Pennant," *The Sporting News*, March 13, 1989.

212 *"If he thinks"*: Murray Chass, "Henderson's Remarks Raise Rhoden's Ire," *New York Times*, March 3, 1989.

"If they're not happy": "Dallas, Rickey, Deion Star in Yankees' Sitcom," *The Sporting News*, March 13, 1989.

213 *"There were 10 reasons"*: "Piniella Tells of '88 Curbs on Drinking by Players," *New York Times*, March 1, 1989.

214 *"The Giants wanted"*: Henderson and Shea, *Off Base*, p. 124.

215 *"All season long"*: Claire Smith, "Yankees Trying to Understand What Makes Their Rickey Tick," *Hartford Courant*, June 21, 1989.

216 *"For two summers"*: Interview with Rob Cohen.

217 *"There is no quarrel here"*: Dave Anderson, "Pinstripes Never Really Fit Rickey," *New York Times*, June 23, 1989.

218 *"It is not easy"*: Riley, *The Red Sox Reader*, p. 257.

"There is not a significant void": Michael Martinez, "Yankees Send Henderson back to Oakland," *New York Times*, June 23, 1989.

Chapter 12

220 *"The stadium was absolutely buzzing"*: Interview with Christopher Sauceda.

221 *"Rickey Henderson"*: Bruce Jenkins, "A Steal of a Deal for Loaded A's," *San Francisco Chronicle*, June 23, 1989.

"The A's bid goodbye": "A's Make Move—But Let's Wait and See," *Dallas Morning News*, June 23, 1989.

224 *"You want to start talking"*: Interview with Dave Stewart.

225 *"They really weren't"*: Interview with Dave Parker.

"I'll tell you one thing": Interview with Dave Stewart.

227 *"The move was worthwhile"*: Moss Klein, "Rickey: Perfect for A's; Worth Rent in NY," *The Sporting News*, July 3, 1989.

230 *"Henderson, one of the game's"*: 1980s Sports Home. "1989 HQ Game 4 . . ." YouTube video. https://www.youtube.com/watch?v=mFdKXaR-C20&t=2565s. Courtesy MLB Productions.

"There was so much going on": 1980s Sports Home. "1989 HQ Game 4 . . ." YouTube video. https://www.youtube.com/watch?v=mFdKXaR-C20&t=2565s. Courtesy MLB Productions.

231 *"Fuck Rickey Henderson"*: Interview with Ernie Whitt.

"No one likes: "Rickey's 'Stylin' Angers Jays," *Sacramento Bee*, October 5, 1989.

"If you think": "Rickey's 'Stylin' Angers Jays," *Sacramento Bee*, October 5, 1989.

"That kind of stuff": Interview with Lloyd Moseby.

232 *"I don't think he can ever"*: "Blue Jays' Song Has Turned into Loud Whine against Athletics," *Edmonton Journal*, October 6, 1989.

234 *"Lou Brock had a couple of years"*: 1980s Sports Home. "1989 HQ Game 4 . . ." YouTube video. https://www.youtube.com/watch?v=mFdKXaR-C20&t=2565s. Courtesy MLB Productions.

235 *"It wasn't just the winning"*: Interview with Dennis Eckersley.

"Come Saturday night": Mike Lupica, "Will the Real Rickey Please Lie Down?," *New York Daily News*, October 12, 1989.

237 *"To tell you the truth"*: Interview with Rickey Henderson; ESPN transcript, July 24, 2009.

238 *"It was turned on to"*: Interview with Claire Smith.

Chapter 13

239 *"I remember one time"*: Interview with Shooty Babitt.

240 *"He's a man"*: Interview with Pamela Henderson.

241 *"There have been so many times"*: Interview with Rickey Henderson.

"This was when": Interview with Jim Guinn.

242 *"He wants more than one year"*: *The Sporting News*, December 4, 1989.

245 *"They put us out"*: Interview with Mike Norris.

"Why? Because he was unemployed": "The Purple Haze Lifts for Norris," *The Sporting News*, April 30, 1990.

"The game got too easy": Interview with Mike Norris.

247 *"Man, I could hit the hair"*: Interview with Dave Stewart.

"I go into the clubhouse": Interview with Dave Stewart.

248 *"When Rickey kept his nose"*: Interview with Dennis Eckersley.

249 *"To keep Jose Canseco"*: "$23.5 Million for Canseco Has Rickey Down in the Wallet," *The Sporting News*, July 9, 1990.

250 *"It's a matter of politics"*: "Canseco Checks Swing on 'Racism,'" *The Sporting News*, May 7, 1990.

"John Simmonds was": Interview with Christopher Sauceda.

251 *"They were just so good"*: Interview with Ellis Burks.

252 *"That meltdown"*: Interview with Dave Stewart.

"We'll never know": Tom Barnidge "A's Frantically Dial Canseco Hotline during Series, but Jose Doesn't Answer," *The Sporting News*, October 29, 1990.

253 *"I feel it was"*: Interview with Tony La Russa.

"It wasn't the team": Interview with Dave Stewart.

255 *"The debate surrounding"*: Moss Klein, "Rickey over Fielder: Result Is Right on Target," *The Sporting News*, December 3, 1990.

256 *"I want to tip my hat"*: "Cecil Second," *Detroit Free Press* (Associated Press), November 21, 1990.

"I did everything I could": "Cecil Wonders What More He Had to Prove," *Great Falls Tribune*, November 21, 1990.

"Years from now": "Memories of Fielder Will Be Most Valuable," *Detroit Free Press*, November 21, 1990.

258 *"I knew when Rickey"*: Interview with Dave Stewart.

259 *"Where the fuck else"*: Interview with Jose Canseco.

260 *"When you're around"*: Lowell Cohn, "Hey Rickey, You're Wrong," *San Francisco Chronicle*, March 7, 1991.

261 *"After he went"*: Interview with Dave Stewart.

"How quickly the good times": Kit Stier, "Canseco Took the Heat, A's Shared All the Blame," *The Sporting News*, December 10, 1990.

262 *"Rickey, I thought your mama"*: Interview with Rickey Henderson.

"Rickey was the guy": Interview with Dave Stewart.

263 This is gonna be bad, *he thought*: Interview with Carney Lansford.

"I was thinking": Interview with Willie Wilson.

264 *"Nobody does it alone"*: Interview with Rickey Henderson.

"I was just the fiancée": Interview with Pamela Henderson.

265 *"When he said that"*: *The Sporting News*, May 13, 1991.

"After I said it": Interview with Rickey Henderson.

Chapter 14

266 *"Rickey had other"*: Interview with Dennis Eckersley.

267 *"To be honest"*: Interview with John Shea.

269   *"I read that"*: Interview with Bob Boone.
       "Nobody had ever": Interview with John Shea.
272   *"Tony tolerated Rickey"*: Interview with Willie Wilson.
273   *"It was tough around here"*: Interview with Cito Gaston.
       "It was starting": Interview with Paul Beeston.
       "I struck Rickey out": Interview with David Cone.
274   *"They did try"*: Interview with Cito Gaston.
       "They got me back": Interview with Dennis Eckersley.
275   *"The team was known for coddling"*: Interview with Pedro Gomez.
       "They said to us": Interview with Joe Carter.
276   *the same speech*: Interview with Rickey Henderson.
       "Rickey Henderson was somebody": Interview with John Olerud.
277   *"When he joined us"*: Interview with Joe Carter.
278   *"He should have been"*: Interview with Joe Carter.
       "What they had": Interview with Paul Beeston.
       "Rickey, I only wish": Interview with Cito Gaston.
279   *"This is just an attempt"*: "Half-Sister Says Rickey Raped Her," *San Francisco Examiner*, August 5, 1994.
       "Our approach is very simple": "Half-Sister Says Rickey Raped Her," *San Francisco Examiner*, August 5, 1994.
280   *"I think he needs to suffer"*: "Allegations of Incest: A Sister's Story," *San Francisco Examiner*, September 20, 1994.
282   *"I really tried"*: Interview with Daniel Horowitz.
       "I grew up in a family": *P. Henderson v. Doe (+Rickey Henderson)*, Alameda County (CA) court filing number c-739133.
       "It was always a comparison thing": "Bobbie Henderson 'Coaches' A's Star," *San Francisco Examiner*, October 9, 1990.
       "Paula's mother would": *P. Henderson v. Doe (+Rickey Henderson)*, Alameda Country (CA) court filing #c-739133.
283   *"There was a lot"*: Interview with Daniel Horowitz.
284   *"IT IS HEREBY ORDERED"*: *P. Henderson v. Doe (+Rickey Henderson)*, Alameda County (CA) court filing number c-739133.
285   *"We lost on everything"*: Interview with Daniel Horowitz.

Chapter 15

289   *"There's a high fly ball"*: MLB. "LAD@SD: Henderson Becomes . . ." YouTube video, https://www.youtube.com/watch?v=1ueNfNu38eg. Courtesy MLB Productions.
290   *"Of all the records"*: Interview with Pamela Henderson.
292   *"I have been connected"*: Howard Bryant, *Shutout: A Story of Race and Baseball in Boston* (New York: Routledge, 2002), pp. 28–29.
294   *"The following premise"*: Bob Ryan, "He Can't Steal Hearts," *Boston Globe*, October 6, 2001.
296   *"Tony Bennett!"*: Interview with Walt McCreary.
297   *"The game has become so boring"*: Interview with Willie Wilson.
       "So I've only been in the league": Interview with J. T. Snow.
299   *"I'd always heard"*: Interview with Jimmy Rollins.
300   *"Rickey had baseball"*: Interview with Pamela Henderson.
301   *"Media-wise, the writers"*: Interview with Terry Steinbach.
302   *"I get there"*: Interview with Walt McCreary.
304   *"If Rickey played today"*: Interview with Jimmy Rollins.
       The fearsome Red Sox slugger: Interview with Mo Vaughn.
305   *"You had to go down the stairs"*: Interview with Bob Alejo.

306   *"Jose went into the trainers' room"*: Interview with Jim Kascinski.
307   *"That's how it would go"*: Interview with Rickey Henderson.
      "He has been a vagabond": Steve Buckley, "Rickey Good for Sox," *New York Daily News*, February 17, 2002.
      "I just remember": Interview with Tim Mead.
308   *"He'd sit there"*: Interview with Pat Borders.
      "If the pitcher's move": Interview with Joe Maddon.
309   *"To me, what you're saying"*: Interview with Rickey Henderson.
      "There's a swing": MLB. "Rickey's Leadoff HRs . . ." YouTube video, https://www.youtube.com/watch?v=9F8tnHyAT5c. Courtesy MLB Productions.
310   *"Tony had given Rickey"*: Interview with Bob Alejo.
      "There's 10 percent": Interview with J. T. Snow.
      "There's not a lot": Interview with Terry Steinbach.
311   *"Rickey was hitting"*: Interview with Buck Showalter.
      I WAS ON SECOND BASE: Interview with Dave Feldman.

Chapter 16

313   *"We were naturally thrifty"*: Interview with Pamela Henderson.
316   *Walt made sure that Rickey's*: Interview with Walt McCreary.
317   *"Where you been?"*: Interview with Billy Beane.
318   *"Rickey's so cut"*: Interview with Jason Giambi.
      "His knees were knocking": Interview with Jim Bloom.
319   *"I was never"*: Interview with Art Howe.
321   *"Because of the fact"*: Interview with Pamela Henderson.
322   *"It was one of the reasons"*: Interview with Pamela Henderson.
323   *"Rickey was very comfortable"*: Interview with Steve Sayles.
324   *"One time we were"*: Interview with Ron Washington.
325   *"Let me tell you"*: Interview with Ron Washington.
      "Rickey was like a big brother": Interview with Bip Roberts.
      "He'd have that burst": Interview with Ron Washington.
326   *"He asked me"*: Interview with Jim Bloom.
327   *"He knew the fans"*: Interview with Jim Bloom.
328   *"The A's honored"*: "Rickey Shows His Worth—for Last Time?," *San Francisco Examiner*, September 27, 1998.
      "The thing I remember": Interview with Art Howe.

Chapter 17

332   *"Rickey Henderson simply"*: Jon Heyman, "Rickey Plays Spoiler," *Newsday*, April 21, 1993.
      "I hit a ball at home": Interview with Rickey Henderson.
333   *"I wore his ass out"*: Interview with Rickey Henderson.
      "He was such a dynamic ballplayer": Interview with Richie Garcia.
      "I think he's embellishing": Interview with Buck Showalter.
337   *"We were done negotiating"*: Interview with Steve Phillips.
338   *"That first year"*: Interview with Steve Phillips.
340   *"Henderson's role in this escapade"*: Lisa Olson, "Throw the Bums Out," *New York Daily News*, October 24, 1999.
341   *"Rickey doesn't have"*: Interview with Bob Alejo.
      "Bonilla wasn't a real Met": Interview with Bob Klapisch.
342   *"It really wasn't"*: Interview with Robin Ventura.
343   *"I was a batboy"*: Interview with Jason Beatty.
345   *"Here's how I heard"*: Interview with John Olerud.

346 *"We were in the trainers' room"*: Interview with Robin Ventura.
348 *"He was every bit as good"*: Interview with Dave Parker.
     Third-person Rickey: Interview with Phil Nevin.
     "on the Padres team bus": Interview with Mark Kotsay.
349 *"After every pitch"*: Interview with David Cone.
350 *"I'm not a big home run hitter"*: "Duque vs. Rickey," *The Record*, March 17, 2002.
351 *"They have to figure out"*: "Rickey Doesn't Like These Numbers," *Hartford Courant*, March 29, 2002.
     "It was just so bizarre": Interview with Glenn Wilburn.
353 *"You want a car"*: Interview with Charles Steinberg.
     "Whose piece of shit": Interview with Mike Port.
355 *"The guy was in his midforties"*: Interview with Michael Collazo.
356 *One day during Rickey's*: Interview with Jim Hague.

Chapter 18

357 *"The reason why"*: Interview with Frank Blackman.
360 *"Hey, hey"*: Transcript of Rickey Henderson, Hall of Fame induction speech, National Baseball Hall of Fame and Museum.
363 *"Basically, I'm reflecting"*: Interview with Jeff Idelson.
364 *"I was analyzed"*: Interview with Rickey Henderson.
366 *"It took a lot of effort"*: Interview with Pamela Henderson.
368 *"If Rickey had done"*: Interview with Dave Stewart.
     "They tried to control him": Interview with Shooty Babitt.
     "Rickey knew his body": Interview with Tony La Russa.
369 *"Tell me something"*: Interview with Rickey Henderson.

Epilogue

374 *"I think he would be"*: Interview with Billy Beane.
375 *"A lot of today's players"*: Interview with Rickey Henderson.
     "The WBC?": Interview with Jeff Idelson.
376 *"He couldn't understand it"*: Interview with Pamela Henderson.

Bibliography

Bagwell, Beth. *The Story of a City*. Oakland: Oakland Heritage Alliance, 1994.

Baylor, Don, with Claire Smith. *Nothing but the Truth: A Baseball Life*. New York: St. Martin's Press, 1989.

Bradford, Amory. *Oakland's Not for Burning*. New York: David McKay Co., 1968.

Cramer, Richard Ben. *Joe DiMaggio: The Hero's Life*. New York: Simon & Schuster, 2000.

Duberman, Martin. *Paul Robeson: A Biography*. New York: New Press, 1989.

Flood, Curt, with Richard Carter. *The Way It Is*. New York: Trident Press, 1971.

Gammons, Peter. *Beyond the Sixth Game*. New York: Penguin, 1986.

Griffey, Ken, and Phil Pepe. *Big Red: Baseball, Fatherhood, and My Life in the Big Red Machine*. Chicago: Triumph Books, 2014.

Henderson, Rickey, and John Shea. *Off Base: Confessions of a Thief*. New York: HarperCollins, 1992.

Hilliard, David, and Donald Weise. *The Huey P. Newton Reader*. New York: Seven Stories Press, 2002.

Hilliard, David, and Lewis Cole. *This Side of Glory: The Autobiography of David Hilliard and the Story of the Black Panther Party*. Boston: Little, Brown and Co., 1993.

Jolliffe, David A., Christian Z. Goering, Krista Jones Oldham, and James A. Anderson Jr. *The Arkansas Delta Oral History Project: Culture, Place, and Authenticity*. Syracuse, NY: Syracuse University Press.

Korach, Ken, and Susan Slusser. *If These Walls Could Talk: Stories from the Oakland A's Dugout, Locker Room, and Press Box*. Chicago: Triumph Books, 2019.

Madden, Bill, and Moss Klein. *Damned Yankees: Chaos, Confusion, and Craziness in the Steinbrenner Era*. Chicago: Triumph Books, 1990.

Martin, Billy, and Phil Pepe. *Billyball*. Garden City, NY: Doubleday, 1987.

Morgan, Joe, and David Falkner. *Joe Morgan: A Life in Baseball*. New York: W. W. Norton, 1993.

Newton, Huey P. *Revolutionary Suicide*. New York: Penguin Classics, 1973.

Pearson, Hugh. *The Shadow of the Panther*. New York: Addison-Wesley, 1994.

Piniella, Lou, with Bill Madden. *Lou: Fifty Years of Kicking Dirt, Playing Hard, and Winning Big in the Sweet Spot of Baseball*. New York: HarperCollins, 2017.

Pointer, Anita, Fritz Pointer, and Dave Smitherman. *Fairytale: The Pointer Sisters' Family Story.* Deadwood, OR: Wyatt-McKenzie Publishing, 2020.

Reed, Ishmael. *Blues City: A Walk in Oakland.* New York: Crown Journeys, 2003.

Rhomberg, Chris. *No There There: Race, Class, and Political Community in Oakland.* Berkeley: University of California Press, 2004.

Riley, Dan, ed. *The Red Sox Reader.* Boston: Houghton Mifflin, 1991.

Robinson, Frank, with Al Silverman. *My Life Is Baseball.* New York: Doubleday and Co., 1968.

Russell, Bill, and Bill McSweeny. *Go Up for Glory.* New York: Berkley Medallion, 1966.

Self, Robert O. *American Babylon: Race and the Struggle for Postwar Oakland.* Princeton, NJ: Princeton University Press, 2004.

Shames, Stephen, and Bobby Seale. *Power to the People: The World of the Black Panthers.* New York: Abrams Books, 2016.

Snyder, Brad. *A Well-Paid Slave: Curt Flood's Fight for Free Agency in Professional Sports.* New York: Viking, 2006.

Tafoya, Dale. *Billy Ball: Billy Martin and the Resurrection of the Oakland A's.* Guilford, CT: Lyons Press, 2020.

Winfield, Dave, with Tom Parker. *Winfield: A Player's Life.* New York: W. W. Norton, 1988.

Index

drafted by A's, 22
drug and alcohol use, 60, 61, 62,
 244–45
family background, 60–61
on Fingers, 99–100
on Finley, 51, 54
friendship with Rollins, 299
intellectual abilities, 59–60
Kennedy and, 54
likable personality, 245
Martin and, 84, 89–91, 94, 116–17
minor leagues, 31, 50–51, 54–55,
 58–59, 61–63, 356
on Pacific Heights, 23
on Rickey's base-stealing, 73, 77, 107
on Rickey's competitiveness, 138
on Rickey's financial discipline, 149
Rickey's Hall of Fame speech,
 363–64
Rickey's minor league career, 50–51,
 54–55, 58–59, 61, 62–63
Rickey's reading skills, 58–59
on salary arbitration, 131
scouting Rickey, 22
Sports Illustrated cover, 95
North, Billy, 84, 107
North Oakland, 3–4, 8, 150. *See also*
 Bushrod Field; Oakland Tech High
 School
Northwest League, 31, 44, 45–46
Nothing but the Truth (Baylor and C.
 Smith), 160, 192

Oakland, California
 attitude of Oakland kids, 27–30, 65
 Black activism, 10
 Black migrants from South, xiii–xvii, 3,
 7, 11, 15, 28–29
 legends, 299, 325, 373
 neighborhoods, 3–4
 segregation, 5–6, 8, 9–10, 28
 youth baseball, 13–14, 19, 26–27,
 71
Oakland Army Base, 5, 7, 10

Oakland A's
 1972 World Series, 17
 1973 World Series, 17
 1974 World Series, 17, 31
 1975 season, 38
 1976 draft, 38–40
 1976 season, 38, 86–87, 104
 1978 season, 67–68
 1979 season, 64–71, 76, 361
 1980 season, 75–86, 118
 1981 season, 91–92, 94–98, 109,
 117–18, 133–34
 1982 season, 103–8, 110, 112–14, 118
 1983 season, 122–23, 128, 133–34, 137
 1984 season, 127–35, 138–42
 1985 season, 164–65
 1986 season, 223
 1988 season, 225–26
 1988 World Series, 226
 1989 season, 220–22, 226–35, 278
 1989 World Series, 234–37
 1990 salaries, 242–43, 249–51
 1990 season, 244–52, 254–55
 1990 World Series, 251–54, 268–69,
 331
 1991 season, 256–57, 260–65
 1992 season, 273–74, 333
 1993 season, 270–71, 309–10, 331–32
 1994 season, 278, 305–6, 311
 1995 season, 284
 1997 season, 316
 1998 season, 312, 315–20, 322–28,
 357–58
 1999 season, 336
 2000 season, 344
 2020 spring training, 372
 ad campaigns, 91–92
 attendance, 71, 92, 103
 Burrell as batboy, 24
 Canseco traded to Texas, 274
 clubhouse dues, 87
 as dysfunctional (1979), 70
 Finley's sale of, 67–68, 76, 98–99
 Guinn as scout for, 31, 35–37

About the Author

HOWARD BRYANT is the author of nine previous books, including *The Last Hero: A Life of Henry Aaron* and *The Heritage: Black Athletes, a Divided America, and the Politics of Patriotism*. He is a senior writer for ESPN and the sports correspondent for NPR's *Weekend Edition*. Bryant is also a four-time nominee for the National Magazine Award for Commentary and a two-time Casey Award winner for best baseball book of the year.